Economic Transformation in Poland and Ukraine

When Poland and Ukraine introduced their political, social and economic system reforms at the beginning of the 1990s, both economies were at a similar level of economic development (GDP $9,500 per capita). However, in 2018, Ukrainian GDP per capita had remained at the same level since 1991, while in Poland, it had increased significantly, to more than $27,000 per capita.

This book assesses the reasons for the growing gap between the level of economic development in Ukraine and Poland. It examines the course of events and evaluates the effectiveness of the system transformations, both in the context of the economy, as a whole, and in individual regions (Polish 'voivodeships' (provinces) and Ukrainian 'oblasts'). It also analyzes the consequences of the 2008–2009 Ukrainian-Russian gas conflict and 2013–2014 Euromaidan events for the Ukrainian economy. Additionally, the authors offer an insight into the migration movements, which have recently been observed in Poland and Ukraine.

This is the first comprehensive, comparative analysis concerning the spatial diversification of economic development in these two countries, and the authors highlight the ways in which these reforms have proved effective in Poland and hardly effective in Ukraine. This analysis helps to identify the basic interrelations between the core macroeconomic variables at the regional level and the impact of political events from both a national and regional perspective.

The book will appeal to academics, researchers and policy makers interested in the economic and political changes in these two countries, in a comparative setting and on national and regional levels, as well as those working on issues of EU integration.

Rafał Wisła is Professor at the Department of Economics and Innovation of the Jagiellonian University, Krakow, Poland.

Andrzej Nowosad is Assistant Professor at the Institute of Journalism, Media and Social Communication of the Jagiellonian University, Krakow, Poland.

Routledge Studies in the European Economy

52 **Digital Transformation and Public Services**
Societal Impacts in Sweden and Beyond
Edited by Anthony Larsson and Robin Teigland

53 **Economic Policy, Crisis and Innovation**
Beyond Austerity in Europe
Edited by Maria Cristina Marcuzzo, Antonella Palumbo and Paola Villa

54 **The Economics of Monetary Unions**
Past Experiences and the Eurozone
Edited by Juan E. Castañeda, Alessandro Roselli and Geoffrey E. Wood

55 **Economic History of a Divided Europe**
Four Diverse Regions in an Integrating Continent
Ivan T. Berend

56 **The Political Economy of Independence in Europe**
Hana Lipovská

57 **The European Monetary Union After the Crisis**
From a Fiscal Union to a Fiscal Capacity
Nazaré da Costa Cabral

58 **Empirical Macroeconomics and Statistical Uncertainty**
Spatial and Temporal Disaggregation of Regional Economic Indicators
Mateusz Pipień and Sylwia Roszkowska

59 **Economic Transformation in Poland and Ukraine**
National and Regional Perspectives
Edited by Rafał Wisła and Andrzej Nowosad

For more information about this series, please visit www.routledge.com/series/SE0431

Economic Transformation in Poland and Ukraine

National and Regional Perspectives

Edited by
Rafał Wisła and
Andrzej Nowosad

Routledge
Taylor & Francis Group
LONDON AND NEW YORK

First published 2020
by Routledge
2 Park Square, Milton Park, Abingdon, Oxon OX14 4RN

and by Routledge
52 Vanderbilt Avenue, New York, NY 10017

Routledge is an imprint of the Taylor & Francis Group, an informa business

British Library Cataloguing-in-Publication Data
A catalogue record for this book is available from the British Library

Library of Congress Cataloging-in-Publication Data
Names: Wisła, Rafał, editor. | Nowosad, Andrzej, editor.
Title: Economic transformation in Poland and the Ukraine / edited by Rafał Wisła and Andrzej Nowosad.
Description: 1 Edition. | New York : Routledge, 2020. |
Series: Routledge studies in the European economy | Includes bibliographical references and index.
Subjects: LCSH: Economic development—Poland. | Economic development—Ukraine. | Poland—Economic policy—1990– | Ukraine—Economic policy—1991- | Labor mobility—Poland. | Labor mobility—Ukraine.
Classification: LCC HC340.3 .E3236 2020 (print) | LCC HC340.3 (ebook) | DDC 338.9438—dc23
LC record available at https://lccn.loc.gov/2020026874
LC ebook record available at https://lccn.loc.gov/2020026875

ISBN: 978-0-367-48493-4 (hbk)
ISBN: 978-0-367-49861-0 (pbk)
ISBN: 978-1-003-04137-5 (ebk)

Typeset in Times New Roman
by codeMantra

The publication was funded by the Priority Research Area Society of the Future under the program "Excellence Initiative – Research University" at the Jagiellonian University in Krakow.

Contents

Figures

Tables

Maps

Contributors

Monika Bolińska is a doctoral student at the Faculty of Management and Social Communication at the Jagiellonian University in Krakow (Poland). She is the author and co-author of 14 academic publications, such as *Spatial diversity of unemployment in Ukraine* (2019), *Demographic forecasts and volatility of investment rates vs. labour productivity trajectories* (2019), *An impact of the variable technological progress rate on the trajectory of labour productivity* (2020). Her research is mainly based on regional development and labor market analysis. In her research, she studies economic development in eastern Poland and western Ukraine.

Olesia Chornenka is a master of economics at the Jagiellonian University in Krakow. She is the author and co-author of over 15 academic publications, such as *Selecting the optimal method to assess the level of financial safety of enterprise* (2018), *Spatial diversification of Ukraine's GDP* (2019), *Spatial diversity of Unemployment in Ukraine* (2019). Her main interests include the impact of socio-political factors to the regional development in Ukraine.

Nataliia Chugaievska is working on her master's degree in Economics at the Jagiellonian University in Krakow, Poland, and is also a student of Law at the Polissia National University, Zhytomyr, Ukraine. She is the author and co-author of over 10 academic publications, such as *Statistical Analysis of the Impact of the Gravitational Effect on the Diversification of the Economic Development of Ukraine* (2017), *Legal regulation of higher education for Ukrainian citizens in Ukraine and Poland* (2018), *Determinants of spatial diversity of wages in Ukraine* (2019). Her scientific papers are devoted to issues of adaptation of Ukrainian economy to global migration processes in Europe.

Svitlana Chugaievska, PhD in Economic (Candidate of Economical Sciences), is Associate Professor of Analysis and Statistics Department at the I. V. Popovich, Polissia National University, Zhytomyr, Ukraine. She is the author and co-author of over 100 academic publications, such as *Statistical* *principles of innovative activity of dairy enterprises, Statistical Analysis of the Impact of the Gravitational Effect on the Diversification of the Economic Development of Ukraine* (2017), *Fundamentals of Economic Analysis: a Training Manual* (2018), *Determinants of spatial diversity of wages in Ukraine* (2019). Her spheres of scientific interests are statistical and analytical assessments of business entities' development; statistical analysis of sustainable development of the regions; statistical and analytical support of innovative processes of enterprises; a business analysis of enterprises in the context of the economic environment variability.

Paweł Dykas is Assistant professor at the Faculty of Management and Social Communication in the Jagiellonian University in Cracow (Poland). He is the author of over 50 academic publications, such as *The neoclassical model of economic growth and Its ability to account for demographic forecasts* (2018), *Demographic forecasts and volatility of investment rates vs. labour productivity trajectories* (2019), *An impact of the variable technological progress rate on the trajectory of labour productivity* (2020). His main interests include the mathematical theory of economic growth, an analysis of the spatial diversity of economic development and an analysis of regional differences in the labor market.

Titus Ferenc is a Assistant and doctoral student at the Institute of Journalism, Media and Social Communication at the Jagiellonian University. His latest articles have dealt with political marketing and political management, and his current research has been focused on the most recent presidential election in the United States, such as *Fake news in the United Kingdom and the United States : a historical-conceptual sketch (*2016), *Fashion politics : the strategic directions of political marketing* (co-author with Teresa Sasińska-Klas 2018), *Unstable democratic arrangements in East-Central Europe: the case of Poland* (co-author with Teresa Sasińska-Klas 2019).

Katarzyna Filipowicz is Assistant professor at the Department of Mathematical Economics of the Jagiellonian University. She is the author and co-author of over 50 academic publications devoted to this issue and the monograph: *The impact of domestic and foreign gravity effects on the diversity of economic development of Poland* (2017), *Diversification of economic development of EU countries on the basis of the gravity growth model* (2018), *The influence of spatial interactions on the differentiation of economic development of Poland* (2019). Her research interests are mathematical models of economic growth and the spatial differentiation of economic development.

Oleksii Kelebaj is a doctoral student of Economy and Finance of the Doctoral School in Social Sciences at the Jagiellonian University in Krakow. His main interests include the regional and local differentiation of economic development and mathematical models of economic growth.

Tomasz Misiak is Assistant professor at the Department of Economics at the Rzeszow University of Technology (Poland). He is the author of over 50 scientific papers, such as *Intra-regional differences in the Polish labour market* (2012), *Determinants of spatial differentiation of selected macroeconomic variables* (2013), *Diversifying of unemployment and employment and changes in GDP in European countries* (2016). His main interests include economic growth, real convergence processes and a spatial analysis of the diversification of economic development with a particular focus on the labor market.

Andrzej Nowosad is Assistant professor at the Institute of Journalism, Media and Social Communication of the Jagiellonian University. He is the author and co-author of over 100 academic publications, such as *Media i władza w Bułgarii* (The Media and the State in Bulgaria, 2008), *Zróżnicowanie rozwoju współczesnej Europy* (The Differentiation of Development in Contemporary Europe, co-author with Rafał Wisła 2016), *Klastery medialne jako kapitał społeczny na Bałkanach* (Media Clusters as Social Capital in the Balkans, 2019) and *Nieformalne komunikowanie o pracy w krajach bałkańskich* (Informal Communication About Work in the Balkan Countries, 2019). His main interests include the differentiations of the paths of regional development and economic, socio-political and media transformation in the world.

Daniela Szczepaniak is doctoral student of Economics at the Jagiellonian University. She is a co-author of *Economic Determinants of Intervoivodeship Migration* (2018). Her research interests are principally in regional development and stock markets.

Tomasz Tokarski is Professor at the Department of Mathematical Economics of the Jagiellonian University in Krakow (Poland). He is the author and co-author of over 200 academic publications, such as *Wybrane modele podażowych czynników wzrostu gospodarczego* (Selected Supply models of Economic Growth)(2005), *Ekonomia matematyczna modele mikroekonomiczne* (Microeconomic models of Mathematical Economics) (2011), and *Ekonomia matematyczna modele makroekonomiczne* (Macroeconomic models of Mathematical Economics) (2011), as well as extensive research and publications dealing with economic growth models and problems related with regional and local development. He is the Director of the Department of Mathematical Economics in the Institute of Economics, Finance and Management at the Jagiellonian University in Krakow. His main interests include gravitational growth models and the differentiation of spatial economic development in Europe.

Turanli Umit is working on an undergraduate degree in international management at the Jagiellonian University, and on a master's degree in intercultural relations at the Institute of Intercultural Studies at the

Jagiellonian University in Krakow (Poland). His main interests include the economic, political, social and intercultural relations between Asia and Europe.

Rafał Wisła is Professor at the Department of Economics and Innovation of the Jagiellonian University in Krakow (Poland). He is the author of over 80 academic publications, such as *Regional Patterns of Technology Accumulation in Central and Eastern Europe Countries* (2014), *Developmental Diversification of Contemporary Europe* (2016), *Innovation in the Pharmaceutical and Medical Technology Industries of Poland* (2018). He is an expert of a task force for the preparation of the 2013–2020 *Małopolska Regional Innovation Strategy* and co-director of the Institute of Economics, Finance and Management of the Jagiellonian University in Krakow. The issues which he deals with are technological changes and innovation activity from a regional perspective.

Introductory remarks

Rafał Wisła and Andrzej Nowosad

Poland and Ukraine are the two most important economies in Central and Eastern Europe, not counting the Russian Federation. Ukraine as a member of the Union of Soviet Socialist Republics gained independence in August 1991 as a result of the collapse of the USSR, while Poland transformed from 1989 as a satellite country of the USSR, and in October 1991 held its first completely free parliamentary elections since World War II (1939–1945). In both countries, 1991 marked the beginning of the transformation of the political and economic systems as well as a metamorphosis in the social fabric of both nations. The Ukrainian GDP per capita (in PPP, at constant prices from 2011) in 1991 amounted to 9.5 thousand USD, just as in Poland. In 1999, it fell to 4.5 thousand USD per capita. In 2017, it still did not return to the level of 1991 (7.9 thousand USD per capita). By comparison, in Poland, the GDP per capita has grown by nearly 190% over the last 27 years, from 9.5 thousand USD in 1991 to 27,000 USD in 2017. In 2018, the Polish GDP per capita was three times higher than in 1991 (The World Bank, 2019).

Both countries, although significantly different in terms of territory (Poland, 312,696 km^2; Ukraine, 603,700 km^2), have a similar population as of 2019 (Ukraine, 37,289,000;[1] Poland, 38,386,000), which places Poland on the 36th and Ukraine on the 37th place in the world in terms of population, taking into account the disputed territories.

Poland, in the early 1990s, had at its disposal several basic relatively scholarly institutions: its own currency, a central bank, the spirit and pragmatism of the free market, a limited form of private property, its own state budget, a solidarity-intellectual elite based on the working class and dissident intelligentsia, capable of developing and carrying out reforms with the help of foreign professionals.

Ukraine, in 1989, was one of the republics of the Union of Soviet Socialist Republics, whose independent economy was part of an inefficient Soviet economic organism. At the beginning of the 1990s, Ukraine did not have any experience in building market economy institutions, or the institutions of parliamentary democracy. Ukrainian society, brought up in a totalitarian system, had to face the extremely difficult task of creating market economy institutions and implementing democratic principles of the rule of law, in a post-soviet sphere of socio-economic development. The collapse of the Union of Soviet Socialist Republics was associated with a violent break in the Soviet supply chain, and economic connections. Internal imbalances (hyperinflation, rapidly rising unemployment, declines in production volume) and external factors (imminent depreciation of national currencies, rapidly growing balance of payments deficit and rising costs of foreign debt) were the macro-characteristics of the first years of systemic changes, not solely in Poland and Ukraine.

The development potential of both economies and the diversification of the level of social and economic life in the regions were examined.

The image of modern Europe is a combination of many processes. Their research turns out to be a problem, so complicated and complex and occurring in so many spheres of political, economic and social life that understanding this issue requires identifying individual areas of its occurrence. The complexity of the problem and the need to separate research areas and tasks in this area require constant returns to research, as well as their continuation in subsequent years. This publication is a continuation of the research interests of a team associated with the Faculty of Management and Social Communication of the Jagiellonian University in Krakow (Poland), and the Department of Mathematical Economics working under the guidance of prof. Tomasz Tokarski. A similar editorial body conducted research in 44 European countries; the results of which were published in Polish in a book entitled *Developmental Diversification of Contemporary Europe*, edited by A. Nowosad, R. Wisła, Kraków: Jagiellonian University Press, 2016.

This book is part of the world research of regional economies, such as the USA (Cox 2016), China (Girardin, Kholodilin 2011; Goodman 2016; Wu 2016), Australia (Coombs 2001), Mexico and Brazil (Alonso, Martin 2019), and especially areas bordering on the European Union, such as the Balkan Region (Duman, Obralić 2016), the Black Sea and Georgia (Zakaradze 2019), Turkey (Berber et al. 2014; Karakılçık 2014) and Russia (Kramorenko 2014; Maksimets, Bukatina 2016). The purpose of this book is to provide research on the regional development of Poland and Ukraine, located in Eastern Europe.

In the methodological layer, the book is an invitation to discuss the methods and techniques for the reader to become acquainted with the economic-political phenomena and processes and mechanisms analyzed from a macro- and meso-regional (regional) perspective. This type of research employs the Estimating and Forecasting with a Dynamic Spatial Panel Data Model methods (see, for example, Longhi, Nijkamp 2007; Girardin, Kholodilin 2011; Baltagi et al. 2016), and other types of spatial research methods and techniques.

In the cognitive layer, it is not only a diagnosis but also an answer to contemporary questions about the condition of Eastern Europe and its opportunities in the global economy. For the authors – representing various academic centers and scientific specialties in the field of economics and political science – the book should provoke and inspire further discussions on the economic potential of Europe in the global economy.

This monograph opens with a chapter devoted to the institutional conditions essential for the functioning of the Polish and Ukrainian economies as a key factor for economic growth and development (Nowosad A., Wisła R., Turanli U.). Recognition of the properties of the institutional order of both countries provides the basis for further analysis. Important issues addressed in the first chapter are the aspect of constitutional economic and political freedoms and real possibilities of exercising them, the multivariate institutional structure, the conditionality of the political and social order and their relationship with features of the respective national cultures, recognized forms of business and consequently with the structural changes of the entire economy and the dynamics of its growth. The authors use the methods of the new institutional economy (see: North 1995; Harris, Hunter, Lewis 1995; Lecours 2005; Staniek 2017).

The problem of the emergence of market economy institutions is continued in Chapter 2 (Chugaievska S., Wisła R., Nowosad A.), which aims to discuss selected institutional charts of changes in the period of economic transformation in Poland and Ukraine. The formation of private property and the capital market – a mechanism supporting privatization – is the main area of analysis in this chapter, using the institutional economics approach (see: Williamson 1985, 2000; North 1993; Richter 2005; Staniek 2017).

A diagnosis of institutional development conditions and an assessment of the level of maturity of market economy institutions assist the reader to understand well the consequences of the institutional immaturity of the state – both in Poland and in Ukraine (see: Lowndes, Roberts 2013).

Poland and Ukraine are very good subjects for this type of analysis. Polish and Ukrainian society had to face the exceptionally difficult task of creating market economy institutions practically from scratch, where the main brakes on GDP growth are the established and stable, informal, non-market institutions which are not conducive to free competition (interest networks of the former political elite groups, clans, oligarchy and an acquiescence for corruption and an autocratic political elite). This hypothesis is tested in the following chapters.

In Chapter 3 (Wisła R., Chugaievska S., Nowosad A., Turanli U.) the direction and dynamics of structural changes in the Polish and Ukrainian economies against the background of other eastern European countries are assessed from a macroeconomic perspective. Poland and Ukraine are observed from the viewpoint of systemically transforming countries (see: Lin 2012; Webster, Dunning 2013; McMillan et al. 2016).

Chapter 4 (Chugaievska N., Kelebaj O., Tokarski T.) opens a regional standpoint for the conducted research. In this chapter, Polish and Ukrainian administrative regions and their groups are discussed and have been analyzed from the angle of their demographic potential (population density, geographical structure of the population and urbanization rates).

In turn, in Chapter 5 (Chugaievska N., Kelebaj O., Tokarski T.), the economic potential of the regions and their groups, as indicated in Chapter 4, is analyzed in Poland, which is already in the EU, and in Ukraine, which is a candidate for membership in the EU (see: Liebscher et al. 2005).

Chapter 6 (Filipowicz K., Tokarski T., Ferenc T.) is a continuation of the analyses carried out in Chapters 3–5. This chapter describes the evolution of gross value added in agriculture, industry, construction and services in Polish voivodeships (in 2004–2015) and in Ukrainian oblasts (in 2004–2016).

The main purpose of the analyses carried out in Chapter 7 (Dykas P., Misiak T., Tokarski T.) is to present the spatial diversity of the situation on regional labor markets in Poland and Ukraine in 2004–2017, demonstrating its specificity (Blien, Wolf 2002; Ganesch 2018). These analyses relate to the diversity and dynamics of economic variables such as labor productivity, wage levels and unemployment rates. Determinants of the spatial difference of labor markets are used.

In Chapter 8 (Chugaievska S., Filipowicz K., Tokarski T., Wisła R.), the authors analyze the spatial diversity of characteristics such as capital-labor ratio and the so-called gravity growth model and labor productivity in the Ukrainian oblasts. These analyses are conducted on the basis of the gravity growth model. The chapter also presents 8 variants of numerical simulations of trajectories for increasing labor productivity in circuits by 2050.

The last in the series of analyses of the labor market is Chapter 9 (Chugaievska N., Szczepaniak D.) devoted to the differentiation of migration inflows and outflows as well as factors affecting these flows – i.e., relative wages and relative unemployment rates.

The book closes with Chapter 10 (Bolińska M., Chornenka O.). The main purpose of this chapter is to assess the spatial diversity of the economic development of voivodeships and oblasts in 2004–2016. The measures of the spatial diversity of economic development of voivodeships and oblasts are made by calculating and analyzing the taxonomic indicators of economic development for these regions.

The level of economic development of the Polish and Ukrainian regions is significantly diversified in both space and time. The results of the analysis conducted in this book show significant disparities in the economic development of these regions. Can they give an answer as to what is their scale, direction and dynamics? What place do Ukraine and Poland occupy in the global and European economy today? The answers are contained in this book.

Unfortunately, based on existing data, we limited our forecasts for these economies to variants of numerical simulations of trajectories of labor productivity growth. The reason is that we began to write the book in relatively stable times, and we are publishing it now, during the global pandemic of Coronavirus (COVID-19). In both countries, strict measures have been introduced to prevent the spread of the virus, and in both countries, this situation has a huge impact on the condition of the economy and society, and thus on the potential increase in the wealth of the countries, regions and markets analyzed here. Product markets and labor markets found themselves in a crisis, and supply chains were broken.

The analyses carried out in this book can be very helpful material for further comparative research.

An important part of the efforts to establish policies for regional development should be focused on the safety and security in the region. Also, the development of intraregional policies (i.e., trade, employment, market) should be prioritized as compared to outer-regional ones, especially in the short term.

This book points out the need for regional economic development policies for the west European region and brings together insights from academics on various economic and social aspects of regional development.

Note

1 On January 23, 2020, the Ukrainian government team for assessing the population of Ukraine presented the results of their research, according to which on December 1, 2019, the number of residents of the country (excluding Crimea and parts of the Donetsk and Luhansk oblasts not controlled by Kyiv) was 37.3 million. On the same day, the State Statistics Service (Derzhstat) announced that the number of residents of Ukraine (excluding Crimea) on December 1, 2020, was 41.9 million.

Acknowledgements

The authors and editors of this volume would like to cordially thank prof. Eugeniusz Kwiatkowski and prof. Krzysztof Malaga, for the valuable comments and advice, which they provided during the inception of this book.

1 Institutional conditions for the functioning of the Polish and Ukrainian economies

Andrzej Nowosad, Umit Turanli and Rafał Wisła

1.1 Introduction

Today's direction and dynamics of economic development play a key role in shaping economic development, not so much traditional cost or resource factors, as qualitative ones as human capital, the innovation capacity of the economy and, above all, the quality of the institutional environment, that is, of the social, political, economic and communication processes.

Institutions in the economy reduce uncertainty by introducing patterns into everyday life. They bring to business a factor of sustainability, continuity and stability through the creation of conditions ensuring the predictability of the results of a particular set of actions and communication patterns. They become a model of human interaction (North 1990: 4). Institutions are also instruments used by individuals to maximize benefits in their efforts to increase individual prosperity and should, according to North, reduce uncertainty and background noise in communication and transaction costs (North 1992: 447–449).

Institutions can be understood not only as dominant ways of thinking, taking into account individual social conditions, individual and community functions (Veblen 1899) but also as collective activities to supervise individual activities (Commons 1934). Institutions are usually referred to as any permanent, organizational or customary condition for repetitive human behavior and human interactions (Pejovich 1995), as well as conventions and social communication. In systemic terms, institutions are evolutionarily educated standards and rules of action often transformed into a set of formal or legally binding restrictions (through legal provisions or constitutions) together with the related mechanisms of their enforcement (WEF 2015).

Institutions are usually divided into formal and informal. The state creates formal institutions by setting out forms of economic activity and economic relations by law, which must also be classified by rules for registration, affiliation and trade union activities, amongst others. It also creates a stimulus system; social impact institutions in terms of functioning institutions can be defined as effective, where the adopted principles are respected and enforced, and inefficient, when institutional principles are not respected, as North writes:

> Institutions and ideology together shape economic performance. Institutions affect economic performance by determining (along with the technology used) the cost of transacting and producing. Institutions are composed of formal rules, informal constraints, and characteristics of enforcing those constraints. While formal rules can be changed overnight by the polity, informal constraints change very slowly. Both are ultimately shaped by people's subjective perceptions of the world around them; those perceptions, in turn, determine explicit choices among formal rules and evolving informal constraints (...) Institutions are the rules of the game in a society; more formally, they are the humanly devised constraints that shape human interaction. Thus, they structure incentives in exchange, whether political, social, or economic. Institutional change shapes the way societies evolve through time and, hence, is the key to understanding historical change.
>
> (North 1992: 447)

While formal institutions are easy to create and change, informal institutions are often resistant to change. These are the usually unwritten rules of human behavior, ways of thinking and a hierarchy of values (Veblen 1899; Commons 1934; North 1992). While every person has his own system of values and behavior, the mere fact that a person is a social unit causes that, with puberty and personal development, he also adopts the characteristic attributes of the specifics of his surroundings and recognizes the accompanying norms, principles and traditions. In other words, institutions are the learning matrix of human individuals and their social groups in different forms of education. Informal institutions therefore include not only regional customs, overt behavior, historically imposed by generations of mothers and fathers, patterns of socially and politically desirable behavior, habits and cultural codes, social habits, a general way of life and customs, but also legal usages, conventions, communication systems and behaviors.

Informal institutions endure from generation to generation and are difficult to change, whereas formal institutions can be created by the state as a system of impulses to the state's desired behavior practically overnight.

Economics does not deal with matters of the functioning of the state itself, and yet institutionally the principles acquired by the state, or developed under the influence of its current and former institutions, created in a certain international environment, have an equally important impact on the functioning of the state and its economy as internal formal and informal institutions. After all, the state's habits of regulating and creating institutions depend on the adopted political system, standards, rules of action, mechanisms for the enforcement of social and economic contracts, and the quality of human capital – that is, the competence of those politicians who manage this country. The political system of communism, which was in force in Poland and Ukraine until the end of the 1980s, created its own set of formal, legally binding restrictions and its own economic system. Its features were a lack of private property, the injunction-resolution system, central planning, all power monopolized by one political party, a totalitarian ideology, full control and supervision of society in all aspects of public and private life and finally, a propagandistic and one-way form of political communication. All economic, communication and ownership initiatives were killed in the individual person, as a separate entity. Since the 1990s the Polish and Ukrainian economies have undergone a systemic transformation. The aim was to create a country with a market economy, characterized by political and economic freedom, and the free exchange of human thoughts in the public and private sphere – a concept which still faces difficulties and creates economic and social problems.

The institutional conditions for the functioning of the Polish and Ukrainian economies are diverse, but in many ways they are similar. Both countries combine a communist heritage, system of prescriptive economy, similar forms of social communication, the privatization of institutions, the creation of principles of economic freedom and the functioning of the state. These are not identical systems. Ukraine now enjoys its own independent state for the first time in its history, while Poland's statehood has been historically shaped.

The purpose of this chapter is to identify the basic institutional characteristics, in the sense of formal and informal institutions, in Poland and Ukraine, which affect the functioning of the economy, and to delineate their specificities. It is also an introduction to this book, which, admittedly, is written by many authors, specialists in their own fields, but is an integral whole of looking at the Polish and Ukrainian economies.

1.2 Poland and Ukraine yesterday and today

Communism was the first political system which, after World War I, extracted Ukraine from the nations surrounding it (1918–1920), while Poland at that time regained its statehood after a hiatus of more than 100 years due largely to a wave of anti-communism. Ukraine failed to defend its independence against the Russian Bolsheviks, but Poland succeeded by retaining its statehood after winning the Polish-Bolshevik War (1919–1921). Although the history of both peoples has been converging for centuries and historical phenomena have occurred, sometimes resulting in direct rivalries, the institutional forms of state and society were different for Poles and Ukrainians. Even during the occupations since 1807, Poland had a substitute for independence in the form of the Duchy of Warsaw, which was transformed in 1815 into the Kingdom of Poland, formally connected by a personal union with Russia, and therefore not a sovereign state, but since 1918 Poland has been a completely self-governing country. Ukraine, on the other hand, has been a sovereign state since 1991. The 73-year difference plays a significant role here in shaping the institutional order of the state, its economy and society. For 71 years, Ukraine had been incorporated into the Union of Socialist Soviet Republics (USSR) – a communist, totalitarian state, with a centrally planned economy, where every manifestation of an individual economic initiative was treated as anti-state activity and punished by years of imprisonment in the gulag, or even by death. In Poland from 1918 to 1939, the institutions of the market economy and of the state were formed and strengthened, while society reacquired its national customs and recovered and implemented the traditions of the Polish nobility, the Church, bourgeoisie and the peasantry, which in communist Ukraine was something utterly unimaginable. The Church was banned, manifestations of religious faith were punished by death or imprisonment in the glugs, and talking about Ukrainian traditions linked with the nobility or land-owning class was punishable by death.

The result of World War II brought peoples closer, but the course and events during World War II widened the separation between them. The Polish-Ukrainian guerrilla wars, ethnic cleansing of civilians carried out on both sides of the border, mutual former resentments and old animosities, meant that even though both countries were in the same orbit of socialist states after 1945 under the dictatorship of the USSR, they produced neither common institutions nor informally traditional attitudes. Poland was in the group of satellite countries of the USSR, and Ukraine was an entity within the USSR itself. The Polish United Workers' Party (PUWP; Polish: Polska Zjednoczona Partia Robotnicza, PZPR) was a party that formed the communist system of institutions in Poland from 1945 to 1990 mainly through the implementation of the guidelines of the Communist Party of the Soviet Union (CPSU, Коммунистическая партия Советского Союза – КПСС, Kommunisticzeskaja partija Sowietskogo Sojuza – KPSS), and it did not treat the oppression of the citizenry entirely seriously, and certainly less seriously than in the Communist Party of Ukraine (KPU), which functioned in a Ukraine and was completely subordinate to Russia.

In Poland, private property was tolerated to a minimal degree, small farms and even small private forests were permitted, and above all, craftsmen and artisans were allowed to carry on their trades, something which didn't appear in Ukraine before 1990. In Poland, it was also not possible to implant in the minds of the people, the concept that the state and its needs were all-important. In Poland, people continued to think for themselves, as individuals (not collectively), about their own private affairs (not state matters), with an emphasis on their private consumer matters, as an element of collective state affairs. In Ukraine, individuality was killed in the fields of social activity as well as in culture, art and language. Another, no less essential matter was the possibility of interacting with the institutions of other countries. In Poland, during communism, there were no problems with trips abroad within the Soviet Bloc of states, whereas in Ukraine, any departure from the USSR was almost impossible. In addition, Poles, for example, when going to Bulgaria for a holiday, could always travel through Ukraine, while Ukrainians could not come to Poland. This was quite significant, because already in communist times the Poles developed an individual economic initiative on an international scale. Poles practiced this so-called border suitcase trade – they bought goods in Poland, which were not in Ukraine, sold them there for rubles, and then in Romania or Bulgaria exchanged these rubles for dollars, thus creating capital, which then allowed them to build their own homes in Poland and to undertake entrepreneurial activity on a small scale, which was permitted by the communist authorities. Ukrainians did not have such an opportunity, and from the point of view of economics, it was difficult for the Ukrainians to understand the existence of the free market, the spontaneous education of sectors of the economy on the basis of individual economic initiatives, individual choices, without any intervention, supervision or direction from the state. Today, nearly 30 years after regaining independence, the reasoning of the principles of the free market economy in Poland and Ukraine is different and barely comparable to each other, as are the informal institutions (paved principles of conduct), the functioning of economic institutions or the transactional principles of the open market. These are entrenched, homegrown ways of thinking which existed in the old system and are still present even today in the young generation.

Literature of the subject, especially Russian language literature, indicates that Ukraine's economy cannot be subjected to comparative studies from the viewpoint of the guidelines adopted by Western Europe and the liberal economies. It would appear that these measures are incomparable, because there are other institutional dependencies. It has been proposed that any research of the economies of those countries which arose after the fall of the USSR should be conducted using the paradigm applied to Asian countries, since the countries of the former-USSR, at least in their institutional behavior, are closest to their Asian counterparts (Lipov 2012). Of course, from a Polish perspective, it can be considered that perhaps there is a lot of evidence to confirm these scientific assertions and opinions, but also it may be the result of the ordinary political line of Russian or Ukrainian research.

There are two main reasons behind the writing of this book. The main aim of this chapter is to explain the institutional behavior and possible inconsistencies that the reader can find in literature on the subject, and research regarding the economies of Poland and Ukraine.

It can be said, with a high degree of probability, that writing and talking about these economies – Polish and Ukrainian – is not free from the local policies of the countries from which the authors or commentators originate. The thought processes of the research plans and categories cited are also subject to the specific customs and habits of the respective regions.

An outstanding book published in Polish on this subject has been edited by Antoszewski et al. (2010), in which Poles write about Polish affairs and

Ukrainians write about Ukrainian affairs (translated into Polish obviously); however, there is one shortcoming. The authors bilaterally take up the same problem; they write in a different scientific code and operate in a different paradigm, which causes the reader to get, on the one hand, two viewpoints of the same things – Polish and Ukrainian – which are completely incompatible and even outright disharmonious, while large fragments are utterly incomprehensible. On the other hand, perhaps the authors really do comprehend the variety of paradigms and thought habits (see: Antoszewski et al. 2010). The mere fact that the editors and authors do not even try to create a common paradigm-narrative for research of the Polish and Ukrainian economies may not be so much an error as an acknowledgment of the lack of one (common paradigm).

Regarding Russian literature, publications in the Journal of Institutional Studies (Zhurnal Institutsional'nykh Issledovaniy, Журнал Институциональных Исследований, from 2009) are noted.

The Journal's editorial board states that only an institutional paradigm can constitute the common ground for research of the economies and states of the former USSR and the Western world, and on institutional assumptions formulates the scientific mission of the research, when they say that:

> Neoclassical recipes to describe economic reforms have shown a very limited effectiveness in almost all post-Soviet countries as early as the 1990s. 20th century economists began to search for a new economic paradigm that would be more relevant to the post-soviet reality and at the same time would allow them to communicate with foreign colleagues "in the same language". Institutionalism (both "old" and "new") has become such a new paradigm.
>
> Wrote the Journal of Institutional Studies, https://www.hjournal.ru/journals/journal-of-institutional-studies.hthttps://www.hjournal.ru/journals/journal-of-institutional-studies.html, ml, access date; 2020–01–10)

The Journal of Institutional Studies highlights the importance of institutional differences in the countries of the former USSR, on the one hand, and points to their institutional convergence with Asian countries, on the other. Unfortunately, there is a paucity of material concerning Ukraine in the Journal, and references to the institutional traditions of Poland or Western Europe, in Ukraine, are not taken into account a priori.

Ukrainian researchers have not developed a common platform for exchanging institutional thought with Western Europe and the world. Regional studies are usually not based on hard data, and their output rarely refers to uniform and comparable data sources. The reason, as indicated in literature, is the inability to carry out comparative studies, because in these very regions of Ukraine, different specificities of economic systems and social institutions have been created. Aggregated data by region, on the other hand, is not subject to consistent econometric modeling (Duma 2017). It is given as effective methods of cognitive maps (Когнітивна карта, cognitive maps) which allow us to determine the distribution of the pulsation process, but do not permit research of the evolution of the process itself (Vyshnevskyi, Dementiev 2010: 41–62; Duma 2017: 176). It has been noted that when simulating the evolution of the process of actual economic systems in Ukraine, there is a problem of time consistency and data inconsistency, and pulsation processes can have different delays for different model variables (Leontev, Ford 2012: 370–400).

In general, there is a substantial amount of literature on the Polish and Ukrainian economies, which enables us to conclude that there is a growing interest in this issue, and although the topic is not new, it is nevertheless the presentation of one more research perspective which can be both interesting and noteworthy for research purposes. A gravitational outlook is proposed in this book.

Many institutional documents from the first period of systemic transformation have been published in Poland (Gomułka 2013; Gomułka, Kowalik 2011), as well as a general look at post-communism in Poland (Staniszkis 2001). With regard to the Ukrainian economy, this type of literature is still lacking. However, scientific literature concerning the Polish transformation has been written in "waves". The majority of works were published between 1997 and 2000 and then 2011–2013; that is, the theme of the Polish transformation returns approximately every ten years to the area of interest of Polish academic research. No such pattern of "waves" has occurred regarding Ukraine. Foreign publications are usually the aftermath of literature and research published in Poland and Ukraine and are written mainly in English by Poles and Ukrainians, which also means that they are, in the majority, concurrent with Polish and Ukrainian views on this systemic transformation (Smalej 2016; Dolińska 2019; Fałkowski, Kurek 2019; Holubiak 2019; Kaźmierska 2019). A special issue of the "Qualitative Sociology Review" Vol 15 (2019) was published to commemorate the 30th anniversary of the transformation in Poland.

Studies of regional development in Poland, using quantitative methods, are quite well documented in the literature of the subject (see: Wisła, Tokarski 2016; Pastuszka, Tokarski 2017; Szczepaniak, Tokarski 2018), while in Ukraine, attention is called to the instability of the application of mathematical and econometric models regarding the various regions of Ukraine. The unstable and fluid character of these regions is given as a barrier to mathematical and economic models; hence, the cognitive map model is proposed.

L. V. Duma writes directly:

> The character of dynamics, pace and proportions of socio-economic indicators in Ukraine are largely under the influence of non-stationary conditions of operation. Some signs of non-stationary structure are

> unstable macroeconomic processes in time, the difficulty of for- normalizing their dynamics, an uncertain future etc. Ignoring these features along with a lack of statistical data renders it impossible to make an evaluation, analysis and forecasting of the dynamics of these macroeconomic processes by classical methods. Therefore, this study aims at reviewing the nature and characteristics of the simulation for analyzing and forecasting the socio-economic development of the country. The results of the study have shown that the basis of such simulations are diagrams, a causality - cognitive map and study of the problem on the basis of a cognitive map is through the distribution of the pulsed process. The authors have also analyzed a number of modern simulation (cognitive) models of regional development proposed in the research literature that demonstrate the use of this tool as the modeling of the dynamics of macroeconomic indicators and indicators of the local economic and social development of the region (…) Applying pulse models can predict the development of specific situations in certain regions and make substantiated recommendations on measures of economic and social policy.
>
> (Duma 2017: 78)

The proposed and implemented gravitational model in the book can be useful for researching the various regions of Ukraine, and for conducting comparative studies.

1.3 The subject of this research and its specificity: Poland–Ukraine

Ukraine, as an independent state, was established on July 16, 1990, when the Supreme Council of the Ukrainian Socialist Soviet Republic (USRR) adopted a Declaration on State Sovereignty (Декларація про державний сувереренітет Украшни). Ukraine became a successor to the USSR, which was part of the Union of Socialist Soviet Republics (USSR) from 1919 to 1991. As part of the USSR, the Ukrainian SSR, alongside the Belarusian SSR and the Russian SSR, was one of three Soviet republics that were a legal entity according to international law, were co-founders of the United Nations and a member of most UN specialized organizations (Osmańczyk 1982; Wiszka 2007).

Polish statehood has a long history. The first historically confirmed date describing the history of Poland is 966, when Poland was baptized and became a Christian state. In 1025, the Kingdom of Poland was established. In 1569, the Republic of Both Nations (Polish Commonwealth) was established, which was one of the largest and most populous countries on the map of 16th- and 17th-century Europe. The Republic ceased to exist as a result of the Third Partition of Poland, in 1795, when its territory was divided between Prussia, Russia and Austria. Poland regained its independence in

1918, immediately after World War I. After World War II, from 1945 to 1989, it functioned as a satellite state of the USSR under the name of the Polish People's Republic (Polish: Polska Rzeczpospolita Ludowa, PRL).

The period of communism analyzed in both countries – Poland and Ukraine – was a command-control economy with a socialist doctrine but in Poland for a considerably shorter period (since 1946) and in a much more mild form than in the USSR, while this system lasted in Ukraine for 25 more years (from 1921 to 1991) and in a more repressive form.

Unlike its Polish counterpart, modern Ukrainian statehood began to take shape at the end of the 1980s. The 20th century, within the framework of the political and economic system of the USSR, was characterized by full market control of the economy and of public life. However, Ukraine as a universally recognized name first appeared in the Middle Ages and signified the borderlands of various geographical regions. By the end of the 16th century, the term "ukraine" was not official and only meant the "borderline" ("boundary line", "state frontier") of individual lands under the control of different countries. The official name "Ukraine" was first used in 1590 in the title of the Sejm (Polish parliament) Constitution of the Republic (Konopczyński 1999: 211).

The Ukrainian SSR had quite a lot of freedom within the Soviet Union itself compared to other soviet republics, such as Tajikistan, Georgia and Moldova, but much less than Poland, during the timeframe of the operation of the PRL (Polish People's Republic). The processes of institutional change in Poland and Ukraine took place at the same time, but with a different intensity, and went in different directions. In Ukraine in 1989, the social organization of the People's Movement of Ukraine (Народний Рух Украшни), formed by Ukrainian writers and dissidents, transformed into a political party with an independence program and in the elections of 1989 scored 9.4%, thereby occupying second place in the local one-chamber parliament, the Supreme Council of Ukraine (Верховна Рада Украшни), gaining a total of about 50 seats. The LRU received the highest support in the regions of western Ukraine bordering on Poland. New forms of the state's institutional system were created by communist activists in weak opposition to Ukrainian writers and dissidents. In the new formula of the nascent Ukrainian state, old communist activists introduced modernized forms of old and proven institutions from the soviet era; however, rejecting forms of total state control, the substantive power of communicating the principles of the functioning of a free state and its economy among Ukrainian writers and journalists was not significant.

In Poland, the transformation of the regime began after 1981, when under pressure from a wave of strikes and social protests, martial law was declared, after which the regime was eliminated and the Round Table meetings took place and elections were held in June 1989. As in Ukraine, Polish dissidents, journalists and writers were in opposition against the old communist institutions. However, the main role in political change and negotiations was played by the trade union "Solidarity", whose members were industrial workers and had a convincing instrument known, since the 1980s, as the general strike whereby they were able to paralyze the country and stop all production in state-run factories. It would be difficult to compare the power of the opposition in Poland and Ukraine.

In both countries, in general, all the transformations commenced in the 1990s and were focused on the creation of a free market, civil society and democratization. The redevelopment of the state has covered almost all spheres of social life, including systemic transformation (implementation of parliamentary institutions and procedures), economic transformation (creation of a free market based on private property), social transformation (social change, acceptance of new rules of social life), as well as privatization in Ukraine, and privatization and reprivatization in Poland. In Ukraine, this transformation had no "shock therapy", but in Poland, due to the huge debt of the state and the requirements of financial institutions associated with the so-called London and Paris clubs, this period took on some of the characteristics of "shock therapy", resulting in a high-speed transformation.

Ukraine adopted a new Constitution (Конституція Украшни) on June 28, 1996, Poland on April 2, 1997. Ukraine has established a presidential-parliamentary system of government (Constitution of Ukraine 1996) and a welfare state-oriented economy (Constitution of Ukraine 1996: Article 13). Poland, on the other hand, has adopted a welfare state-oriented market economy by enshrining in Article 10(2) of Regulation (EC) No 1250/2003 and article 20 of the Polish Constitution of 7 April 1997, that the welfare state-market economy is based on freedom of economic activity, private property and solidarity, dialogue and cooperation of social partners, and these pillars forms the basis of the economic system of the Republic of Poland (Constitution of the Republic of Poland, Article 20). Constitutional records coincide, but for the functioning of the state and society, the welfare state-oriented economy (Ukraine) and the welfare state-market economy based on the freedom of economic activity (Poland) gave rise to the creation of completely different institutions and behavior during this economic transformation; this situation has lasted for nearly three decades, with significantly different economic results.

Literature on the subject points out that the Constitution of Ukraine was written very broadly, and the exercising of the rights arising thereof was to a great extent impossible. In both countries, all political forces with a particularly large-scale involvement of the media participated in writing the constitution. These parties were post-communist in origin, whereas in Poland the Solidarity workers' movement, whose symbol was Lech Walesa, elected him as the first president of an independent Poland (1990–1995). In Poland, Lech Walesa was an authority, a leading opposition politician during the communist period, co-founder and first chairman of the Independent Self-governing Trade Union "Solidarity" (Polish: Niezależny Samorządny Związek Zawodowy "Solidarność"), and winner of the Nobel

Peace Prize in 1983, with strong national and foreign support. As president, Walesa effectively blocked any moves by those who nurtured nostalgia for communism, and had full public support. Ukraine did not possess such a leader. The first President of Ukraine was Leonid Kravchuk (Леонід Кравчук) (1991–1994), who helped maintain communism in the USSR during the soviet period. From 1958, he was a member of the CPSU (Communist Party of the Soviet Union). He had worked in the communist party's department of propaganda since the 1980s. In the 20th century he was a member of the Central Committee of the Communist Party of Ukraine. From 1988 to 1990 he served as head of the propaganda department and II secretary of the Central Committee, in 1989 he became a deputy member, and in 1990 he was a member of the Political Bureau of the Central Committee of the Communist Party of Ukraine. As president, he did not modify political customs which had been for him, de rigueur. While Walesa broke all formal and informal institutions which had arisen in communist Poland, in Ukraine Leonid Kravchuk (Леонід Кравчук) attempted to preserve these institutions by any means possible. This was significant since the constitutions in both Poland and Ukraine delineated the authority of the highest state officials in a broad manner, without establishing the specific limits of these powers, which in later years resulted in an overlapping not only of jurisdictions and political friction between the president, parliament and federal government but also of the courts and local government administration units in both Poland and Ukraine. In Poland, regional self-government was encouraged, whereas in Ukraine, attempts were undertaken to stifle this local self-government.

The processes of narrowing and expanding competence were ameliorated in Ukraine throughout this period (from 1990 to 2019), but especially in the amendment of the constitution, developed by President Leonid Kuchma and adopted in 2004 with insufficient votes of MPs in parliament (294 voted for, with a required minimum of 300), alternating the adoption of the system from one which was on the parliamentary-presidential border to an "oligarchization" of power, while in Poland this became especially evident only in 2014–2020, when the Law and Justice (Polish: Prawo i Sprawiedliwość) party expropriated the competence of a majority of the institutions of the state and transformed them into organs of (their) political party, without taking into consideration the rule of law, minimal electoral thresholds or the credibility which the voters held in parliament

In Ukraine, it was difficult to implement the provisions in the Constitution whereby Ukraine was to be a democratic state with a rule of law, in which society has an extensive social safety net; however, in Poland it has become difficult to maintain those provisions imposing an obligation of social solidarity. In Poland, social solidarity materialized regarding groups of extreme poverty with the 500+ package for large families, and the 13 monthly pension payments, which tackled the problem of income inequality, only in principle, since 2016.

Poland has been part of the European Union since May 1, 2004, under the Accession Treaty signed on April 16, 2003. In addition, the agreement between Ukraine and the European Union establishing a more profound and comprehensive free trade area (DCFTA), which is the most important and largest part of the Association Agreement between Ukraine and the EU, was signed in June 2014, and entered into force on January 1, 2016. Under the agreement, Ukraine has pledged to secure the free movement of capital and create a level playing field for companies from EU countries, which has de facto led to the break-up of free trade agreements with Russia and the Commonwealth of Independent States (CIS) (ros. Содружество Независимых Государств).

In 2013, Ukraine's attempt to strengthen ties with the EU led to a Russian-Ukrainian trade and energy war. Ukraine has not yet become a member of the European Union, and the withdrawal of public authorities from an accession treaty to the EU in 2013 led to the tragic events known as the Euromaidan (Ukrainian: Євромайдан), which began in Kyiv on November 21, 2013. The reason for the Euromaidan was precisely the failure to sign the Association agreement between Ukraine and the European Union by President Viktor Yanukovych, who served from 2010 to 2014 and after the Euromaidan, was forced to flee to Russia.

Today's institutional circumstances of the functioning of the Ukrainian economy are mainly due to its historical dependence, habits and social customs and the well-worn practices of exerting state power. For Ukraine today, the most important factor is the loss of territorial unity and the state's communication network, infrastructure and the breakdown of energy networks and other sectors of the economy, as well as the transfer of technology.

As regards the functioning of administrative units in Ukraine, Article 10(1) of Regulation (EC) No 1250/1999 shall be adopted in accordance with the procedure laid down in Article 132 of the Constitution which defines the territorial structure of the state based on the principles of unity and territorial integrity, composed of: The Autonomous Republic of Crimea (Ukrainian: Автономна Республіка Крим), oblasti (області), districts (райони), cities (міста), districts in cities (райони в містах), rural areas (селища) and villages (села) (Official interpretation of Article 133 of the Constitution). The cities of Kyiv and Sevastopol have been awarded a special status, as will be referred to later in this chapter. The military conflict in eastern Ukraine between pro-Russian separatists from eastern Ukraine, supported by the Russian Federation and forces loyal to the legitimate authorities of Ukraine. Led to new administrative map. The conflict led to self-proclation of The Donetsk People's Republic (DPR or DNR; Russian: Донецкая Народная Республика) and The Luhansk People's Republic (alternatively spelled as Luhansk People's Republic; Ukrainian: Луганська Народна Республіка), thereby severing political and economic relations with Ukraine for Russia, and also to Russia's annexation of Crimea by using her armed forces in 2014.

Formally, the territory of Ukraine is still divided into 24 circuits (Ukr. Область, Oblast), separated cities (Kyiv and Sevastopol) and one autonomous republic (Autonomous Republic of Crimea); in row II, Ukraine is divided into 490 districts (ukr. Район, rayon) and 185 cities separated from the districts (u. місто обласного значення – misto oblasnoho znachennia). In March 2014, Sevastopol and the Autonomous Republic of Crimea were unilaterally incorporated into Russia under a provision of the Verkhovnaya Rada Avtonomnoy Respubliki Krym (Postanovleniye ot 17 marta 2014 goda № 1745–6/14 O nezavisimosti Kryma); (Verkhovnaya Council avtonomnoy Respubliki Crimea, Postanovleniye ot 17 marta 2014 goda No 1745–6/14 About the Autonomy of Crimea). However, in Ukraine and in the international community, these regions are still considered to be a part of Ukraine. It is worth pointing out that Crimea was transferred to Ukraine by Russia in 1954 (Order of the USSR of 26.04.1954 O peredache crimea oblasti and sostava RSFSR v sostav Ukrainskoy SSR).

The districts in Ukraine are divided into councils: rural (two types: селищна рада – selishchna rada and сільська рада – sils'ka rada), and district and urban councils.

In Poland, the country's new territorial division was carried out on January 1, 1999, on the basis of a three-stage establishment of local authorities (regions, counties and municipalities (powiats)). Level I units are composed of 16 provinces, Level II units 380 districts and Level III units 2477 municipalities.

The general principles of the functioning of local authorities enshrined in the Constitution were developed in Ukraine by the Law of 24 April 1997, which repeats many provisions of Ukraine's ratified European Charter of Territorial Self-government from November 1996. In Poland, in turn, only part of the local and regional tasks are carried out by governmental agencies, which directly (hierarchically) are subject to the Council of Ministers, the Prime Minister or individual ministers. Today, in an increasingly centralized Poland, only that part of the administrative tasks, which is not of national importance, is carried out by the local government.

While territorial units are easily comparable in Poland, in Ukraine it is considerably more difficult. The dynamics, pace and proportions of Ukraine's economic indicators are largely influenced by unstable conditions for the functioning of regions and the market, which renders an analysis and proper forecasting of the dynamics of macroeconomic processes for Ukraine by classical methods, and especially in some regions, impossible (Duma 2017: 174). Even without the fear of separatist regions, literature on the subject draws attention to the functioning of the following five different regional systems (five classes of regions) in Ukraine based on modeling principles:

1 subsidized by the State with an internal potential for targeted changes;
2 chronically depressive, virtually devoid of economic potential;

3 developed, export-oriented;
4 isolated, mainly based on import substitution strategies;
5 shadow (тіньові), whose development is determined by factors not controlled by the structures of state power (see Duma 2017: 174–178).

In Ukraine, it is recommended to explore the economy in terms of survival, profit, earnings per share, return on investment (total or shareholders), volume of sales, growth (in sales, number of employees, capital employed or profit), efficiency, productivity (i.e., output per unit of some input), market position, product quality, product leadership, employee attitudes, employee morale and job satisfaction, accident rates, absenteeism and labor turnover, posture (i.e., ability to adapt to changing circumstances), social responsibility, and the most important points are:

1 profitability;
2 market position;
3 productivity
4 product leadership
5 personnel development
6 employee attitudes
7 public responsibility
8 balance between long-run and short-run goals

(see: Emmanuel et al. 1990: 33–34; Duma 2017).

The entire area of post-Soviet countries is characterized by subsidized regions, chronically depressive and shadow regions, forgotten by state authorities, or which conduct economic development independently of formal authorities, or are subordinated to large clans of the oligarchies. Duma and Dement'yev write that the state government in Ukraine is incapable of directly influencing the institutions, the size of investments, social programs, the size of the money supply or tax rates and tax collection, in general, in each and every region (Dement'yev, Vyshnevskyi 2010; Duma 2017: 174).

In the case of subsidized regions, there is a decrease in production and an increase in external development factors; however, they are unable to fill the budget. Spending is increasing and industrial production is insignificant, while social programs are also inefficient.

In chronically depressed regions, there is a lack of practical economic potential. Production is low and the standard of living is also low, leading to the need to build external development factors, not always targeted to the interior of the country, but often outside its borders (Russia, Belarus, Poland, Turkey).

In crisis-affected regions, physical growth in production does not lead to an acceleration of technological progress.

External sources of development are weakening with increased production costs, tax rates and macroeconomic risks, and this, in turn, promotes an increase in shadow structures. Investment is declining in shadow regions, and the region's fiscal budget is a facade. A general feature in Ukraine is that companies do not have sufficient resources for innovation and development, and business spending on research and development is comparable, if not worse, than state spending, for activities regarding the maintenance of political parties Dement'yev, Vishnevskiy 2010: 82). A more extensive explication of this problem is contained in Chapter 2.

In Poland, European Union support programs function in the regions, based on a subsidization of the sustainable development of the poorest regions of the European Union.

1.4 Powerful institutions: oligarchy and network

In the transforming economies of Poland and Ukraine, exceptionally powerful informal and formal institutions arose – informal, because they have never formally demonstrated their structure or principles of action or the values they are guided by, and formal, because they could usually be identified by name recognition, as the names of these companies oftentimes were combined with the names of politicians or businessmen. In Poland, these groups are not uniformly defined, whereas in Ukraine they are usually referred to by the name of their oligarchy or clan.

Oligarchies, as institutionally informal groups, were established on the basis of those who formally served in the soviet military or police, who worked "under cover" or with the quiet participation of politicians and the newly established security services, and they are characterized by an instrumental treatment of the state and society, and therefore a criminalization of the public sphere. In connection with these institutions, there were also institutional features of political corruption connected with these organizations, which fostered a lack of respect for the law, an erosion of social values and, most importantly, an undermining of social trust in political power from the public as a whole. The institutions described above were most exposed during the period of privatization and (re)privatization, which in Ukraine was conducted in one of the worst manners conceivable, the so-called mass privatization (coupon), which in terms of social justice was terrible, as it, on the one hand, allowed state property to be gradually expropriated by the former communist authorities, the former police and military (the KGB in Ukraine) and, on the other hand, permitted those criminal spheres associated with them to penetrate the state apparatus (Kolodii 2010; Nikulin 2012; Dolbneva 2019). In Poland, privatization was a priority for state policy, but no comprehensive solution to the problem of reprivatization was undertaken. Since the fall of the PRL (Polish Peoples' Republic), reprivatization has been carried out on the basis of administrative decisions and judgments. However, this applies only to cases where the acquisition of property was unlawful (e.g., lack of a legal basis or crossing the nationalization limits). In Poland, this has resulted in numerous social conflicts and a resort to extra-legal recovery methods, as well as to the unlawful acquisition of real estate. Poland remains the only country of the former Soviet bloc that has not systematically settled the subject of compensation for private property confiscated by the communist system. Often, huge estates find their way into "unknown" hands. Social injustice is facilitated by the lack of clearly written provisions in the criminal codes in both Poland and Ukraine, and in particular regarding bribery (divesting), that is, the acceptance of material benefits in connection with someone's fulfilling his public function or discrepancies concerning privatization (reprivatization).

In both Poland and Ukraine, groups related to the ambiguity of reprivatization have been created (Miszewski 2001; Nikulin 2012; Dolbneva 2019). From the level of ordinary awareness of the "oligarch" is someone who possesses a lot of capital, obtained in a manner which is not in accordance with the law, and has considerable political influence. The spoils are allocated among a chosen circle of people close to those in power, who act only in their own interests with the support of organized groups of people, of which they are the rulers. In Ukraine, groups of this type are referred to as clan-oligarchical, and relations formed in these groups are patronal-clientele. In this manner, both informal groups and officially registered associations, parties and even unions and parliamentary factions may be established. Oligarchy also appears where a specific financial and industrial group controls entire manufacturing industries together with the decision-making process of the state; that is, it becomes a financial-industrial-political group (Dolzhenkov 2000, 2002). In Poland, one refers rather to a group of network links. In both Poland and Ukraine, overt organized, special interest groups are of little importance (see: Lisnichuk 2002). There are, however, many types of pressure groups that operate in the shadows, and the four types of possible dysfunctional consequences from the activities of such pressure groups are (1) social protectionism (i.e., the tendency of groups to demand the preservation of positions and rights); (2) stagnations in management when government actions and initiatives are blocked; (3) denying collective discipline (i.e., when each group seeks to shift the burden of national expenditure to other groups); (4) changes in the balance of power, where the equality of power between different regions can be overturned, since each pressure group provides an unequal means of influence (Balabayeva 2015: 221).

The main areas of influence of these forces on governments are:

- influence on the government and making political decisions for them,
- influence on parties that control power and on their political decisions,
- influence on public opinion, influencing those in power and their political decisions (mainly by concentrating the mass media in their hands) (Teleshun, Reyterovych 2008).

The principles arising from state policy on restructuring the economy were and are still unclear in Poland and Ukraine, in particular those entrusted specifically for this purpose by politicians and relegated by politicians to agencies which in many cases have been allotted the powers of ministries. Numerous agencies have also received supervision regarding important processes for the economy. The multiplicity of such institutions and the transparency of legal regulations on the principles of their functioning allow us to pose a legitimate question even about their ordinary economic rationality, especially since they are quasi-market institutions operating in a live economic framework on an equal basis with the other participants of the market game, and partly supported by staff and financed by certain state structures or by an oligarchy or by a network. In the context of the current role of the state in the economic system, it seems essential to bear in mind that state officials who are directors of state-owned enterprises and, as may be assumed, are police/intelligence officers, and not necessarily from the highest level of power, would ever initiate a process of self-expropriation (Zalewa 2008: 114–115). The empowerment of the former communist elites is an institutionalized political process that over time has evolved into the empowerment of political elites in Poland regardless of political provenance (Jarosz 2004: 44), and in Ukraine according to regional clans and a trans-regional oligarchy (Szapowałenko 2010).

Countries have been created within a country with a network structure, whereby a group of people connected by a common interest, having a common purpose, be they a party or social and business links, are a fundamental element of the network (Staniszkis 2001: 94). The activities of these structures are also influenced by the highest authorities in the state (the president, for example, approves a specific person as chairman of the board of a large company, although his impact on the economic life of the country in terms of the system is constitutionally of minor significance). It seems, writes Zaza, that for the effectiveness of the economic system it is not important which party dominates the business-political system. More important is the progressive encapsulation of systems that foster the patronage-client system, with the patron having certain goods or leverage, and the customer is an entity who desires to obtain a profit through a specific transaction. It was in this way that the institution of political and economic clientele was created in Poland and Ukraine. The public interest, in theory, is supposed to be protected by the state. Thanks to state functionaries however, the state has been replaced by the sum of the interests of the members of a given structure – that is, oligarchy, clan, etc. (Gadowska 2002; Zalewa 2008: 117–118) – which strongly distorts the functioning of the political and economic mechanisms of democracy and the free market. The main conflicts and problems of individual groups of the network and oligarchical-clan are concentrated around those who will be the first to master a given segment (market) that will take over its character and how it is organized, all the while with shrinking resources at the disposal of the networks, oligarchies and clans.

There has also been a rather limited political participation and legitimization for at least ten years, by both Poles (Sobkowiak 2008) and Ukrainians

(Bortnikow 2010), which is caused by a lack of social faith in the functioning of democracy and a negative attitude towards politicians in general. In Poland, in the only national poll of this type, conducted in 2003, 74% of those surveyed said that politicians are dishonest, 76% that they were not credible and 82% that politicians cared only about their own interests, constitute a unified clique (network), linked to many common interests and were engaged in "various types of economic scandals" (44%) (CBOS 2003). A similar type of survey has yet to be carried out in Ukraine. It can only be assumed that the above-mentioned indicators are similar or even higher in Ukraine. In both Poland and Ukraine, the elections of the highest authorities are only the ritual of a new, emerging arrangement from a network of associations and of clan-oligarchic structures. Based on arbitrariness, an asymmetry of economic magnitude was established in Ukraine, which means that there is a surplus of power among some people and economic structures and a lack of power in others (Dement'yev, Vishnevskiy 2010: 89), which also interferes with the influx of foreign investment (Nosova 2012: 14–20). In Poland, these problems are perhaps not quite as magnified, but they are of a similar nature.

The period of the Orange Revolution (2004–2010) in Ukraine is described as "the initial stage of an anti-oligarchical struggle to preserve the direction of democratic development" (Kolodii 2010: 35). During this period, there was an institutional expansion of civil liberties, but there was also a continuing crisis of political power that had institutional characteristics. The effectiveness of institutional functioning (institutional performance) was diminishing, the indeterminacy of the powers and responsibility of these institutions had also increased, while citizens had a sense of a lack of real power and of the volatility of developments. The political life was overwhelmed with chaos and permeated with elements of anarchy, and on the other hand, with neo-patrimonial relations and the aspirations of influential political and business leaders to usurp power. In both Poland and Ukraine, manipulative democracy is growing to a greater extent than before, and there is no one fighting for true democracy (Kolodii 2010: 35). It may be affirmed that one of the causes of this situation is the passive attitude of society. In Ukraine, for example, protests during the Orange Revolution (in 2004), Euromaidan (in 2013), or the numerous protests in Poland (from 2015 to 2020) mobilized many people, but the vast majority of citizens approached them and the values they represented, as something foreign which, only introduced unnecessary chaos in the state. Poles felt the mechanisms of manipulative democracy in 2015–2019, under the rule of the Law and Justice party, a national-conservative, Christian and right-wing populist political organization in Poland. During this period, the neo-patrimonial relations and aspirations of influential leaders in politics, to usurp power, were intensified in Poland. The opposition was weak and fragmented, while that element of society which was protesting heretofore was exhausted. Nearly 50% of Polish society supported the authoritarian actions of the Law and Justice party, and thus expresses a need to retreat from the principles of democracy. In both countries, institutions of irresponsible social pluralism and the institutions affirming an undemocratic regime were established (Carothers 1999: 160–170; Carothers Th., de Gramont, D. 2013; Carothers, O'Donohue 2019).

Legislative assistance mainly consisted of programs for expanding the capacity of legislators and legislative staff, physical infrastructure improvement and support for watchdog NGOs and the media (Carothers 1999, 177–187). Expanding the capacity of legislators and legislative staffers involved training on the essence of democratic governance and its methods. Support for infrastructure, such as libraries and office equipment, is also necessary. Assistance for NGOs and the media ensures their watchdog function to encourage transparency and accountability in legislative bodies (Ichihara 2017). Such an infrastructure has not been created in Ukraine.

In Ukraine, separatism took over the Crimea and eastern Ukraine on April 6, 2014, when the so-called Donetsk People's Republic (Донецкая Народная Республика) was proclaimed, and on April 27, 2014, the self-proclaimed Luhansk People's Republic (Луганская Народная Республика)' was created, while in Poland "separatism" appears via an "internal" isolation from the problems of the state and society, an "internal exile", which has become especially evident in the last ten years.

Both Poland and Ukraine have adopted formal institutional arrangements, which are largely at odds with informal institutions, that is, social customs, habits or established principles of social coexistence. What is important for one nation and less important for another was not discussed when establishing constitutional or state regulations, which resulted in large social groups being systematically excluded from the decision-making process. In Ukraine, there were national and linguistic minorities, as well as less educated workers' and peasant masses, whereas in Poland, there were the poorly educated and heavily religious social masses of small towns and villages. Today, it turns out that in both countries, the voice of the excluded is beginning to play an increasingly important role, causing among "internal refugees" a general erosion of trust in the institutions of the state, on the one hand, and nationalism and real and "internal" separatism, on the other.

It should be noted that in Poland and Ukraine, the network and oligarchical-state system are relatively stable. Parliamentary and local government elections make certain reshufflings within the system, while the various structures are interested in its continuance, regardless of the political outcome. The weakness of state institutions leads to, amongst others, a growing interest in the networks of formal and informal ties and links, which thereby become one of the main resources of the transformative institutions of the economies of both those countries mentioned here.

With regard to Poland, Z. Krasnodębski writes that

> the greatest threat to democracy, to our freedom and our prosperity flows not from the underclass of the III Republic, but from its cultural,

> political and economic center, not from the bottom, but from the very top, from the post-communist and partially from the post-Solidarity network of "oldboys".
>
> (Krasnodębski 2003)

P. Zalewa writes that

> the non-market nature of the Polish economic system promotes the maintenance of individual network nodes.... In Poland, too many areas of economic life depend on the "kindness" on all levels of government officials and too much of the state's money is used to finance specific elements of the state network.
>
> (Zalewa 2008: 123–124)

Transparency International which publishes the "Corruption Perceptions Index" points out that in both Poland and Ukraine, social acceptance of political corruption is high (Ukraine Score 32/100; Rank 120/180, Poland Score 60/100; Rank 36/180 in 2018) (https://www.transparency.org/cpi2018).

Poland and Ukraine are not countries with a free market economy. There is quite a lot of economic freedom, but there is also, at the same time, a considerable lack of economic freedom. In Poland and Ukraine, the state, to a high degree, controls the market and its components to a great extent and imposes a framework for economic activities on the individual.

The legal and tax systems are not transparent, and the checks on taxpayers and penalties imposed on them often have a political basis. The most striking fact of the Polish and Ukrainian economies are the ambiguous legal and tax rules regarding the form and scope of economic activity. Regulations are contradictory, and sometimes the huge penalties imposed by the state on the taxpayer are the result of an individual interpretation of the law. The taxpayer is helpless in the face of the heartless state-fiscal machine, which oftentimes functions under the political dictatorship of party leaders or of officials who occupy a certain position in the state bureaucracy, and often don't act in the public interest, but rather in their own interest or in that of the network (clan) to which they belong. Both in Ukraine and Poland, the tax code is often created under the auspices of a particular taxpayer, oligarchy or other member of the network; however, this law does in fact become universally applicable. Often after meeting the needs of oligarchs and networks, certain laws are withdrawn or become dead letters, but they may be brought back to life if and when another oligarch or member of the network requires them. In Poland and Ukraine an institution called "legal privacy" exists. This is where a universally binding law is created for the private needs of those in power, or of people linked with them. Economic courts are not independent, and the taxpayer feels defenseless in face of the state apparatus. The institution of distrust in courts and state authorities, as well as the volatility and contradiction of the legislation passed, does not allow for long-term business strategies, without increasing transaction costs (including the price of corruption) (see: Kondratowicz 2013).

In 2019, Poland directly violated the standards of the European Union, which is a condition for Poland's membership in the organization, concerning the independence of the judiciary, including the economic judiciary. In the Finsberg Report (1990), the independence of the courts is indicated as an important and fundamental guarantee of the protection of civil rights and obligations.

In recent years, the aspirations of political parties to express their own worldview and imposing a lifestyle on society have been growing in Poland and Ukraine, and the intensity and scope of the political discussions is little related to the decision-making political policies in this regard. The "weltanschauung" of the Polish political elite of the Law and Justice party is authoritarian-conservative, based on the worldview of the conservative Catholic Church in Poland (prohibition of abortion, even after rape, prohibition of civil partnerships, legal and systemic protection for priest-pedophiles and common criminals associated with the Catholic Church). In Ukraine, the worldview is still ethnocentrist-nationalist and statist, in accordance with the principle of the "state above all".

The Economist Intelligence Unit's Democracy Index 2018 lists Poland among countries with a "flawed democracy", but Poland, according to the index, is only slightly above the threshold designating a group of countries called "hybrid regimes", while Ukraine is in the "hybrid regime" group, just slightly below the limit separating "flawed democracy" countries, where Poland is (Democracy Index 2018, https://www.eiu.com/topic/democracy-index, access date: 2020–01–10). The disparity in the index between the two countries is not statistically significant enough to recognize this difference as a lack of a possibility to compare Poland with Ukraine (Ukraine (5.69) in 2018, Poland (6.67) in 2018), at the border between these groups 6.00, for our research, nevertheless, this discrepancy should not be borne in mind. Douglas North points out that ideology not only plays an essential role in political choices (North 1990) but is also a key to those individual choices that affect economic performance. Individual perceptions concerning the fairness and justice of the rules of the game obviously affect performance (North 1992: 479).

In both Poland and Ukraine, difficulties are observed in the implementation of state-proposed institutional attitudes, but on the other hand there is less and less economic freedom, greater taxation of economic activities, difficulties with the bureaucracy and corruption. All these factors have an impact on regional development.

The institutional conditions of Poland and Ukraine should be looked at from different points of view and according to a variety of scales. In principle, it can be considered that these are areas which are alien to each other, and disproportionate to homogeneously accepted research paradigms. Russian- and Ukrainian-speaking authors, like Japan's Masahiko Aoki and Carothers, point out the complementary conditionality of corporate, political and social governance in Asian states, and those countries created after the fall of the USSR and their relationship with the features of their respective national cultures (Aoki 2002; Bessonova 2006; Lipov 2012; Carothers, Th., O'Donohue 2019). However, the research mainly deals with Kazakhstan and Russia, but not with Ukraine. With regard to Ukraine, it indicates that it has a multivariant structure of an institutional order of socio-political and corporate governance. There is one type of institutional structure in eastern Ukraine, another in the central part of the country and yet another in western Ukraine. It is even accepted that, indeed, this multivariant structure may have been the basis of the separatist movements, resulting from the fear of an unknown institutional order, put forward by the European Union or in the absence of EU acceptance, the institutional conditions of the Asian-post-Soviet structure in the countries formed after the fall of the USSR.

It can be concluded that three institutional and organizational cultures – acceptable, observed and implemented – clash in Poland and Ukraine. An acceptable order is the old post-Soviet order in the process of transformation and the quest for a new order. An observed order is an order which should be pursued but it has not been implemented. It could be an order of the new member states of the EU or an order of authoritarian states such as Russia, Belarus, etc. Once this order has been implemented, this is the kind that penetrates into the system in a regulated form, for example, the association treaties with the EU, or on the basis of institutional solutions developed by other countries, such as in the case of Poland, by Turkey or Hungary, and in the instance of Ukraine, by Russia. It should be noted that the system of Soviet countries has been in place, at least since the 1980s, and the desirability of the culture of the organizational order of the countries of Southeast Asia has appealingly permeated other countries, is attractively intersects, and on the other hand the culture of the social economy and institutional governance characteristic of the transaction culture of post-Ottoman states (mainly Turkey, Azerbaijan in the context of the order found in Iraq and Iran), and the least understandable in the post-Soviet countries, including Ukraine, is the so-called "European order", which, in fact, has been examined, only since the 1990s within the confines of its synergies. In many respects, after all, in Ukraine and Poland, this order is still more declaratory than implemented.

The source of this contradiction lies in the very human way of thinking – abstract, symbolic and above all in the diverse and multivariant perception of the world. In Poland and Ukraine, only people who have lived and worked for several years in other countries can accept this multivariant world, but these people also create the broad depths of differences between those who perceive the world solely on the basis of old, traditional values (in Poland clericalism and networks, in Ukraine a welfare state and oligarchy) and the newly acquired features of individualism versus those of collectivism.

As part of these institutional circumstances, habits, and socially worn out values, mankind is developing rational-logical thinking and creating its own cognitive alternative. Ultimately, priorities which have been established institutionally can only arise at a stage when society has attained an economic and political modernization, and the completion of this process may take several generations. It does not occur overnight. These are long-term processes, against which there is also strong social resistance. There is no, as M. Friedman and F. Hayek have already demonstrated, economic freedom without political and social freedom, and the latter must be liberated in man (Friedman 1962, 1993, 2002; Friedman, Friedman 1985; Hayek 1939, 1944, 1960). It is just as difficult to exchange worn out thinking and behavior for thinking and behavior which are institutionally desirable. This confrontation reflects the principle of unity in the struggle of opposites. Characteristic features of institutional behavior are the reactions and interactions, stimuli and conditional reactions – when some gain strength, others loose theirs. In terms of political and economic freedoms, A. Nowosad writes that the lines of political and economic freedom in Europe are negatively tilted towards the east of Europe (Nowosad 2016: 166–168).

The dialectic of alternative relationships (individualism/collectivism) or the principles of social orientation within the framework of the structural complementarity of socio-economic systems implies the existence of a certain state-geared social orientation, which can be called institutional. In such large, culturally and systemically multifaceted and, above all, young countries like modern Ukraine or Poland, this targeted social orientation is lacking something, as evidenced by a social and economic separatism, which in Kyiv led to the Maidan values, in the Donbas to separatism and civil war, and in Poland to "internal exile", that is, to a society becoming separated from state affairs. Both countries are in the process of transformation, but that does not mean that they are headed in the same or even a similar direction. In Poland, there is a distinct retreat from the western values cherished in recent years towards a more well-known authoritarian (which does not mean for the better) direction; however, Ukraine seeks to return to a western direction while at the same time recognizing that western values are considered to be unachievable.

1.5 Summary

The nature of the inclusion in the institutional system of factors affecting the composition of institutional elements and their interaction, as well as the choice of the level of analysis of institutional complementarity, suggests an allocation of endogenous and exogenous complementarity of economic systems. Endogenic complementarity reflects the interaction of institutions in an institutional system, subsystem, institution and exogenous – the quality of the institutional system's interaction in an external environment, the elements of which may be both other institutional systems as well as non-institutional economic phenomena that affect the functioning of the whole system. A key role in them is played by the system's social, political, material, technological and environmental conditions.

Freedom House in 2019 ranked both Poland and Ukraine as free electoral democracies, but not as liberal ones. Poland was rated at 84/100, which ranks it among countries such as Argentina, Panama, Mongolia, and Ghana. In 2018, Poland had six points of freedom less than Hungary (70) and the least among all European Union countries, and its new institutional solutions are moving towards remedies already known among the countries formed after the fall of the USSR: Ukraine (60), Kazakhstan (22) Russia (20). In Poland and Ukraine, the old system of thinking still exists, in a sense. O. Inshakov and D. Frolov opine that where the essence of the institution is not so much that of change, but a perpetuation of a way of doing things, is where a way of thinking emanates from. This is the level of relationship between form and function. The specificity of the institutional form is determined by its assigned function. In turn, the function depends on the institutional form (Kidrina 2001: 57–73; Inshakov, Frolov 2010: 67; Lipov 2012: 26–40). The presence of a functional gap is the starting point for the creation of a new institution and a new way of communicating institutional, political and economic governance. Fundamental institutions in system-transforming economies are, on the one hand, new and not known and, on the other, deep, historically stable and constantly reproducing social relationships. Not only they ensure the integration of different types of societies, but they also create their diversity. The function of the institution is the regulation of basic social subsystems, increasingly used for a channeled ideology, politics and the economy, both on a national and regional scale.

2 Ownership transformations in Poland and Ukraine

Svitlana Chugaievska, Rafał Wisła and Andrzej Nowosad

2.1 Introduction

In August 1991, Ukraine gained independence for the first time in its history. In October 1991, the first completely free parliamentary elections since World War II were held in Poland. Changes to the socio-economic system commenced (it can be said symbolically) in the same year in Poland and Ukraine, and they had a common denominator – the Gross Domestic Product (GDP) per capita[1] in both countries was at the same level (9.5 thousand USD, PPP,[2] in prices of the year 2011[3]). However, it is difficult to find other similarities.

Poland, in the early 1990s, had at its disposal several basic relatively scholarly institutions: its own currency, a central bank, the spirit and pragmatism of the free market, private ownership, its own state budget, a solidarity-intellectual elite based on the working class and a dissident intelligentsia, capable of developing and implementing reforms with the help of US professionals, and access to relatively reliable statistical data.

Ukraine, after the fall of the Union of Soviet Socialist Republics (hereinafter: the USSR), in the early 1990s, had no experience in building a market economy institution. Ukrainian society, brought up in a totalitarian system, had to face the extremely difficult task of creating a market economy institution and implementing democratic principles of the rule of law in a post-Soviet sphere of socio-economic development. It never possessed the conditions essential for the creation of democratic institutions. It is worth recalling that it went directly from a system of authoritarian monarchy (tsardom-autocracy) in Tsarist Russia – after the February Revolution (Russian: Февра́льская револю́ция, 1917) and the October Revolution (the October Revolution, officially known in Soviet historiography as the Great October Socialist Revolution, 1917), and the killing of Tsar Nikolai II Alexandrovich Romanov (May 18 [O.S. 6 May], 1868–July 17,1918) and the entire Tsarist-Imperial family, Russia (followed by Russian-occupied Ukraine) immediately began to build a communist state. At a time when these events took place, it was a modern idea, and the doctrine of the state was to be based on social justice, the protection used by the owners of the workers' capital, but quickly became the basis for one of the world's most terrifying and repressive totalitarian regimes.

The dissolution of the USSR in the 1990s surprised many in the republics that were part of the USSR as well as the leaders of the USSR itself. For the leaders of Ukraine, Russia and Belarus, however, it was no surprise because they initiated and signed the dissolution of the USSR, even though this was a surprise to many of the citizens of the USSR. Free market institutions, private property, financial markets and individual entrepreneurship were created from scratch, without the help of American specialists.

The many difficulties in institutional changes in Ukraine and Poland have been the subject of extensive research, and the basic literature on the subject has been presented in Chapter 1. The aim of this chapter is to provide a synthetic discussion of the process of ownership transformations in Poland and Ukraine, and the role of the capital market in the process of ownership between 1990 and 2015. The development of two selected institutions of the economy – private property and the capital market, a mechanism supporting privatization – is the main area of analysis in this chapter.

2.2 Privatization

The process of the ownership structure transformations in the Polish and Ukrainian economies is an important area of major institutional changes that took place in the sectors studied during the period of systemic transition from a communist regime, and a centrally planned economy, to a democratic regime and a free market. Both economies experienced nationalization at that time, a form of state-expropriation through which the state acquired the rights and ownership of land, businesses and capital under a legal act. Nationalization was carried out mainly without payment of compensation for existing owners, or for a symbolic remuneration. In Bolshevik Russia, in 1918, after the revolution, private property was nationalized without any compensation for private companies-owners, which was also extended to soviet-occupied Ukraine in the 1920s. (The opposite of nationalization is privatization.)

In Poland, nationalization was implemented in 1946 on the basis of the Law on the Acquisition of the Basic Branches of the National Economy (Act of 1946) and the Decree amending the Act, dated January 3, 1946, on the acquisition of the main branches of the national economy by the state. The processes of nationalization were accompanied, both in Poland and in Ukraine, by expropriation and confiscation, that is, a forced (without compensation or payment) deprivation of private property. These processes were conducted under the banner of building communism. The Communist Party manifesto announced that "communists can express their theory in one phrase: 'destruction of private property'" (знищенння приватної власності). In Ukraine, the processes of nationalization and expropriation began in 1919 and was a continuation of the process that began in Russia in

1918, on the basis of a decree of the High Council of the People's Economy (Вища Рада Народного Господарства)[4] and whose guidelines were sent to Ukraine, after its seizure by soviet troops, to the Ukrainian Council for The People's Economy (Українська Рада Народного Господарства).[5] In the process of nationalization and expropriation, the Ukrainian Council led the work of 45 faculties (відділ) with an extensive network of departments, management and centers and 10,720 regional units of active property collection. It was an intensive process which resulted in many victims and was concluded in 1921.

After the collapse of the USSR, both in Poland and in Ukraine, one of the most important tasks of the transformation was the privatization of state-owned enterprises and the privatization of property in general.

2.2.1 Privatization in Poland

Privatization in Poland, which began in 1990, was a number of diverse actions aimed at changing the ownership of private property while reducing state involvement in the economy (Bałtowski 2002: 17).

In July 1990, a law on the privatization of state-owned enterprises was passed in Poland[6] – the basic legal act triggering the process of ownership transformation in the country.

In the following years, laws were passed: on the management of agricultural property of the State Treasury,[7] on the ownership transformations of certain state-owned enterprises of particular importance for the economy,[8] on national investment funds (NFI) and their privatization.[9] These regulations enabled proprietary transformations using three basic privatization approaches:

1 Capital privatization – consisting of the conversion of a state-owned enterprise into a single-owner company of the State Treasury and subsequently its privatization by selling shares or stakes (often using the capital market) or transferring them to the NFI (National Investment Fund)
2 Privatization by liquidation – consisting of the liquidation of a state-owned enterprise for the sale of its assets, transfer to a company or putting it into non-gratuitous use
3 The inclusion of assets in the Agricultural Property Resources of the State Treasury – consisting of the liquidation of an agricultural enterprise and the acquisition of its assets by the Agricultural Property Agency of the State Treasury (Agencja Własności Rolnej Skarbu Państwa)

Poland when initiating, in the early 1990s, the process of ownership transformation encountered difficulties due to the lack of a bona fide register of state property.[10] Most of the production assets were the responsibility of

49 provincial offices (Urząd Wojewódzki). The grassroots initiatives of the workers' council or of the director of a state enterprise were not generally blocked by the provincial administration. For example, privatization in the Jelenia Góra region covered about 53% of state-owned enterprises by the end of 1995.

The most dynamic was the privatization processes in 1992 and 1994. Information about ownership transformations at the provincial level did not always go to the State Treasury Ministry, and if it was transmitted, the ministry did not maintain any database on the original formal and legal status of privatized assets, the number of transformations carried out and many other detailed bits of information on the basis of which a credible, myth-free image of the dynamics of privatization in Poland could have been created.

A much more reliable picture of the ownership transformation processes emerges from those ownership changes that took place directly under the supervision of the Ministry of the Treasury (Resort Skarbu Państwa). The Statistical Bulletin of the GUS (Biuletyn Statystyczny GUS) from 1991 reports that there were 8,453 state-owned enterprises operating at the end of 1990 in Poland. Between August 1, 1990, and the end of December 2015, 6,003 state-owned enterprises were included in the ownership transformation programs. At the end of 2015, the number of state-owned enterprises was 41, including 19 active business enterprises.[11]

Between 1991 and 2015, 1,756 state-owned enterprises were commercialized (29.3% of all converted enterprises), 2,308 applications for direct privatization (38.4% of all converted enterprises) were commercialized, and 1,939 state-owned enterprises were liquidated due to their poor financial condition under Article 19 of the Law on the privatization of state-owned enterprises in the absence of opposition from the Ministry of Property Transformation or the Ministry of the Treasury (32.3% of the total companies by at the end of 1990).[12] The grand total was some 6,003 state-owned enterprises. In 2013, the GUS[13] provided a specific number, that is, 7,555 entities that were covered by the privatization process between 1990 and 2012.

As a result of the commercialization of state-owned enterprises between 1990 and 2012, 1,710 companies were established.[14] Most companies were created in the Śląskie (306) and Mazowieckie (230) provinces, the least in the Lubuskie (35) and Warmińsko-Mazurskie (37). At the end of 2012, 1,047 companies were operating as a result of commercialization (in 2011 – 1097), including 178 single-member Companies of the State Treasury (there were 228 a year earlier).

At the end of 2015, the Minister of the State Treasury (Minister Skarbu Państwa) exercised ownership rights in 206 companies which were conducting economic activity (excluding 67 companies with only employee shares). The State Treasury's share was 100% in 87 companies out of the 206 "active" operating companies, in 29 companies the State Treasury held a majority stake, and in 90 companies the State Treasury held a minority stake.

In 217 companies, legal proceedings were conducted aimed at terminating their operations: in 73 companies the liquidation process was continuing, 68 companies went bankrupt, and 76 companies were not in operation.[15]

The experience of 25 years of economic transformation allows an overall positive assessment of Polish privatization. Although the Ministry of the Treasury did not possess, in the 1990s, a structured list of state-owned enterprises – that is, a register of its assets – the state's share as owner of the means of production between 1990 and 2015 decreased radically, according to both MSP and GUS data.

A comparison of the course and effects of Polish privatization with the same process conducted in Ukraine indicates that the path adopted and the methods used were generally appropriate. Numerous empirical studies and GUS statistics indicate that privatized companies are better managed than state-owned companies, and thus achieve better financial results. The effectiveness of the various privatization paths in Poland varies. Privatization with a strategic investor was the most effective method. The path of labor privatization was significantly less effective. By far the least effective method of ownership transformation turned out to be the NFI Programs – Programs of Universal Privatization (Stępniak-Kucharska 2015: 142).

One of the criticisms of the privatization process in Poland was the fact that the rules of privatization were not clearly defined, which led to numerous abuses. The state retained the right to decide the fate of a company as a whole, that is to say, the liquidation, merger with another entity or its sale (Zalewa 2008: 67) and the fact of top-down privatization, not bottom-up, which resulted in an asymmetry of information among entities and transformation for private purposes used by the previous communist mangers and, above all, by the directors of enterprises and employee's councils. This process in the 1990s was commonly referred to as the "pillaging of the economy" because a company's assets were sold for symbolic quotas – that is, pennies on the dollar, regardless of the condition of the company. It is worth mentioning that in Poland since 1987 the law has allowed the possibility of converting state-owned enterprises into commercial partnership companies, provided that the shareholders will be from various state organizations (Fedorowicz 1990: 25), and the Act of 24 February 1989 on certain conditions of consolidation of the national economy contained a general declaration as to the transfer to natural and legal persons of state-owned enterprises, for the purpose of doing business[16] (Guzek 1994).

The institutional framework for the privatization process was being prepared in Poland for at least five years before its formal initiation, by drafting the appropriate legislative acts. The laws were adopted under a specific recipient, and the form of the companies created was called "nomenclature companies", since it was only former communist party directors who established and conducted private activities using state assets (Gomułka 2013; Długosz 2014). It is also pointed out that for privatization purposes, a large number of institutions were established in Poland that functioned as companies and had the powers of ministries and were not under any real public control, such as the Agricultural Market Agency, 1990–2017, in 2017, merged with the Agricultural Real Estate Agency and transformed into the National Agricultural Support Centre; The Agricultural Property Agency of the State Treasury (1991–2017; converted in 2003 into the Agricultural Real Estate Agency; the Military Real Estate Agency (2005, transformed into the Military Property Agency in 2015); the State Coal Agency Joint Stock Company (1990, in 2003 converted into the Coal Company Joint Stock Corporation, in 2016 acquired by the Polish Mining Group Joint Stock Company), etc. It is already clear from the names of the agencies that they can be segregated by the economic sectors in which the state has retained supervision, and their task was to carry out privatization. Today, they are among the largest companies in Poland. It is worth noting that the functions, tasks and competences of such enterprises with the competence of the ministries were created as companies with public money, which is a characteristic of Polish privatization, although in Poland none of these network systems are officially referred to as an oligarchy. Nevertheless, these are networks of shadow systems, of old political arrangements and of state-policy-business-privatization links. The state apparatus has great legal, semi-legal and illegal capabilities in Poland to fight organized crime; however, the ministry-companies and their privatizations were never the subject of a criminal investigation conducted by the public prosecutor's office. The Polish security services and the judiciary not only do not combat such phenomena, but are also interested in maintaining and supporting them. "Protection" of the system according to the patron-client principle is a characteristic of the privatization era (see: Gadowska 2002; Jarosz 2004: 44; Zalewa 2008: 117).

2.2.2 Privatization in Ukraine

In 1991, Ukraine regained its independence and began to reform both the political and legal, as well as the economic systems. The dissolution of the Soviet Union led to the creation of more than a dozen independent states, resulting in the disintegration of dependencies within the Union of Soviet Socialist Republics, including the dissolving of dependencies between former soviet republics and the businesses operating in their territory. One of the most important challenges – institutional changes – on the path to systemic and economic change has become the privatization of the state sector – a key element of the socialist system.

The reference point for the proposed ownership transformations in Ukraine in the early 1990s was the experience of decentralizing the public sector of the economies of the Western European countries of the 1970s and 1980s. However, ownership changes in western European countries have taken place under the conditions of a structured and mature private property institution, while in Ukraine it was necessary to construct this institution almost from scratch, by creating adequate legal bases and forming the relevant institutions, a process which continues to this day.[17]

At the initial stage of the ownership transformation process – national privatization, based on the Law on the Privatization of State Property (1992) – the transfer of "property titles" to part of the state assets in the form of a new type of securities, that is, privatization coupons, was organized.

The main reasons were (1) the taking up of public and managerial functions in privatized companies by the former bureaucratic apparatus, (2) questionable valuations of companies intended for coupon privatization and (3) a profound pauperization of society. Under the conditions of hyperinflation, combined with the unpunctual payment of wages, the reprivatization coupons were often exchanged in "currency kiosks" for an amount of money equal to the cost of three to four loaves of bread.

In 1995, in the industrial processing sector of Ukraine, where the process of ownership transformation took place at the fastest pace, state-owned enterprises, nevertheless, continued to dominate. At the beginning of the ownership transformation process, they were estimated to be around 8,900 companies, that is, approximately 70% of the total number of state-owned enterprises. By 1995, 3,701 companies had been commercialized; only one of them was completely privatized.[18] In 1997, the classification of legal entities changed; hence, the existing organizational and legal forms in the early 1990s and those in force after 1997 are quite difficult to compare.

In 1996, the Company register was created (Єдиний державний реєстр фізичних осіб-підприємців та громадських формувань – JPRPOU) – that is a system for collecting, accumulating and processing data on enterprises and organizations operating in all legally permitted forms of ownership. Since 1997, the process of ownership transformation has taken on a faster pace. It should be noted, however, that the consolidation of data sets concerning corporate entities was not started until 1998, hence the lack of data for 1995. Since 1996, UKRSTAT has kept a record of data for all economic operators together, in one group, without distinguishing between forms of ownership in the manufacturing processing sector. The dynamics of changes in the number of economic operators according to different forms of ownership between 2000 and 2015[19] are presented in Table 2.1.

The number of state-owned enterprises decreased significantly during the analysis period. In 2000, The State Property Fund of Ukraine (Фонд державного майна України, Fond derzhavnoho mayna Ukrayiny) reported nearly 10,000 state-owned enterprises on its balance sheet. After 15 years, this number has fallen to 4,042 companies. The increasing number of limited liability companies is explained by their attractive legal and business construction, commonly used in business activities in Ukraine. A very significant decrease in the number of public limited liability companies between 2010 and 2015 can be explained by the mass closure due to the break-up of trade relations with the Russian Federation, and a

Table 2.1 Number of economic entities in Ukraine between 2000 and 2015 (in thousands)

Indicator	*2000*	*2005*	*2010*	*2015*[20]
State sector				
• State-owned enterprises	9.9	7.8	6.8	4.0
• Public utility	…	16.5	16.0	11.5
Private sector				
• Private companies (entrepreneurs)	175.9	2380	283.7	201.9
• Public limited liability companies (spółki akcyjne)	35.2	34.6	30.2	15.9
• Limited liability companies (spółki z o.o.)	198.1	302.9	418.1	453.9

Source: State Statistics Service of Ukraine: http://www.ukrstat.gov.ua.

strong increase in the prices of Russian raw materials (2013–2014) used by Ukrainian industry.

In 2008, the Center for Economic Development (Центр економічного розвитку, Tsentr ekonomichnoho rozvytku) based in Kyiv conducted a retrospective analysis of the effects of the privatization processes in Ukraine. During the timeframe considered, three main stages of the ownership transformation process were identified. Stage one (1992–1994) was characterized by a slow pace of privatization and the gradual buyback of previously leased state property. Stage two was mass privatization using privatization coupons (1995–1998). At this stage, the securities trading market was established, while the base of state assets intended for privatization employing privatization coupons was expanding. The main barriers to effective privatization at this stage were a low standard of living (hence the rapid resale of privatization coupons), a dearth of knowledge on the rules of how a market economy functions and hyperinflation. The third phase, from 1999 to 2004, was characterized by a decrease in the average state revenue from the sale of medium and large state property entities and a reduction in the sale of state-owned enterprises to strategic industrial investors (see Paskhaver et al. 2008: 85).

The last decade has seen the creation of large Ukrainian business groups with an agricultural, industrial and financial profile. This is linked to the formation of a new Ukrainian elite – representatives of "big business", which use the intensive involvement of foreign capital by Ukrainian companies on the external market for their modernization and expansion. The last few years have manifested a marked increase in the value of direct foreign investment in Ukraine, but also of considerable Ukrainian capital investment abroad (see: Leonov, Zhuk 2005: 135; Andriychuk 2015: 12–22).

According to data from the State Property Fund of Ukraine (Фонд державного майна України, Fond derzhavnoho mayna Ukrayiny (SPFU), a central body of executive power with special status and being administered by the Cabinet of Ukraine, in 1992–2017 more than 132,700 entities were privatized. Of these, 29,610 were state entities, and 103,090 were municipal property facilities. The total budgetary revenue from the privatization of state property during the analysis of ownership conversions was 67 billion UAH (SPFU 2018).

Since 2017, there has been an online platform for the sale of small privatization facilities https://prozorro.sale/ (ProZorro.Продажі). A mechanism has been put in place to block rogue entities from participating in the state property rental competition. Currently, 18,906 state-owned economic facilities are leased (as of January 2018; SPFU 2018).

At the end of 2017, 3,893 state companies were registered in the SPFU and public utility companies numbered 11,640. The state has majority packages in approximately 500 capital companies (SPFU 2018). The issue of ownership changes of large and strategic state-owned enterprises and an increase in the efficiency of the management of Ukraine's agricultural property are still not resolved.

The current geopolitical situation and the declining average living standard create a social and economic situation and social sentiment reminiscent of those from 1995 to 1998, that is, the risk of selling off state and private assets below their fair value, and are therefore not conducive to stabilization.

In general, any assessment of the current process in the ownership transformation in Ukraine and its results is not unambiguous. Two opposing forces are clashing. On the one hand, a strong pro-market stimulus has been unleashed, which has contributed to a radical change in the political and economic system, including the construction of a private property sector from scratch, and the emergence of national production capital, which played a particularly positive role in ensuring a high pace of economic growth in the period of 2005–2008 (Chenash 2013: 55–60; Khoma, Kondakova 2013: 280–286). On the other hand, the privatization methods employed, the lack of proper control over their course and corruption caused tensions in Ukraine's social fabric. The gap between the narrow group of "winners" and a broad group of "losers" in the process of ownership transformation (Paskhaver et al. 2008) became one of the causes of the political crisis in the country – the Orange Revolution (Ukrainian: Помаранчева революція, Pomarancheva revolyutsiya) 2004 and the Euromaidan (Євромайдан, Yevromaidan) in 2013–2014.

2.3 The capital market – a mechanism to support ownership transformation

Long-term finance capital is understood to be one of the tools of the equity path of ownership transformation and the mechanism for converting national savings into corporate sector investments. A mature and efficient capital market is also a mechanism: economic optimization and rationality, trans-economic turnover and the financial supply for projects with above-average economic risks (new business models, new product solutions)

The aim of this part of the chapter is to generally diagnose the potential of the Polish and Ukrainian equity and debt securities equity, as a mechanism used to increase the allocative and dynamic efficiency of the huge long-term capital finance required.

The following assumptions are made in the subsection: (1) a well-functioning and developed capital market contributes to economic growth and job creation, (2) companies present on the capital market as issuers of equity and/or debt securities are characterized by a higher than average intensity in R&D activities, (3) a well-functioning and developed capital market supports fair economic turnover.

The development of the Polish capital market is closely observed by Polish and Ukrainian economists (see: Madej 1998; Krasnov 2001; Arkhireyev 2006; Harutyunyan 2017), and the results of its analysis in Poland were regularly published in the journal *Rynek Kapitałowy: miesięcznik analiz polskiego rynku kapitałowego* (Capital Market: a monthly analysis of the Polish capital market, 1998–2008), and by the National Bank of Poland in recurring reports entitled "The Financial Market in Poland" (1998–2018);[21] in Ukraine in "Visnyk of the National Bank of Ukraine" (Вісник Національного банку України), since 1994.

2.3.1 The Polish capital market

Individual operating segments of the financial market have been developing in Poland since the early 1990s. The interbank market will be the first to develop the following segments: interbank deposits, treasury bills and currency exchange. In parallel with the interbank market, the market for equity and debt capital is developing within the market governed by securities trading. The main driving force behind the development of the equity market was privatization, while for the debt securities market, it was the issuing of treasury bonds.

The development of the financial capital market depends not only on economic conditions but also on the quality of created institutions – i.e. the durability and efficiency of regulatory solutions resistant to the dynamics of changes in an economic environment. Capital market institutions in the 1990s of the 20th century, just before accession to the European Community, as well as during the period of full membership of the EU's internal capital market, are characterized by high volatility.

The ratification of the Europe Agreement establishing an association between the Republic of Poland and the European Communities (1992)[22] has necessitated a consistent alignment in the manner national institutions operate, in comparison with those institutions already developed in nations within the European Community. In the 1990s, with regard to the capital market, significant changes in capital market regulations were observed. These activities were linked with the development of the internal market or from the single-currency zone within the European Community.

In 1999, the European Financial Services Action Plan (FSAP) was adopted by the European Commission. In 2000, the European Council recognized it as an important part of the so-called Lisbon Strategy. According to the original assumptions, the majority of the actions taken under the FSAP related to the capital market and retail financial services. In the preceding period, as well as during the creation of the FSAP, these areas were the least integrated with the European financial market.

The following directives adopted by the European Parliament and the Council of the EU are among the most important capital market regulations during this period: (1) regarding prospect uses (2003/71/EC), (2) regarding markets in financial instruments (Markets in Financial Instruments Directive – MiFID; 2004/39/EC), and (3) regarding transparency and information obligations (2004/109/EC). All these changes in EU capital market regulations are fully reflected in the Polish legal order, that is, in the 2005 package of laws: (1) on the trading of financial instruments,[23] (2) on the public offer and conditions for the introduction of financial instruments into an organized trading venue and on public companies[24] and (3) supervision of the capital market.[25]

Among European countries, the capital market in Poland is in tenth place (±2 places depending on the year) according to the criterion of the capitalization of companies and the value of trading in shares.[26] Europe's biggest markets are currently Euronext with a market capitalization of nearly $4 trillion and the London Stock Exchange Group with a capitalization of $3.8 trillion at the end of 2018. The market value of listed companies on the Warsaw Stock Exchange is about USD 160 billion, and the capitalization of the Ukrainian Stock Exchange (Українська біржа, Ukrayinska birzha) is 4.4 billion USD. Similar levels of capitalization are found in the Cyprus Stock Exchange ($3.3 billion) and the Ljubljana Stock Exchange ($7.1 billion). At the end of 2018, there were 854 companies listed in Warsaw and 86 in Kyiv.

In the EU, the level of individual capital markets development and their importance in the local economy varies greatly, which is best reflected in stock market capitalization, the number of listed companies or the ratio of capitalization of exchanges to GDP. In Poland, this relationship is about 38%. By comparison, in the United States it is about 160%; around 150% in the UK; around 100% in France, Finland and Belgium; and less than 10% in Lithuania, Latvia, Cyprus and Slovakia. For Ukraine, this ratio is currently difficult to determine.[27]

2.3.2 *The Ukrainian capital market*

The position in the ranking of the capitalization of the Ukrainian Exchange against the background of the Warsaw Stock Exchange (WSE) (Polish: Giełda Papierów Wartościowych w Warszawie – and other European exchanges) prompts one to search for the reasons for the observed weak competitive position in the area of securities trading in Europe. Harutyunyan proposes a periodization of the stages of development of the Ukrainian capital market, which can assist us to understand the causes of the observed weak competitive position of the Ukrainian capital market (Harutyunyan 2017).

Between 1990 and 1999, a mass privatization of state-owned enterprises was carried out, which created the National Bank of Ukraine (Ukrainian: Національний банк України, Natsionalnyy bank Ukrayiny) and the first Stock Exchange (Trading Information System (Ukrainian Торгівельно-інформаційна Система, Torhovelno-informatsiyna Systema).[28] In 1997, the National Securities and Stock Market Commission began to operate (Ukraine) (Ukrainian: Національна комісія з цінних паперів та фондового ринку, Natsionalna komisiya z tsinnykh paperiv ta fondovoho rynku).

Between 2000 and 2009 the infrastructure framework of Ukraine's institutional financial system was revised. The banking system was developed and the legal bases for the activities of exchanges were standardized. It was only at this stage that the process of educating the private shareholders of the largest industrial companies, combined with a noticeable and deliberate transformation of national savings into investments by companies, began. However, capital control and corruption were among the major barriers to capital market development during this period.

Institutional changes in the financial sphere coincided with a good economic situation in the real economy. Between 2001 and 2007, real GDP per capita in Ukraine increased by 60.7%. Such favorable results were mainly due to the undertaken economic reforms related to the conversion of the Ukrainian currency (UAH), stabilization of inflation, increasing the competitiveness of domestic production and the creation of favorable conditions for the development of innovation and entrepreneurship (Pustovoit 2016: 86–109). The equity securities market and the debt market were discounting the overall prosperity. The issue of a new series of shares and bonds (government and corporate) expanded from UAH 47.3billion (in 2000) to UAH 95.6 billion (in 2010). The liquidity of the securities market dramatically increased from UAH 39.2 billion (in 2000) to UAH 1 537.8 billion (in 2010). Over the whole of the year under consideration, there was a marked increase in the share of government bond issuance and their increasing share of total securities turnover (46.4% in 2010).[29] The economic prosperity of this decade created a climate of trust in the institutions of the financial system. In October 2008, a consolidated Ukrainian Exchange was established (Українська біржа, Ukrayinsa birzha) in Kyiv. The main motivation was to create a transparent securities trading platform conducive to corporate governance, to attract foreign capital and to integrate securities market operators into international competition.

The last decade (2009–2019) was characterized by political instability, nationalization trends (the case of PrivatBank, ПриватБáнк), a decrease in confidence in the financial system, a weak economic downturn, the depreciation of the UAH, difficulties in fulfilling the conditions of cooperation with the International Monetary Fund (IMF), continuing restrictions on capital turnover, the inoperable criminal justice system and corruption.

In these circumstances, any development of the capital market is extremely difficult. In a development strategy paper entitled: "A Comprehensive Development Program for the Finance Sector of Ukraine by 2020" (Комплексна програма розвитку фінансового сектору України до 2020 р.; Compleksna prohrama rozvytku finansovoho sectoru Ukrainy do 2020), the need for an evolution based on those standards developed in the western part of Europe is stressed.[30] From the perspective of 2018, the biggest weaknesses of the Ukrainian capital market include the downward trend in trading volume, the low level of free float, the limited and decreasing number of investors, and the construction of the main stock market index (Акції в Індексі UX) based in 72% on the results of the shares quotations of 3 companies (Центренерго,[31] Мотор Січ,[32] Укрнафта[33]).

The Polish capital market is the largest and most developed market in Central and Eastern Europe and is an important element in the corporate development financing system. Compared to the largest capital markets in Europe, Poland is a relatively small market with little capitalization and turnover. The Warsaw Stock Exchange is more than ten times smaller than the stock exchange in Switzerland, and the scale may compare with the markets in Turkey or Norway, but it is 35 times the size of the Kyiv Stock Exchange. Only macroeconomic stabilization combined with the implementation of the standards and principles of the member states of the European Union can change the competitive position of the capital market and its impact on the Ukrainian economy.

The Ukrainian capital market is still not an important tool for ownership transformation and an efficient mechanism for converting national savings into investments in the business sector, nor does the creation of transparency augment economic turnover.

2.4 Summary

The experience of the last 25 years allows for an overall positive assessment of the Polish way of ownership transformation and the development of private property institutions. The share of the Polish State as owner of the means of production between 1990 and 2015 decreased radically.

In general, an assessment of the heretofore process of ownership transformation in Ukraine and its results is not clear. On the one hand, the process of ownership transformation is still far from completed, and is considered an important impetus for the development of a market-oriented political and economic system; on the other hand, selected privatization paths, a lack of proper control over its course and corruption have caused great dissatisfaction and a lack of the universal public acquiescence required to continue this process by the methods employed until now. Privatization in Ukraine is an unfinished process.

The Polish capital market during the first two decades of the economic transformation was significantly involved in the process of the privatization of the public sector. The sale of shares of state-owned companies was one of the most important changes in the whole process of the transformation of the ownership structure of Polish companies. The Ukrainian capital market is much less involved in the process of the ownership transformation of the Ukrainian economy and its entities. It is to be assessed as a barely efficient mechanism for supporting private sector development in Ukraine.

Notes

1 The GDP per capita is based on the purchasing power parity (PPP). The PPP GDP is the gross domestic product converted to international dollars using purchasing power parity rates. An international dollar has the same purchasing power over GDP as the US dollar has in the United States. The GDP at the purchaser's prices is the sum of the gross value added by all resident producers in the economy plus any product taxes, and minus any subsidies not included in the value of the products. It is calculated without making deductions for the depreciation of fabricated assets or for the depletion and degradation of natural resources. Data are in current international dollars based on the 2011 ICP round.

2 Purchasing power parities (PPPs) are indicators of price level differences across countries. PPPs tell us how many currency units a given quantity of goods and services costs in different countries. PPPs can thus be used as currency conversion rates to convert expenditures expressed in national currencies into an artificial common currency (the Purchasing Power Standard, PPS), eliminating the effect of price level differences across countries.

The main use of PPPs is to convert national accounts aggregates, like the Gross Domestic Product (GDP) of different countries, into comparable volume aggregates. Applying nominal exchange rates in this process would overestimate the GDP of countries with high price levels relative to countries with low price levels. The use of PPPs ensures that the GDP of all countries is valued at a uniform price level and thus reflects only differences in the actual volume of the economy.

3 The prices of the so-called base year prices, 2011 = 100, serve to determine physical changes in the size of the aggregate economic volumes (GDP, investment) in a valuable sense. The purpose of applying the prices of the base year is to eliminate the impact of current price developments on the dynamics of the categories tested. The prices of the base year ensure the comparability of changes over different periods

4 *Entsyklopediya istoriyi Ukrayiny*: Vol. 1: A-V/Redkol.: V. A. Smoliy (holova) ta in. NAN Ukrayiny. Instytut istoriyi Ukrayiny. – K.: V-vo "Naukova dumka", 2003. – 688, Access: http://www.history.org.ua/?termin=Vyscha_Rada (18.01.2020).

5 Marochko V. *Ukrayins'ka Rada Narodnoho Hospodarstva – 2*, Access: http://www.history.org.ua/?termin=Ukrainska_hospodarstva

6 Ustawa z dnia 13 lipca 1990 r. o prywatyzacji przedsiębiorstw państwowych, Dz. U. z 1990 r. nr 51, poz. 298.

7 Ustawa z 19 października 1991 r. o gospodarowaniu nieruchomościami rolnymi Skarbu Państwa (Dz. U. 1991, nr 107, poz. 464).

8 Ustawa z 5 lutego 1993 r. o przekształceniach własnościowych niektórych przedsiębiorstw państwowych o szczególnym znaczeniu dla gospodarki państwa (Dz. U. 1993, nr 16, poz. 69).

9 Ustawa z dnia 30 kwietnia 1993 r. o narodowych funduszach inwestycyjnych i ich prywatyzacji (Dz. U. 1993, nr 44, poz. 202).

10 Before they proceeded with the process of ownership transformation, the Czechs first drew up a detailed register of state property (including craft workshops and other small businesses engaged in sectors of the service industry).

11 State-owned enterprises entered in the register of entrepreneurs

12 Ownership transformations of state-owned enterprises, MSP, 2016, Access: 2018-12-01, https://bip.msp.gov.pl/bip/raporty-analizy/przeksztalcenia-wlasnos/10245, stan-na-dzien-31-grudnia-2015-roku.html]

13 *Prywatyzacja przedsiębiorstw państwowych w 2012 roku, Notatka informacyjna*, GUS, 2013, p. 1.

14 Ibidem.

15 *Ownership transformations of state-owned enterprises*, MSP, 2016, Access: https://bip.msp.gov.pl/bip/raporty-analizy/przeksztalcenia-wlasnos/10245.

16 *Ustawa z dnia 24 lutego 1989 r. o niektórych warunkach konsolidacji gospodarki narodowej oraz o zmianie niektórych ustaw*, Dz.U. 1989 nr 10 poz. 57.

17 *Zakon Ukrayiny Pro pryvatyzatsiyu derzhavnoho mayna*, Vidomosti Verkhovnoyi Rady Ukrayiny 1992, No. 24, p. 348 (Закон України Про приватизацію державного майна (Відомості Верховної Ради України (ВВР), 1992, № 24, ст. 348), Access: http://zakon.rada.gov.ua/laws/show/2163-12.

Zakon Ukrayiny; Pro Derzhavnu prohramu pryvatyzatsiyi, Vidomosti Verkhovnoyi Rady Ukrayiny (Закон України; Про Державну програму приватизації, Відомості Верховної Ради України (ВВР), 2000, N 33–34:. 272) Access:: http://zakon.rada.gov.ua/laws/show/1723-14.

Zakon Ukrayiny, Pro Derzhavnu prohramu pryvatyzatsiyi (Закон України, Про Державну програму приватизації) 2010–2014 from 5.08.2010, Source: http://www.spfu.gov.ua/documents/962.html

Zakon Ukrayiny, Pro pryvatyzatsiyu derzhavnoho i komunal'noho mayna (Vidomosti Verkhovnoyi Rady (Закон України, Про приватизацію державного і комунального майна (Відомості Верховної Ради (ВВР), 2018, № 12, ст.68) from 18.01.2018 r Source: http://zakon.rada.gov.ua/laws/show/2269-19.

18 The statistical yearbook "Ukraine in numbers" (Rocznik statystyczny "Ukraina w liczbach"). Source: http://www.UKRSTAT.gov.ua. Personal conversation with employees UKRSTATu. http://www.UKRSTAT.gov.ua. Personal conversation with employees of UKRSTAT.

19 Consolidated datasets About Legal People started only in 1998, hence the lack of data for 1995. Since 1996, UKRSTAT has kept a record of data for all economic operators together, without distinguishing between the forms of ownership in the manufacturing-processing sector.

20 Data for year 2015 does not contain information on occupied Crimea and the ATO territory.

21 Financial System Development Reports, Access: https://www.nbp.pl/homen.aspx?f=/en/systemfinansowy/rozwoj.html.

22 Ustawa z dnia 4 lipca 1992 r. *o ratyfikacji Układu Europejskiego ustanawiającego stowarzyszenie między Rzecząpospolitą Polską a Wspólnotami Europejskimi i ich Państwami Członkowskimi*, sporządzonego w Brukseli dnia 16 grudnia 1991 r. (Dz. U. 1992, nr 60, poz. 302).

23 Dz. U. z 2005 r., nr 183, poz. 1538.

24 Dz. U. z 2005 r., nr 184, poz. 1539.

25 Dz. U. z 2005 r., nr 183, poz. 1537.

26 These are estimates based on World Bank Data (2019), and the World Federation of Exchanges database (Access: 2019-01-07, https://data.worldbank.org/indicator/CM.MKT.LCAP.CD?view=chart); StockMarketClock.com (2019), List of Stock Exchanges (Access: 2019-01-07, https://www.stockmarketclock.

com/exchanges) and World Federation of Exchanges (2019), Market Statistics – December 2018 (Access: 2019-01-07, https://focus.world-exchanges.org/issue/december-2018/market-statistics).

27 See. http://www.ux.ua/en/ (Market Capitalization, UAH, bln).

28 Stock trading, however, in Ukraine dates back to 1992. Until 2008, the "Exchange" did not have a guaranteed system for the execution of transactions. The trading technology was based on bulletin boards or a message exchange system. This generated a huge operational risk for securities trading.

29 Along with annual reports of Natsional'na Komisiya Z Tsinnykh Paperiv Ta Fondovoho Rynku (Національна Комісія З Цінних Паперів Та Фондового Ринку). Access: http://www.ssmsc.gov.ua/).

30 Kompleksna prohrama rozvytku finansovoho sektoru Ukrayiny do 2020 roku: Postanova Pravlinnya Natsional'noho banku Ukrayiny vid 18 chervnya (*Комплексна програма розвитку фінансового сектору України до 2020 року: Постанова Правління Національного банку України від 18 червня 2015*). *Retrieved from: https://bank.gov.ua/doccatalog/document?id=43352266*; Lyashenko, S. V. (2011), *Capital market in Ukraine and ways of cooperation with the countries of the commonwealth of independent states (CIS).* Economic Herald of the Donbas, Vol. 4 (26), s. 151–162.

31 http://www.centrenergo.com/.

32 http://www.motorsich.com/ukr/.

33 https://www.ukrnafta.com/.

3 Structural changes in the Polish and Ukrainian economies against the background of other Central and Eastern European countries

Rafał Wisła, Svitlana Chugaievska, Andrzej Nowosad and Umit Turanli

3.1 Introduction

In June 1989, communism ended in Poland. The inflation rate was 640% per annum, the Polish currency did not have a widely accepted internal exchangeability – the market converted it to dollars – and shop shelves were bare. Poland was threatened with an economic catastrophe. The free market, fight against inflation, budgetary discipline, politically independent monetary policy, opening up to foreign trade and sanctioning unemployment were the main assumptions and tools of Poland's new economic policy. In the early 1990s, the Polish economy underwent a revolution.

In 1989, Ukraine was one of the republics of the Union of Soviet Socialist Republics (USSR) whose independent economy was part of an inefficient Soviet economic organism. As a result of the 1990s systemic transformation in Ukraine was overtaken by conglomerates, while output in all production sectors decreased by more than 50%. Hyperinflation in the early 1990s was the result of, amongst others, a lack of independence of the Central Bank of Ukraine, which led to a destabilization of the state's finances and a significant devaluation of the Ukrainian currency.

In Ukraine the 1990s were a period of deep economic recession. The situation in Ukraine was also indirectly exacerbated by the Russian financial crisis of 1998, which did not have much impact on Poland. The Ukrainian GDP per capita (in PPPs, at fixed prices from 2011) fell from 9,500 USD in 1991 to 4,500 USD in 1999. In 2017, it did not retain its 1991 level – 7,900 USD per capita. By comparison, in Poland, the GDP per capita has grown by nearly 190% over the last 27 years from 9,500 USD in 1991 to 27,000 USD in 2017 (Figure 3.1). In 2018, the Polish GDP per capita was three times higher than in 1991 (The World Bank 2019).

Between 2000 and 2007, the real GDP per capita increased by 83% in Ukraine. The Russian financial crisis combined with the gas conflict with Russia led to a one-year, significant recession in Ukraine in 2009 (nearly

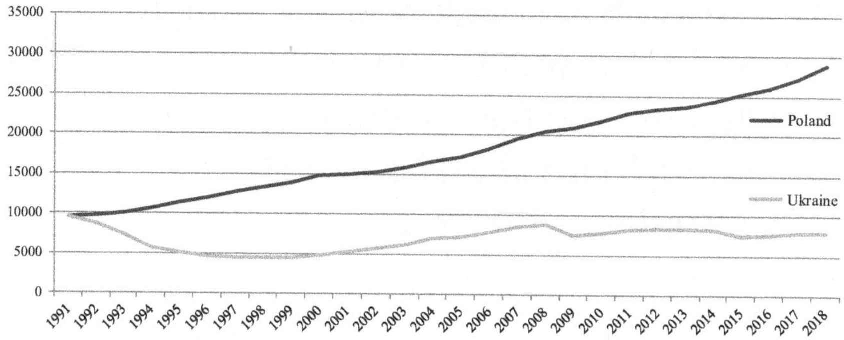

Figure 3.1 GDP per capita in Poland and Ukraine between 1990 and 2018 (USD, PPPs, in 2011 prices).

Source: The World Bank Group, Indicators, (2019). (https://data.worldbank.org/indicator/NY.GDP.PCAP.PP.KD?locations=UA-PL&view=chart, access: 2019-12-30).

a 15% decrease), after which, in 2010, the Ukrainian economy returned to the path of economic growth until 2013. The cumulative real GDP per capita growth during this period was 11.2%. This upward trend was halted after the Euromaidan (2013–2014), Russia's annexation of the Crimea and the fight against pro-Russian separatists in eastern Ukraine, as mentioned in Chapter 1. In 2014–2015, the real GDP per capita of Ukraine decreased by nearly 10%. In 2018, the GDP per capita in Ukraine was on the level of tiny, former soviet states, such as Moldova, Georgia and Armenia (according to purchasing power parity), and was three times lower than in Poland.

The financial sector was affected by the crisis resulting from abovementioned events. The value of deposits in 2015 decreased by 2/3 compared to the value of deposits of 2013. There was a devaluation of the UAH, the foreign debt exceeded $47.5 billion, and the total debt was $75 billion. This political crisis affected the real economy (an approximately 50% decrease in investment, and an increase in unemployment by around 3%). In 2018, the state budget spent the largest expenses on servicing the foreign debt. After the events of 2014, the Ukrainian economy was declining. Negotiations with the International Monetary Fund (IMF) required the implementation of difficult reforms in exchange for further loan tranches. One of the conditions of the IMF was the unfreezing (deregulation) of natural gas prices. In practice, this meant that a sharp increase is gas prices. This in turn resulted in an increase in inflation (Figure 3.2).

The aim of this chapter is to present and discuss the structural changes in the GDP of Poland and Ukraine as a consequence of the institutional changes referred to in Chapters 1 and 2.

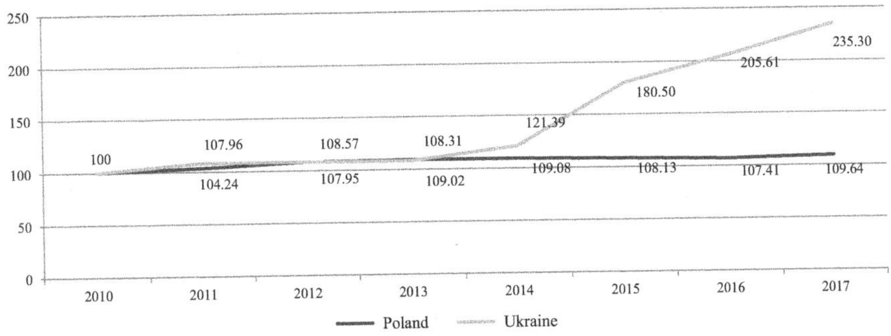

Figure 3.2 Consumer price index (2010 = 100), Poland and Ukraine, 2010–2017.
Source: The World Bank Group, Indicators, (2019). (https://data.worldbank.org/indicator/FP.CPI.TOTL?end=2017&locations=PL-UA&start=2010, access: 2019-12-30).

3.2 Share of the industrial sector in GDP

The share of the industrial sector (mining, industrial processing, energy, construction) in the Ukrainian economy in the early 1990s was high; at the same time, however, it was characterized by significant volatility. In 1991, the share dropped to 55%, in 1990 – 42%, and between 1997and 1998, it fell to a level of approximately 30.5% of GDP.

The sharp decline in the GDP share of Ukrainian industrial sector between 1991 and 1998 was a consequence of:

- the slow process of ownership transformation (privatization) of state-owned industrial enterprises,
- difficulties in expanding into foreign markets and the decapitalization fixed assets.

The low competitiveness of industrial products in the conditions of this transition and of the world market which was increasingly open to Ukraine led to a radical reduction in this sector's share of the Ukrainian GDP (Figure 3.3).

During the period of 1998–2017, there was a constant decline in the competitiveness of the Ukrainian industrial sector reinforced by political turmoil and domestic demand variability, a weakening of international competitiveness, violations of the free competition rules (unlawful enrichment of a very narrow social group) and corruption.

Over this same period, the Polish industrial sector held a stable average annual GDP share of 29%. At the end of 2017 the share of the industrial sector in the Polish economy was 29.5%, while in the Ukrainian economy it was 23.3%.

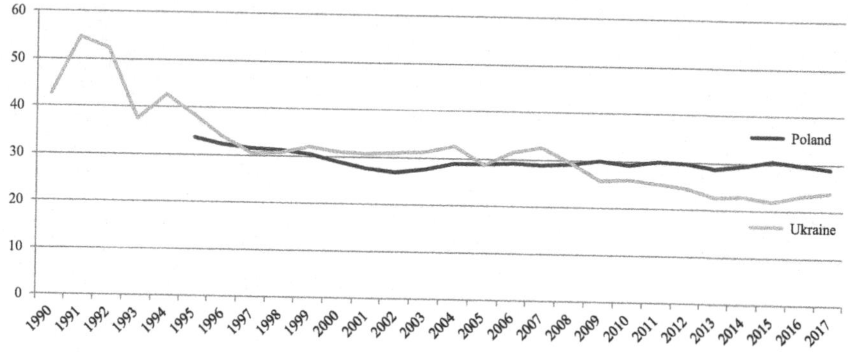

Figure 3.3 Changes in the gross value added of the industrial sector (ISIC: 10–45) in GDP (in %), Poland and Ukraine.

Source: The World Bank Group, Indicators, (2019). (https://data.worldbank.org/indicator/NV.IND.TOTL.ZS?locations=PL-UA&view=chart, access: 2019-12-30).

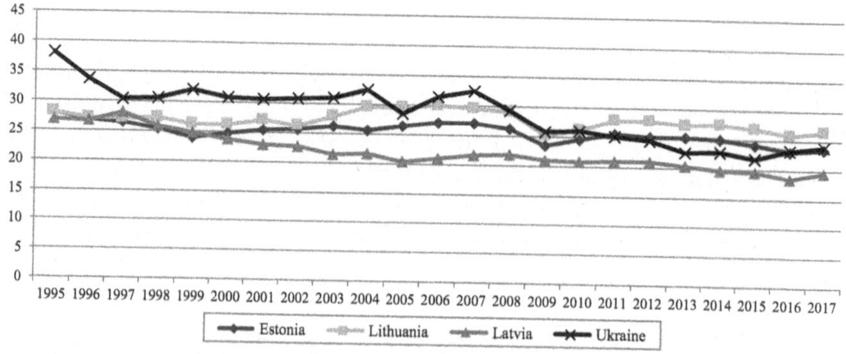

Figure 3.4 Changes in the gross value added of the industrial sector (ISIC: 10–45) in GDP (in %), 1995–2017, The Baltic states and Ukraine.

Source: The World Bank Group, Indicators, (2019). (https://data.worldbank.org/indicator/NV.IND.TOTL.ZS?locations=UA-EE-LT-LV&view=chart, access: 2019-12-30).

In the emergent countries of the former USSR – which, like Poland, became members of the European Union, namely Lithuania, Latvia and Estonia – the GDP share of the industrial sector decreased steadily between 1995 and 2017. This process ran relatively calmly (Figure 3.4).

In the case of Lithuania, this share decreased by 1.8% points (pp), Estonia by 4.7 pp and Latvia by 7.3 pp. Against this background, Ukraine stands out with an almost 14 pp decrease over the last 23 years, as shown in Figure 3.5.

During the period considered, the Visegrád Group countries (Visegrád Four, V4) – Czechia, Hungary, Poland and Slovakia – were characterized by a stable GDP share of the industrial processing sector. In the case of

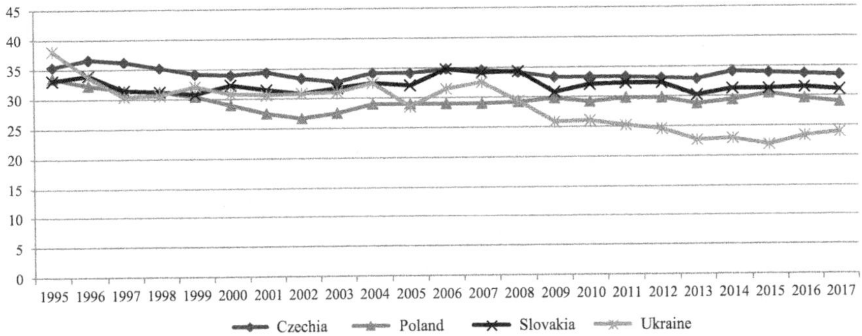

Figure 3.5 Changes in the gross value added of the industrial sector (ISIC: 10–45) in GDP (in %), 1995–2017, The Visegrád group and Ukraine.

Source: The World Bank Group, Indicators, (2019). (https://data.worldbank.org/indicator/NV.IND.TOTL.ZS?locations=UA-PL-HU-CZ-SK&view=chart, access: 2019-12-30).

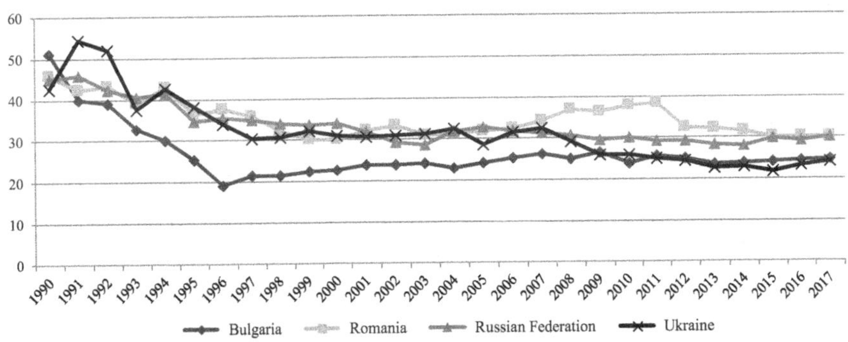

Figure 3.6 Changes in the gross value added of the industrial sector (ISIC: 10–45) in GDP (in %), 1990–2017, Bulgaria, Romania, Russia and Ukraine.

Source: The World Bank Group, Indicators, (2019). (https://data.worldbank.org/indicator/NV.IND.TOTL.ZS?locations=UA-RU-BG-RO&view=chart, access: 2019-12-30).

Hungary, both in 1995 and 2017, this share remained at the same level of 26%. Similarly, in Czechia, in 1995, this share was 35.3%; however, over 23 years it decreased slightly to 33.5% – the largest GDP share in the group as a whole. Slovakia was the last country to start reform and has taken the longest in the V4 group. However, Slovakia has been dependent on the raw materials and the economy of Russia; therefore, this change was just above 1 pp over the entire 22-year period (Figure 3.6).

A common feature of Ukraine, Russia, Romania and Bulgaria was the sharp collapse in the economic activity of industrial companies in the first half of the 1990s. The hardest collapse was experienced by Bulgarian industry, down from a nearly 52% share of GDP (1990) to barely a 19% share in 1996. In 2017, industry produced a 24% stream of the global production of the Bulgarian economy.

The slow, systematic decline in the Russian industrial GDP share over the last 3 decades indicates evolutionary changes in the GDP structure, rather than a sharp collapse in its competitiveness. Romania has had the highest volatility regarding the industry GDP share of industry. At the beginning of the 1990s, as in the case of the other countries, this share was high, close to 46% of GDP. In 2000, it fell to its lowest level (30.1%); however, it increased by 8.5% over the next 11 years. In 2017, it returned to its 2000 level.

3.3 GDP share of the agricultural sector

The share of the agricultural sector in the Ukrainian economy in the early 1990s was close to 25%, while the industrial processing sector accounted for a total of 80% of the stream of GDP produced. Between 1995 and 2001, the share of agriculture hovered between 14.5% and 12%; in 2007, it fell to its lowest level in Ukraine's history (6.6%). The period 2008–2015 manifested a consistent marked increase in the share of agricultural production in GDP (an increase of 5.5% points). In 2017, this share was 10.1% (Figure 3.7).

In the same period, production of the Polish agricultural sector reduced its share of GDP from 5.5% to 2.8%. The importance of agricultural work

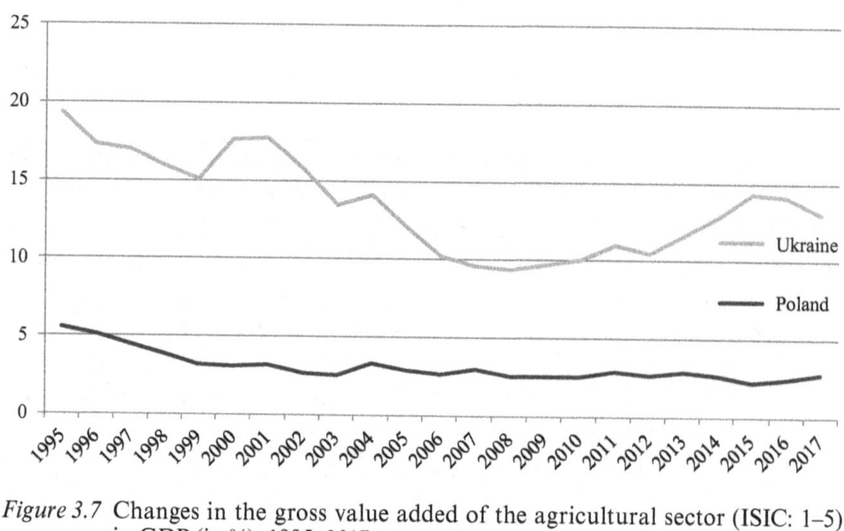

Figure 3.7 Changes in the gross value added of the agricultural sector (ISIC: 1–5) in GDP (in %), 1995–2017.

Source: The World Bank Group, Indicators, (2019). (https://data.worldbank.org/indicator/NV.AGR.TOTL.ZS?locations=PL-UA&view=chart, access: 2019-12-30).

measured by the gross value per employee was one of the lowest compared to other EU Member States. It was a consequence:

- of the fragmentation of Polish agriculture,
- an unfavorable agriculture structure,
- the low economic strength of agricultural holdings, as well as
- a lack of modern machinery and equipment on the farms.

The proportion of workers employed exclusively in Polish agriculture has been steadily declining since the early 1990s, when around 100,000 people worked in this sector of the economy, 27% of the total number of those employed. In 2004, about 100,000 people worked in agriculture, that is, 16.5% of the total number of employees, or 2.1 million people. In 2018 this number increased to 1.6 million people (i.e., 9.7% of the total workforce in the national economy) (Figures 3.8 and 3.9).

In the Baltic States, between 1995 and 2017, the share of the agricultural sector in GDP decreased steadily:

- in Lithuania from 10% (1995) to 3% (in 2017),
- in Latvia from 8% to 3.4%, and
- in Estonia from 5% to 2.5%.

Following the accession of the Baltic states (Lithuania, Latvia and Estonia) and the EU V4 countries, the share of agricultural production in GDP has remained stable at 3% (±1%). The decline in the share of the agricultural sector in GDP over the last 23 years has been gradual and was the result of a more rapid growth in the remaining sectors. At the end of 2017, the share of the agricultural sector in GDP in Hungary and Slovakia was 3.3%, in Poland it was 2.8%, and in Czechia it was 2.2% (Figure 3.10).

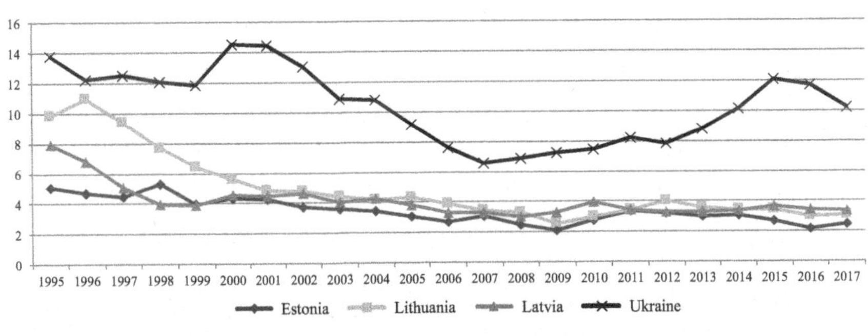

Figure 3.8 Changes in the gross value added of the agricultural sector (ISIC: 1–5) in GDP (in %), 1995–2017, the Baltic states.

Source: The World Bank Group, Indicators, (2019). (https://data.worldbank.org/indicator/NV.AGR.TOTL.ZS?locations=UA-EE-LT-LV&view=chart, access: 2019-12-30).

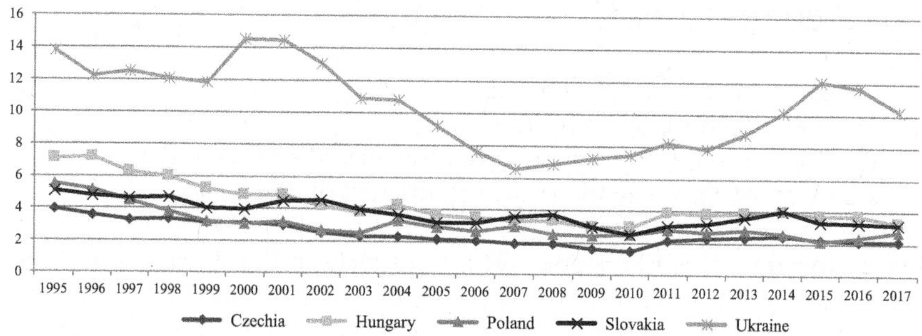

Figure 3.9 Changes in the gross value added of the agricultural sector (ISIC: 1–5) in GDP (in %), 1995–2017, the Visegrád Group.

Source: The World Bank Group, Indicators, (2019). (https://data.worldbank.org/indicator/NV.AGR.TOTL.ZS?locations=UA-PL-HU-CZ-SK&view=chart, access: 2019-12-30).

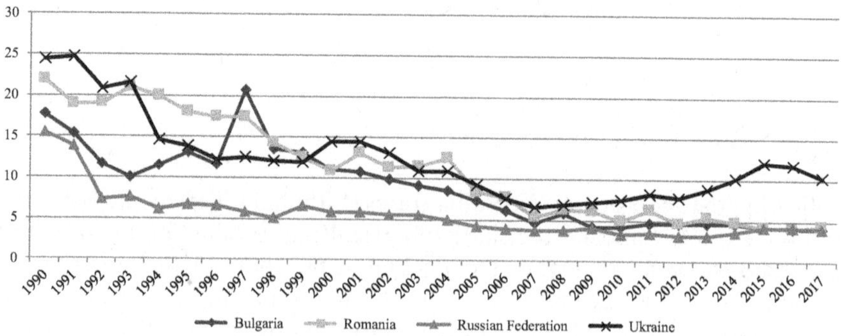

Figure 3.10 Changes in the gross value added of the agricultural sector (ISIC: 1–5) in GDP (on %), 1990–2017, Bulgaria, Romania, Russia and Ukraine.

Source: The World Bank Group, Indicators, (2019). (https://data.worldbank.org/indicator/NV.AGR.TOTL.ZS?locations=UA-RU-BG-RO&view=chart, access: 2019-12-30).

The common feature of Ukraine, Russia, Romania and Bulgaria was a much more significant decrease in the share of the gross value added of the agricultural sector in GDP compared to the other groups of countries analyzed. The share of the agricultural sector in the Ukrainian economy in the early 1990s was close to 25% of GDP. In 2017, this share decreased to10.1% of GDP. In the case of Romania, there was a decrease from 22% of the share of GDP (in 1990) to 4.3% (2017 and 2018). In Bulgaria, in 1990, the agricultural sector's share of GDP was 17.7% and decreased to 9.2% in 1995, and in 1997, it increased to its highest level (20.6%) during the period of economic transition. At the end of 2017, it was only 4%.

The reduction in the gross value-added share of the agricultural sector in Russian GDP was relatively calm, outside the 1990 period (15.4%

share) – 1998 (5.1%). Between 1999 and 2017, this share decreased by 3.4% points, that is, to 3.1% of GDP.

3.4 GDP selected components from the distribution side

3.4.1 Total investment expenditure

The investment[1] rate in Poland between 1995 and 2018 ranged from 17.5% (1995, 2017) to 24% (1999–2000). The average investment rate in Poland for this period was 20.2% of GDP. This was significantly lower than Estonia's average of 28.1% and that of Latvia, 24.2%. The average value of this parameter for the Lithuanian economy was 21%, and for the Ukrainian economy 19.1%.

The group's highest investment rates in 2007 were a common feature for all the countries analyzed. Over the next decade, the investment rates of these countries have not come close to the level of 2007.

- Estonia, Latvia approx. 36.5% of GDP (2007), 2018 – Estonia 23.9%, Latvia 22.8%
- Lithuania 28.5% (2007), 19.3% in 2018
- Ukraine 26.1% (2007), 17.2% in 2018
- Poland 22.5% (2007), 11 years later, 18.2%.

The average investment rate for EU Member States in 2018 was around 20.5%, while for the Euro zone it was 20.8%.

The general regularities emerging from Figure 3.11 were (1) during the analyzed period (1995–2018), investment rates in Ukraine and Poland were almost lower in each year and often significantly lower than in Czechia, Slovakia and Hungary; (2) the average annual investment rate in Czechia was the highest in the group under consideration at 28.3% of GDP, for Slovakia it was 26.1%. Hungary's average investment rate (22.8%) was also significantly higher than in Poland and Ukraine (Figure 3.12).

The average investment rates for the period of 1995–2018 for Ukraine (19.1%), Russia (19.8%), and Poland and Bulgaria (in both cases 20.2%) are relatively close to each other. Romania (24.1%) is characterized by a significantly higher average investment rate. Bulgaria (4.5% in 1996; 33% in 2008) and Romania (18% in 1999; 37.2% in 2008) had the highest volatility of annual investment rates (Figure 3.13).

Investment rates in Poland and Ukraine are lower than in the other countries of Central and Eastern Europe. From the point of view of international competitiveness and the development prospects of both economies, this is a negative factor. Part of the difference between the investment rate in Poland and Ukraine, and the other countries of the region, is the sectorial structure of these economies. If the share of individual sectors in creating added value in Poland and Ukraine was at the average of EU countries in general, their

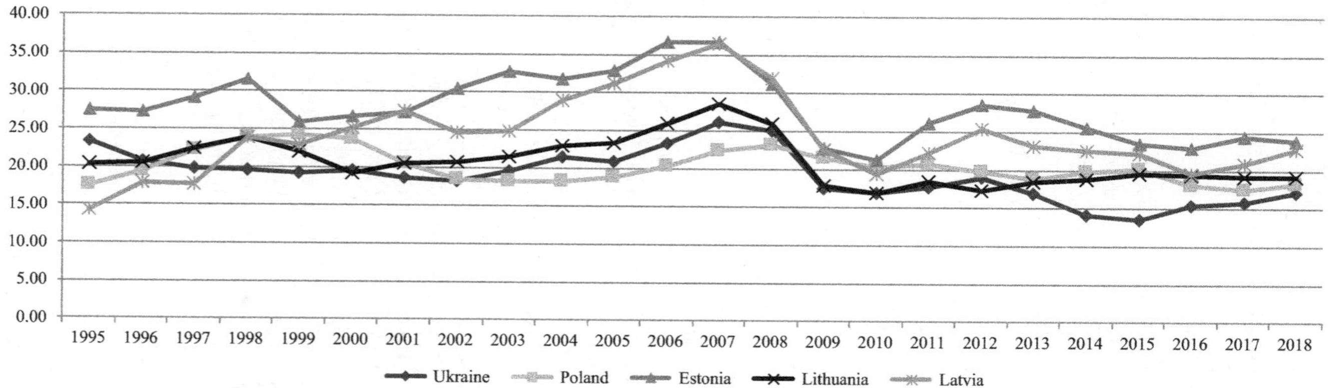

Figure 3.11 Investment rates of Ukraine, Poland and the Baltic states, 1995–2018 (%).

Source: The World Bank Group, Indicators, (2019). (https://data.worldbank.org/indicator/NE.GDI.FTOT.ZS?end=2018&locations=UA-PL-EE-LT-LV&start=1995, access: 2019-12-30).

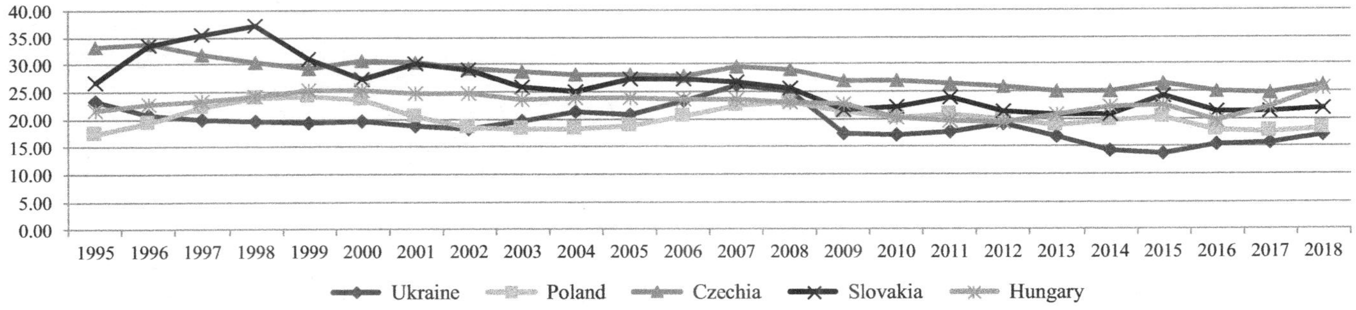

Figure 3.12 Investment rates of Ukraine and Visegrád group countries, 1995–2018 (%).

Source: The World Bank Group, Indicators, (2019). (https://data.worldbank.org/indicator/NE.GDI.FTOT.ZS?end=2018&locations=UA-PL-CZ-SK-HU&start=1995, access: 2019-12-30).

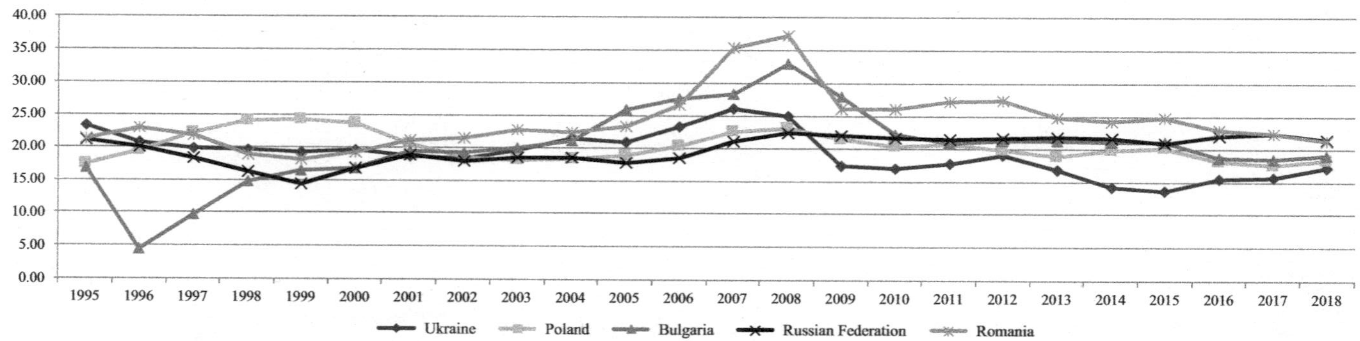

Figure 3.13 Investment rates of Ukraine, Poland, Bulgaria, Russia and Romania, 1995–2018 (%).

Source: The World Bank Group, Indicators, (2019). (https://data.worldbank.org/indicator/NE.GDI.FTOT.ZS?end=2018&locations=UA-PL-BG-RU-RO&start=1995, access: 2019-12-30).

investment rates would probably be higher. The investment economic fluctuations in Poland between 1995 and 2018 are highly synchronized with the EU (0.54) and, in particular, with the Euro zone. The correlation of GDP is around 0.6. This relationship weakened significantly after 2008 (0.15), when the pro-cyclicality of investments in Poland decreased. On the other hand, the degree of synchronization of the economic cycle between Poland and the EU remained high.

What is surprising is the level of the correlation index (Pearson) for Ukraine and the EU. For the period of 1995–2018 it was 0.80, and for 2008–2018 it rose to 0.84. Between 1995 and 2007, this synchronization was 0.41.

The correlation rate of the investment rate changes in Poland and Ukraine, for the period 1995–2018 was 0.29; in 2008–2018 it rose to 0.65. Between 1995 and 2007, this interdependence was negative (−0.09).

3.4.2 R&D expenditure

Research and development expenditure (R&D) spending in Poland, as well as for software and databases, remains particularly low. This is a negative factor from the point of view of the development prospects of the Polish economy.

R&D outlays relative to GDP have not increased significantly since Poland entered the EU. In 2004 it reached 0.55%, and in 2017 it increased to 1% of GDP. In the EU, the average level is twice as high (2.1%), and the average value of this share for the Visegrád Four, without Poland, is about 1.4%. Recognizing that R&D capital expenditure promotes an increase in the total productivity of input and consequently economic growth, measures are systematically taken to support the activity and innovation of enterprises, including those of R&D centers of global corporations. Such a process, although relatively slow, has been observed in Poland (Figure 3.14).

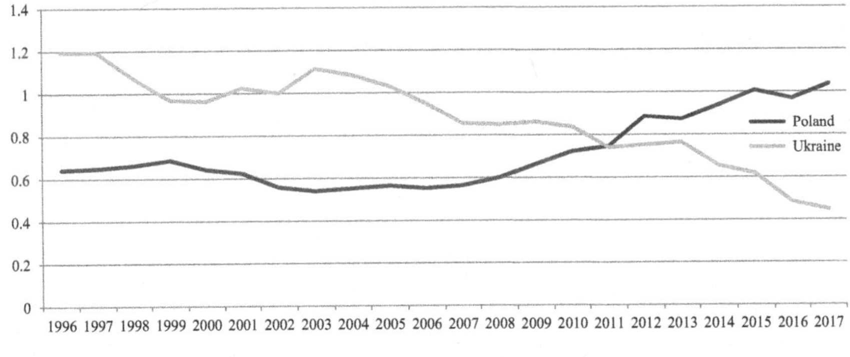

Figure 3.14 Changes in the share of R&D expenditures in GDP (in %), 1996–2017, Poland and Ukraine.

Source: The World Bank Group, Indicators, (2019). (https://data.worldbank.org/indicator/GB.XPD.RSDV.GD.ZS?locations=UA-PL&view=chart, access: 2019-12-30).

In the case of Ukraine, the R&D investment expenditure level is consistently becoming less and less important; more than 1% in 2004, it was down to just 0.4% in 2017. Based on such a trend, it is possible to infer the fading potential for the development of the Ukrainian economy, with a source of technological progress and growth in productivity.

From the point of view of economic development prospects, both the investment rate and its structure are important. Against this background, in highly developed countries in recent decades, there is a noteworthy trend of systematic growth in the role of investment in intellectual property products, that is, research and development, computer software and databases. R&D and software outlays display significantly higher growth rates than overall investment. The increase in investment rates in intellectual property products, from a theoretical point of view, is linked to an increase in the innovative potential of the economy.

3.4.3 National defense spending

Poland has spent 2% of GDP on defense per annum, on average, over the last 25 years. With an average annual 4% economic growth during this period, this means, in practice, a systematic increase in real defense spending for Poland. In most geopolitically stable countries in the world, defense spending is approximately 1% of GDP (Figure 3.15).

In 1993, the share of defense spending in Ukraine's GDP was 0.44%, while the real value was $642.4 million (in fixed 2010 prices). In 1997, this share increased to 4%, which in fact meant an expenditure of $3.44 billion (in fixed 2010 prices). Between 1993 and 1997, Ukraine's GDP decreased from $146 billion to $86 billion. Between 1997 and 2013, military spending decreased to a level of 2.4% of GDP, with a real value at the 1997 level.

Figure 3.15 Changes in the share of defense spending in GDP (in %), 1993–2017, Poland and Ukraine.

Source: The World Bank Group, Indicators, (2019). (https://data.worldbank.org/indicator/MS.MIL.XPND.GD.ZS?end=2017&locations=UA-PL&start=1993&view=chart, access: 2019-12-30).

The political tensions that Ukraine has been embroiled in since 2013 pushed defense spending up again to 4% of GDP in 2015, that is, to $4.84 billion in real terms (in fixed 2010 prices). In 2017, this value fell to $4.1 billion, or 3.24% of GDP. Social and political instability after the Euromaidan of 2013–2014, Russia's annexation of Crimea and the fight against pro-Russian separatists in eastern Ukraine have resulted in a marked increase in this category of public spending in 2014–2015 (by about $1.4 billion).

3.5 Summary

Poland, after the period of a centrally planned economy (1946–1989), in the early 1990s, had at its disposal several basic or well-trained institutions typical of a market economy.

At the beginning of the 1990s, Ukraine did not have any institutions with experience in building a market economy, or the institutions of parliamentary democracy. Ukrainian society had to face the extremely difficult task of creating market economy institutions from scratch. In Poland, the GDP per capita has increased by 190% over the last almost 30 years from 9,500 dollars (1991) to 27,300 dollars (2017). When we consider 2018, the Polish GDP per capita is three times the value of 1991.

The Ukrainian GDP per capita in 2017 has still not returned to its 1991 level. GDP per capita in Ukraine is currently at the level of Moldova, Georgia and Armenia and is three times lower than in Poland. The main brake on Ukraine's GDP growth is established informal non-market institutions, which are not conducive to free competition (clan interest networks and corruption).

Between 1991 and 2017, the low competitiveness of industrial products combined with the lack of managerial competence to operate under a growing market economy resulted in a radical reduction in the share of the processing sector in the Ukrainian GDP. This trend was reinforced by political turmoil and the volatility of domestic demand. Between 1991 and 2017, the Polish industrial sector held a stable 29% of average annual GDP. At the end of 2017, the share of the industrial sector in the Polish economy was 29.5%, while in the Ukrainian economy, it was 23.3%.

The share of the agricultural sector in the Ukrainian economy in the early 1990s was close to 25%. In 2017, this share was 10.1%. During the same period, the agricultural sector's share of Polish GDP was reduced from 5.5% to 2.8%. The productivity of agricultural labor, measured by the gross value per employee, was one of the lowest, when compared to other EU Member States.

Economic fluctuations in investment in Poland (1995–2018) are highly synchronized with the average investment rate of EU Member States (0.54); by comparison, the similarly calculated GDP correlation is around 0.6. For Ukraine and all EU Member States, this interdependence is at an even higher level (0.84). R&D spending relative to GDP has increased since Poland's entry into the EU. In 2004, it was 0.55% and increased to 1% of GDP in 2017. In the case of Ukraine, a contrary trend is observed – from more than a 1% share in 2004, R&D spending fell to just 0.45% in 2017.

Note

1 Gross expenditure per fixed assets to GDP.

4 The demographic potential of Polish voivodeships and Ukrainian oblasts

Nataliia Chugaievska, Oleksii Kelebaj and Tomasz Tokarski

4.1 Introduction

The aim of this chapter is to characterize the absolute and relative demographic potential of Polish and Ukrainian regions. In Poland, there are voivodeships (województwo), and in Ukraine oblasts (область). These analyses concern 2004–2017 (or 2004–2016) depending on the availability of statistics from the Central Statistical Data Bank (hereinafter BDL GUS, https://bdl.stat.gov.pl/https://bdl.stat.gov.pl/) and the Ukrainian Statistical Office (Державна Служба Статистики України) (hereinafter ДССУ, http://www.ukrstat.gov.ua/http://www.ukrstat.gov.ua/).

This chapter analyzes the demographic potential of the population, population density and the division of the population into urban and rural areas. It also takes into consideration the spatial diversity and dynamics of both the population numbers and the urbanization rate.

4.2 Administrative divisions of Poland and Ukraine

Since January 1, 1999, Poland has been divided into 16 voivodeships. For analytical purposes, these voivodeships are divided into four groups:

- Mazowieckie,
- five voivodeship in eastern Poland (Lubelskie, Podkarpackie, Podlaskie, Świętokrzyskie and Warmińsko-Mazurskie),
- five in central Poland (Kujawsko-Pomorskie, Łódź, Małopolskie, Pomorskie and Śląskie),
- five western Polish voivodeships (Dolnośląskie, Lubuskie, Opolskie, Wielkopolskie, and Zachodniopomorskie (Map 4.1).

The Mazowieckie Voivodeship was treated as a separate entity, as it is atypical as a voivodeship. This is because it contains the capital of Poland-Warsaw and the very economically vigorous city of Płock (mainly due to the largest Polish oil company "Orlen" being based there) and the fairly weak, economically, agricultural environs surrounding Warsaw, Płock and Radom.

Map 4.1 Administrative division of Poland.
Source: https://pl.wikipedia.org/wiki/Podzial_administracyjny_Polska.

Eastern Poland includes areas belonging to the poorest in the European Union, which therefore benefit from the special funds provided by the European Union.

The remaining voivodeships were divided into two parallel groups consisting of the voivodeships of central and western Poland. Through the voivodeships of central Poland run the main north-south transportation routes (railway and road) connecting the Tri-city region (Tri-city – Gdańsk, Gdynia and Sopot) with Bydgoszcz, Toruń, Łódź, the Górny Śląsk-Zagłębie agglomeration and Kraków. On the other hand, the areas of the current voivodeships of western Poland were before World War I in the German partition, and in the interwar period (except for the voivodeship of Wielkopolskie) belonged to Germany (for more information on the specifics of these Polish voivodeships see: Filipowicz, Tokarski 2015, Filipowicz 2017, 2019 or Szczepaniak, Tokarski 2018).

Ukraine is divided into 24 oblasti, the Autonomous Republic of Crimea (Автономна Республіка Крим, ARC) with its capital city of Simferopol and two cities with a specific status (міста зі спеціальним статусом): Kyiv and

Map 4.2 Administrative division of Ukraine.
Source: http://www.ukrexport.gov.ua/eng/about_ukraine/admin/?country=ukr.

Sevastopol. Since 2014, the Autonomous Republic of Crimea and Sevastopol have been occupied by Russia (Map 4.2).

The names of most Ukrainian regions are adjectives derived from the names of their capitals, except the regions of Dnipropetrovsk Oblast, Kirovohrad Oblast, Volyn Oblast and the Zakarpattia Oblast. The capital city of the Dnipropetrovsk Oblast region is the city of Dnipro (which until 2016 was called Dnipropetrovsk) and the Kirovohrad Oblast Kropyvnytskyi (until 2016 called Kirovohrad). The capital city of the Volyn Oblast is Lutsk, while the Zakarpattia Oblast's capital is Uzhhorod. In these cases, the names of oblasts are historically contingent. The boundaries of the Volyn Oblast largely coincide with the Volyn Oblast's border of the interwar period,[1] whose capital city at the time was Lutsk. The Zakarpattia Oblast belonged to the Kingdom of Hungary (a part of the Austro-Hungarian Empire) before World War I, and in the interwar period, it was in Czechoslovakia. The historic capital of the Zakarpattia region is Uzhhorod, which is currently the capital city of the Zakarpattia Oblast.

The oblasts of Ukraine are divided into five groups:[2]

- There are eight oblasts in western Ukraine (Khmelnytskiy, Chernivtsi, Ivano-Frankivsk, Lviv, Rivne, Ternopil, Volyn and Zakarpattia),
- The north Ukrainian oblasts (Kyiv with the regions of Chernihiv, Kyiv, Sumy and Zhytomyr),

- There are four oblasts in eastern Ukraine (Kharkiv, Donetsk, Luhansk and Zaporizhzhya),
- The south of Ukraine has the following regions: the Autonomous Republic of Crimea, Kherson Oblast, Mykolayiv Oblast, Odesa Oblast and Sevastopol,
- Finally, there are five oblasts in central Ukraine (Cherkasy, Dnipropetrovsk, Kirovohrad, Poltava and Vinnytsya).

Located in Volyn (Волинь), the Volyn Oblast (Волинська область) and Rivne Oblast (Рівненська область) before World War I were located in the Russian Empire, near the border, while in the interwar period, they were in Poland along its eastern border. The Ivano-Frankivsk Oblast, Lviv Oblast and Ternopil Oblast until 1918 were the easternmost part of the Kingdom of Galicia and Lodomeria belonging to the Austro-Hungarian Empire (Habsburg Monarchy), while in the interwar period, this region was in Poland. Located in Bukovina (Буковина), the Chernivtsi Oblast in the years 1849–1918 was part of the Austrian Empire's Duchy of Bukovina, while between World Wars I and II, this district belonged to Romania. The Zakarpattia Oblast, until 1918, was part of the Kingdom of Hungary, while in the interwar period, Czechoslovakia. The Khmelnytskiy Oblast, located in Podilla, was in the Romanov Empire before World War I, and was part of the Soviet Union in the interwar period. After World War II (until Ukraine regained its independence in 1991), all the oblasts of western Ukraine were part of the Ukrainian Soviet Socialist Republic, which in turn was part of the Soviet Union.

It can be concluded that the oblasts of western Ukraine over the past 200 years have been the outermost areas of the countries to which they belonged. This was not an aid in fostering neither their social or political stability nor their economic development (see: for example, Hrycak 2000; Serczyk 2001 or Hud 2018).

The districts belonging to the remaining provinces (in particular those areas located in Ukraine, on the right (west) bank of the Dnieper River[3] and the coastal oblasts, i.e., of the Odesa Oblast, Mykolayiv Oblast and Kherson Oblast) in the19th and 20th centuries were much more (than the oblasts of western Ukraine) politically and economically integrated first with tsarist Russia, and subsequently with the USSR. Therefore, their history, social, political and economic relations differed significantly from what was taking place in western Ukraine (see Hrycak 2000; Serczyk 2001; Wyszczelski 2015 or Hud 2018).

4.3 The demographic potential of the Polish voivodeships

Statistical data describing the voivodeships and the above-mentioned groups of voivodeships relate to the area and population at the beginning and end of the time period considered in this chapter.

From statistical data, it can be concluded that:

- the largest voivodeships in terms of area are the Mazowieckie (11.4% of Poland), Wielkopolskie (9.5%) and Lubelskie (8.0%). The smallest voivodeships include the Śląskie (3.9%), Świętokrzyskie (3.7%) and Opolskie (3.0%);
- The voivodeships of eastern Poland occupy 31.7% of the country's area, while those of western Poland 30.7% and central Poland 26.2%;
- On average, in the years 2004–2017 the largest population was recorded in the Mazowieckie Voivodeship (13.7% of the Polish population), followed by the Śląskie (12.1%) and Wielkopolskie (9.0%) voivodeships. The lowest number of inhabitants was found in the following voivodeships: the Podlaskie (3.1%), Opolskie (2.7%) and Lubuskie (2.6%) (Map 4.3);
- At the time, 38.7% of Poland's population lived in central Poland, the provinces of western Poland had 26.3%, while eastern Poland had only 21.3% of the country's overall population.
- Between 2004 and 2017, the population in 10 of the 16 voivodeships increased, while in the others, it decreased. The largest relative increases were recorded in the following voivodeships: Pomorskie (5.9%), Mazowieckie (4.6%), Małopolskie (4.0%) and Wielkopolskie (3.7%)

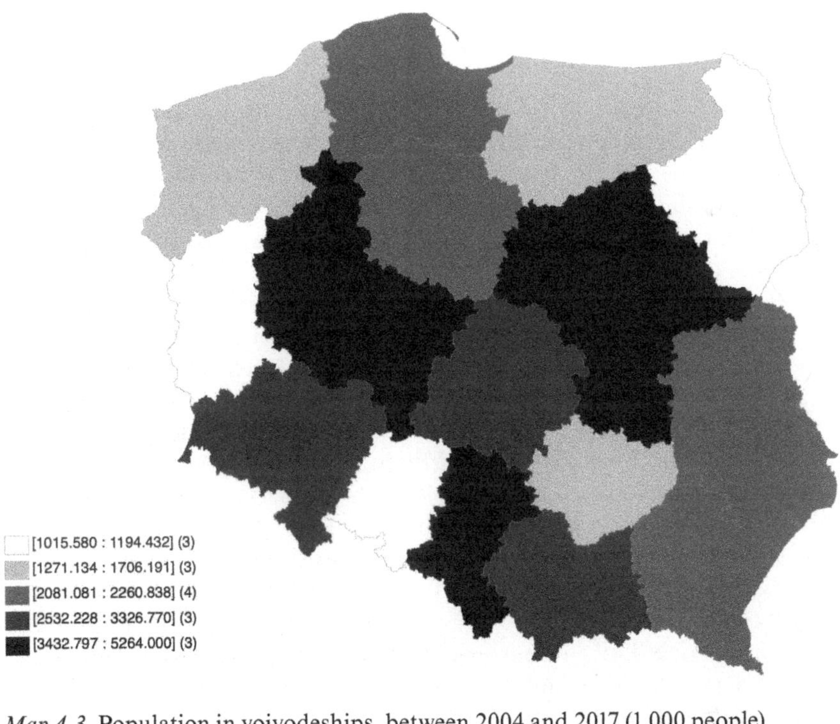

Map 4.3 Population in voivodeships, between 2004 and 2017 (1,000 people).
Source: Our own estimates based on: https://bdl.stat.gov.pl/BDL/start (access: 2019-12-30).

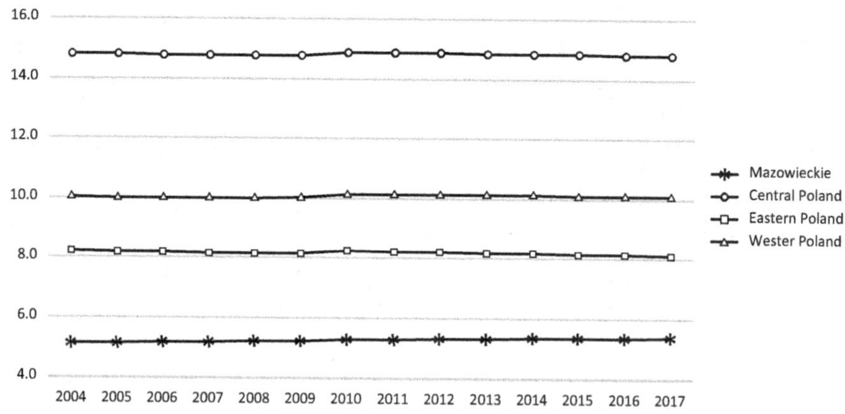

Figure 4.1 Population in groups of voivodeships, between 2004 and 2017 (million people).

Source: Our own estimates based on: https://bdl.stat.gov.pl/BDL/start (access: 2019-12-30).

The highest decreases were recorded in the Opolskie Voivodeship (a decrease of 5.8%), followed by the Łódzkie (4.3%), Śląskie and Świętokrzyskie (3.2%), Lubelskie (2.7%) and Podlaskie (1.5%) voivodeships (Figure 4.1). Hence we may come to a more general conclusion that in the years 2004–2017, Polish population growth was mainly characterized by those voivodeships with demographically and economically strong urban centers (Warsaw, Kraków, Poznań and the Tri-City area), while a decline in population occurred in either the post-industrial voivodeships (Łódzkie and Śląskie) or the voivodeships of eastern Poland (see: Trojak, Tokarski 2013; Filipowicz, Tokarski 2015; Trojak 2015; or Szczepaniak, Tokarski 2018).

- Regarding the groups of voivodeships, in western Poland the population in the research period increased by 0.9%, in central Poland by 0.1%, while in the voivodeships of eastern Poland decrease by 1.0%.
- In 2017, the Śląskie Voivodeship had the highest population density (369.8 persons/km^2,), with an average population density in Poland of 122.9 persons/km^2. The next in order were the following provinces: Małopolskie (223.1 persons/km^2), Mazowieckie (151.3 persons/km^2), Dolnośląskie (145.9 persons/km^2) and Łódzkie (136.1 persons/km^2). The lowest value of this characteristic (i.e., less than 100 people/km^2) was recorded in the following voivodeships: Lubelskie (84.7 people/km^2), Warmińsko-Mazurskie (59.3 people/km^2) and Podlaskie (58.6 people/km^2) in eastern Poland, and the Zachodniopomorskie (74.5 people/km^2) and Lubuskie (72.6 people/km^2) voivodeships in western Poland.

- The average population density of central Poland was 180.8 people/km^2 and in western Poland 105.3 people/km^2, while eastern Poland had only 82.0 people/km^2.
- The areas of eastern Poland are characterized by a much lower demographic potential (measured both in population and in population density) than in other regions of Poland.
- Below are the statistical data on the population of cities that in 2004 or 2017 had more than 200,000 inhabitants.
- In 2004, there were 18 cities in Poland of over 200,000 and in 2017, only 16 cities (the population of Gliwice and Kielce dropped below 200,000[4]). Among these cities, both in 2004 and 2017, there was one city of over a million (Warsaw), and four with a population between 500,000 and one million people (Kraków, Łódź, Wrocław and Poznań) and 13 cities in 2004 and 11 cities in 2017 with a population between 200,000 and 500,00 people.
- In total, 21.5% of the Polish population in 2004 and 20.9% in 2017 lived in the analyzed group of cities. Those cities with a population exceeding 500,000 persons were inhabited by some 11.6% (2004) and 11.4% (2017) of the Polish population in general.
- In the Mazowieckie Voivodeship, two cities with a population of over 200,000 persons (Warsaw and Radom) had 37.3% of the inhabitants of this voivodeship in 2004 and 36.8% in 2017. Similar indicators for the remaining groups of voivodeships were as follows: in eastern Poland three cities in 2004 (Lublin, Białystok and Kielce) and two cities in 2017 (Lublin and Białystok) constituted (respectively) 10.5% and 7.8% of the population of these voivodeships. Central Poland had ten cities in 2004 (Kraków, Łódź, Gdańsk, Bydgoszcz, Katowice, Gdynia, Częstochowa, Sosnowiec, Toruń and Gliwice), and nine in 2017 (those previously listed with the exception of Gliwice), 25.8% of their respective voivodeship populations in 2004, and 23.3% in 2017. In western Poland three cities (Wrocław, Poznań and Szczecin) had 16.2% of their respective voivodeship populations in 2004, and 15.6% in 2017.
- In five Polish cities, the population in 2017 was higher than in 2004: Warsaw had an increase in the number of inhabitants by 4.2%, Białystok 1.8%, Kraków 1.3%, Gdańsk 1.1% and Wrocław 0.4%. The largest relative decreases in population were recorded in Częstochowa and Gliwice (a decrease of 9.5%), and in Sosnowiec (10.6%) and Łódź (10.8%).
- It is worth noting that the decrease in the population in some of these cities (with the exception of Częstochowa, Łódź, Radom and the cities of the Górny Śląsk-Zagłębie agglomeration, i.e., Gliwice, Katowice and Sosnowiec) was compensated for by an increase in the population in the districts neighboring these cities. The total population of Warsaw with neighboring municipalities increased from 2.5 million people in 2004 to 2.9 million people in 2017 (i.e., by 8.9%), Poznań and the Poznań

district grew from 851.700 persons to 920.300 persons (8.0%), the Tri-City region with neighboring districts went from 1.3 million people up to 1.4 million people (7.4%), Kraków and neighboring districts with 1.2 million people increased to 1.3 million people (6.1%), Wrocław and its surroundings with 1.0 million people went up to 1.1 million people (5.2%), Toruń and the Toruń district from 295.400 persons up to 308.200 persons (4.3%), Białystok and the Białystok district from 431.200 persons up to 444.300 persons (3.0%), Szczecin and neighboring district from 755.200 persons up to 767.800 persons (1.7%) or Bydgoszcz and the Bydgoszcz district from 461.100 persons to 468.300 persons (1.6%). The population of Kielce and the Kielce district did not change in 2004–2017 (it amounted to 406.900 people), while in Lublin and the Lublin district the number of inhabitants dropped from 567.300 persons to 565.600 persons (0.3%), in Radom and the Radom district from 372.000 persons to 366.500 persons (1.5%), in Czestochowa and the Czestochowa district from 381.900 persons to 359.600 persons (5.8%), in Łódź with its neighboring districts from 1.1 million people down to 1.0 million people (by 6.4%) and in the urban districts of the Górny Śląsk-Zagłębie agglomeration this chart dropped from 2.3 million people to two million people (by 7.1%).

- In the Mazowieckie Voivodeship, the population of Warsaw and Radom together with their surrounding areas increased by 7.7%, in the large cities of western Poland and neighboring districts this chart increased by 5.1% and in eastern Poland by 0.8%, while in central Poland this chart fell by 1.0%.
- The total population in the 18 large Polish cities and the neighboring districts mentioned above increased in 2004–2017 from 14.1 million people to 14.4 million people (by 2.2%). It can be stated that some inhabitants of large Polish cities change their place of residence by moving to districts neighboring these cities.
- In 2004, 46.5% of the population of those cities of over 200,000 lived in central Poland, 23.4% in Mazowieckie, 19.7% in western Poland and only 10.9% in eastern Poland. In 2017, these indicators were (respectively) 45.1% central Poland, 25.9% Mazowieckie Voivodeship, 20.7% western Poland and 8.3% eastern Poland. This leads to the conclusion that the voivodeships of eastern Poland not only have a lower demographic potential but also have a much weaker potential of the population living in cities of over 200,000.

Tables 4.1 and 4.2 present statistical data on the number of people living in cities and in the countryside, both in individual voivodeships and in the previously distinguished groups of voivodeships in 2004 and 2017. Data regarding the number of inhabitants are divided into urban and rural districts.

Table 4.1 Basic data about the Polish voivodeships

Voivodeship	*Region's area*		*Population*				*Population 2017 (2004 = 100)*
			2004, year		*2017, year*		
	1,000 km²	*Poland = 100*	*1,000 people*	*Poland = 100*	*1,000 people*	*Poland = 100*	
Mazowieckie	**35.6**	**11.4**	**5146.0**	**13.5**	**5,384.6**	**14.0**	**104.6**
Kujawsko-Pomorskie	18.0	5.7	2068.3	5.4	2,082.9	5.4	100.7
Łódzkie	18.2	5.8	2587.7	6.8	2,476.3	6.4	95.7
Małopolskie	15.2	4.9	3260.2	8.5	3,391.4	8.8	104.0
Pomorskie	18.3	5.9	2194.0	5.7	2,324.3	6.0	105.9
Śląskie	12.3	3.9	4700.8	12.3	4,548.2	11.8	96.8
Central Poland	**82.0**	**26.2**	**14,811.0**	**38.8**	**14,823.1**	**38.6**	**100.1**
Lubelskie	25.1	8.0	2,185.2	5.7	2,126.3	5.5	97.3
Podkarpackie	17.8	5.7	2,098.0	5.5	2,129.1	5.5	101.5
Podlaskie	20.2	6.5	1,202.4	3.1	1,184.5	3.1	98.5
Świętokrzyskie	11.7	3.7	1,288.7	3.4	1,247.7	3.2	96.8
Warmińsko-Mazurskie	24.2	7.7	1,428.7	3.7	1,433.9	3.7	100.4
Eastern Poland	**99.0**	**31.7**	**8,203.0**	**21.5**	**8,121.7**	**21.1**	**99.0**
Dolnośląskie	19.9	6.4	2,893.1	7.6	2,902.5	7.6	100.3
Lubuskie	14.0	4.5	1,009.2	2.6	1,016.8	2.6	100.8
Opolskie	9.4	3.0	1,051.5	2.8	990.1	2.6	94.2
Wielkopolskie	29.8	9.5	3,365.3	8.8	3,489.2	9.1	103.7
Zachodniopomorskie	22.9	7.3	1,694.9	4.4	1,705.5	4.4	100.6
Western Poland	**96.1**	**30.7**	**10,013.9**	**26.2**	**10,104.2**	**26.3**	**100.9**
Poland	**312.7**	**100.0**	**38,173.8**	**100.0**	**38,433.6**	**100.0**	**100.7**

Source: Our own estimates based on: https://bdl.stat.gov.pl/BDL/start (access: 2019-12-30).
Bold represents group of regions.

Table 4.2 The population of Polish cities with more than 200,000 inhabitants in 2004 and 2017 (1,000 people)

City	*Voivodeship or group of voivodeships*	*Year*		*Population in 2017 (year 2004 = 100)*
		2004	*2017*	
Warszawa	Mazowieckie	1,692.9	1764.6	104.2
Kraków	Małopolskie	757.4	767.3	101.3
Łódź	Łódzkie	774.0	690.4	89.2
Wrocław	Dolnośląskie	636.3	638.6	100.4
Poznań	Wielkopolskie	570.8	538.6	94.4
Gdańsk	Pomorskie	459.1	464.3	101.1
Szczecin	Zachodniopomorskie	411.9	403.9	98.1
Bydgoszcz	Kujawsko-Pomorskie	368.2	352.3	95.7
Lublin	Lubelskie	356.0	339.9	95.5
Białystok	Podlaskie	292.2	297.3	101.8
Katowice	Śląskie	319.9	296.3	92.6
Gdynia	Pomorskie	253.3	246.3	97.2
Częstochowa	Śląskie	248.0	224.4	90.5
Radom	Mazowieckie	227.6	214.6	94.3
Sosnowiec	Śląskie	228.2	204.0	89.4
Toruń	Kujawsko-Pomorskie	208.3	202.6	97.3
Kielce	Świętokrzyskie	209.5	196.8	94.0
Gliwice	Śląskie	200.4	181.3	90.5
Mazowieckie		1,920.5	1,979.2	103.1
Central Poland		3,816.8	3,629.2[a]	95.1[a]
			3,447.6[b]	90.3[b]
Eastern Poland		857.6	833.9[c]	97.2[c]
			637.1[d]	72.3[d]
Western Poland		1,618.9	1581.1	97.7
Poland		8,213.8	8,023.4[e]	97.7[e]
			7,645.3[f]	93.1[f]

Source: Our own estimates based on: https://bdl.stat.gov.pl/BDL/start (access: 2019-12-30).

a With Gliwice.
b Without Gliwice.
c With Kielce.
d Without Kielce.
e With Gliwice and Kielce.
f Without Gliwice and Kielce.

From statistical data, it can be concluded that:

- Both in 2004 and 2017, the quartile group[5] with the largest population living in cities included the following voivodeships: Śląskie, Mazowieckie, Dolnośląskie and Wielkopolskie. These values were at a level of 3.7 million people in 2004 and 3.5 million people in 2017 in the Śląskie Voivodeship, 3.3 million people and 3.5 million people in the Mazowieckie Voivodeship, 2.1 million people and 2.0 million people in the Dolnośląskie Voivodeship and 1.9278 million persons, and 1.9034 million persons in the Wielkopolskie Voivodeship, whereas the quartile group with the smallest value of the variable analyzed here was composed of two voivodeships in eastern Poland and two in western Poland. In the cities, in the Podlaskie Voivodeship, there were in 2004 – 710.800 people and in 2017 – 719.200 people, in Lubuskie Voivodeship in 2004 – 648.200 people and in 2017 – 659.700 people, in Świętokrzyskie Voivodeship in 2004 – 586.700 people and in 2017 – 556.200 people, while in the Opolskie Voivodeship in 2004 – 554.000 people and in 2017 – 522.600 people.

- In five voivodeships, the number of urban residents in 2017 was higher than in 2004, while in the remaining 11 voivodeships, it was lower. The population of cities increased the fastest in the Mazowieckie (by 4.0%), Podkarpackie (3.2%), Lubuskie (1.8%) and Podlaskie (1.2%) voivodeships. However, the population of cities fell the fastest in the following voivodeships: Świętokrzyskie (by 5.2%), Śląskie (5.6%), Opolskie (5.7%) and Łódź (7.3%).
- In 2004, 41.6% of the inhabitants of Polish cities lived in the cities of central Poland, 27.1% in western Poland, 17.1% in eastern Poland, and the remaining 14.2% of the urban population in the Mazowieckie Voivodeship. In 2017, these percentage rates were 40.7% in central Poland, 27.1% in western Poland, 17.3% in eastern Poland and 15.0% in the Mazowieckie Voivodeship.
- In 2017, the number of urban residents in the Mazowieckie Voivodeship was 4.0% higher than in 2004, while in other groups of voivodeships the value of this demographic variable decreased. In the voivodeships of central Poland, the value of this trait decreased in 2004–2017 by 3.6%, in western Poland by 1.7% and in eastern Poland – by 1.0%.
- When analyzing the number of inhabitants of cities that are in urban districts, it turns out that in 2017 this chart fell in Poland by 1.8% compared to 2004. It should be noted, however, that declines of this magnitude were not evenly distributed geographically. In the voivodeships of western Poland the value of this variable increased by 2.6%, in the Mazowieckie Voivodeship by 2.3%, while in the voivodeships of eastern Poland by 1.1% and central Poland by 5.3% (mainly as a result of processes of demographic trends taking place in the post-industrial Śląskie and Łódzkie voivodeships).
- In six voivodeships (Dolnośląskie, Lubuskie, Podkarpackie, Mazowieckie, Podlaskie and Małopolskie) the number of inhabitants of urban districts increased, while in the remaining voivodeships it decreased. The largest relative increases (by more than 5%) in the value of this variable considered here between 2004 and 2017 were recorded in the Dolnośląskie (by 12.4%) and Lubuskie (8.2%) voivodeships in western Poland and the Podkarpackie (6.3%) Voivodeship in eastern Poland. The largest decreases were recorded in the Wielkopolskie Voivodeship (a 5.5% drop) in western Poland, in the Świętokrzyskie Voivodeship (6.0%) in eastern Poland and (as already mentioned) the post-industrial Śląskie (8.1%) and Łódzkie (by 9.9%) voivodeships in central Poland.

- The population of cities in rural voivodeships between 2004 and 2017 in Poland fell by 1.2%. In the Mazowieckie Voivodeship the value of this variable increased by 7.2%, while in the other groups of voivodeships it decreased. In the voivodeships of western Poland, the population of cities in rural districts fell by 4.6%, in eastern Poland by 0.9%, while in central Poland by 0.6%. In the voivodeships of central Poland, the number of people living in towns in rural districts decreased in 2004–2017 by 4.6%, in western Poland by 0.9% and eastern Poland by 0.6%.
- In seven voivodeships (except for the Mazowieckie Voivodeship, also in the voivodeships: Pomorskie, Wielkopolskie, Małopolskie, Podkarpackie, Podlaskie and Zachodniopomorskie), the value of the variable considered here increased, in the others it decreased. The highest relative increases were recorded in the Pomorskie (by 2.6%) and Małopolskie (2.3%) voivodeships in central Poland, while the largest decreases were recorded in the following voivodeships: Łódzkie (4.1%) in central Poland, Świętokrzyskie (4.7%) in eastern Poland and Opolskie (7.2%) and Dolnośląskie (13.0%) in western Poland.
- In 2017, 4.2% more people lived in the Polish countryside than in 2004. The fastest growing population living in the countryside was in central Poland (by 7.2%), then in Mazowieckie (5.8%) and western Poland (5.4%), while in rural eastern Poland the value of this variable dropped by 1.0%.
- In 11 voivodeships the percentage of those living here increased, while in the remaining five voivodeships (Lubuskie, Świętokrzyskie, Lubelskie, Podlaskie and Opolskie) it decreased. The highest relative increments of this variable were recorded in the following voivodeships: Pomorskie (17.1%), Wielkopolskie (10.3%), Dolnośląskie (7.9%) and Kujawsko-Pomorskie (7.1%). In the Lubuskie Voivodeship, the population living in the countryside dropped by 1.1%, in Świętokrzyskie by 1.5%, Lubelskie by 2.3%, Podlaskie by 5.3% and Opolskie by 6.0%.

Map 4.4 shows the geographic diversity of urbanization rates in Poland, on the average, in 2005–2017, while Figure 4.2 shows the trajectories of these rates in the groups of the voivodeships researched in the period of time analyzed here. From the map and graph mentioned here as well as statistical data on urbanization rates in these voivodeships, the results are as follows:

- The highest urbanization rates in the years 2005–2017 were recorded in central Poland (64.6%), followed by Mazowieckie (64.4%), and western Poland (62.5%), while the lowest values of this feature were recorded in the agricultural voivodeships of eastern Poland (only 49.1%, with an average percentage for Poland as a whole of 60.7%).
- The quartile group with the highest urbanization rates included the following voivodeships: Śląskie (77.7%), Dolnośląskie (69.9%), Zachodniopomorskie (68.8%) and Pomorskie (65.6%). However, the quartile group

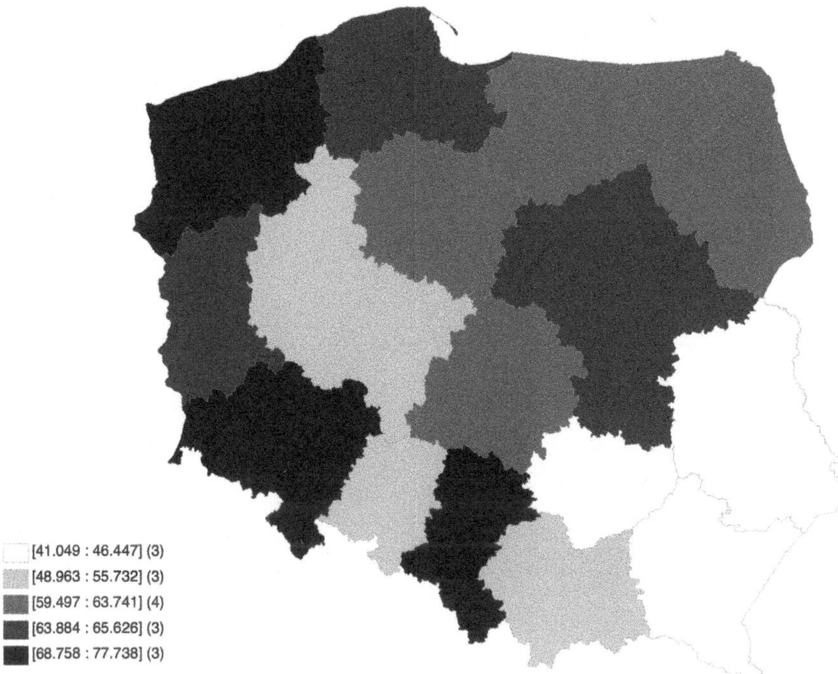

Map 4.4 Average urbanization rates in voivodeships in 2005–2017 (%).
Source: Our own estimates based on: https://bdl.stat.gov.pl/BDL/start (access: 2019-12-30).

with the lowest value of this variable was composed of the Małopolskie Voivodeship[6] (49.0%) in central Poland and three voivodeships in eastern Poland: the Lubelskie (46.4%), Świętokrzyskie (45.0%) and Podkarpackie (41.0%).

- Urbanization rates in the agricultural voivodeships of eastern Poland were over 15 percentage points lower than in the Mazowieckie Voivodeship, whereas in the voivodeships of western Poland these rates were almost 2 percentage points lower than in the aforementioned voivodeship. Urbanization rates in the Mazowieckie Voivodeship and central Poland were similar.
- In the least urbanized voivodeships of eastern Poland, the urbanization rate increased by 0.1% point between 2005 and 2017. In other groups of voivodeships, this rate was falling. In the Mazowieckie Voivodeship, the urbanization rate dropped by 0.4% point, in western Poland by 1.5 percentage points and central Poland by 2.2 percentage points (mainly as a result of the de-urbanization of the Śląskie and Łódzkie voivodeships).
- When comparing the urbanization rates in individual voivodeships in 2017 with those recorded in 2005, it turns out that in 3 voivodeships

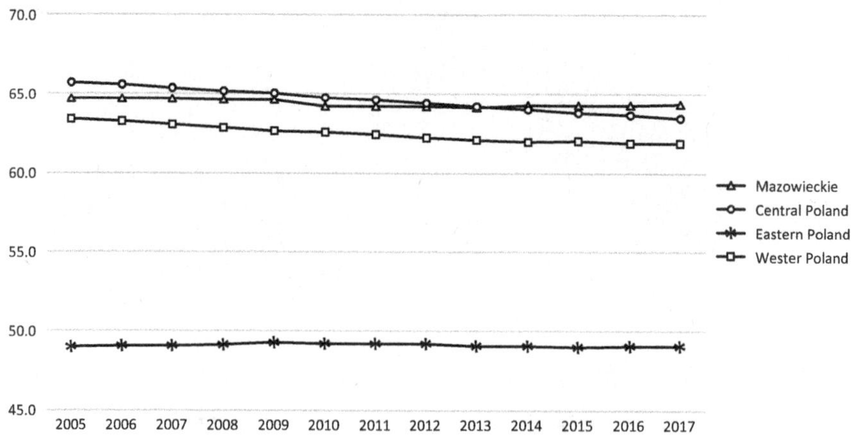

Figure 4.2 Urbanization rates in 2005–2017 (%).
Source: Our own estimates based on: https://bdl.stat.gov.pl/BDL/start (access: 2019-12-30).

(Podlaskie, Podkarpackie and Lubuskie) these rates increased, while in the others they fell. In the Podlaskie Voivodeship, the urbanization rate increased by 1.5 percentage points, while in the Podkarpackie and Lubuskie voivodeships by 0.8 percentage point. The largest decreases in the rate considered here were recorded in the Kujawsko-Pomorskie (2.2 percentage points), Dolnośląskie (2.3 percentage points), Wielkopolskie (2.5 percentage points) and Pomorskie (3.4 percentage points) voivodeships. In Poland, the urbanization rate then fell by 1.3 percentage points.

4.4. Demographic potential of the Ukrainian oblasts

Tables 4.3 and 4.4 present basic statistical data describing oblasts and group of oblasts. These data relate to the area and population at the beginning and end of the time period considered in this chapter and in 2013, that is, the last year in which the Autonomous Republic of Crimea and Sevastopol were actually part of Ukraine.

From statistical data it can be concluded that:

- The largest quartile group includes the following oblasts: Odesa in southern Ukraine (5.5% of Ukraine, 5.8% of Ukraine without the Autonomous Republic of Crimea and Sevastopol), Dnipropetrovsk Oblast (5.3%, 5.5%) in central Ukraine, Chernihiv Oblast (5.3%, 5.5%) in northern Ukraine, Kharkiv Oblast (5.2%, 5.4%) in eastern Ukraine, Zhytomyr Oblast (4.9%, 5.2%) in northern Ukraine and the Poltava Oblast (4.8%, 5.0%) in central Ukraine. The special status cities were the smallest in terms of area of the oblasts: Kyiv (0.1%, 0.1%) in northern Ukraine

Table 4.3 Population of cities and villages in 2004 and 2017 (1,000 people)

Voivodeship	*2004, year*				*2017, year*				*Year 2017 (year 2004 = 100)*			
	Cities	*Cities in urban districts*	*Cities*	*Village rural districts*	*Cities*	*Cities in magistrate districts*	*Cities in rural districts*	*Village*	*Cities*	*Cities in urban districts*	*Cities in rural districts*	*Village*
Mazowieckie	**3,329.9**	**2,179.5**	**1,150.4**	**1,816.1**	**3,463.5**	**2,229.8**	**1,233.7**	**1,921.1**	**104.0**	**102.3**	**107.2**	**105.8**
Kujawsko-Pomorskie	1,276.9	796.7	480.1	791.4	1,235.0	762.3	472.7	847.9	96.7	95.7	98.5	107.1
Łódzkie	1,674.9	902.8	772.1	912.8	1,553.4	813.0	740.4	922.9	92.7	90.1	95.9	101.1
Małopolskie	1,621.6	960.2	661.4	1,638.6	1,637.9	961.0	676.8	1,753.5	101.0	100.1	102.3	107.0
Pomorskie	1,481.4	851.7	629.7	712.7	1,484.8	838.6	646.3	839.4	100.2	98.5	102.6	117.8
Śląskie	3,702.6	2,741.8	960.8	998.1	3,496.0	2,548.4	947.6	1,052.1	94.4	92.9	98.6	105.4
Central Poland	**9,757.3**	**6,253.2**	**3,504.2**	**5,053.6**	**9,407.1**	**5,923.3**	**3,483.9**	**5,415.9**	**96.4**	**94.7**	**99.4**	**107.2**
Lubelskie	1,020.0	549.4	470.6	1,165.2	988.4	525.1	463.3	1,138.0	96.9	95.6	98.4	97.7
Podkarpackie	848.7	325.0	523.8	1,249.3	876.2	345.5	530.8	1,252.9	103.2	106.3	101.3	100.3
Podlaskie	710.8	425.1	285.7	491.6	719.2	429.9	289.2	465.4	101.2	101.1	101.2	94.7
Świętokrzyskie	586.7	209.5	377.2	702.0	556.2	196.8	359.4	691.6	94.8	94.0	95.3	98.5
Warmińsko-Mazurskie	858.8	301.5	557.3	569.9	846.4	294.0	552.5	587.5	98.6	97.5	99.1	103.1
Eastern Poland	**4,025.0**	**1,810.5**	**2,214.6**	**4,177.9**	**3,986.4**	**1,791.2**	**2,195.1**	**4,135.3**	**99.0**	**98.9**	**99.1**	**99.0**
Dolnośląskie	2,053.4	830.1	1,223.4	839.6	1,996.4	932.6	1,063.8	906.2	97.2	112.4	87.0	107.9
Lubuskie	648.2	244.1	404.1	361.0	659.7	264.1	395.6	357.1	101.8	108.2	97.9	98.9
Opolskie	554.0	128.9	425.2	497.5	522.6	128.1	394.5	467.5	94.3	99.4	92.8	94.0
Wielkopolskie	1,927.8	824.6	1,103.2	1,437.4	1,903.4	779.3	1,124.1	1,585.8	98.7	94.5	101.9	110.3
Zachodniopomorskie	1,174.3	560.8	613.6	520.5	1,170.2	552.6	617.6	535.3	99.6	98.5	100.7	102.8
Western Poland	**6,357.9**	**2,588.4**	**3,769.5**	**3,656.0**	**6,252.2**	**2,656.7**	**3,595.5**	**3,852.0**	**98.3**	**102.6**	**95.4**	**105.4**
Poland	**23,470.1**	**12,831.5**	**10,638.6**	**14,703.7**	**23,109.3**	**12,601.1**	**10,508.2**	**15,324.3**	**98.5**	**98.2**	**98.8**	**104.2**

Source: Our own estimates based on: https://bdl.stat.gov.pl/BDL/start (access: 2019-12-30).

Table 4.4 Basic data about the Ukrainian oblasts

Oblast	*Region's area*			*Population*									
				2004, year			*2013, year*			*2017, year*			*Population 2017 (2004 = 100)*
	1,000 km²	*Ukraine*	*Ukraine without the ARC*	*1,000 people*	*Ukraine*	*Ukraine without the ARC*	*1,000 people*	*Ukraine*	*Ukraine without the ARC*	*1,000 people*	*Ukraine*	*Ukraine without the ARC*	
Cherkasy Oblast	20.9	3.5	3.6	1,364.8	2.9	3	1,264.4	2.8	2.9	1,225.8	2.9	2.9	89.8
Dnipropetrovsk Oblast	31.9	5.3	5.5	3,489.5	7.4	7.7	3,300.1	7.3	7.6	3230.8	7.6	7.6	92.6
Kirovohrad Oblast	24.6	4.1	4.3	1,092	2.3	2.4	991.4	2.2	2.3	961	2.3	2.3	88
Poltava Oblast	28.8	4.8	5	1,581.5	3.3	3.5	1,463	3.2	3.4	1,420.3	3.3	3.3	89.8
Vinnytsya Oblast	26.5	4.4	4.6	1,728.2	3.6	3.8	1,622.7	3.6	3.8	1,583.1	3.7	3.7	91.6
Central Ukraine	**132.7**	**22**	**23**	**9,256**	**19.5**	**20.5**	**8,641.6**	**19**	**20**	**8,421**	**19.8**	**19.8**	**91**
Kharkiv Oblast	31.4	5.2	5.4	2,857.5	6	6.3	2,740.8	6	6.4	2,697.6	6.3	6.3	94.4
Donetsk Oblast	26.5	4.4	4.6	4,696.4	9.9	10.4	4,359.7	9.6	10.1	4,222.3	9.9	9.9	89.9
Luhansk Oblast	26.7	4.4	4.6	2,456.4	5.2	5.4	2,248	4.9	5.2	2,181.5	5.1	5.1	88.8
Zaporizhzhya Oblast	27.2	4.5	4.7	1,884.9	4	4.2	1,780.5	3.9	4.1	1,731.3	4.1	4.1	91.9
Eastern Ukraine	**111.8**	**18.5**	**19.4**	**11,895.2**	**25.1**	**26.4**	**11,129**	**24.5**	**25.8**	**10,832.7**	**25.5**	**25.5**	**91.1**
Chernihiv Oblast	31.9	5.3	5.5	1,197.3	2.5	2.7	1,072.3	2.4	2.5	1,026.7	2.4	2.4	85.8
Kyiv	28.1	4.7	4.9	1,786.4	3.8	4	1,723.8	3.8	4	1,744.4	4.1	4.1	97.6
Sumy Oblast	23.8	3.9	4.1	1,252.8	2.6	2.8	1,138.1	2.5	2.6	1,099.4	2.6	2.6	87.8
Zhytomyr Oblast	29.8	4.9	5.2	1,352.5	2.9	3	1,265.7	2.8	2.9	1,235.9	2.9	2.9	91.4
Kyiv	0.8	0.1	0.1	2,652.7	5.6	5.9	2,856.9	6.3	6.6	2,930.1	6.9	6.9	110.5
North Ukraine	**114.5**	**19**	**19.9**	**8,241.7**	**17.4**	**18.3**	**8,056.8**	**17.7**	**18.7**	**8,036.5**	**18.9**	**18.9**	**97.5**
The ARC	26.1	4.3	-	1,999.7	4.2	-	1,966.2	4.3	-	-	-	-	98.3
Kherson Oblast	28.5	4.7	4.9	1,144	2.4	2.5	1,075.4	2.4	2.5	1,051.3	2.5	2.5	91.9
Mykolayiv Oblast	24.6	4.1	4.3	1,235	2.6	2.7	1,170.9	2.6	2.7	1,145.7	2.7	2.7	92.8
Odesa Oblast	33.3	5.5	5.8	2,422.9	5.1	5.4	2,395.8	5.3	5.6	2,384.8	5.6	5.6	98.4
Sevastopol	0.9	0.1	-	378.5	0.8	-	384.7	0.8	-	-	-	-	101.6

Southern Ukraine	**113.3**	**18.8**	**15**	**7,180.1**	**15.1**	**10.7**	**6,993**	**15.4**	**10.8**	**4,581.8**	**10.8**	**10.8**	**63.8**
Khmelnytskiy Oblast	20.6	3.4	3.6	1,394.6	2.9	3.1	1,310.5	2.9	3	1,279.8	3	3	91.8
Chernivtsi Oblast	8.1	1.3	1.4	913	1.9	2	907.8	2	2.1	907.4	2.1	2.1	99.4
Ivano-Frankivsk Oblast	13.9	2.3	2.4	1,395.7	2.9	3.1	1,381.9	3	3.2	1,378.7	3.2	3.2	98.8
Lviv Oblast	21.8	3.6	3.8	2,593.2	5.5	5.8	2,539.6	5.6	5.9	2,531.8	6	6	97.6
Rivne Oblast	20.1	3.3	3.5	1,162.4	2.4	2.6	1,157.9	2.5	2.7	1,161.7	2.7	2.7	99.9
Ternopil Oblast	13.8	2.3	2.4	1,123.1	2.4	2.5	1,075.3	2.4	2.5	1,055.8	2.5	2.5	94
Volyn Oblast	20.1	3.3	3.5	1,046.8	2.2	2.3	1,040.6	2.3	2.4	1,039.7	2.4	2.4	99.3
Zakarpattia Oblast	12.8	2.1	2.2	1,249.8	2.6	2.8	1,255.6	2.8	2.9	1,258.5	3	3	100.7
Western Ukraine	**131.3**	**21.7**	**22.8**	**10,878.6**	**22.9**	**24.1**	**10,669.2**	**23.5**	**24.7**	**10,613.4**	**25**	**25**	**97.6**
Ukraine	**603.5**	**100**	-	**47,451.6**	**100**	-	**45,489.6**	**100**	-	**42,485.5**	**100**	-	**89.5**
Ukraine without the ARC and Sevastopol	**576.6**	**95.5**	**100**	**45,073.4**	**95**	**100**	**43,138.7**	**94.8**	**100**	**42,485.5**	**100**	**100**	**94.3**

Source: Our own estimates based on: http://www.ukrstat.gov.ua/ (access: 2019-12-30).

and Sevastopol (0.1%) in southern Ukraine and the following oblasts in western Ukraine: Chernivtsi (1.3%, 1.4%), Zakarpattia (2.1%, 2.2%), Ternopil (2.3%, 2.4%) and Ivano-Frankivsk (2.3%, 2.4%).

- The largest part of Ukraine is the oblast of central Ukraine (22.0% of Ukraine, 23.0% of the country without the Autonomous Republic of Crimea and Sevastopol). Next in terms of the value of this feature are the oblasts of western Ukraine (21.7%, 22.8%), northern Ukraine (19.0%, 19.9%), southern Ukraine (18.8%, 15.0%) and eastern Ukraine (18.5%, 14.9%).
- In 2004, the quartile group with the greatest demographic potential was composed of the Donetsk Oblast in the east of Ukraine (9.9% of the population of the country), Dnipropetrovsk in the center (7.4%), Kharkiv in the east (6.0%), Kyiv in the north (5.6%), and the Lviv Oblast in the west (5.5%) and the Luhansk oblast in the east of Ukraine (5.2%). Sevastopol (0.8%) in the south of Ukraine and the following oblasts: Chernivtsi (1.9%) and Volyn (2.2%) in western Ukraine, and Kirovohrad (2.3%) in central Ukraine belonged to the oblasts with the lowest population numbers at the time, Ternopil (2.4%) in western Ukraine and Kherson (2.4%) in southern Ukraine.
- 25.1% of the population of Ukraine lived at that time in the eastern Ukrainian oblasts, 22.9% in western Ukraine, 19.5% in central Ukraine, 17.4% in northern Ukraine and 15.1% in southern Ukraine.
- In 2013 (and thus in the last year for which the DSSU (ДССУ) statistics on the population of the Autonomous Republic of Crimea and Sevastopol are available), the quartile group with the largest population overlapped with the quartile group of the oblasts with the highest population in 2004. This situation was similar at the time to the quartile group of the least populated oblasts.
- This year, 24.5% of the population of Ukraine (or 25.8% of the population of the country without the Crimean Peninsula) lived in eastern Ukraine, 23.5% in western Ukraine (24.7%), and central Ukraine 19.0% (20.0%), northern Ukraine 17.7% (18.7%) and southern Ukraine 15.4%. The population of the Autonomous Republic of Crimea and Sevastopol at that time was about 2.4 million people, which constituted 5.2% of the country's population (Map 4.5).
- In 2017 (i.e., three years after Russia's annexation of the Crimean Peninsula), the group of 6 oblasts with the highest demographic potential included once again the Donetsk Oblast in eastern Ukraine (9.9% of the population of Ukraine without the Crimean Peninsula), Dnipropetrovsk in central Ukraine (7.6%), Kyiv (6.9%), the Kharkiv Oblast in eastern Ukraine (6.3%), Lviv in the west of Ukraine (6.0%) and Odesa in the south (5.6%). The oblasts with the lowest demographic potential were Chernivtsi in western Ukraine (2.1%), Kirovohrad in central Ukraine (2.3%), Chernihiv in northern Ukraine (2.4%), and Volyn in western Ukraine (2.4%), Kherson in southern Ukraine (2.5%) and Ternopil in western Ukraine (2.5%).

Map 4.5 Population in oblasts between 2004 and 2017 (1,000 people).
In the case of the ARC and Sevastopol in 2004–2013.
Source: Our own estimates based on: http://www.ukrstat.gov.ua/ (access: 2019-12-30).

- In 2017, 25.5% of the population of Ukraine lived in eastern Ukraine, 25.0% in western Ukraine, 19.8% in central Ukraine, 18.9% in northern Ukraine and 10.8% in southern Ukraine. The population of Ukraine between 2004 and 2017 fell from 46.5 million people to 42.5 million people (i.e. a decline of 10.5%). If we consider the population of Ukraine without the Crimean Peninsula, then in 2004–2017 it fell from 45.1 million people to 42.5 million people (i.e. by 2.6 million people). Also taking into account the fact that in the years 2004–2017, the population of the capital of Kyiv increased from 2.6 million people to 2.8 million people, it will turn out that the population in the provinces of Ukraine (except for Kyiv and the Crimean Peninsula annexed by Russia) dropped from 42.4 million people to 39.6 million people, that is, by 2.9 million people (roughly the population of Kyiv) or 6.8% of the population of this part of Ukraine.
- If we compare the population in 2004 and 2017 in the oblasts of Ukraine, it will turn out that only in two oblasts (Kyiv in the north and the Zakarpattia oblasts in the west of Ukraine) the population increased, while in others it decreased. In Kyiv, the population increased by 10.5%, while in the Zakarpattia Oblast by 0.7% (which in absolute numbers results in only 8.7 thousand people). The largest (exceeding 10%) relative declines in the population were recorded in the following oblasts: Chernihiv (14.2%) and Sumy (12.2%) in northern Ukraine, Kirovohrad (12.0%) in central Ukraine and Luhansk (11.2%) in eastern Ukraine, Cherkasy (10.2%) and Poltava (10.2%) in central Ukraine and Donetsk (10.1%) in eastern Ukraine.

- In 2017, the capital city Kyiv definitely had the highest population density (3,600 people/km^2). High values of this characteristic were also noted in the following regions: Donetsk (eastern Ukraine, 159.3 persons/km^2), Lviv (western Ukraine, 116.1 persons/km^2), Chernivtsi (western Ukraine, 112.0 persons/km^2) and Dnipropetrovsk (central Ukraine, 101.3 people/km^2). The lowest population density (below 45 people/km^2) was observed in the following oblasts: Chernihiv (32.2 people/km^2) in the north of Ukraine, Kherson Oblast (36.9 people/km^2) in the south, and the Kirovohrad Oblast (39.1 people/km) km^2) and Zhytomyr Oblast (41.5 people/km^2) in the north of Ukraine. In the Russian-occupied Crimean Peninsula in 2013, the population density in 2013 was 427.4 persons/km^2 in Sevastopol and 75.3 persons/km^2 in the ARC, respectively.
- The eastern Ukrainian oblasts had the highest population density in 2017 (96.9 people/km^2). The next most important were the regions in the west of Ukraine (80.8 people/km^2), the north (70.2 people/km^2) and in the center (63.5 people/km^2), and the lowest population density was in the southern Ukrainian (oblasts: Odesa, Mykolayiv and Kherson, 53.0 people/km^2).[7]

Figure 4.3 illustrates the trajectories of the population in groups of Ukrainian oblasts. The following conclusions can be drawn from this chart. First of all, there were declines in population in all the groups of Ukrainian oblasts in the years 2004–2017. Second, the largest losses were recorded in the south of Ukraine (where the population dropped from 7.2 million in 2004 to 4.6 million at the end of the period researched). However, this was mainly due to the annexation of Crimea in 2014. In the remaining oblasts of southern Ukraine

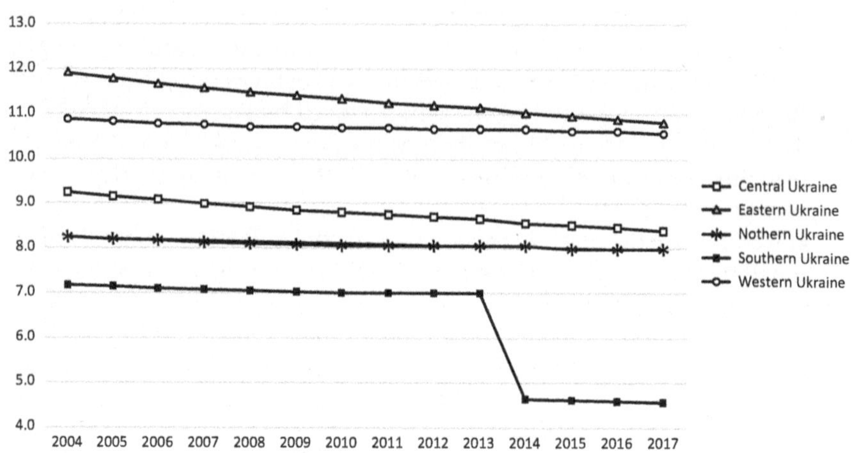

Figure 4.3 Population in groups of oblasts, between 2004 and 2017 (million people).
Source: Our own estimates based on: http://www.ukrstat.gov.ua/ (access: 2019-12-30).

(i.e., Odesa, Mykolayiv and Kherson), the population dropped from 4.8 million people in 2004 to 4.6 million people in 2017 (i.e. by 233,300 people). Third, in eastern Ukraine the number of inhabitants in the given time period decreased by 1.1 million persons, in central Ukraine by 863,300 persons, in the west by 302,400 people and in the north of Ukraine by 262,200 people. Fourth, if you consider the fact that in the years 2004–2017 the population of Kyiv increased by 236,000 people, it turns out that in the oblasts of northern Ukraine with the exception of Kyiv (i.e., Chernihiv, Kyiv, Sumy and Zhytomyr) the population dropped by almost 500,000 people.

Table 4.5 summarizes statistical data on the population of Ukrainian cities with a population exceeding 200,000 residents in 2001 and 2017. From statistical data it can be concluded that:

- In 2001, 32 Ukrainian cities had a population of over 200,000. In 2017 (after the annexation of the Crimean Peninsula by Russia) there were 30 such cities, as Simferopol and Sevastopol have been de facto, outside of Ukraine's jurisdiction since 2014.
- In both 2001 and 2017, the capital City of Kyiv was by far the largest Ukrainian city. Over the 16 years considered, the population of Kyiv increased by 12.0%.
- In 2001, the population of 4 cities in Ukraine (except Kyiv) exceeded one million people. They were Kharkiv (1.5 million people) and Donetsk (1.0 million people) in eastern Ukraine, Dnipro (1.1 million people) in central Ukraine and Odesa (1.0 million people) in southern Ukraine.
- The largest city with a population of between 500,000 and one million inhabitants is Zaporizhzhya in the east, followed by Lviv in the west, Kryvyi Rih in the center and Mykolayiv in the south of Ukraine.
- Out of the remaining cities with over 200,000 inhabitants, six were located in central Ukraine (Vinnytsya, Poltava, Cherkasy, Kamianske, Kropyvnytskyi and Kremenchuk), four in eastern Ukraine (Mariupol, Luhansk, Makiyivka and Horlivka), four in northern Ukraine (Chernihiv, Sumy, Zhytomyr and Bila Tserkva), three in southern Ukraine (Simferopol, Sevastopol and Kherson) and six cities in western Ukraine (Khmelnytskiy, Rivne, Chernivtsi, Ternopil, Ivano-Frankivsk and Lutsk).
- 29.5% of those living in cities of more than 200,000 lived in eastern Ukraine, 22.0% in northern Ukraine (of which 70.7% in Kyiv), 20.6% in central Ukraine, 15.3% in southern Ukraine and 12.7% in western Ukraine.
- In 2017, the situation changed (compared to 2001) to the extent that the cities of Dnipro and Donetsk ceased to maintain a population of over one million (the population of the Dnipro fell by 8.3% to 976,500 people, and Donetsk by 8.8% to 927,200 people), while Mykolayiv ceased to be a city of over half a million (the population of this city dropped by 4.5% to 490,800 people).

- In the last period surveyed, 29.0% of people living in cities of over 200,000 lived in eastern Ukraine, 25.1% in northern Ukraine (of which 73.9% in Kyiv), 20.6% in central Ukraine, 13, 8% in western Ukraine and 11.4% in southern Ukraine (not counting around 650,000 – the populations of Simferopol and Sevastopol).
- Comparing the population of the cities analyzed here, it turns out that the population of seven of these cities increased, while the remaining decreased. Growing populations were noted in (as was already mentioned) Kyiv (an increase of 12.0%) in northern Ukraine; Chernivtsi (10.6%), Ivano-Frankivsk (6.9%) and Khmelnytskiy (5.7%) in western Ukraine; Vinnytsya (4.5%), in central Ukraine; Lutsk (3.9%) in western Ukraine; and Bila Tserkva (3.8%) in northern Ukraine. The largest (exceeding 10%) population decreases were recorded in Horlivka (15.2%), Makiyivka (10.8%) and Luhansk (10.7%) in the Donbass and Kherson (10.7%) in the south of Ukraine.
- In 2017, the number of people living in cities of more than 200,000 fell by 6.1%, (excluding the number of inhabitants of Simferopol and Sevastopol) where this chart dropped by 2.1%. In northern Ukraine, the value of this statistic increased by 7.2%, and in western Ukraine by 2.2%. In the remaining groups of oblasts, the population living in cities of more than 200,000 fell by 5.8% in central Ukraine, 7.4% in the east of Ukraine and 29.8% in the south, respectively (excluding Simferopol and Sevastopol, where a drop of 4% was recorded).

Figure 4.4 illustrates the trajectories of the urban population in groups of oblasts in 2004–2017. The following conclusions can be drawn from this figure:

- The largest percentage of the urban population in Ukraine was in eastern Ukraine (nine to ten million people). Next came the oblasts of northern and central Ukraine (5.7–6.2 million people, respectively), and western Ukraine (approx. 5.3 million people). The least numerous were the cities of the southern Ukrainian oblast (3.0–4.7 million people).
- In the north of Ukraine, the population living in cities increased by 165,000 people. However, this was mainly due to the growing number of residents of the capital, Kyiv. In other cities of northern Ukraine, this chart fell by 107,400 people.
- Also, in western Ukraine, the number of urban residents increased (by 50,000 people).
- In the remaining groups of Ukrainian oblasts, the number of city dwellers was falling. In central Ukraine, this chart fell by 354,300 people, and in eastern Ukraine by 759,000 people.
- The largest decreases in the population in cities in 2004–2017 were recorded in southern Ukraine. There was a decrease in this volume, of approximately 1.7 million people. However, this decline was mainly due to the annexation of the Crimean Peninsula. In the Odesa, Mykolayiv and Kherson oblasts, the population living in cities fell (between 2004 and 2017) from 3.1 million people to 3.0 million people.

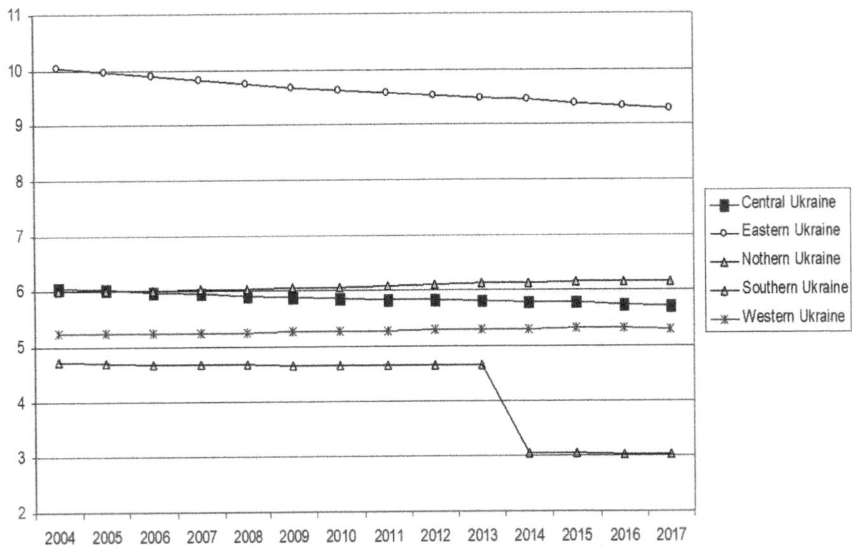

Figure 4.4 Population in groups of oblasts, between 2004 and 2017 (million people).
Source: Our own estimates based on: http://www.ukrstat.gov.ua/ (access: 2019-12-30).

Figure 4.5 illustrates the trajectories of the population living in the countryside in groups of Ukrainian oblasts in 2004–2017. The following conclusions can be drawn from the data illustrated in this figure:

- In contrast to the population living in cities, the highest part of the rural population in Ukraine was located in western Ukraine. In the years 2004–2017 about 5.3–5.6 million people lived in the countryside. In central Ukraine, around 2.7–3.2 million people lived in the countryside, in northern Ukraine about 1.8–2.2 million people and in the east only 1.5–1.9 million people. In southern Ukraine, on the other hand, mainly as a result of the Russian armed intervention of 2014 and the annexation of the Crimean Peninsula, the number of people living in villages fell from 2.5 million people, in 2014, to 1.5 million people in 2017 (in 2013, i.e., directly before the annexation of Crimea, the number of the rural population in the Crimean Peninsula was 756,700 people).
- The rural population is steadily decreasing in all groups of Ukrainian oblasts. The largest absolute decreases in the population living in the countryside were recorded in the south of Ukraine (914,400 people between 2004 and 2017), then in central Ukraine (509,000), northern Ukraine (427,900 persons), western Ukraine (352,400 persons), while the smallest was in eastern Ukraine (337,400 persons).

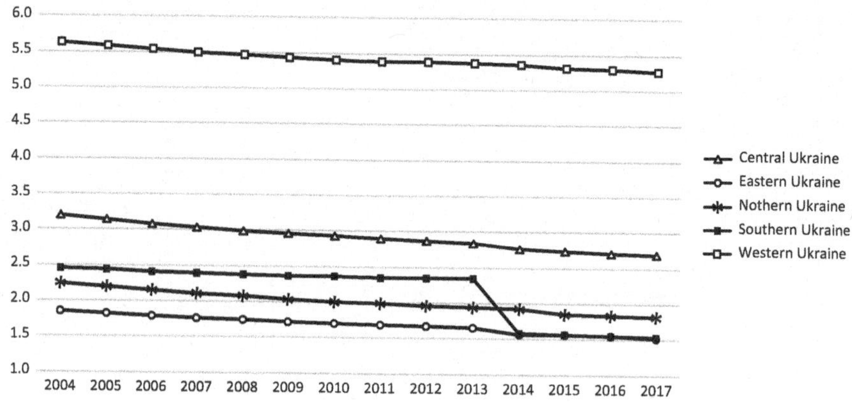

Figure 4.5 Village population in oblast groups in 2004–2017 (million people).
Source: Our own estimates based on: http://www.ukrstat.gov.ua/ (access: 2019-12-30).

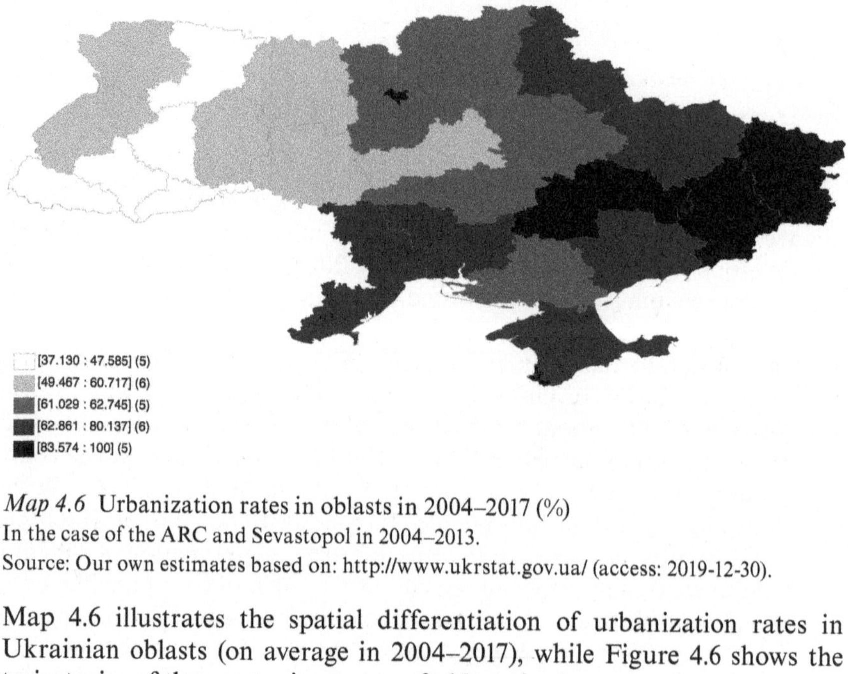

Map 4.6 Urbanization rates in oblasts in 2004–2017 (%)
In the case of the ARC and Sevastopol in 2004–2013.
Source: Our own estimates based on: http://www.ukrstat.gov.ua/ (access: 2019-12-30).

Map 4.6 illustrates the spatial differentiation of urbanization rates in Ukrainian oblasts (on average in 2004–2017), while Figure 4.6 shows the trajectories of these rates in groups of oblasts in the researched timeframe. The following map and the chart show as follows:

- What is natural, by far the highest urbanization rates were recorded in those cities with a special status (i.e. Kyiv and Sevastopol). In Kyiv, this rate was 100%, while in Sevastopol (on average in 2004–2013) 93.9%.
- Very high urbanization rates were also recorded in the Donbass (Donetsk 90.7% and Luhansk 86.8%) in eastern Ukraine, the Dnipropetrovsk

Oblast (83.6%) in central Ukraine and the Kharkiv (80.1%) and Zaporizhzhya (76.9%) oblasts in eastern Ukraine.

- In six oblasts, urbanization rates were lower than 50%. These were the following oblasts: Zakarpattia (37.1%), Chernivtsi (42.1%), Ivano-Frankivsk (43.2%), Ternopil (43.8%) and Rivne (47.6%) in western Ukraine and the Vinnytsya Oblast (49.5%) in central Ukraine, bordering on both western Ukraine[8] and Moldova.
- A more general conclusion can be drawn from this, that is, that the oblasts of the left-bank and southern Ukraine, more strongly integrated in the past with Russia or the Soviet Union, are still characterized by a much higher level of urbanization than the right-bank part of this country (see also data in Table 4.5 and Figure 4.6).

Figure 4.6 shows the trajectories of urbanization rates in groups of Ukrainian oblasts in 2004–2017. From statistical data it can be concluded that:

- Eastern Ukrainian oblasts had by far the highest rates of urbanization (around 85%). Lower urbanization rates were around 10 percentage points in the north of Ukraine, which was mainly due to the demographic potential of the capital City of Kyiv.
- In the oblasts of central Ukraine, the average urbanization rates in 2004–2017 were about 66.8%, while in central Ukraine 66.2%. The lowest urbanization rates were recorded in the peripheral western Ukraine (49.3%), where (as has already been mentioned) there is only one large city.
- Urbanization rates were increasing in all oblasts groups. These rates increased the fastest in northern Ukraine (by 4.5 percentage points), then in central Ukraine (2.5 percentage points), western (1.9 percentage points), eastern (1.5 percentage points) and southern Ukraine (0.5 percentage points).
- The increase in urbanization rates in northern Ukraine is mainly due to the very dynamic increase in the population of Kyiv, combined with the gradual depopulation of the rest of this part of Ukraine. In the remaining groups of oblasts, the increasing rates of urbanization are mainly due to the fact that Ukrainian villages are depopulating faster than Ukrainian cities.
- In all 25 Ukrainian regions (except the Autonomous Republic of Crimea and Sevastopol), urbanization rates were higher in 2017 than in 2004. These rates increased the fastest (by over 3 percentage points) in the Chernihiv region (by 6.3 percentage points) in northern Ukraine, Khmelnytskiy (5.0 percentage points) in western Ukraine, Vinnytsya (4.3 percentage points) in central Ukraine, Sumy (3.8 percentage points) in northern Ukraine, Poltava (3.4 percentage points) in central Ukraine, Kyiv (3.2) in northern Ukraine and Cherkasy (3.0 percentage points) in central Ukraine. In the whole of Ukraine, the urbanization rate increased by 2.1 percentage points.

Table 4.5 The population in Ukrainian cities with more than 200,000 inhabitants in 2001 and 2017 (1,000 people)

City	*Oblast*	*Population in a year*		*Population in 2017 (year 2001 = 100)*
		2001	*2017*	
Kyiv (*Київ*)	City of Kyiv	2,611.3	2,925.8	112.0
Kharkiv (*Харків*)	Kharkiv Oblast	1,470.9	1,439.0	97.8
Odesa (*Одеса*)	Odesa Oblast	1,029.0	1,010.8	98.2
Dnipro (*Дніпро*)	Dnipropetrovsk Oblast	1,065.0	976.5	91.7
Donetsk (*Донецьк*)	Donetsk Oblast	1,016.2	927.2	91.2
Zaporizhzhya (*Запоріжжя*)	Zaporizhzhya Oblast	815.3	750.7	92.1
Lviv (*Львів*)	Lviv Oblast	732.8	728.0	99.3
Kryvyi Rih (*Кривий Ріг*)	Dnipropetrovsk Oblast	669.0	636.3	95.1
Mykolayiv (*Миколаїв*)	Mykolayiv Oblast	514.1	490.8	95.5
Mariupol (*Маріуполь*)	Donetsk Oblast	492.2	449.5	91.3
Luhansk (*Луганськ*)	Luhansk Oblast	463.1	413.4	89.3
Vinnytsya (*Вінниця*)	Vinnytsya Oblast	356.7	372.7	104.5
Makiyivka (*Макіївка*)	Donetsk Oblast	389.6	347.4	89.2
Kherson (*Херсон*)	Kherson Oblast	328.4	293.3	89.3
Poltava (*Полтава*)	Poltava Oblast	318.0	292.0	91.8
Chernihiv (*Чернігів*)	Chernihiv Oblast	305.0	291.6	95.6
Cherkasy (*Черкаси*)	Cherkasy Oblast	295.4	281.5	95.3
Khmelnytskiy (*Хмельницький*)	Khmelnytskiy Oblast	254.0	268.5	105.7
Zhytomyr (*Житомир*)	Zhytomyr Oblast	284.2	267.4	94.1
Chernivtsi (*Чернівці*)	Chernivtsi Oblast	240.6	266.0	110.6
Sumy (*Суми*)	Sumy Oblast	293.1	265.6	90.6
Horlivka (*Горлівка*)	Donetsk Oblast	292.3	247.9	84.8
Rivne (*Рівне*)	Rivne Oblast	248.8	247.4	99.4
Kamianske (*Кам'янське*)	Dnipropetrovsk Oblast	255.8	237.2	92.7
Ivano-Frankivsk (*Івано-Франківськ*)	Ivano-Frankivsk Oblast	218.4	233.4	106.9
Kropyvnytskyi (*Кропивницький*)	Kirovohrad Oblast	254.1	229.6	90.4
Kremenchuk (*Кременчук*)	Poltava Oblast	234.1	222.3	95.0
Ternopil (*Тернопіль*)	Ternopil Oblast	227.8	217.9	95.7
Lutsk (*Луцьк*)	Volyn Oblast	208.8	217.0	103.9
Bila Tserkva (*Біла Церква*)	Kyiv Oblast	200.1	207.7	103.8
Simferopol (*Сімферополь*)	ARC	343.6	–	–
Sevastopol (*Севастополь*)	City of Sevastopol	342.5	–	–
Central Ukraine		3,448.1	3,248.2	94.2
Eastern Ukraine		4,939.5	4,575.1	92.6
North Ukraine		3,693.8	3,958.1	107.2
South Ukraine		2,557.6	1,794.8	70.2
Western Ukraine		2,131.2	2,178.1	102.2
Ukraine		16,770.1 16,084.1[a]	15,754.4	93.9 97.9[a]

Source: Our own estimates based on: http://www.ukrstat.gov.ua/ (access: 2019-12-30).

a Ukraine without the ARC and Sevastopol.

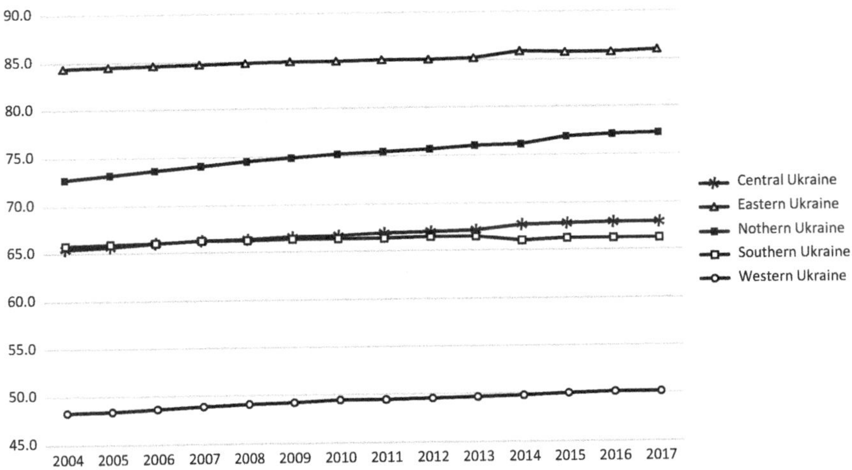

Figure 4.6 Urbanization rates in oblast groups in 2004–2017 (%).
Source: Our own estimates based on: http://www.ukrstat.gov.ua/ (access: 2019-12-30).

4.5 Summary

The considerations can be summarized as follows:

i The Mazowieckie, Śląskie and Wielkopolskie voivodeships were characterized by the largest demographic potential. The lowest potential was found in the Opolskie, Lubuskie, Świętokrzyskie and Podlaskie voivodeships.

ii The group of oblasts with the highest demographic potential was composed of the Donetsk region in the east of Ukraine, Dnipropetrovsk in central Ukraine and the Kharkiv oblasts in the east of that country. Sevastopol in the Crimea and the Chernivtsi and Volyn oblasts in western Ukraine were characterized by having the lowest population.

iii In the voivodeship groups, the largest population was recorded in the voivodeships of central Poland (about 15 million people), followed by Western Poland (about ten million people) and eastern Poland (about eight million people). In the voivodeships of western and central Poland, the population had a slight upward trend, while in eastern Poland it was decreasing.

iv In 2017, about a quarter of the population of Ukraine lived in the east of this country, ¼ in the west, almost 20% in central and northern Ukraine and just over 10% in southern Ukraine.

v All oblast groups in the years 2004–2017 suffered a decrease in population. The population declined by far the fastest in southern Ukraine (due to the Russian annexation of the Crimean Peninsula), and then in the oblasts of the pro-Russian separatists in the regions of eastern Ukraine (Donbas). The lowest drops in population were recorded in the west and north of Ukraine.

vi The voivodeships of central Poland had the highest population density, followed by Mazowieckie Voivodeship, the western Poland voivodeships, and the smallest value of this variable (over two times lower than in Central Poland) was in the voivodeships of eastern Poland.

vii In 2017, the industrial oblasts of eastern Ukraine were by far the highest in population density. Next in line (due to the value of this variable) were the oblasts of western, northern, central and southern Ukraine.

viii In 2004, there were 18 cities in Poland with a population exceeding 200,000 persons, and in 2017 there were 16 (the population of Gliwice and Kielce fell below 200,000). Among the largest Polish cities, the population of Warsaw is growing the fastest, while Łódź and the cities of the Górny Śląsk-Zagłębie agglomeration are depopulating the fastest. What's more, the total population of all cities of over 200,000 inhabitants in eastern Poland was lower than the population of Warsaw. The situation was similar with the total population of cities of over 200,000 in western Poland.

ix In 2001, there were 32 cities in Ukraine over 200,000; since 2014 (after the Russian annexation of the Crimean Peninsula, in which Sevastopol and Simferopol are located), the number of these cities has dropped to 30. By far, the fastest growth in population in the years 2001–2017 was noted in the capital of Kyiv and in the city of Chernivtsi, located near the borders with Romania and Moldova, in the province of Bukovina. The population of Ivano-Frankivsk and Khmelnytskiy in western Ukraine, Vinnytsya in central Ukraine, Lutsk in western Ukraine and Bila Tserkva in northern Ukraine also increased. The population of Horlivka, Makiyivka and Luhansk in Donbas and Kherson in the south of Ukraine fell the fastest. In 2017, the total population of cities of more than 200,000 in western or southern Ukraine was smaller than the population of Kyiv.

x The highest rates of urbanization were found in central Poland (mainly due to the Górny Śląsk-Zagłębie agglomeration) and the Mazowieckie Voivodeship (due to the Warsaw agglomeration), followed by western Poland, and the lowest (in the case of population density) was in the agricultural voivodeships of eastern Poland (where these rates were more than 15 percentage points lower than in the Mazowieckie Voivodeship).

xi In the most industrialized regions of eastern Ukraine, urbanization rates were around 85%. Next in terms of urbanization rates were the oblasts located in the north of Ukraine (about 75%), in central and southern Ukraine (over 65%) and the lowest (below 50%) in the oblasts of western Ukraine.

xii In all groups of voivodeships (except for the voivodeships of eastern Poland) urbanization rates fell in 2004–2017. This resulted mainly from the fact that a part of the population of the urban districts moved to neighboring villages. On the other hand, the growing urbanization rates in eastern Poland were the result of the fact that the number of the rural population in this part of Poland fell slightly faster than the number of the urban population.

xiii In contrast, in Ukraine, urbanization rates were rising in all oblasts groups. This resulted from the fact that Ukrainian villages depopulated in the analyzed period of time, much faster than Ukrainian cities.

Notes

1 At that time, the Volhynian Voivodeship also included the city of Rivne, which is now the capital of the Rivne Oblast.

2 For a more extensive description of the general characteristics and division of Ukrainian provinces into group of oblasts see, e.g. Tokarski, Chugaievska, Chugaievska (2019).

3 Left-bank Ukraine (Right Bank Ukraine) is the part of Ukraine that lies on the left (right) of the largest Ukrainian river – the Dnieper. In left-bank Ukraine there are therefore the following oblasts: Sumy, Chernihiv, Kharkiv, Luhansk, Donetsk, most of the Zaporizhia oblasts, the eastern parts of the Kyiv, Cherkasy and Dnipropetrovsk regions, the south-eastern part of the Cherkasy oblast and the Autonomous Republic of Crimea.

4 The population of Gliwice fell below 200,000 persons in 2005, and Kielce in 2013.

5 The first (second, third, fourth) quartile group will be understood hereinafter as a set of provinces or oblasts characterized by the value of the analyzed statistical feature higher than the third quartile (between the third and fourth quartiles, between the second and third quartiles, lower than the third quartile).

6 It seems that the low level of urbanization in the Małopolskie voivodeship results from the mountainous terrain found in the southern part of this voivodeship.

7 In 2013, the population density of the southern Ukraine oblasts together with the ARC and Sevastopol was 61.7 people/km^2.

8 Urbanization rates were also low in other western Ukrainian oblasts. In the Volyn oblast, the average urbanization rates in 2004–2017 were 51.6%, in the Khmelnytskyi oblast 54.6%, and only in the Lviv oblast (mainly due to the urban potential of Lviv) did these rates exceed 60% (on average in the period considered here they were 60.7%).

5 The economic potential of Polish voivodeships and Ukrainian oblasts

Nataliia Chugaievska, Oleksii Kelebaj and Tomasz Tokarski

5.1 Introduction

The purpose of this chapter is to analyze the spatial diversity of the economic potential of Polish voivodeships and Ukrainian oblasts. Absolute economic potential is equated with the amount of GDP. Relative economic potential is understood as GDP per capita.

The timeframe and sources of statistical data are the same as those used in Chapter 4.

5.2 Economic potential of Polish voivodeships

Map 5.1 illustrates the spatial diversity of GDP in voivodeships in 2004–2016. The following conclusions can be drawn from this map and data on this macroeconomic variable:[1]

- The highest levels of GDP in 2004–2016 were recorded in the Mazowieckie (PLN 331.4 billion, 21.6% of Polish GDP), Śląskie (PLN 196.8 billion, 12.8%) and Wielkopolskie (PLN 146.9 billion, 9.6%) voivodeships. A high level of this variable was also recorded in the Dolnośląskie (127.8 billion PLN, 8.3%), Małopolskie (118.7 billion PLN, 7.7%) and Łódzkie (PLN 94.3 billion, 6.1%) voivodeships.
- The group of voivodeships with a low value of this variable included the Zachodniopomorskie (PLN 59.0 billion, 3.8%) Warmińsko-Mazurskie (PLN 41.9 billion, 2.7%) and Świętokrzyskie (PLN 38.9 billion, 2, 5%) voivodeships. However, the group of voivodeships with the lowest value of this variable was composed of the Podlaskie (PLN 34.8 billion, 2.3%), Lubuskie (PLN 34.8 billion, 2.3%) and Opolskie (PLN 33.6 billion, 2.2%) voivodeships.
- When comparing GDP data for 2004 and 2016 in individual voivodeships, it turns out that the value of this variable increased in each of these voivodeships. The largest (exceeding 60%) increases in this macroeconomic variable were recorded in the following voivodeships:

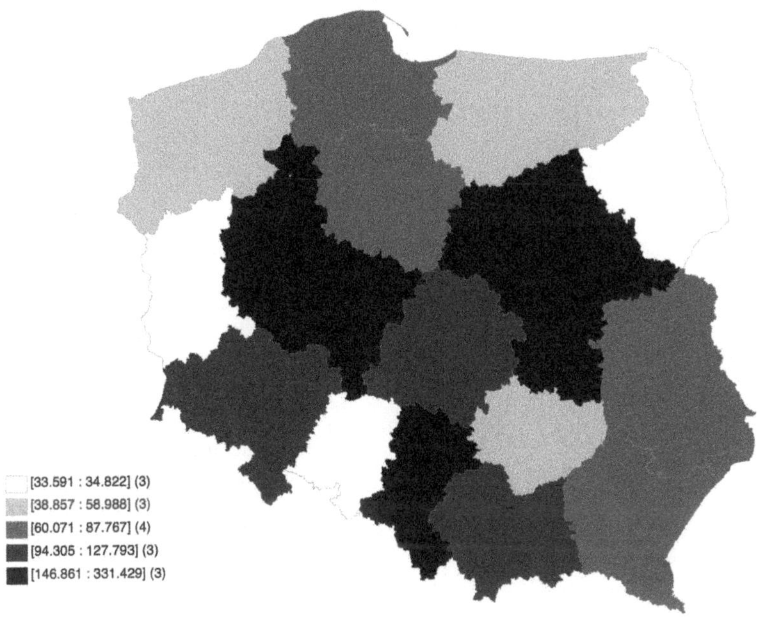

Map 5.1 GDP in voivodeship groups in 2004–2016 (PLN billion, according to 2015 prices)

Source: Our own estimates based on: https://bdl.stat.gov.pl/BDL/start (access: 2019-12-30).

Mazowieckie by 70.1% (4.2% on average annually), Dolnośląskie by 70.5% (4.5%), Małopolskie by 64.6% (4.2%), Wielkopolskie by 63.7% (4.2%) and Pomorskie by 61.5% (4.1%). The lowest increases in this variable were recorded in the Śląskie 39.9% (2.8%), Opolskie 36.6% (2.6%) and Świętokrzyskie 35.7% (2.6%) voivodeships.

- In the voivodeships of central Poland, in the years 2004–2016, 36.9% of the Polish GDP was generated, in the voivodeships of western Poland it was 26.2%, in the Mazowieckie Voivodeship 21.5%, while in the five voivodeships of eastern Poland only 15.4%.
- Figure 5.1 illustrates the trajectories of GDP in the Mazowieckie Voivodeship and other groups of voivodeships. This graph shows the following:
- In the voivodeships of central Poland, GDP increased from PLN 450.6 billion in 2004 to PLN 678.2 billion in 2016. In the voivodeships of western Poland the value of this macroeconomic variable increased from PLN 306.3 billion to PLN 487.1 billion, in the Mazowieckie Voivodeship from PLN 241.6 billion to PLN 413.1 billion, while in the voivodeships of eastern Poland from 188.7 billion PLN billion to PLN 276.8 billion.

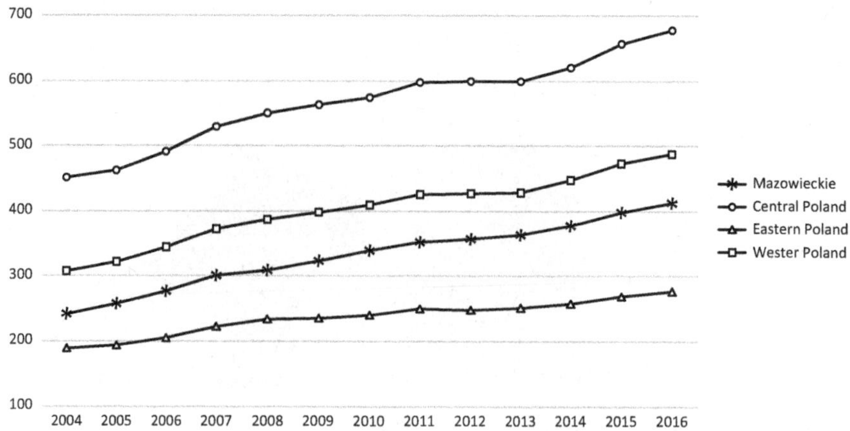

Figure 5.1 GDP in voivodeship groups in 2004–2016 (PLN billion, according to 2015 prices).

Source: Our own estimates based on: https://bdl.stat.gov.pl/BDL/start (access: 2019-12-30).

- On average, in 2004–2016, the Polish GDP grew at a rate of 3.8%. The value of this variable was rising the fastest before the global crisis, that is, before 2009 (the average annual GDP growth rate was 5.1% at the time). In 2010–2013, the growth rate of this variable in Poland dropped to 1.9%, before rising to 4.2%.
- In 2004–2009, GDP grew the fastest in the Mazowieckie Voivodeship (6.0%), then in the voivodeships of western Poland (5.4%) and central Poland (4.6%), and the slowest in the voivodeships of eastern Poland (4.5%).
- During the economic slowdown (2009–2013) caused by the global financial crisis, the Mazowieckie Voivodeship continued to develop the fastest (2.9%) followed by the voivodeships of western Poland (1.9%) and central Poland and eastern Poland (1.6% each).
- Starting from 2013, the average annual GDP growth rate in the Mazowieckie Voivodeship increased to 4.4%, in western Poland to 4.3%, in central Poland to 4.2% and in eastern Poland to 3.3%.
- As a result of these changes, the shares of the Mazowieckie Voivodeship and the voivodeships of western Poland in the creation of the Polish GDP increased, while in the other two groups of voivodeships it decreased. And so the share of the Mazowieckie Voivodeship grew from 20.4% to 22.3% and in the voivodeships of western Poland from 25.8% to 26.3%. The share of the voivodeships of central Poland in GDP fell from 38.0% to 36.6%, while in the voivodeships of eastern Poland it declined from 15.9% to 14.9%.

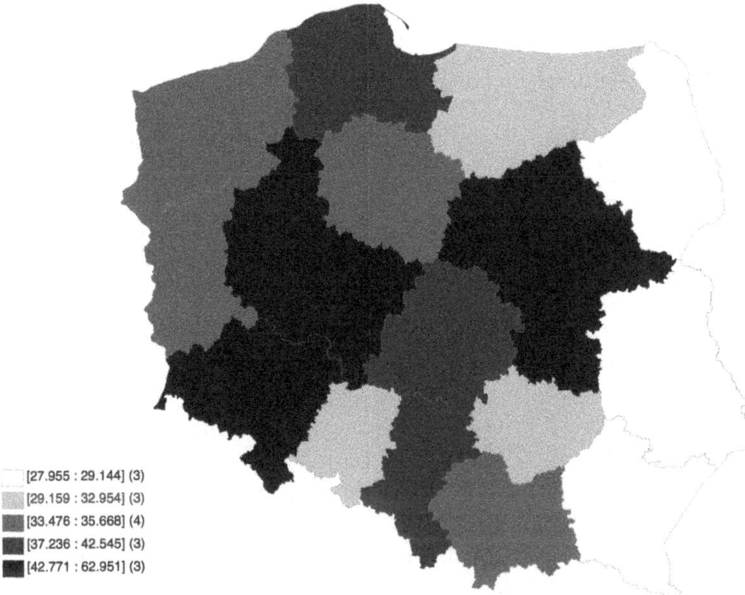

Map 5.2 GDP per capita in voivodeships in 2004–2016 (PLN, in thousands, according to 2015 prices)

Source: Our own estimates based on: https://bdl.stat.gov.pl/BDL/start (access: 2019-12-30).

Map 5.2 illustrates the spatial differentiation of GDP per capita in Poland's voivodeships in the research period (see also Figure 5.2 – in the groups of Poland's voivodeships). The following conclusions can be drawn from this figure (see also, for example, Tokarski 2005a; Trojak, Tokarski 2013; Mroczek et al. 2014; Filipowicz, Tokarski 2015; Trojak 2015 or Filipowicz 2017, 2019):

- The Mazowieckie Voivodeship had by far the highest GDP per capita (PLN 63.0 thousand), which resulted mainly from the economic potential of Warsaw together with the Warsaw agglomeration and the city of Płock. The Dolnośląskie (44.1 thousand) and Wielkopolskie (PLN 42.8 thousand) voivodeships in western Poland were also characterized by very high levels of this variable.
- The group of voivodeships with a high GDP per capita included the three voivodeships of central Poland: Śląskie (PLN 42.5 thousand), Pomorskie (PLN 38.8 thousand) and Łódzkie.
- However, the group of voivodeships with a low, and the lowest GDP per capita, included the Opolskie Voivodeship (PLN 33.0 thousand) from western Poland and five voivodeships from eastern Poland: Świętokrzyskie (30.5 thousand PLN), Warmińsko-Mazurskie (29.2 thousand) PLN),

Podlaskie (PLN 29.1 thousand), Podkarpackie (28.4 thousand PLN) and Lubelskie (28.0 thousand PLN).

- As in the case of GDP, the GDP per capita in 2016 in each voivodeship was higher than in 2004. The fastest GDP per capita increase was in Dolnośląskie (by 69.9%, i.e., 4.5% on average per year), Mazowieckie (64.0%, 4.2%), Małopolskie (58.7%, 3.9%), and Wielkopolskie (58.3%, 3.9%) and Łódzkie (57.5%, 3.9%). The lowest increases in this variable were recorded in the following voivodeships: Opolskie (44.6%, 3.1%), Zachodniopomorskie (44.3%, 3.1%), Śląskie (44.2%, 3.1%), Kujawsko–Pomorskie (43.9%, 3.1%) and Świętokrzyskie (39.6%, 2.8%).

Figure 5.2 presents the trajectories of GDP per capita in voivodeship groups. The following conclusions can be drawn from this figure:

- The shape of these trajectories was similar to the trajectory of GDP, as the variability of GDP was much greater than the variability of the population.
- The GDP per capita of the Mazowieckie Voivodeship in 2004 was higher than the value of this variable in each of the other groups of voivodeships at the end of the research period.
- The GDP per capita of the voivodeships of western Poland in 2004 accounted for 65.2% of the value of this variable in the Mazowieckie Voivodeship, whereas in central Poland it was 64.8% and in eastern Poland only 49.0%. In 2016, these indicators were (respectively) 62.6% (western Poland), 59.4% (central Poland) and 44.2% (eastern Poland).

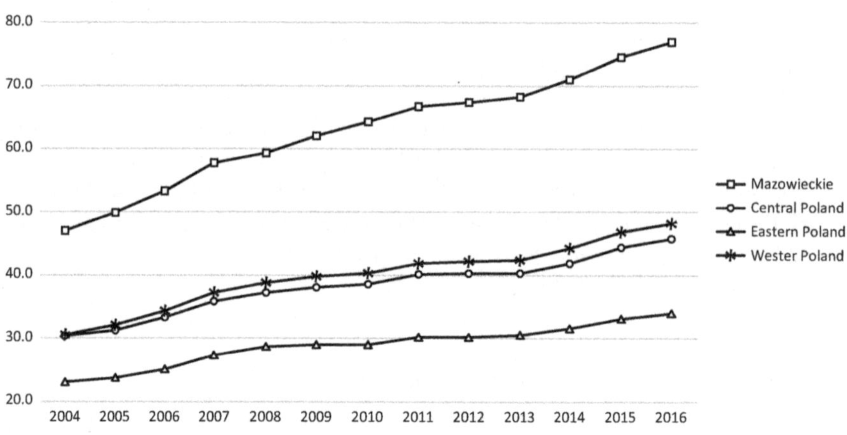

Figure 5.2 GDP per capita in voivodeship groups in 2004–2016 (PLN, in thousands, according to 2015 prices).

Source: Our own estimates based on: https://bdl.stat.gov.pl/BDL/start (access: 2019-12-30).

5.3 Economic potential of Ukrainian oblasts

Map 5.3 illustrates the spatial differentiation of GDP in the oblasts of Ukraine in 2004–2017. The following conclusions can be drawn from this map (see also Chugaievska, Tokarski 2018; Tokarski et al. 2019 or Anilovska et al. 2019):[2]

- Almost every five UAH (20%) of the Ukrainian GDP is produced in the capital of Kyiv (which is both the administrative and political center as well as the scientific, educational, service, communication and financial center of Ukraine).[3] On average, in 2004–2017 Kyiv's GDP was about 0.5 trillion UAH (19.5% of Ukrainian GDP).
- The group of oblasts with a GDP of 100–300 billion UAH included Donetsk (271.3 billion UAH, 10.5% of Ukraine's GDP), Kharkiv (154.8 billion UAH, 6.0%) and Zaporizhzhya (108.0 billion UAH, 4.2%) in eastern Ukraine; Dnipropetrovsk (261.6 billion UAH, 10.1%) and Poltava (105.4 billion UAH, 4.1%) in central Ukraine; Odesa (123.6 billion UAH, 4.8%) in southern Ukraine; Kyiv (111.5 billion UAH, 4.2%) in the north of Ukraine; and Lviv (106.9 billion UAH, 4.1%) in the west of Ukraine.
- In 11 oblasts and one city with a special status (Sevastopol), the average annual GDP in 2004–2017 (or 2004–2013 in the case of Sevastopol) did not exceed UAH 50 billion. The statistics in the following oblasts were as follows: Khmelnytskyi (47.0 billion UAH, 1.8% of Ukraine's GDP), Rivne (40.4 billion UAH, 1.6%), Zakarpattia (36.7 billion UAH, 1.4%), Volyn (36.4 billion UAH, 1.4%), Ternopil (31.3 billion UAH, 1.2%) and

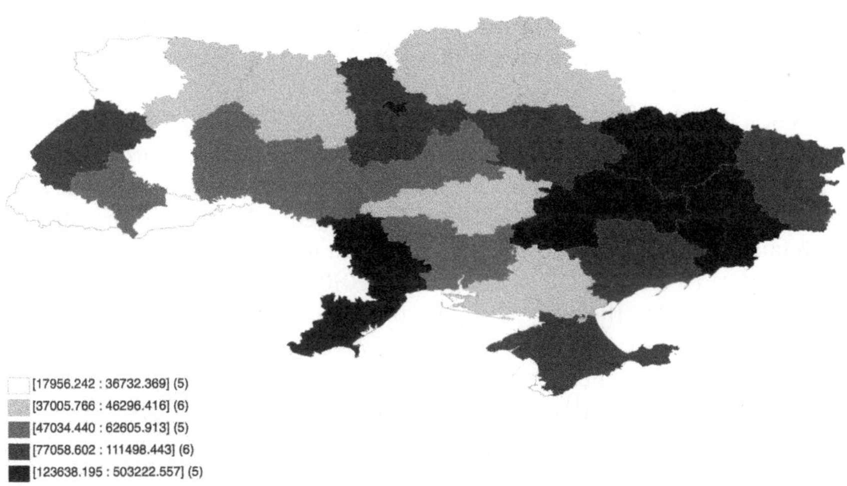

Map 5.3 GDP in oblasts in 2004–2017 (UAH million, according to 2016 prices)
Source: Our own estimates based on: http://www.ukrstat.gov.ua/ (access: 2019-12-30).

Chernivtsi (23.6 billion UAH, 0.9%) in western Ukraine; Sumy (46.3 billion UAH, 1.8%), Zhytomyr (44.4 billion UAH, 1.7%) and Chernihiv (43.0 billion UAH, 1.7%) in northern Ukraine; Kirovohrad (41.2 billion UAH, 1.6%) in central Ukraine; and Kherson (37.0 billion UAH, 1.4%) and a city with a special status, that is Sevastopol[4] (18.0 billion UAH, 0.7%), in the south of Ukraine.

- Regarding the oblast groups, the oblasts of northern Ukraine generated on average 29.3% of the Ukrainian GDP in 2004–2013 (Kyiv itself, as already mentioned, had 19.5%), eastern Ukraine 24.4%, central Ukraine 20.6%, western Ukraine 14.7% and southern Ukraine 11.1%.
- Hence, we may come to a more general conclusion that the greatest economic potential of Ukraine was concentrated in Left-bank Ukraine (Kyiv, the Kyiv region, the city of Dnipro, the Donbas, Kharkiv, Zaporizhzhya), in two coastal oblasts (Odesa and Mykolayiv) and the Lviv Oblast in western Ukraine. Kyiv, as already mentioned, is an administrative, communication center of Ukraine. The city of Dnipro is the center of financial services of the country, and an important center of political, cultural and educational life in central Ukraine. Kharkiv, Zaporizhzhya and Donbas are the main centers of the Ukrainian heavy and mining industries. The high level of economic development of the Odesa Oblast is mainly associated with the port of Odesa. Mykolayiv and the Mykolayiv region are a very important communication junction (road, rail, sea, river and air) in the south of Ukraine, and Lviv is by far the most prominent, demographically and economically, city in the west of the country (see also Chugaievska et al. 2017, 2019 or Chugaievska, Tokarski 2018).

Figure 5.3 illustrates the trajectories of GDP in the oblasts on average in 2004–2017. This graph shows the following:

- When analyzing the development of the GDP trajectory in oblast groups, the timeframe analyzed here should be divided into five subperiods. In the years 2004–2008, the Ukrainian economy was developing very dynamically. However, in the years 2008–2009 the global financial crisis and the Russian-Ukrainian gas conflict led to a significant decline of the GDP in Ukraine. In 2010–2013, the Ukrainian economy returned to the path of rapid economic growth, while in 2014–2015 (i.e., the first years after the Euro-Maidan) a deep recession occurred in the Ukrainian economy as a result of the political and military conflict with Russia (Crimea) or pro-Russian separatists (Donbas). However, in 2016–2017 the Ukrainian GDP slowly began to increase again.
- In the years 2004–2008, the oblast groups of eastern and northern Ukraine were characterized by the highest absolute economic potential (in the order of 600–800 billion UAH). The average, according to Ukrainian conditions, were those regions located in the center of

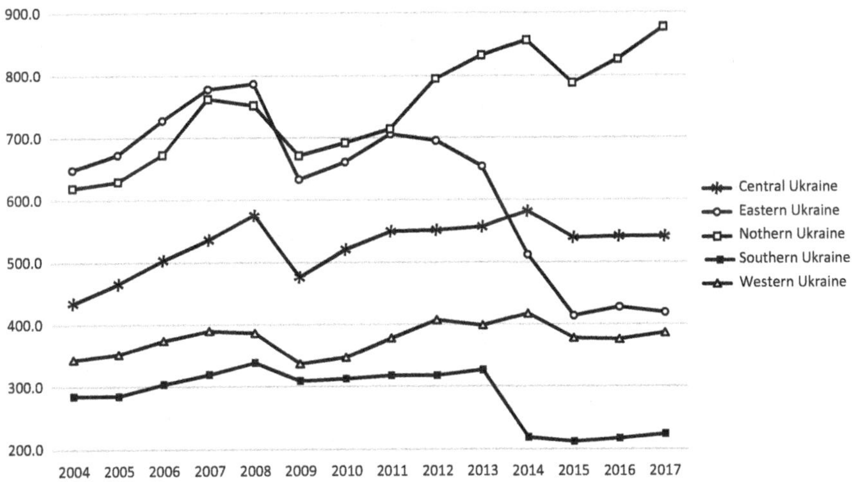

Figure 5.3 GDP in oblast groups in 2004–2017 (UAH billion, according to 2016 prices).

Source: Our own estimates based on: http://www.ukrstat.gov.ua/ (access: 2019-12-30).

Ukraine (430–580 billion UAH), while the lowest were the regions of western Ukraine (340–390 billion UAH) and the southern part of the country (280–340 billion UAH).

- In 2004–2008, the GDP grew the fastest in central Ukraine (at a 7.2% yearly average), followed by northern (5.0%), eastern (4.9%), and southern Ukraine (4.4%), with the slowest GDP increase noted in western Ukraine (3.0%). As a result, the share of individual oblast groups in the production of the Ukrainian GDP changed as follows: the share of central Ukraine increased from 18.6% to 20.2%, northern Ukraine remained unchanged (26.5%), eastern Ukraine fell from 27.8% to 27.7%, southern Ukraine decreased from 12.3% to 11.9%, and western Ukraine fell from 14.7% to 13.6%.
- The global financial crisis combined with the Ukrainian-Russian gas conflict affected quite significantly the most highly industrialized regions of eastern Ukraine (where GDP fell by 19.3%) and central Ukraine (a decline of 17.1%). In western Ukraine, the GDP fell by 12.7%, in the north by 10.8% and in the oblasts of southern Ukraine only by 8.8%. This resulted in an increase in the share of western Ukrainian oblasts in the Ukrainian GDP by 1.1 percentage points, southern Ukrainian oblasts by 0.8 of a percentage points, western oblasts by 0.3 of a percentage point and a decrease in the share of central Ukrainian oblasts by 0.6 of a percentage point and eastern Ukraine by 1.6 points.
- An economic recovery after the Russian-Ukrainian gas conflict resulted in the development of the regions of northern Ukraine (5.5% yearly

average) the fastest, then western (4.2%), central (4.0%), and southern Ukraine (1.4%), and the slowest progress in oblasts located in the east of the country (only 0.8%). In 2013, the oblasts in the north of Ukraine already produced 30.1% of Ukraine's GDP (an increase of 3.5 percentage points compared to 2004), the east 23.6% (a decrease of 4.2 percentage points), the center 20.1% (an increase of 1.4 percentage points), the west 14.4% (a decrease of 0.3 of a percentage point) and the south 11.8% (a decrease of 0.4 of a percentage point).

- The political-military conflict with Russia after the Euro-Maidan also strongly influenced the country's economy. It affected (most obviously) the eastern Ukrainian oblasts (where the struggle with pro-Russian separatists in the Donbas is still ongoing, with a greater or lesser intensity) and southern Ukraine (the annexation of the Autonomous Republic of Crimea with Sevastopol).
- In eastern Ukraine oblasts, in 2014–2015 the GDP fell by 20.5% at a per annum average. However, the decrease in this macroeconomic value was not equal in all regions of this part of Ukraine. In the Luhansk region, the GDP in 2015 was as much as 72.0% lower than in 2013, in the Donetsk region by 55.0%, in the Kharkiv region by 5.6%, and in the Zaporizhzhya region by 5.7%.
- In the oblasts located in the south of Ukraine, the GDP in 2013–2015 fell by 35.4%. However, this was mainly the result of the annexation of the Crimean Peninsula by Russia. If one compares the total GDP of the three remaining regions of this part of Ukraine (i.e., Kherson, Mykolayiv and Odesa), it turns out that in 2013–2015, the GDP fell by 5.2%.
- In the remaining groups of oblasts in the first two years after the Euro-Maidan, drops in the GDP were not as drastic as in the east and south of Ukraine. The average annual rates of decline of this macroeconomic variable in central Ukraine were 1.5%, in northern Ukraine 2.7% and in the western part of the country 2.5%.
- As a result of these changes, the share of northern Ukrainian oblasts in the generation of Ukraine's GDP increased to 33.8%, the central part of the country to 23.1%, western Ukraine to 16.2%, while the share of eastern Ukrainian oblasts fell to 17.7% and in the south to 9.1%.
- In 2016–2017, the Ukrainian economy began to expand again. The GDP in northern Ukraine grew at an average annual rate of 5.5%, while in the south by 2.9%. The value of this variable increased much more slowly in western (1.1%), eastern (0.6%) and central Ukraine (0.2%).
- The effect of these changes was that the GDP in 2017 in three out of the five oblast groups considered here was higher than in 2004. In the regions of northern Ukraine, the value of this variable increased by 41.6% (2.7% annual average), central Ukraine by 24.4% (1.7%) and western Ukraine by 12.8% (0.9%). In eastern Ukraine, the GDP in 2017 was lower than at the beginning of the research period by 35.6% (an average annual decrease of 3.3%), while in southern Ukraine by 21.7%

(a decreases of 1.9%). However, if we consider only the Mykolayiv, Odesa and Kherson oblasts, it turns out that the GDP increased here between 2001 and 2017 by 9.8% (a 0.7% yearly average).

- When comparing the absolute value of GDP in 2004 and 2017 in the 25 regions of Ukraine (excluding the Autonomous Republic of Crimea and Sevastopol), it turns out that in 21 of these regions the GDP increased and in four regions it fell (in Chernivtsi and Zakarpattia in western Ukraine and in Donetsk and Luhansk in eastern Ukraine). The highest (exceeding 30%) increases in this macroeconomic variable were recorded in the Kyiv Oblast (68.6%, 4.1% per annum), in the City of Kyiv (44.9%, 2.9%) in the north of Ukraine and in the Vinnytsya (37, 3%, 2.5%) and Cherkasy (30.2%, 2.0%) oblasts, in the center of the country (Map 5.4). In the Luhansk Oblast, the GDP fell by as much as 72.7% (9.5% on average per year), in the Donetsk Oblast by 58.7% (6.6%), in the Zakarpattia Oblast by 10.0% (0.8%) and in the Chernivtsi Oblast by 3.7% (0.3%).
- In Sevastopol, the GDP in 2013 was 34.4% higher than in 2001 (and therefore the GDP grew annually at a rate of 3.3%), while in the Autonomous Republic of Crimea, it increased at this time by 26.0% (an average annual growth of 2.6%).
- Map 5.1 illustrates the spatial diversity of GDP per capita in oblasts during 2004–2017 (see also Figure 5.4). The following conclusions can be drawn from this figure:
- The capital of Kyiv had by far the highest value of this macroeconomic variable (179.9 thousand UAH). However, if we aggregate the GDP per

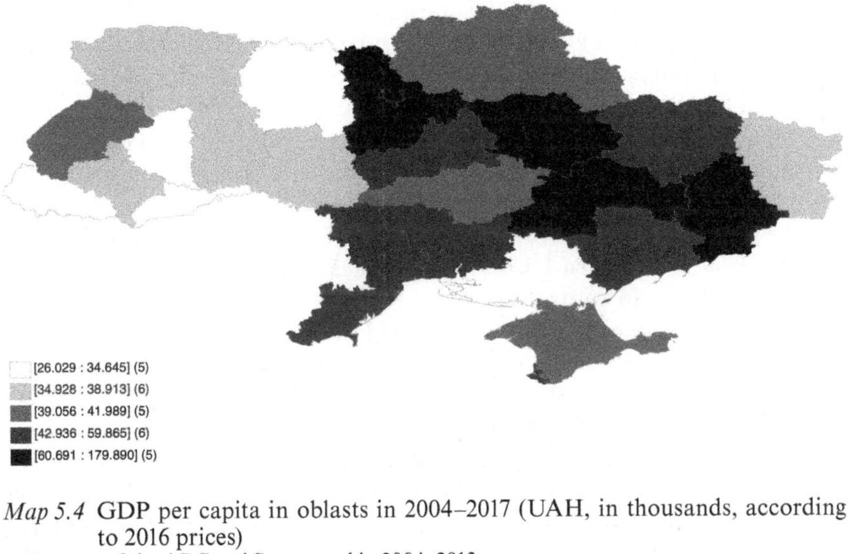

Map 5.4 GDP per capita in oblasts in 2004–2017 (UAH, in thousands, according to 2016 prices)

In the case of the ARC and Sevastopol in 2004–2013.

Source: Our own estimates based on: http://www.ukrstat.gov.ua/ (access: 2019-12-30).

capita of an inhabitant of Kyiv together with the Kyiv Oblast (which may be compared with the capital-Mazowieckie Voivodeship in Poland, or with the Kharkiv, Odesa or Dnipropetrovsk oblasts in Ukraine), the average GDP per capita falls here to a level of 129.3 thousand UAH.

- The Dnepropetrovsk (78.3 thousand UAH), Poltava (70.9 thousand UAH) and Kyiv (64.3 thousand UAH) had a rather high GDP per capita (for Ukrainian conditions), a result which was also characteristic of the Donetsk region in the Donbas (60,700 UAH).
- Those oblasts located in the Dnieper valley (except for the Kherson Oblast), eastern Ukrainian oblasts and the Odesa and Mykolayiv coastal oblasts were characterized by the highest level of the macroeconomic variable analyzed here(GDP per capita). This is due to the fact that (first of all) in this part of Ukraine there are nine of the ten largest Ukrainian cities (except Lviv) and (second) the region of the Dnieper valley is very strongly influenced by the economic ripple effects from the rest of Ukraine (Chugaievska et al. 2017).
- Of the five oblasts with the lowest GDP per capita, three were located in the west, and one in the north and south of Ukraine. These oblasts were Zakarpattia (29.4 thousand UAH), Ternopil (28.9 thousand UAH) and Chernivtsi (26.0 thousand UAH) in western Ukraine; Zhytomyr (34.6 thousand UAH) in northern Ukraine; and Kherson (33.9 thousand UAH) in southern Ukraine.
- In general, the oblasts of Left-bank Ukraine together with the Black Sea oblasts of Odesa and Mykolayiv were characterized by a higher level of GDP per capita than the Right-bank oblasts (with the exception of the Lviv Oblast, which maintained an average GDP per capita of 42,000 UAH).
- Comparing the data on GDP per capita in 2017 with the value of this variable from 2001, in 25 out of 27 Ukrainian oblasts (excluding the Autonomous Republic of Crimea and Sevastopol), it turns out that – as in the case of GDP – in 21 of these oblasts the value of this variable increased, while in four (the Chernivtsi and Zakarpattia oblasts in western Ukraine, and the Donetsk and Luhansk oblasts in eastern Ukraine) this value fell.
- The highest (exceeding 30%) per capita GDP growth was recorded in the following oblasts: Kyiv (an increase of 73.3%, average annual growth of 4.3%)[5] in northern Ukraine, Vinnytsya (50.5%, 3.2%) and Cherkasy (45.4%, 2.9%) in central Ukraine, Khmelnytskyi (35.8%, 2.4%) in the west of Ukraine, Dnipropetrovsk (34.3%, 2.3%) in central Ukraine, Zhytomyr (34, 0%, 2.3%) and in City Kyiv (33.1%, 2.2%) in the north of Ukraine, while in the Kirovohrad (32.7%, 2.2%) and Poltava (32.1%, 2.2%) oblasts in central Ukraine.
- In the Chernivtsi Oblast, the GDP per capita in 2017 was 2.8% lower than in 2001 (an average annual decrease of 0.2%), in the Zakarpattia region it fell by 10.4% (0.8% annual average), in the Donetsk GDP it fell by 53.9% (5.8% on average per year), while in the Luhansk Oblast, the GDP declined by as much as 69.2% (8.6%).

- In Sevastopol, the 2013 GDP per capita was 32.3% higher than in 2001 (and therefore the GDP grew annually at a rate of 3.2%), while in the Autonomous Republic of Crimea as a whole, it increased by 21.8% (an average annual growth of 2.6%).
- Figure 5.4 illustrates the trajectories of GDP per capita in groups of Ukrainian oblasts. This graph shows the following:
- Trajectories of GDP per capita in oblast groups are similar in shape to the trajectory of GDP. This is due to the fact that in the research period in Ukraine (as in Poland), the variability of GDP in the oblast groups was much greater than the volatility of the population.
- By far the highest GDP per capita (mainly due to Kyiv and, to a lesser extent, the Kyiv Oblast) was recorded in the group of oblasts of northern Ukraine. Moreover, no other group of oblasts in 2004–2017 attained the level of GDP per capita of the oblasts of northern Ukraine from 2004.
- In the group of industrial oblasts of eastern Ukraine (characterized by the GDP per capita in 2004, the highest after that of northern Ukraine), as a result of the gas conflict with Russia in 2009 and the struggle with pro-Russian separatists in Donbas, the value of this variable dropped from 54.5 thousand UAH in 2004 to 38.7 thousand UAH in 2017 (therefore by 29.0%).
- The GDP per capita in the central Ukrainian oblasts was (on average throughout the entire research period) about 32.9% higher than in southern Ukraine and 70.4% higher than in western Ukraine. However, in relation to the GDP per capita of northern Ukraine, the value of this variable in central Ukraine amounted to 64.9%.

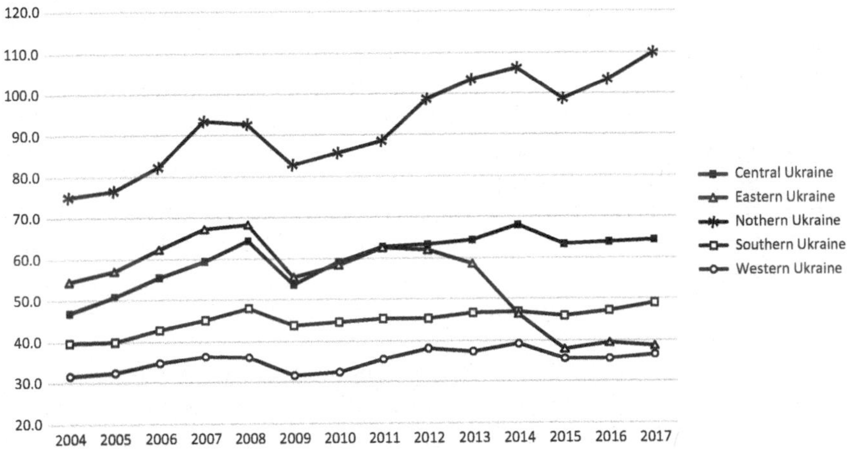

Figure 5.4 GDP per capita in oblast groups in 2004–2017 (UAH, in thousands, according to 2016 prices).

Source: Our own estimates based on: http://www.ukrstat.gov.ua/ (access: 2019-12-30).

5.4 Summary

- i As in the case of demographic potential, the largest economic potential (measured in GDP) was recorded in the Mazowieckie, Śląskie and Wielkopolskie voivodeships. The lowest economic potential was recorded in the Podlaskie, Lubuskie and Opolskie voivodeships.
- ii By far the highest GDP level in 2004–2017 was recorded in the capital City of Kyiv, where literally every 5th UAH (20%) of Ukraine's GDP was generated. A high level of this macroeconomic variable was also recorded in the Donetsk, Kharkiv and Zaporizhzhya regions located in eastern Ukraine. Nevertheless, the lowest absolute economic potential was found in the Zakarpattia, Volyn, Ternopil and Chernivtsi oblasts in western Ukraine as well as in Kherson and in the special status city of Sevastopol in southern Ukraine.
- iii The largest part of the Polish GDP in 2004–2016 was generated by the voivodeships of central Poland (36.9%), followed by western Poland (26.2%), the Mazowieckie Voivodeship (21.5%), and the smallest part by the voivodeships of eastern Poland (15.4%).
- iv In Ukraine (mainly due to Kyiv and, to some extent, the Kyiv Oblast), the largest part of GDP was generated by the northern regions of the country (29.3% of Ukrainian GDP). Next in line were (the most industrialized) oblasts of eastern Ukraine (24.4%), the oblasts of central Ukraine (20.6%), and those of western Ukraine (14.7%). However, the oblasts of southern Ukraine had the lowest economic potential (11.1%).
- v The GDP in voivodeship groups rose the most rapidly prior to the global financial crisis, and grew the slowest during the crisis itself.
- vi On the other hand, the Ukrainian economy (and groups of oblasts) developed the fastest right up until the global financial crisis and the Russian-Ukrainian gas conflict. After a one-year recession in 2009, the economy returned to a path of economic growth, which was interrupted by a deep recession resulting from the political and military conflict with Russia and the pro-Russian separatists. This recession hit the two oblasts of Donbas particularly hard, which significantly weakened the economic potential of eastern Ukraine.
- vii By far the highest GDP per capita in 2004–2016 was recorded in the Mazowieckie Voivodeship. A high GDP was also recorded in the Dolnośląskie and Wielkopolskie voivodeships. The lowest GDP per capita was recorded in the Opolskie Voivodeship and the five voivodeships of eastern Poland.
- viii As in the case of absolute GDP, the capital City of Kyiv had the highest GDP per capita, by far. Next in line were the Dnipropetrovsk, Poltava and Kyiv oblasts lying in the Dnieper valley. The least developed, economically, parts of Ukraine are the Zakarpattia, Ternopil and Chernivtsi oblasts in western Ukraine, Zhytomyr in northern Ukraine, and Kherson in southern Ukraine.

ix During the research period, the GDP per capita of the voivodeships of western Poland accounted for about 62–65% of the value of this variable in the Mazowieckie Voivodeship, central Poland 60–65% and eastern Poland only 45–50%. What's more, because the GDP per capita in the most affluent voivodeship, that is, the Mazowieckie Voivodeship, in 2004–2016 increased by 64.0%, in the provinces of western Poland by 57.6%, central Poland by 50.4% and the poorest group of those voivodeships in eastern Poland by only 47.9%, on the one hand, the development gap between the best-developed Mazowieckie Voivodeship and the rest of the country is growing and, on the other hand, the gap between the least-developed voivodeships of eastern Poland and other groups of voivodeships is also increasing.

x In Ukraine in 2004, the GDP per capita of the eastern Ukrainian oblasts constituted 72.6% of the value of this variable in northern Ukraine, and it was in central Ukraine 61.9%, southern Ukraine 53.0%, and western Ukraine only 42.0%. In 2004–2017, the most prosperous regions of northern Ukraine were developing the fastest (total GDP per capita growth by 46.2%), followed by central Ukraine (37.2%), and then southern (23.1%) and western Ukraine (16.0%). In contrast, the GDP per capita of the eastern Ukrainian oblasts fell by as much as 29.0% during this timeframe. As a result, the development gap between the north of Ukraine and the rest of the country widened. In 2017, the GDP per capita of central Ukraine already accounted for only 61.9% of the value of this variable in northern Ukraine, while in southern Ukraine it was 45.6%, eastern Ukraine 38.1% and in western Ukraine 34.2%.

Notes

1 All charts given in this section regarding GDP or GDP per capita of the voivodeships are expressed in constant prices from 2015.

2 In 2016, Ukraine's nominal GDP amounted to 2,385.4 billion hryvnia, while Poland's was PLN 1,861.1 billion. The real GDP of Ukraine at PPP and fixed prices from 2010 was at that time USD 6,281.1 billion, and in Poland USD 917.8 billion (see https://w3.unece.org/). Therefore, the dollar was (according to PPP) was valued at 3.798 hryvnia or 2.010 PLN. From this comes the conclusion that 100 hryvnia from 2016, after including PPP, equaled PLN 52.9.

3 The fact that the capital of the state is also the most developed city (as is the case in both Poland and Ukraine) is by no means the rule. For example, the best developed cities of Germany are Hamburg and Munich, not the capital Berlin (Pastuszka 2016, 2017; Gomółka et al. 2017), while in Italy, the capital region of Lazio is much less developed than Lombardy or the province of Trentino-Alto Adige (Pastuszka, Tokarski 2017).

4 In 2004–2013, the average value of GDP generated in the Crimean Peninsula (i.e., in the Autonomous Republic of Crimea and Sevastopol) amounted to UAH 95.0 billion (3.6% of the Ukrainian GDP).

5 In Kyiv, together with the Kyiv Oblast, the GDP per capita increased by 42.7%, that is, 2.7% on average per annum.

6 Product market structures

Katarzyna Filipowicz, Tomasz Tokarski and Titus Ferenc

6.1 Introduction

This chapter is a continuation of the analyses carried out in Chapters 3–5. Chapter 3 presents and discusses the structural changes in the product stream and investments in Poland and Ukraine in macroeconomic terms. Chapters 4 and 5 began a series of meso-economic analyses. The division of a complex, multidimensional and dynamic structure, that is the national economy into smaller elements such as regions and sectors of regional economies, permits a better understanding of the ongoing changes in space and its economic structure.

The next parts of this chapter describe changes in the gross value added in the following sectors of the economy: agriculture, industry, construction and services in Polish voivodeships (2004–2015) and in Ukrainian oblasts (2004–2016). In the conducted regional analyses, these voivodeships and oblasts were divided into groups according to the same criteria as in Chapters 4 and 5. The data used in this chapter come from the Local Data Bank, Statistics Poland, (GUS)[1] and the State Statistics Service of Ukraine (ДССУ).[2]

The analyses conducted in this chapter concern both the absolute and relative potential of various sectors of the regional economy. The absolute potential of these sectors is measured by the gross value added of individual sectors in voivodeships and oblasts, while the relative potential is the share of the gross value added in a given sector in the gross value added of four major sectors of the region's economy.

6.2 Sector structure of the product market in Poland

6.2.1 Added value in agriculture

Figure 6.1 presents the gross value added in agriculture in voivodeship groups in 2004–2015. The shape of their trajectory indicates that the value added in agriculture has fluctuated significantly in all groups of voivodeships throughout the entire research period. The course of the trajectory on the graph is probably the result of many factors, the most important of which (in the context of the agricultural sector) being climate fluctuations

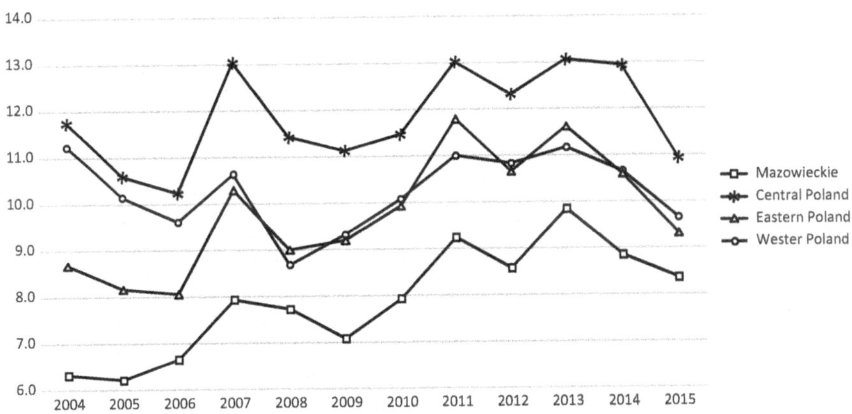

Figure 6.1 Gross value added in agriculture in voivodeship groups in 2004–2015 (PLN billion, according to 2015 prices).

Source: Our own estimates based on: https://bdl.stat.gov.pl/BDL/start (access: 2019-12-30).

and agricultural policy. It is worth noting that the agricultural potential of eastern Poland oscillated in the range of 8.1–11.8 billion PLN and was comparable or lower than the potential of western Poland (9.5–12.4 billion PLN) or central Poland (9.4–12.0 billion PLN). The Mazowieckie Voivodeship had the lowest added value in agriculture (6.2–9.2 billion PLN). In addition, the value added in agriculture increased in the Mazowieckie Voivodeship (by 32%) and in the voivodeships of eastern Poland (by 7%) in 2015 compared to 2004; in the other two groups there was a decrease in the value of this variable in the years under consideration.

On average, in the years 2004–2015, the highest absolute values of the variable under consideration were recorded in the following voivodeships: Mazowieckie (7.9 billion PLN), Wielkopolskie (5.7 billion PLN) and Łódzkie (3.24 billion PLN). In turn, the lowest values were observed in the following voivodeships: Lubuskie (1.08 billion PLN), Opolskie (1.07 billion PLN) and Podkarpackie (1.00 billion PLN, see Map 6.1). The low added value in agriculture in the Lubuskie and Opolskie voivodeships was probably associated with the low demographic potential of these voivodeships.

Figure 6.2 shows the share of gross value added in agriculture (in gross value added in all sectors of the economy) in groups of voivodeships. The share of the agricultural sector in GVA was falling in every group of voivodeships. The largest decrease was recorded in the group of voivodeships of western Poland (by approx. 2% points), then in central Poland (approx. 1% point). The voivodeships of eastern Poland had the highest share of this sector in the generated gross value added (from 5.2% in 2004 to 3.9% in 2015). In turn, the share of the agricultural sector was the lowest in the voivodeships of central Poland (in 2004 it was 2.7%, while in 2015 it was only 1.7%).

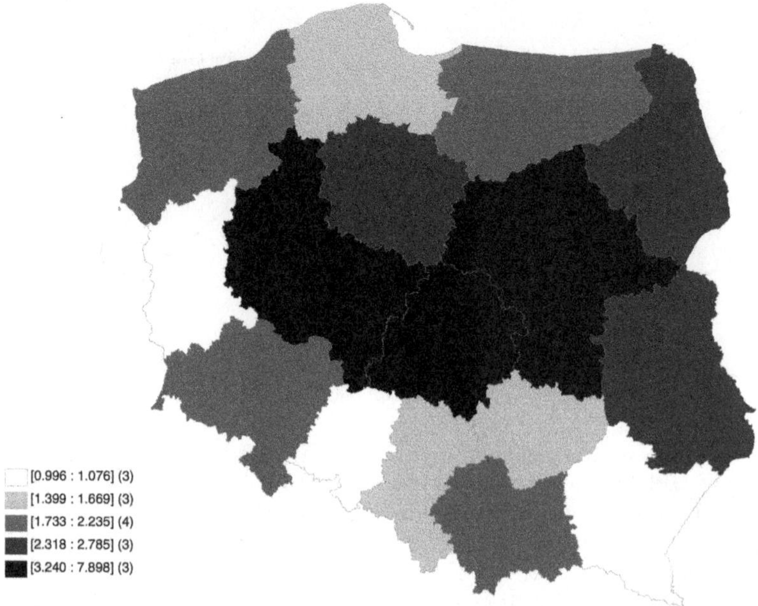

Map 6.1 Gross value added in agriculture in voivodeships in 2004–2015 (PLN billion, according to 2015 prices).

Source: Our own estimates based on: https://bdl.stat.gov.pl/BDL/start (access: 2019-12-30).

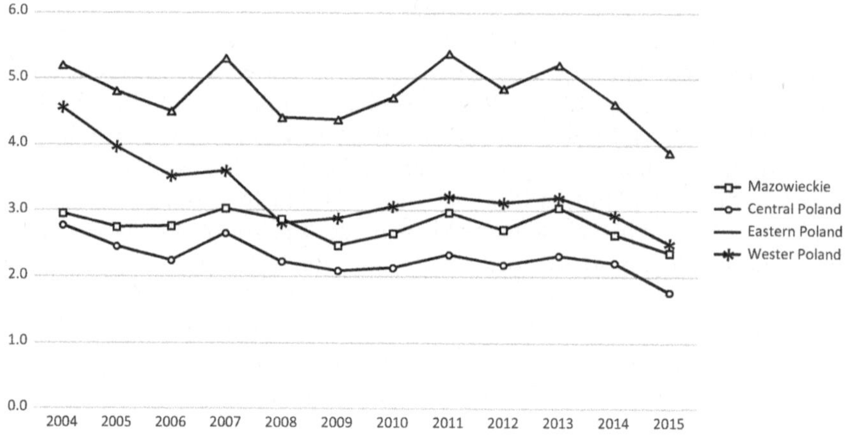

Figure 6.2 Share of gross value added in agriculture in voivodeship groups in 2004–2015 (%).

Source: Our own estimates based on: https://bdl.stat.gov.pl/BDL/start (access: 2019-12-30).

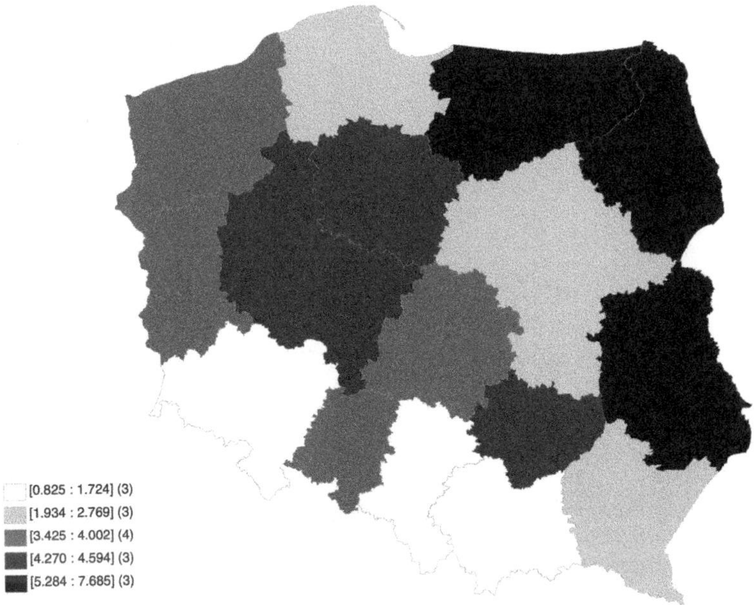

Map 6.2 Share of gross value added in agriculture in voivodeships on average in 2004–2015 (%).

Source: Our own estimates based on: https://bdl.stat.gov.pl/BDL/start (access: 2019-12-30).

The average share of gross value added in agriculture in Poland in the years 2004–2015 was 3.0%, so for the entire economy this sector was rather marginal. Nevertheless, there are significant differences in the importance of this sector on the level of individual voivodeships. The highest share of gross value added in agriculture was found in the following voivodeships: Podlaskie (7.7%), Warmińsko-Mazurskie (6.2%) and Lubelskie (5.3%). In turn, the agricultural sector had the least significance in the generated gross value added in the following voivodeships: Małopolskie (1.7%), Dolnośląskie (1.6%) and Śląskie (0.8%, i.e., over seven times less than in Podlaskie, see also Map 6.2).

6.2.2 Added value in industry

Figure 6.3 shows the gross value added in industry in voivodeship groups. It can be observed that in the years 2004–2015, in all groups of voivodeships there was an increase in gross value added in industry. The largest increase was recorded in the Mazowieckie Voivodeship and in the voivodeships of western Poland (an increase of approx. 78% in 2015, compared to 2004). The value added in industry is a procyclical variable; in all groups of voivodeships there was a decrease in the growth rate after 2008, that is, during the global financial crisis. Throughout the entire analyzed period, the highest

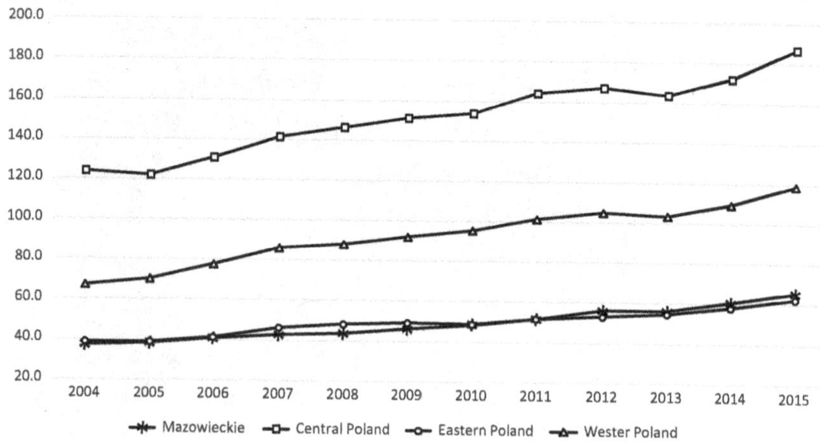

Figure 6.3 Gross value added in industry in voivodeship groups in 2004–2015 (PLN billion, according to 2015 prices).

Source: Our own estimates based on: https://bdl.stat.gov.pl/BDL/start (access: 2019-12-30).

value added in industry was recorded in the voivodeships of central Poland (PLN 114.6–175 billion). In addition, the potential of industry located in the five eastern Polish voivodeships (PLN 38.6–62.9 billion) was comparable to the potential of the industrial sector in the Mazowieckie Voivodeship (PLN 37.0–65.8 billion).

On average, in the years 2004–2015 the highest value added in industry was recorded in the following voivodeships: Śląskie (PLN 59.9 billion), Mazowieckie (PLN 49.0 billion) and Dolnośląskie (PLN 37.7 billion). The lowest values were recorded in the following voivodeships: Opolskie (PLN 9.0 billion), Świętokrzyskie (PLN 8.8 billion) and Podlaskie (PLN 6.2 billion, see Map 6.3).

Figure 6.4 presents the share of gross value added in industry in voivodeship groups. The shape of all trajectories is similar, but one can see a slight decrease in these shares after 2008 (associated with the global financial crisis) and then, from 2013, a renewed increase in the importance of this sector in all groups of voivodeships. When comparing 2015 to 2004, an increase in the share of gross value added in industry in all groups can be observed, with the largest increase in the variable considered being recorded in the provinces of western Poland (by 3.9% points) and eastern Poland (by 3.2% points). The industrial sector was of the greatest importance for the provinces of western Poland and central Poland. The shares of this sector in 2004–2015 in these groups changed in the range of 27.3–31.2%. In the voivodeships of eastern Poland, the level of the feature considered fluctuated between 22.9% and 26.3%. The lowest share of gross value added in

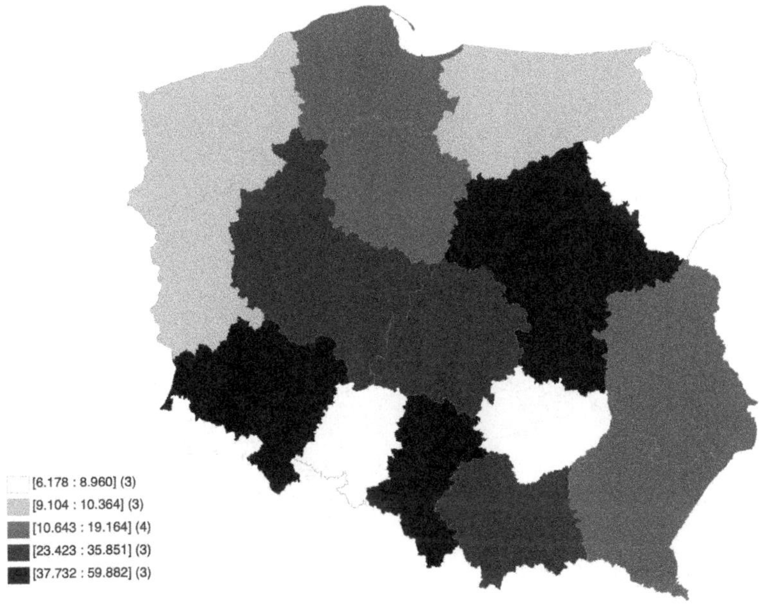

Map 6.3 Gross value added in industry in voivodeships in 2004–2015 (PLN billion, according to 2015 prices).

Source: Our own estimates based on: https://bdl.stat.gov.pl/BDL/start (access: 2019-12-30).

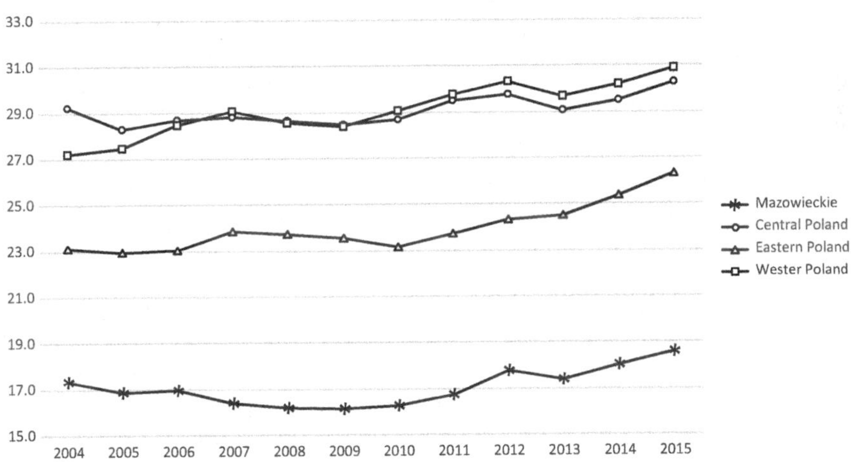

Figure 6.4 Share of gross value added in industry in voivodeship groups in 2004–2015 (%).

Source: Our own estimates based on: https://bdl.stat.gov.pl/BDL/start (access: 2019-12-30).

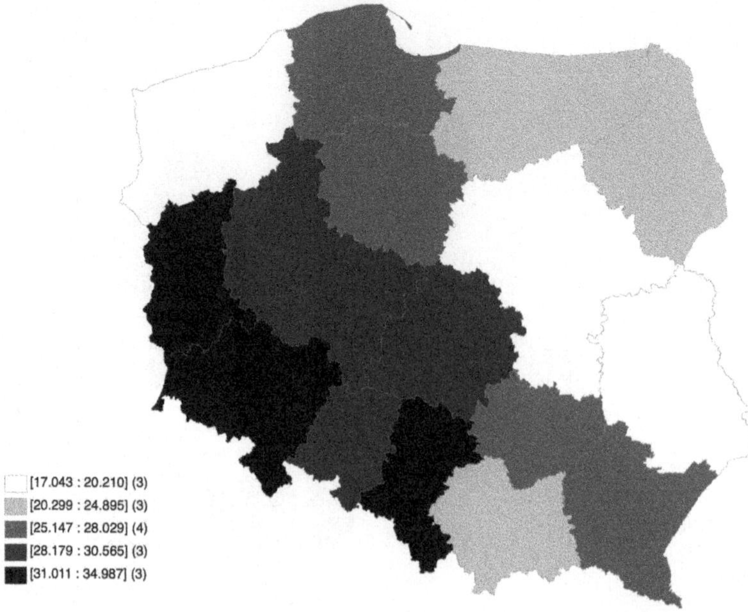

Map 6.4 Share of gross value added in industry in voivodeships in 2004–2015 (%).
Source: Our own estimates based on: https://bdl.stat.gov.pl/BDL/start (access: 2019-12-30).

industry was recorded in the Mazowieckie Voivodeship; in the entire analyzed period it did not exceed 19%.

The average share of gross value added in industry in Poland in 2004–2015 was 25.7%. The industrial sector had a significant share in the generated gross value added in the Śląskie (35.0%), Dolnośląskie (33.8%) and Lubuskie (31.0%) voivodeships. The lowest shares of the gross value added of the considered sector were recorded in the following voivodeships: Lubelskie (20.2%), Zachodniopomorskie (20.1%) and Mazowieckie (17.0%, more than twice less than in the Śląskie Voivodeship (see Map 6.4)).

6.2.3 *Value added in construction*

Figure 6.5 presents the gross value added in construction in groups of voivodeships in the years 2004–2015. The shape of the trajectories of these macroeconomic variables allows us to conclude that the value added in this sector did not fall after 2008, which means that the sector did not react to the global financial crisis. The effects of the crisis have probably been neutralized by significant infrastructure investments throughout Poland related to the organization of the Euro 2012 football tournament. A decrease in this variable can be perceived only in 2011–2013. In the last two analyzed years, the value added in construction increased once again in all groups of

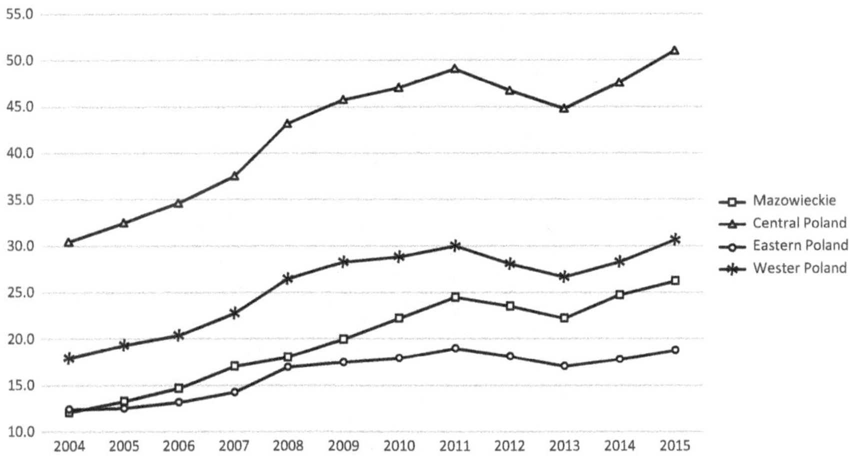

Figure 6.5 Gross value added in construction in voivodeship groups in 2004–2015 (PLN billion, according to 2015 prices).

Source: Our own estimates based on: https://bdl.stat.gov.pl/BDL/start (access: 2019-12-30).

voivodeships. Definitely the highest values of the variable under consideration were obtained in central Poland (PLN 28.7–48.7 billion), followed by western Poland (PLN 19.6–32.9 billion), Mazowieckie (PLN 12.1–26.2 billion) and the voivodeships of eastern Poland (PLN 12.4–18.7 billion). It is worth noting that the value added in the construction sector in the Mazowieckie Voivodeship in 2004 was similar to the value of this variable in the five voivodeships of eastern Poland. However, in the following years, there was a much more rapid growth of the construction sector located in the Mazowieckie Voivodeship, and in 2015 its potential was already about 40% greater than the potential of this sector in the voivodeships of eastern Poland.

Map 6.5 illustrates the spatial diversity of gross value added in voivodeships in 2004–2015. The following conclusions can be drawn from this map: The highest value added in construction was recorded in the Mazowieckie (PLN 19.9 billion), Śląskie (PLN 13.3 billion) and Wielkopolskie (PLN 10.1 billion) voivodeships. In turn, the Opolskie (PLN 2.3 billion), Podlaskie (PLN 2.3 billion) and Lubuskie (PLN 2.2 billion) voivodeships recorded the lowest values of this variable.

Figure 6.6 shows that the share of the gross value added in the construction sector in the voivodeships of eastern, central and western Poland was very similar. In the years 2004–2007, it oscillated in the range of 7.2–7.7%, and then in 2011 it attained a level of almost 9%, while over the next two years it fell and in 2013 it was at a level of 7.5–8.0%. The share of the construction sector in the Mazowieckie Voivodeship was slightly lower; however, in

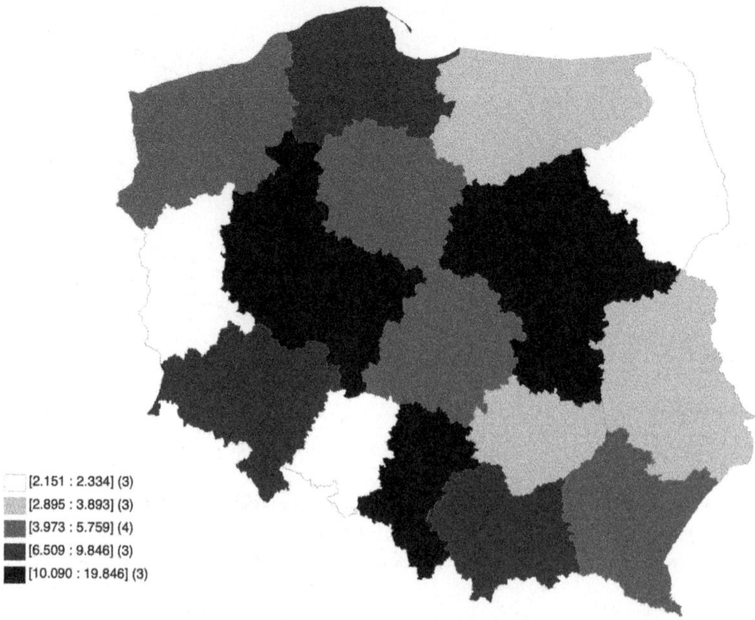

Map 6.5 Gross value added in construction in voivodeships in 2004–2015 (PLN billion, according to 2015 prices).

Source: Our own estimates based on: https://bdl.stat.gov.pl/BDL/start (access: 2019-12-30).

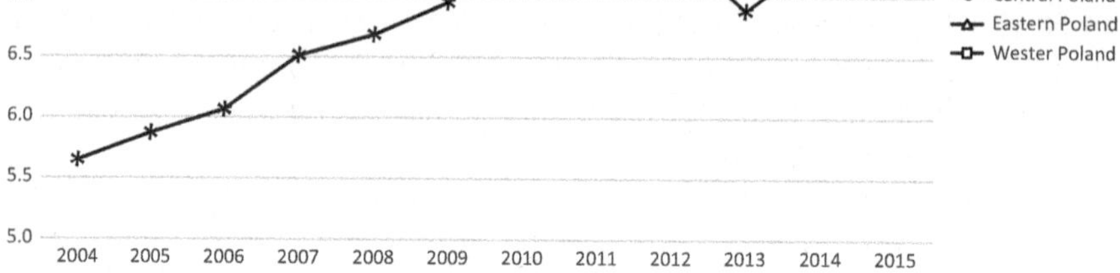

Figure 6.6 Share of gross value added in construction in groups of voivodeships in 2004–2015 (%).

Source: Our own estimates based on: https://bdl.stat.gov.pl/BDL/start (access: 2019-12-30).

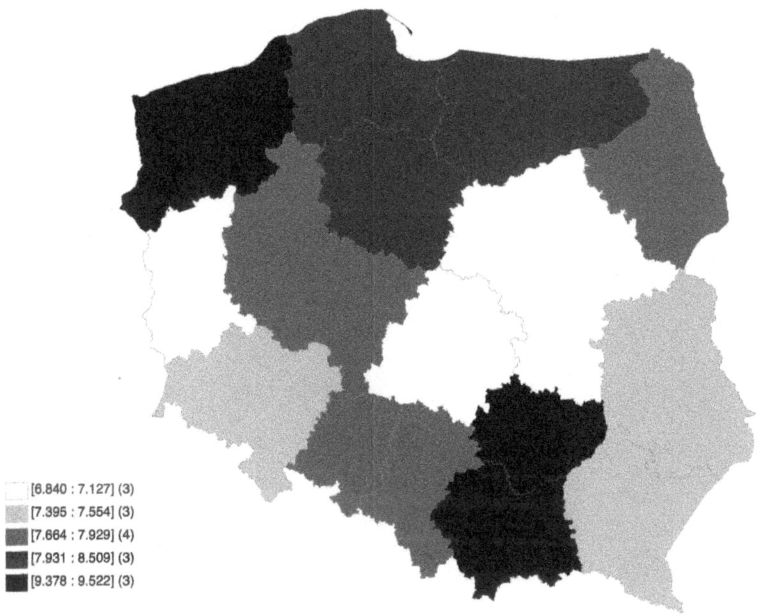

Map 6.6 Share of gross value added in construction in voivodeships on average in 2004–2015 (%).

Source: Our own estimates based on: https://bdl.stat.gov.pl/BDL/start (access: 2019-12-30).

2004–2011 it increased from 5.6% to 7.9%, then fell and in 2013 was at 6.9%. In recent years, the importance of the construction sector is growing again in all voivodeship groups. In addition, when referring to 2004 to 2015, an increase in the variable under consideration by approx. 1.7% points in the Mazowieckie Voivodeship, 1.2% points in central Poland voivodeships and below 1% point in the remaining groups of voivodeships can be observed.

The average gross value added in construction in Poland in the years 2004–2015 was 7.8%. The highest gross value added in construction was recorded in the following voivodeships: Małopolskie (9.5%), Zachodniopomorskie (9.5%) and Świętokrzyskie (9.4%). In turn, this sector (construction) had the least significance for the economies of the Lubuskie (7.1%), Łódzkie (7.0%) and Mazowieckie (6.8%) voivodeships (Map 6.6).

6.2.4 Added value in services

The service sector is definitely the most important component of gross value added in the Polish economy. Figure 6.7 presents the added value in services in 2004–2015 in groups of voivodeships. In the analyzed period, in all groups of voivodeships, the value of this variable increased (by approx. 60% in the Mazowieckie Voivodeship, by 49% in western Poland, by 44% in central

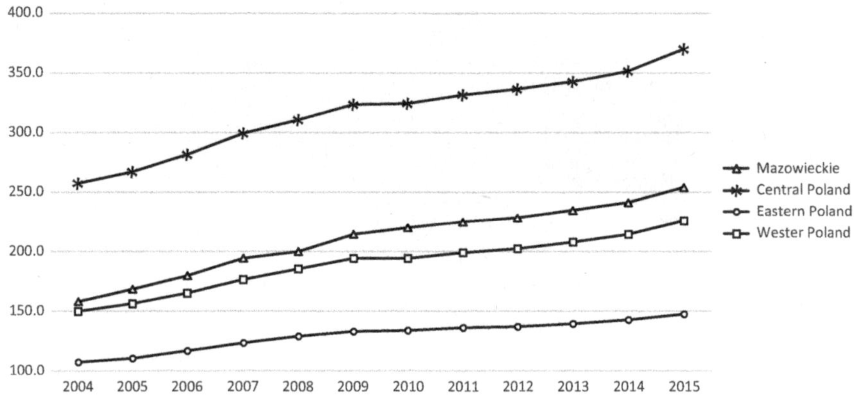

Figure 6.7 Gross value added in services in voivodeship groups in 2004–2015 (PLN billion, according to 2015 prices).

Source: Our own estimates based on: https://bdl.stat.gov.pl/BDL/start (access: 2019-12-30).

Poland and by 38% in eastern Poland). In addition, analyzing the trajectory of this variable, one can observe their response to the global financial crisis (a slowdown in the value of this variable) after 2008. This reaction results from the close links of this sector (primarily the financial and insurance industry) with the global economy. The highest added value in services in the whole analyzed period was recorded in the voivodeships of central Poland (PLN 242.4–349.9 billion). Voivodeships in eastern Poland had the lowest values of this trait (PLN 107.2–148.1 billion). It is also worth noting that the potential of the services sector in the Mazowieckie Voivodeship is similar to the potential of five voivodeships of western Poland and definitely higher than the potential of five voivodeships of eastern Poland.

By far the highest average value added in services was the Mazowieckie Voivodeship (PLN 209.7 billion). The following voivodeships were also distinguished by the high values of the analyzed variable: Śląskie (96.7 billion PLN) and Wielkopolskie (75.2 billion PLN). The lowest added values in services were recorded in the following voivodeships: Opolskie (PLN 2.3 billion), Podlaskie (PLN 2.3 billion) and Lubuskie (PLN 2.2 billion, see Map 6.7), which is mainly due to the low demographic and economic potential of these voivodeships.

Figure 6.8 presents the share of gross value added in groups of voivodeships in 2004–2015. In all groups this share remained at a stable, high level, although it should be emphasized that there was a slight decrease in this analyzed feature after 2008, which (as previously mentioned) was associated with the global financial crisis. The service sector is by far the most important for the Mazowieckie Voivodeship (in the analyzed period the shares of this sector were in the range of 71.6–74.5%). In eastern Poland, the share of the services sector throughout the entire period changed between 61.9% and 65.2%.

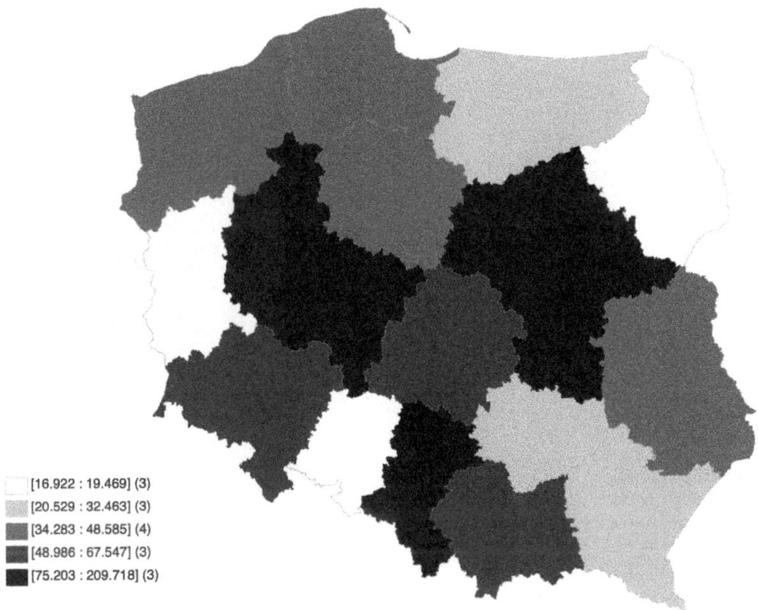

Map 6.7 Gross value added in services in voivodeships in 2004–2015 (PLN billion, according to 2015 prices).

Source: Our own estimates based on: https://bdl.stat.gov.pl/BDL/start (access: 2019-12-30).

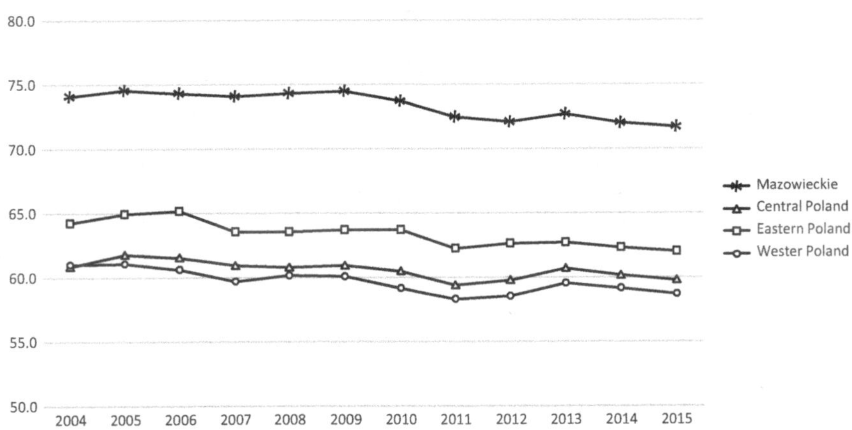

Figure 6.8 Share of gross value added in services in voivodeship groups in 2004–2015 (%)

Source: Our own estimates based on: https://bdl.stat.gov.pl/BDL/start (access: 2019-12-30).

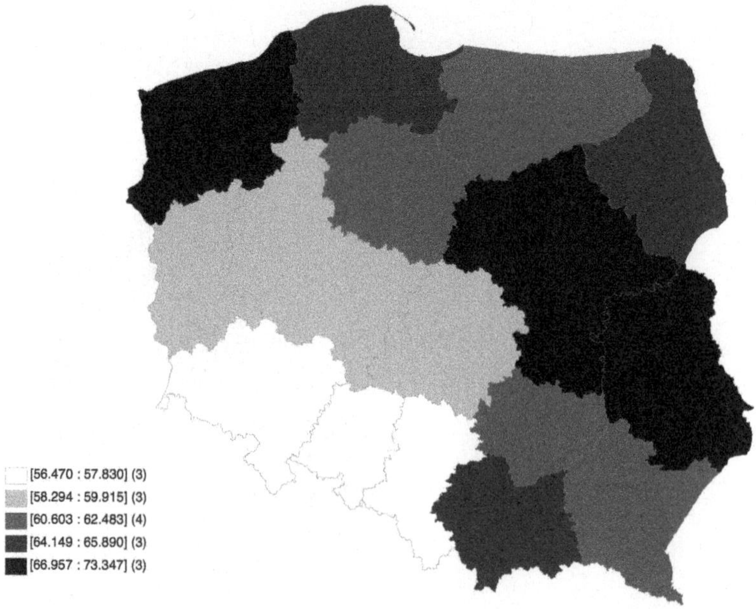

Map 6.8 Share of gross value added in services in voivodeships on average in 2004–2015 (%).

Source: Our own estimates based on: https://bdl.stat.gov.pl/BDL/start (access: 2019-12-30).

In the other two groups, the level of this variable fluctuated around 60%. Comparing 2015 with 2004, it turns out that in all groups of voivodeships the share of gross value added in services decreased (by 2.6% points in western Poland, by 2.4% points in the Mazowieckie Voivodeship, by 2.3% points and by 0.8% point in central Poland).

The average share of gross value added in the service sector in Poland in the years 2004–2015 was 63.5%, and therefore this is the sector which definitely dominated in the economy. The service sector was of the greatest importance for the following voivodeships: Mazowieckie (73.4%), Lubelskie (67.1%) and Zachodniopomorskie (67.0%). The lowest shares of the service sector in the gross value added were recorded in the following voivodeships: Opolskie (57.8%), Dolnośląskie (57.1%) and Śląskie (56.5%, see Map 6.8).

6.3 Sector structure of the product market in Ukraine

6.3.1 Added value in agriculture

Figure 6.9 illustrates the trajectories of gross value added in agriculture in groups of Ukrainian oblasts in 2004–2016. This graph shows the following: First, at the beginning of the period under consideration, the highest value

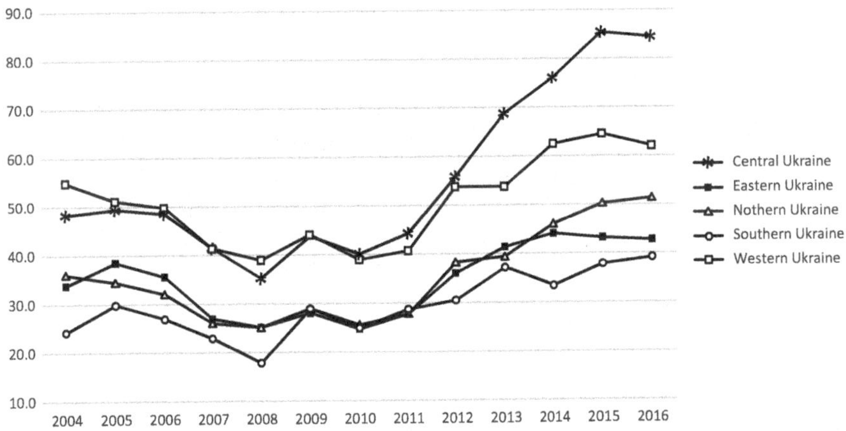

Figure 6.9 Gross value added in agriculture in oblasts groups in 2004–2016 (UAH billion, according to 2016 prices).

Source: Our own estimates based on: http://www.ukrstat.gov.ua/ (access: 2019-12-30).

of this macroeconomic variable was observed in the oblasts of western and central Ukraine (about 50 billion UAH). Second, in 2004–2008, the gross value added in agriculture fell (as a tendency) in all groups of regions. This can (paradoxically) be associated with a good economic situation in the non-agricultural sectors of the Ukrainian economy. During this period, the UAH strengthened against global currencies,[3] which led to a relative decline in the price of imported food products, a decrease in demand for domestic products and a decrease in domestic agricultural production. Third, after 2010, agricultural production basically increased in all oblasts groups. This can be explained by a reverse process to that which occurred in 2004–2009. During that period, the exchange rate rose to a level of 27.224 UAH for the euro in December 2016. Fourth, in 2004–2016 the value added in agriculture grew the fastest in the regions of central (by 75.2%) and southern Ukraine (by 61.5%), while the slowest in the eastern (by 26.1%) and western (by 13.2%) regions of Ukraine.

However, Map 6.9 (illustrating the spatial differences in gross value added in agriculture on average in 2004–2016) shows that the largest (exceeding 10 billion UAH) value of this macroeconomic variable was observed in the Kyiv region (13.1 billion UAH) in northern Ukraine, in the Vinnytsya (12.9 billion UAH) and in Dnipropetrovsk (12.3 billion UAH) oblasts in central Ukraine, in the Kharkiv Oblast (11.8 billion UAH) in eastern Ukraine and in the Poltava Oblast (11.5 billion UAH). The lowest absolute agricultural potential (except for Kyiv and Sevastopol) was found in the Rivne (5.9 billion UAH), Ivano-Frankivsk (5.6 billion UAH) and Volyn oblasts (5.4 billion UAH) in western Ukraine, in the Luhansk

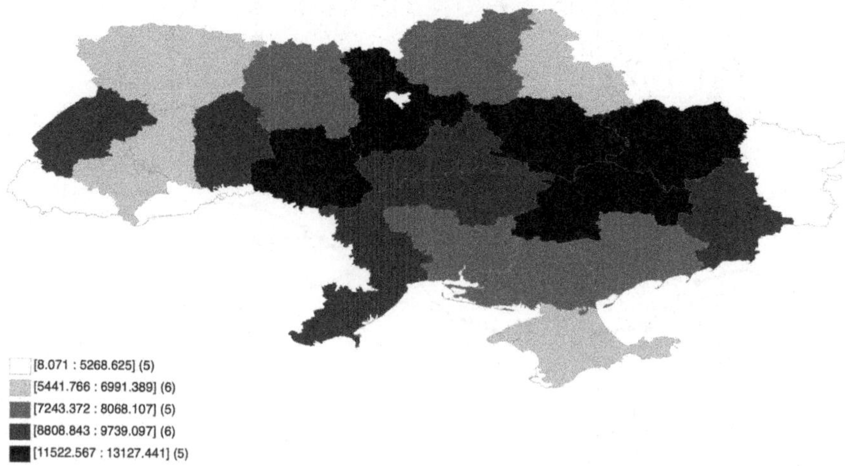

Map 6.9 Gross value added in agriculture in oblasts in 2004–2016 (UAH million, according to 2016 prices).

In the case of the ARC and Sevastopol in 2004–2013.

Source: Our own calculations based on data from the website http://www.ukrstat.gov.ua/ (access: 2019-12-30).

Oblast (5.3 billion UAH) in the east of Ukraine, as well as the Zakarpattia (4.9 billion UAH) and Chernivtsi oblasts (4.2 billion UAH) in the west. Thus, the agricultural potential of western Ukraine (much less urbanized than the other parts of the country) is lower than the potential of central or northern Ukraine.

Figure 6.10 shows the trajectories of the shares of gross value added in agriculture in total gross value added in groups of regions in 2004–2016. From this figure one can draw the following conclusions: First of all, in periods of good/bad economic situations in the Ukrainian economy, the share of gross value added (GVA) in agriculture in total (GVA) decreases/increases. This is due to the fact that, then, the value added in non-agricultural sectors of the economy usually increases (decreases) rapidly. In addition, in periods of good (bad) economic conditions there is a nominal appreciation (depreciation) of the UAH against foreign currencies. This, in turn, leads to a decrease (increase) in the relative prices of foreign food products compared to the prices of domestic products, and domestic consumers exchange domestic (foreign) products for foreign (domestic) products. Second, western, central and southern Ukrainian oblasts are characterized by a much higher share of agriculture in gross value added than the industrial oblasts of eastern Ukraine or the service-oriented oblasts of central Ukraine (mainly due to Kyiv together with the Kyiv Oblast). Third, the share of agriculture in gross value added in Ukrainian oblasts is much higher than in Polish voivodeships (see also Table 6.1).

Table 6.1 Share of gross value added in groups of voivodeships (in 2003–2015) and groups of oblasts (in 2004–2016) in Poland and Ukraine (in %)

Group of voivodeships and oblasts	*Agriculture*	*Industry*	*Construction*	*Services*
Mazowieckie	2.8	17.0	6.8	73.3
Eastern Poland	4.8	24.0	7.9	63.4
Central Poland	2.3	29.1	8.1	60.6
Western Poland	3.3	29.1	8.0	59.6
Poland	**3.0**	**25.7**	**7.8**	**63.5**
Central Ukraine	13.6	42.8	2.8	40.8
Eastern Ukraine	7.6	44.4	3.0	44.9
North Ukraine	6.5	16.0	4.7	72.8
South Ukraine	13.5	19.7	4.5	62.2
Western Ukraine	16.7	23.3	4.6	55.5
Ukraine	**10.5**	**30.3**	**3.8**	**55.4**

Source: own calculations based on data from the website https://bdl.stat.gov.pl/BDL/start (access: 2019-12-30) and http://www.ukrstat.gov.ua/ (access: 2019-12-30).
Bold indicates whole country.

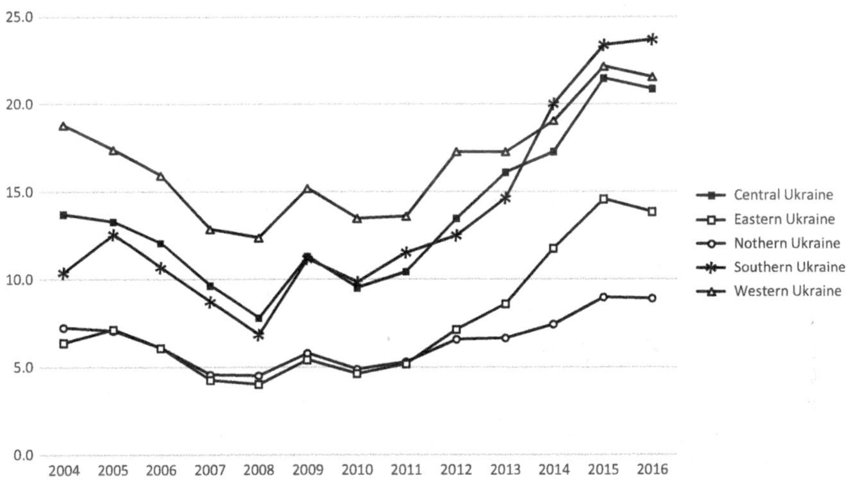

Figure 6.10 Share of gross value added in agriculture in oblasts in 2004–2016 (%).
Source: Our own calculations based on data from the website http://www.ukrstat.gov.ua/ (access: 2019-12-30).

Map 6.10 shows that the highest shares of gross value added in agriculture (in total gross value added) in 2004–2016 were observed in the Kyiv Oblast (26.2%) in central Ukraine, Kherson Oblast (also 26.2%) in southern Ukraine, Vinnytsya Oblast (25.4%) in central Ukraine and the Ternopil Oblast (24.0%) in western Ukraine. The lowest values of this indicator (excluding Kyiv and Sevastopol) were recorded in the Zaporizhzhya (9.8%) and Luhansk (9.5%) oblasts in eastern Ukraine, Odesa (9.5%) in the south, and Dnipropetrovsk (6.3%) in Central Ukraine and Donetsk (4.9%) in eastern

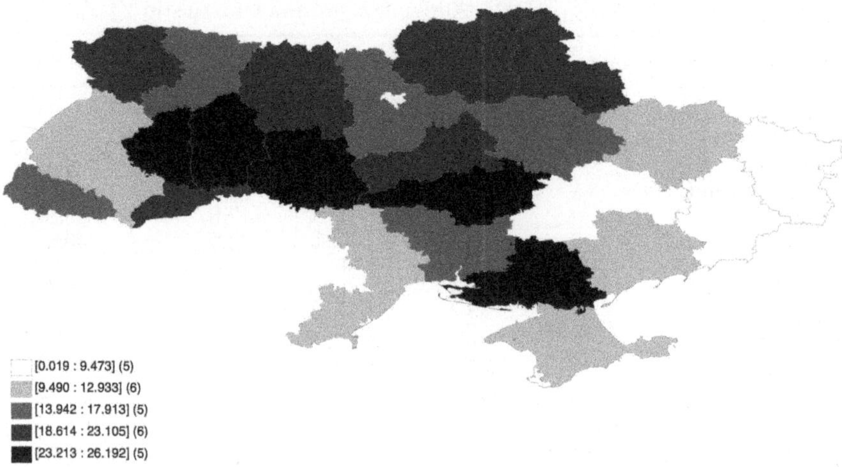

Map 6.10 Share of gross value added in agriculture in the oblasts on average in 2004–2016 (%).

In the case of the ARC and Sevastopol in 2004–2013.

Source: Our own calculations based on data from the website http://www.ukrstat.gov.ua/ (access: 2019-12-30).

Ukraine. Therefore, the more urbanized oblasts of the Left-bank Ukraine (except for the Kirovohrad and Kherson oblasts) are generally characterized by a lower share of gross value added generated in agriculture than the oblasts of Right-bank Ukraine.

6.3.2 Added value in industry

Gross value-added trajectories in oblast groups in 2004–2016 are presented in Figure 6.11. The following conclusions can be drawn from this graph: First, at the beginning of the period under consideration, the highest gross value added in industry was found in (the most highly urbanized and most industrialized) oblasts of eastern Ukraine. The value of this macroeconomic variable increased in eastern Ukraine from 252.2 billion UAH in 2004 to 314.8 billion UAH in 2007. Second, the high value of this feature was characteristic of the central Ukrainian oblasts, where the gross value added in industry increased from 141.4 billion UAH to 196.0 billion UAH. Third, the lowest gross value added in industry was recorded in the southern oblasts of Ukraine, where the value of this characteristic increased from 51.2 billion UAH in 2004 to 59.8 billion UAH in 2008. Fourth, the global financial crisis combined with the Ukrainian-Russian gas crisis led to a decrease in the value of this macroeconomic variable in 2008 or 2009.

The highest gross value added in 2007–2009 fell in western Ukraine (by 33.4%), and the slowest in southern Ukrainian oblasts (by 13.2%) (Amosha et al. 2017). Fifth, in the years 2010–2013, the oblasts of central, northern

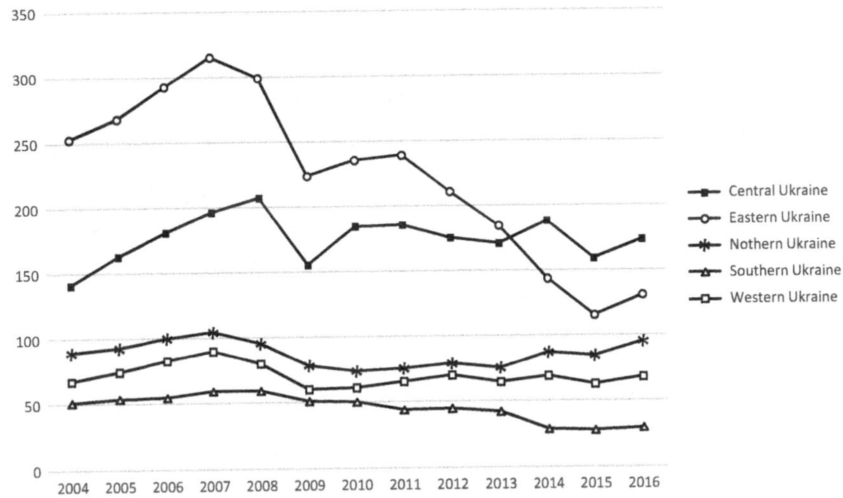

Figure 6.11 Gross value added in industry in oblasts groups in 2004–2016 (UAH billion, according to 2016 prices).

Source: Our own calculations based on data from the website http://www.ukrstat.gov.ua/ (access: 2019-12-30).

and western Ukraine were characterized (as a tendency) by a growing gross value added in industry. Sixth, in the years 2013–2015, in all groups of oblasts (with the exception of central Ukraine) the value of the analyzed variable decreased. Seventh, in the east of Ukraine, the gross value added in industry has been falling since 2012 (in 2016 the value of this macroeconomic variable was as much as 45.3% lower than in 2011). This resulted from both the Russian-Ukrainian conflict in the Donbas and from falling investments in this part of the country (in 2017, investments in eastern Ukraine constituted only 44.6% of the value of this macroeconomic variable in 2011).

Map 6.11 shows the spatial differentiation of gross value added in industry in the oblasts of Ukraine on average in 2004–2016. This map shows that the group of oblasts with the highest value of this macroeconomic variable was composed of cities with a special status, that is, Kyiv (119.1 billion UAH) and of the following oblasts: Donetsk (43.6 billion UAH), and Dnipropetrovsk (41.6 billion UAH), Kyiv (33.9 billion UAH) and Kharkiv (26.2 billion UAH). The lowest gross value added in this sector of the economy was recorded in another city with a special status, that is, Sevastopol (3.8 billion UAH), and in the Chernivtsi (5.2 billion UAH), Ternopil (5.4 billion UAH), Kherson (5.8 billion UAH) and Chernihiv oblasts (6.0 billion UAH). From Map 6.11 one can also draw a more general conclusion that the better urbanized regions of the Left-bank of Ukraine were characterized by a much higher absolute potential of the industrial sector than the regions of the Right-bank of Ukraine.

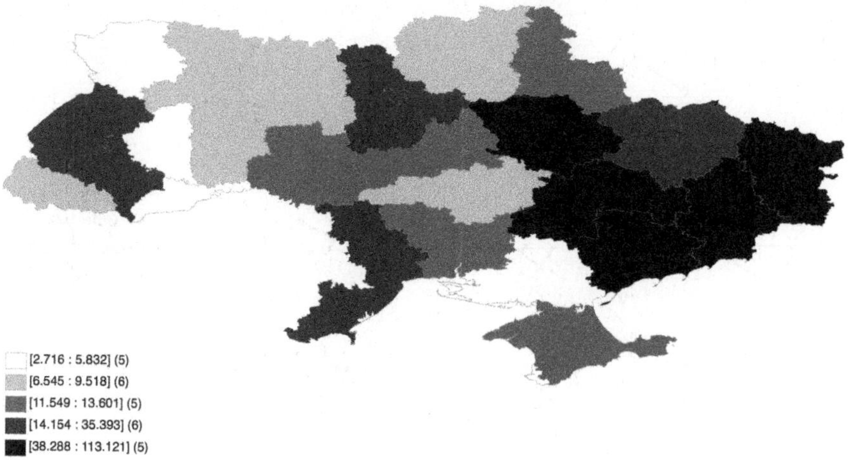

Map 6.11 Gross value added in industry in oblasts in 2004–2016 (UAH billion, according to 2016 prices).
In the case of the ARC and Sevastopol in 2004–2013.
Source: Our own calculations based on data from the website http://www.ukrstat.gov.ua/ (access: 2019-12-30).

Figure 6.12 illustrates the share of gross value added in industry in total gross value added in groups of oblasts in the research period. This graph shows the following: Until 2009, the oblasts of eastern Ukraine were characterized by the highest (generally exceeding 45%) share of gross value added in industry. At that time, the region of central Ukraine was characterized by a high value, exceeding 40%. Starting from 2010, the share of gross value added in these two groups of oblasts was at a similar level. This was mainly due to the fact that since 2009, industrial production in eastern Ukraine has been systematically falling (see Figure 6.11). The lowest percentage of gross value added generated in industry was recorded in northern Ukraine. This is due to the fact that in this part of Ukraine, gross production is produced in Kyiv and the Kyiv Oblast. There, and in particular in Kyiv, the service sector is the dominant sector of the economy. It is also worth noting that (except for the oblasts of northern Ukraine after 2013) the share of gross value added in industry in this research decreased.

The highest share of gross value added in industry (in total gross value added) in 2004–2016 was observed in the following oblasts: Dnipropetrovsk (51.8%), Donetsk (50.1%), Luhansk(50.0%), Poltava (49.1%) and Zaporizhzhya (47.3%). The lowest value of this feature was recorded in the city with a special status, that is, Kyiv (10.0%), and in the following oblasts: Chernivtsi (13.7%), Odesa (16.6%), Ternopil (17.0%) and Volyn (18.5%). Thus, the more highly urbanized oblasts located in Left-bank Ukraine were characterized by a higher share of gross value added in construction than those oblasts of the Right-bank Ukraine (see Map 6.12).

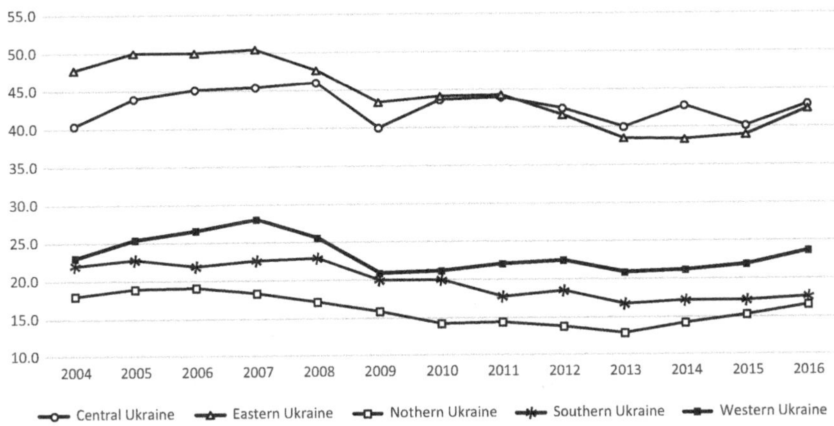

Figure 6.12 Share of gross value added in industry in oblasts in 2004–2016 (%).
Source: Our own calculations based on data from the website http://www.ukrstat.gov.ua/ (access: 2019-12-30).

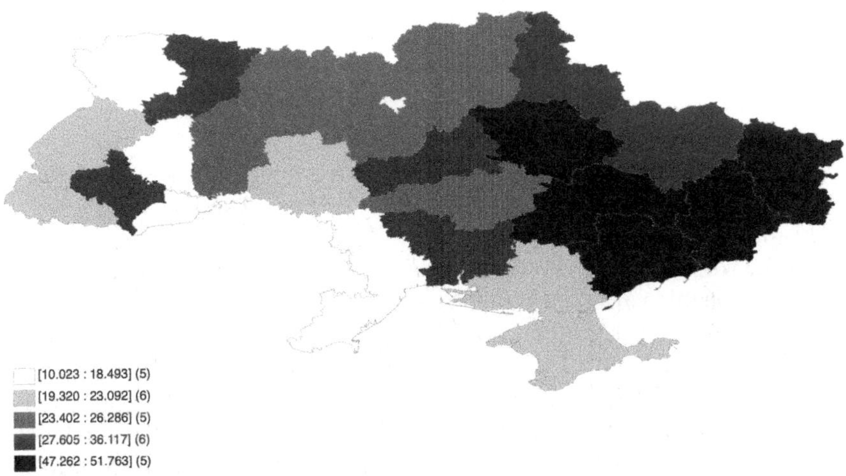

Map 6.12 Share of gross value added in industry in oblasts in 2004–2016 (%).
In the case of the ARC and Sevastopol in 2004–2013.
Source: Our own calculations based on data from the website http://www.ukrstat.gov.ua/ (access: 2019-12-30).

6.3.3 Added value in construction

Figure 6.13 illustrates gross value-added trajectories in construction in oblast groups. From this figure one can draw the following conclusions: First, the construction sector is characterized by the highest procyclicality among the four sectors of the Ukrainian economy. Second, the oblasts of

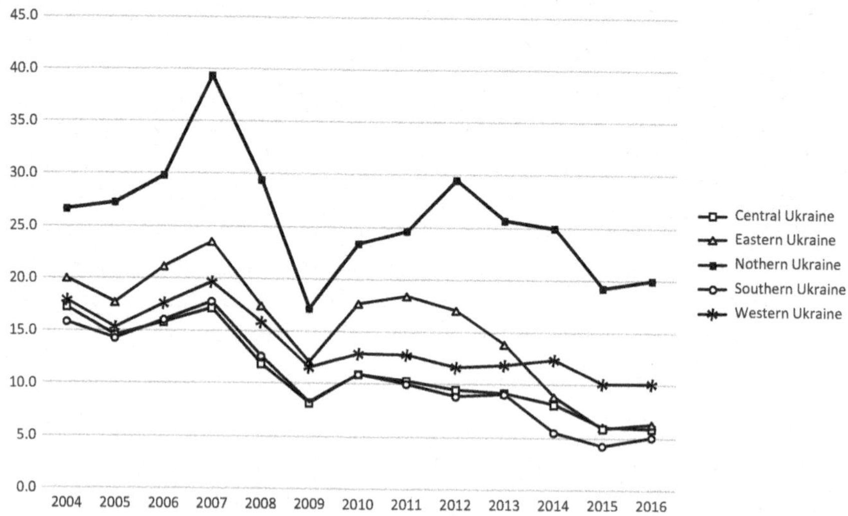

Figure 6.13 Gross value added in construction in oblasts groups in 2004–2016 (billion UAH, according to 2016 prices).

Source: Our own calculations based on data from the website http://www.ukrstat.gov.ua/ (access: 2019-12-30).

northern Ukraine had by far the highest value of this feature (mainly due to Kyiv and partially due to the Kyiv Oblast).

Third, the lowest value of this feature was recorded in the group of oblasts of south and central Ukraine and (after the Euro-Maidan) in the east of Ukraine.

In the whole research period, the capital of Kyiv definitely had the highest value of this variable (18.6 billion UAH). Next in line were the following oblasts: Donetsk (6.9 billion UAH), Odesa (5.0 billion UAH), Kharkiv (4.9 billion UAH) and Dnipropetrovsk (4.6 billion UAH). These are the oblasts in which the largest Ukrainian cities are located (except Lviv). However, the lowest value of this feature was recorded in the Kherson Oblast (0.7 billion UAH), a city with a special status, that is, Sevastopol (0.7 billion UAH), Ternopil (0.9 billion UAH), Sumy (0.9 billion UAH) and the Chernihiv Oblast (1.0 billion UAH). Moreover, Left-bank Ukraine was characterized by a higher absolute potential of the construction sector than Right-bank Ukraine (see Map 6.13).

Analyzing the share of the gross value added in the construction sector in the gross value added of the entire Ukrainian economy, it turns out that the eastern and central Ukrainian oblasts were characterized by a much lower value of this characteristic than the other oblast groups. Moreover, the share of this sector in total gross value added in all groups of oblasts decreased significantly during the Russian-Ukrainian gas conflict. In addition, it should be noted that after the Polish-Ukrainian Euro 2012 football

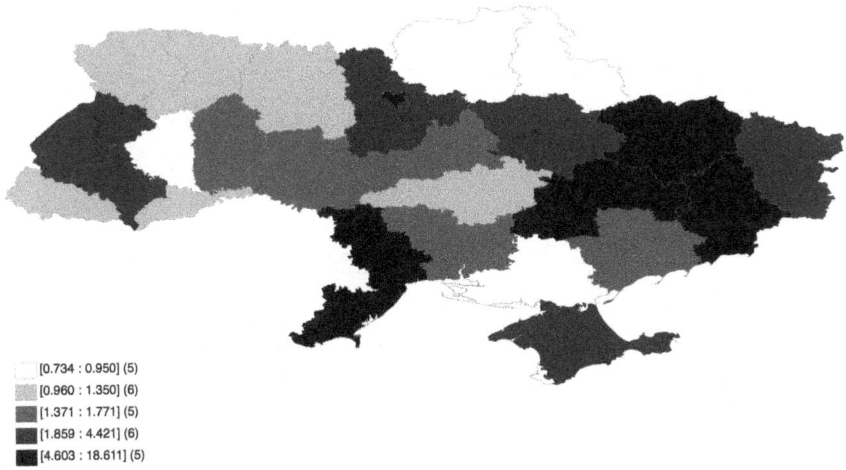

Map 6.13 Gross value added in agriculture in oblasts in 2004–2016 (UAH billion, according to 2016 prices).

In the case of the ARC and Sevastopol in 2004–2013.

Source: Our own calculations based on data from the website http://www.ukrstat.gov.ua/ (access: 2019-12-30).

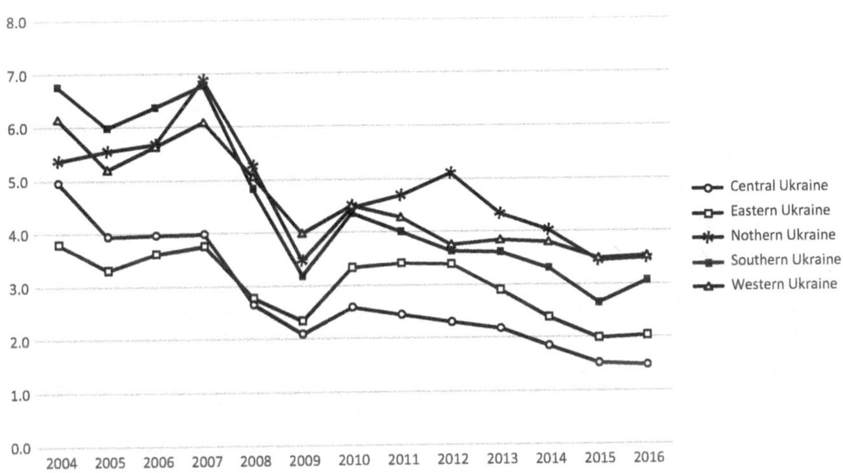

Figure 6.14 Share of gross value added in construction in oblasts groups in 2004–2016 (%).

Source: Our own calculations based on data from the website http://www.ukrstat.gov.ua/ (access: 2019-12-30).

tournament, in all oblast groups, the value of this analyzed macroeconomic variable manifested a tendency to decrease (see Figure 6.14).

On average, in the entire period under consideration, the highest share of construction in the gross value added generated was recorded in the

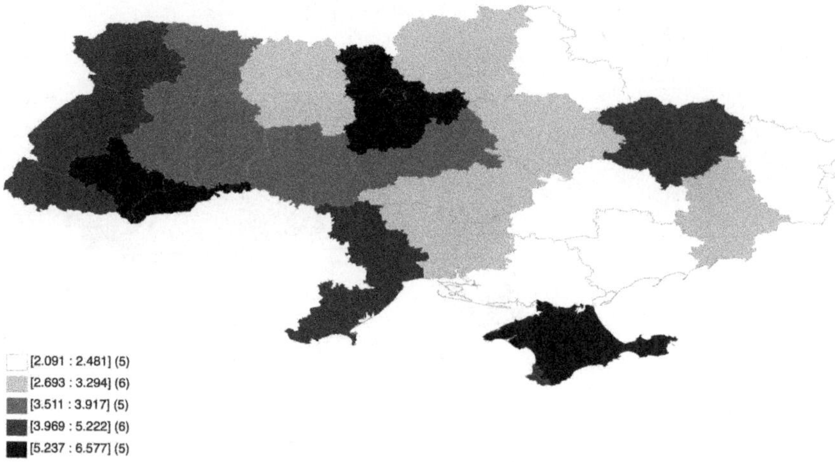

Map 6.14 Share of gross value added in industry in oblasts in 2004–2016 (%). In the case of the ARC and Sevastopol in 2004–2013.

Source: Our own calculations based on data from the website http://www.ukrstat.gov.ua/ (access: 2019-12-30).

Ivano-Frankivsk Oblast (6.6%), the Autonomous Republic of Crimea (5.9%), the Chernivtsi Oblast (5.9%) and Kyiv Oblast (5.4%) and in the City of Kyiv. The lowest value of this feature was observed in the Zaporizhzhya (2.1%), Dnipropetrovsk (2.3%), Luhansk (2.4%), Sumy (2.5%) and Kherson (2.5%) oblasts. Moreover, the spatial differentiation of this feature (in contrast to the analogous index for industry) does not show a clear division of Ukraine into its right and left bank (see Map 6.14).

6.3.4 Added value in services

Figure 6.15 illustrates the gross value-added trajectories in the service sector. The following conclusions can be drawn from this graph. First of all, the oblasts of northern Ukraine had by far the highest value of this feature (roughly in the range of 350–450 billion UAH). This is due to the fact that Kyiv and the Kyiv Oblast are located in the north of Ukraine (on average, in 2004–2016, the value added of the services sector in Kyiv accounted for approx. 27% of the value of this variable throughout Ukraine, while in Kyiv together with the Kyiv Oblast over 31%). Second, up to the time of the Euro-Maidan, the oblasts of eastern Ukraine were characterized by a high potential of the construction sector (the gross value added of services was at a level of 200–250 billion UAH). However, the conflict in Donbas led to a decrease in the value of this feature in eastern Ukrainian oblasts in 2013–2016 by approximately 100 billion UAH (and therefore by about 40%). Third, as a result of the annexation of Crimea, the gross value added in southern Ukrainian oblasts fell after 2013 by approximately 50 billion UAH, and thus

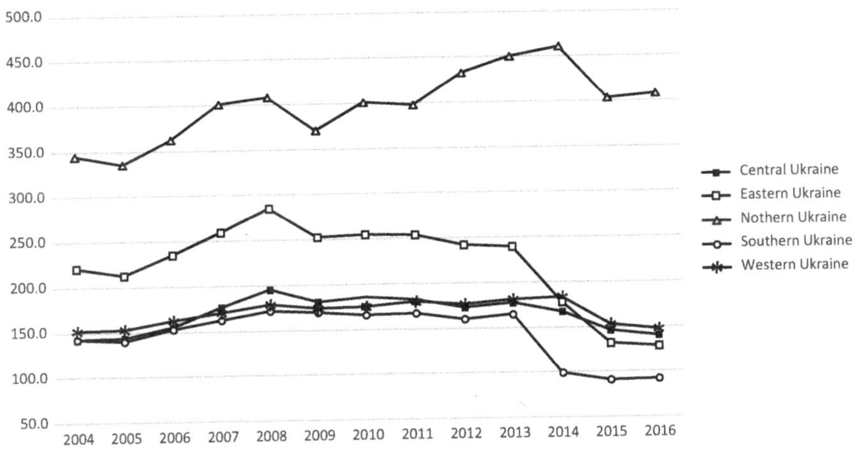

Figure 6.15 Gross value added in services in oblast groups in 2004–2016 (billion UAH, according to 2016 prices).

Source: Our own calculations based on data from the website http://www.ukrstat.gov.ua/ (access: 2019-12-30).

Map 6.15 Value added in services in oblasts on average in 2004–2016 (billion UAH, according to 2016 prices).

In the case of the ARC and Sevastopol in 2004–2013.

Source: Our own calculations based on data from the website http://www.ukrstat.gov.ua/ (access: 2019-12-30).

roughly 1/3 of its value before the Euro-Maidan. Fourth, the service sector in Ukraine is characterized by a prominent procyclicality.

Map 6.15 illustrates the spatial differentiation of gross value added in the oblasts of Ukraine in 2004–2016. This map and data on that feature show

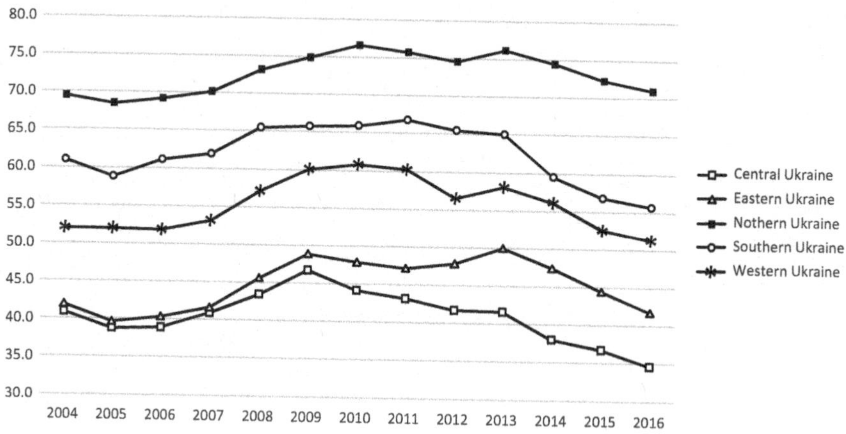

Figure 6.16 Share of gross value added in construction in oblast groups in 2004–2016 (%).

Source: Our own calculations based on data from the website http://www.ukrstat.gov.ua/ (access: 2019-12-30).

that the capital City of Kyiv had by far the highest gross value added in services (UAH 300.5 billion), among oblasts. A high value of this variable was also observed in the following oblasts: Donetsk (92.5 billion UAH), Dnipropetrovsk (79.7 billion UAH), Kharkiv (69.2 billion UAH), Odesa (66.6 billion UAH) and Lviv (51.5 billion UAH). So, this group is composed of oblasts in which the largest Ukrainian cities are located. However, the group of oblasts with the lowest service potential was composed of a city with a special status of Sevastopol (11.1 billion UAH) and the following oblasts: Chernivtsi (11.6 billion UAH), Ternopil (14.3 billion UAH), Kherson (15.4 billion UAH) and Kirovohrad (16.0 billion UAH). Thus, the level of the potential of the service sector (as well as of the industrial sector) on the left bank of Ukraine is much higher than in the oblasts located on the right bank of the Dnieper.

Figure 6.16 shows the trajectories of the shares of gross value added in agriculture in total gross value added in groups of oblasts in 2004–2016. From this figure one can draw the following conclusions: First, the oblasts of northern Ukraine had by far the highest value of this macroeconomic variable (68.5–76.5%). Second, the lowest share of gross value added in services was recorded in central (34.6–46.7%) and eastern Ukraine (39.6–50.0%). Third, this share is much less procyclical than in the case of the corresponding shares of the industrial and construction sectors.

Map 6.16 illustrates the share of gross value added in total gross value added in 2004–2016. This map shows that Kyiv (84.7%) possessed by far the highest value of this trait, followed by Sevastopol (75.6%), the Odesa Oblast (68.6%), the Autonomous Republic of Crimea (64.3%) and the Lviv Oblast

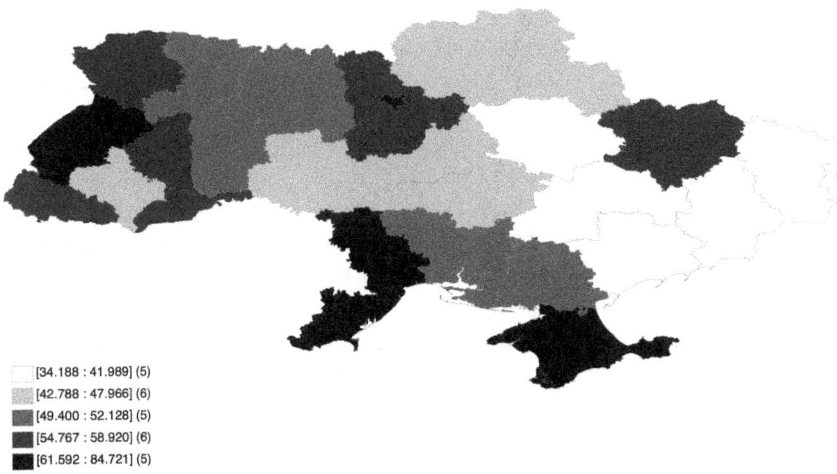

Map 6.16 Share of gross value added in industry in oblasts in 2004–2016 (%). In the case of the ARC and Sevastopol in 2004–2013.

Source: Our own calculations based on data from the website http://www.ukrstat.gov.ua/ (access: 2019-12-30).

(61.6%). The lowest share of gross value added in total gross value added was recorded in the following regions: Poltava (34.2%), Luhansk (38.2%), Dnipropetrovsk (39.6%), Zaporizhzhya (40.8%) and Donetsk (42, 0%).

6.4 Summary

Table 6.1 summarizes the data on sectoral product market structures in groups of voivodeships and regions during the research period of this chapter. The following conclusions can be drawn from this map:

- i The share of the service sector in the gross value added generated in Poland was higher than in Ukraine, while the share of agriculture was significantly lower. This means that the sectoral structure of the product market in Poland is more similar than in Ukraine to the more economically developed countries of western Europe.
- ii In Poland, the share of agriculture is by far the highest in the least developed economically voivodeships of eastern Poland, while in Ukraine in the western and southern oblasts of the country. This is because both in Poland and Ukraine, these regions are the least urbanized.
- iii The industrial sector is best developed in central and western Poland, while in Ukraine in the oblasts of eastern Ukraine (Donbas and Kharkiv) and in central Ukraine (Dnieper).
- iv The spatial differentiation of the percentage of gross value added generated in construction in both Poland and Ukraine is much smaller

than the differentiation of similar percentages in other sectors of the economy. In Poland, these percentages were between 6.8% in the Mazowieckie Voivodeship and 8.1% in the voivodeships of central Poland, while in Ukraine between 2.8% in central Ukraine and 4.6% in the west of the country.

v The service sector in Poland is best developed in the Mazowieckie Voivodeship, while in Ukraine in its northern oblasts. This is mainly due to the fact that Warsaw is in the Mazowieckie Voivodeship and Kyiv in northern Ukraine, which are the administrative centers and economically the most developed cities in their respective countries.

vi In other groups of Polish voivodeships, the share of gross value added in services oscillated around 60%, in Ukraine between 40.8% in central Ukraine and 62.2% in the coastal oblasts of southern Ukraine.

Notes

1 https://bdl.stat.gov.pl/BDL/start (access: 2019-12-30).
2 http://www.UKRSTAT.gov.ua/ (access: 2019-12-30).
3 In January 2004, the nominal exchange rate of the hryvnia against the euro was 6.183, while in December 2008 it was only 3.301 (www.exchangerate-euro.com/currency/UAH-hryvnia-ukraine/).

7 Determinants of the spatial differentiation of labor markets in Poland and Ukraine

Paweł Dykas, Tomasz Misiak and Tomasz Tokarski

7.1 Introduction

The labor market is one of the integral elements of the modern economy. Its characteristic features are, a high heterogeneity, and high sensitivity to the economic cycle or political turmoil and migration issues, amongst others. In spatial terms, it is characterized by a large diversity of basic variables defining the situations on the labor market. The spatial diversity of local or regional labor markets is not only a feature of countries undergoing systemic transformation but also applies to developing and highly developed countries (Bradley and Taylor 1997; Egger et al. 2005; Arntz and Wilke 2009; Marelli et al. 2012).

The most important variables determining the situation and prospects of the labor market are most often labor productivity, the level of wages or unemployment rate and employment. The above-mentioned macroeconomic categories are shaped by many determinants. The authors' attempt to endogenize selected variables of the labor market such as increases in unemployment rates or gross real wages by ascertaining the basic determinants resulting from the Solow 1979 efficiency wage mode, and the neoclassical growth model of Solow (1956) and its generalizations or directly from the definition of the unemployment rate. The Solow–Swan model is an economic formula of long-run economic growth set within the framework of neoclassical economics. It attempts to explain long-run economic growth by looking at capital accumulation, labor or population growth and increases in productivity, which are commonly referred to as technological progress. Determinants resulting from theoretical models are then verified empirically using the econometric methods for panel data.

The main purpose of the analyses carried out in this chapter is to compare the spatial diversity of regional labor markets in Poland and Ukraine in the first two decades of the 21st century. These analyses relate to changes in the number of people employed, the trajectory of unemployment rates, diversity and dynamics of labor productivity (measured by GDP per employee), variability of wages and regional unemployment rates, and an estimation of the equation parameters taking into account basic determinants of real wages and any crease in unemployment rates.

7.2 The labor market in Poland and Ukraine in the XXI century

The basic factor that determined the volume of employment and unemployment in Poland in 2001–2018 was the GDP dynamics. In prosperous times, the number of people employed usually increased, and the number of unemployed and the unemployment rate fell.

Figures 7.1 and 7.2 present the dynamics of GDP, the number of employed persons and the trajectory of the unemployment rate in Poland.[1] The following conclusions can be drawn from these figures.

In the years 2001–2002, as the result of a cooling down of the economy (and a quite restrictive fiscal policy of the government) at the end of the 20th century and due to a restrictive monetary policy of the National Bank of Poland (Narodowy Bank Polski), the growth rate of Polish GDP was low (in 2002 the GDP growth rate was 2.0%, in 2003, 3.6%). This, with the rapidly increasing labor productivity (5.2% in 2002 and 4.8% in 2003), translated into a decline in labor demand, a decrease in employment and an increase in the unemployment rate. In the years 2001–2003 the number of employed in Poland fell by 4.1% (with an increase of GDP by 5.7%), while the unemployment rate increased from 18.3 to 19.8%. This can be explained by the fact that with high labor productivity growth rates and much lower GDP growth rates (and product market demand), employers reduced employment. The unemployment rate in Poland (next to Spain and Slovakia) in 2003 was among the highest in central and western Europe.

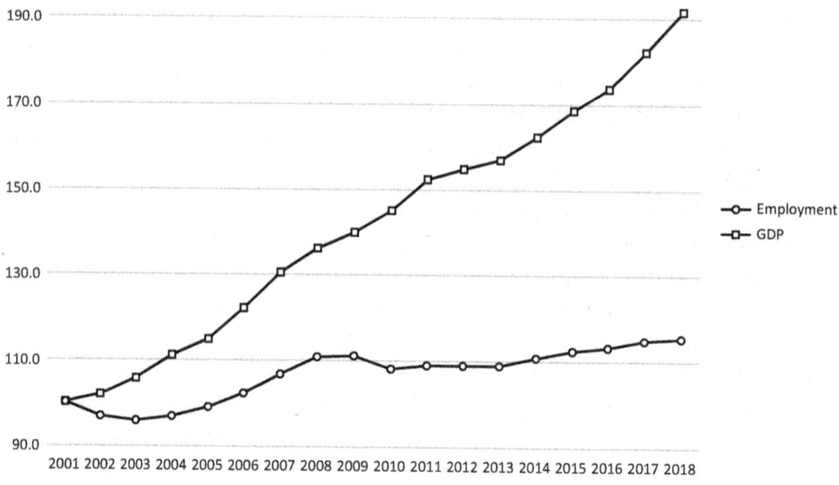

Figure 7.1 Dynamics of GDP and employment in Poland in the 21st century (2001 = 100)

Source: Our own estimates based on https://w3.unece.org/ reading data: 2019-12-30).

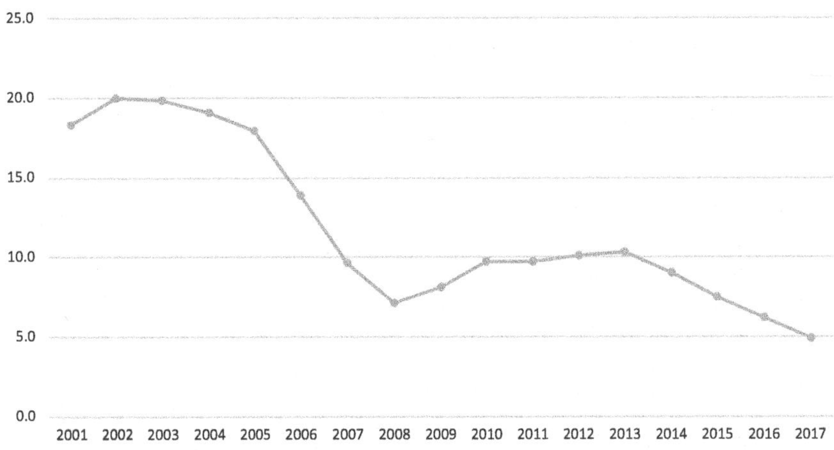

Figure 7.2 Unemployment rates in Poland in the 21th century (%).
Source: Our own estimates based on https://w3.unece.org/ reading data: 2019-12-30).

Poland's accession to the EU in 2004 combined with a period of prosperity in the global economy led to a significant acceleration of economic growth in Poland. The average annual GDP growth rate in 2004–2007 increased to 5.5%. This, in turn, led to an increase in labor demand, an increase in employment and a decrease in unemployment (in 2003–2008 the unemployment rate in Poland fell from 19.8 to 7.1%, while the number of employed rose at this time by 15.6%, i.e., by about 2.1 million people).

The global financial crisis translated into a significant slowdown in economic growth in Poland (in 2007–2013 the average annual GDP growth rate fell to a level of 3.1%). This caused a reduction in employment and an increase in unemployment, which lasted until 2013 (when the unemployment rate was 10.3%).

In the years 2013–2018, largely due to a favorable economic situation in the global economy, the GDP growth rate in Poland increased to 4.1%, which led to a cumulative increase in the number of employed in Poland by 22.0% (approx. 0.9 million persons) and a drop in the unemployment rate to 4.6% in 2017. This rate is currently one of the lowest in the EU.

The situation was different in Ukraine. Ukraine in the 1990s, due to strong links with the other economies of the former Soviet Union and a failure to undertake significant market and structural reforms, underwent a deep recession. Ukraine's GDP in 1999 accounted for only 41.0% of the value of this variable from 1990 (by comparison, in Poland the GDP increased by 37.6% during this period).[2] The first signs of economic recovery in Ukraine, apparently paradoxically, were the result of the Russian financial crisis of 1998. This crisis led to a strong depreciation of the Russian ruble and the Ukrainian UAH (the average annual USD/UAH exchange rate in 1997 was

1.86; in 1998, 2.45; in 1999, 4.13; and in 2000, 5.44).[3] The depreciation of the UAH resulted in a surge in prices of products imported into Ukraine, when counted in UAH. This, in turn, caused that part of the demand of Ukrainian business entities (in particular households and enterprises) to shift from foreign to domestic products. This move led to the creation of a Keynesian multiplier mechanism, which revived the economy.

In the years 2001–2007, the average annual growth rate of the Ukrainian GDP was 7.5% (a decrease in the high growth rate in this period took place only in 2005, which was a direct result of the political and social crisis following the Orange Revolution at the turn of 2004/2005). The rapid GDP growth in Ukraine in 2001–2007 led to an increase in the number of employed in 2008 by 5.0% compared to 2001 (i.e., by about one million people) and a decrease in the unemployment rate from 10.9 to 6.4% (Figs. 7.3 and 7.4).

The Russian-Ukrainian gas conflict 2008–2009[4] led to a one-year recession (a 15.1% decrease in GDP in 2009), which translated into a decrease in the number of employed by 3.7% (around 0.8 million people) and an increase in the unemployment rate from 6.4 to 8.8%.

In the years 2010–2013 (i.e., between the Russian-Ukrainian gas conflict and the Euromaidan), the Ukrainian GDP began to increase again (cumulative growth was then 6%), which translated into a 1% increase in the number of people employed combined with a decrease in unemployment by 1.5% points.

The direct consequences of the Euro-Maidan at the turn of 2013 and 2014 were the Russian annexation of the Crimean Peninsula (i.e., the Autonomous Republic of Crimea with Sevastopol) in the first half of 2014, and a social

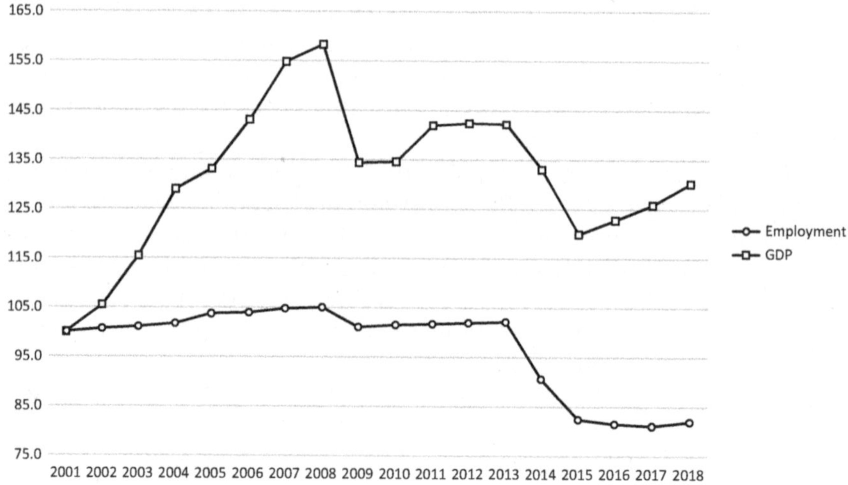

Figure 7.3 Dynamics of GDP and employment in Ukraine in the 21st century (2001 = 100).

Source: Our own estimates based on https://w3.unece.org/ reading data: 2019-12-30).

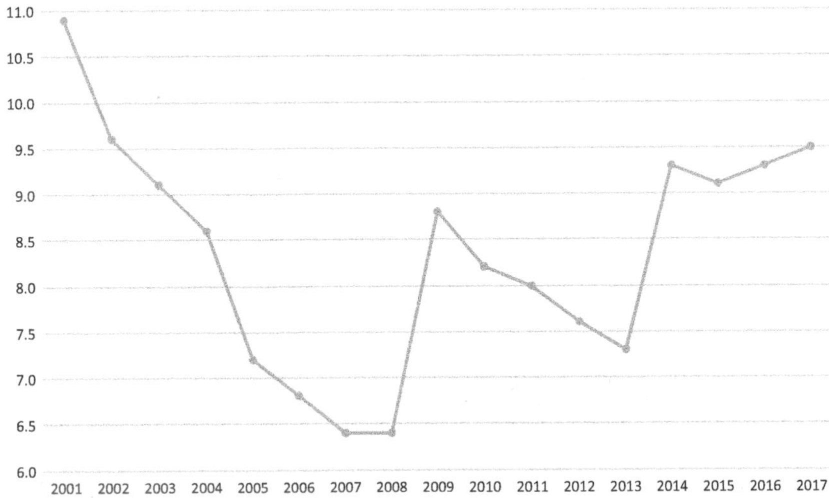

Figure 7.4 Unemployment rates in Ukraine in the 21th century (%).
Source: Our own estimates based on https://w3.unece.org/ reading data: 2019-12-30).

and political crisis, which led to open warfare with the pro-Russian separatists in the Donbas (Donetsk and Luhansk oblasts). As a result, Ukraine has again experienced a deep economic recession. In 2014, the Ukrainian GDP fell by 6.6%, while the number of people employed decreased by 11.4%. This reduction in the number of people employed resulted from the annexation of Crimea, fighting in the Donbas and the economic recession.[5] The unemployment rate increased abruptly by 2% points (to 9.3%). After 2014, despite an increase in the GDP in 2015–2018, the number of employed has stabilized at around 16.3–16.4 million people, and the unemployment rate at around 9.3–9.5%.

7.3 Differentiation in labor productivity, wages and unemployment rates

Map 7.1 illustrates the spatial diversity of labor productivity in Poland on average for 2004–2016. In contrast, Figure 7.5 shows the trajectories of this variable in groups of voivodeships. The following map and graph show what ensued (see also Tokarski 2005a, b, 2008; Mroczek, Tokarski 2013; Trojak, Tokarski 2013; Trojak 2015; Mroczek et al. 2014 or Filipowicz 2017, 2019):

7.3.1 Differentiation in labor productivity, wages and unemployment rates in Poland

- As in the case of GDP per capita, the Mazowieckie Voivodeship also had by far the highest level of labor productivity (PLN 128.8 thousand).

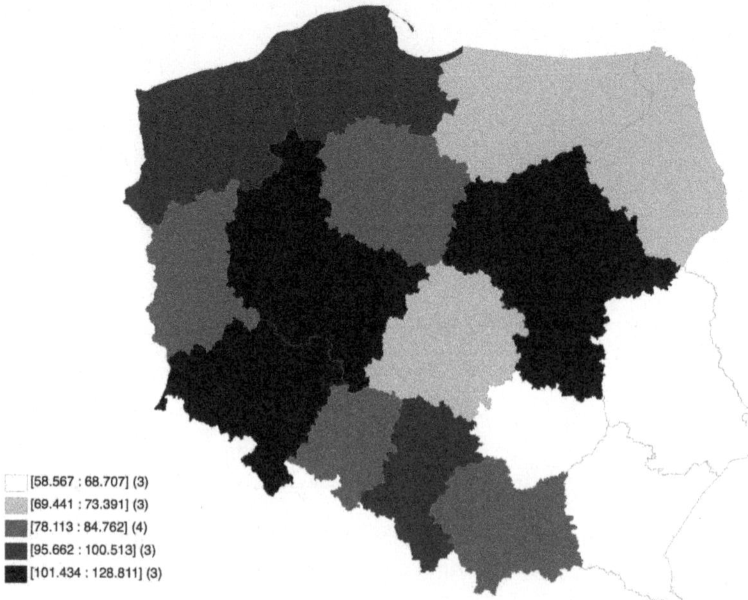

Map 7.1 Labor productivity in Polish voivodeships in 2004–2016 (1,000 PLN, according to 2015 prices).

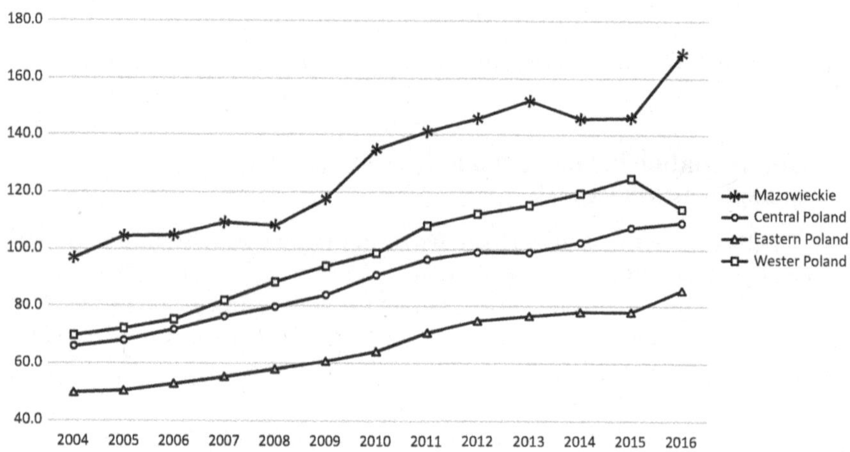

Figure 7.5 Labor productivity in Polish voivodeships groups in 2004–2016 (1,000 PLN, according to 2015 prices).

Source: Our own estimates based on: https://bdl.stat.gov.pl/BDL/start (access: 2019-12-30).

In addition, in the Dolnośląskie (107.2 thousand PLN), Wielkopolskie (101.4 thousand PLN) and Śląskie (100.5 thousand PLN) voivodeships, the value of the macroeconomic variable considered here exceeded 100 thousand PLN. In the Pomorskie (PLN 98.1 thousand) and Zachodniopomorskie (PLN 95.7 thousand) voivodeships, the average production per employee was higher than 90 thousand PLN.

- The group of voivodeships with low labor productivity was composed of the following voivodeships: Lubuskie (78.1 thousand PLN), Warmińsko-Mazurskie (73.4 thousand PLN) and Łódzkie (72.3 thousand PLN). The lowest value of this feature was recorded in three voivodeships of eastern Poland: the Podlaskie (69.4 thousand PLN), Świętokrzyskie (63.7 thousand PLN) and Lubelskie (58.6 thousand PLN).
- Such spatial diversity of the macroeconomic variable analyzed for Poland was mainly due to the spatial differentiation of capital-labor ratio and (to a lesser extent) the diversity of gravity effects (see Tokarski 2005b; Mroczek, Tokarski 2013; Trojak, Tokarski 2013; Trojak 2015; Mroczek et al. 2014 or Filipowicz 2017, 2019).
- Between 2004 and 2016, an increase in labor productivity was recorded in all voivodeships. The fastest-growing value of this macroeconomic variable grew in the following voivodeships: Lubelskie (a cumulative growth equal to 94.7%, an average annual growth of 5.7%), then in Łódzkie (92.3% and 5.6%, respectively), Małopolskie (81.3%, 5.1%), Mazowieckie (74.4%, 4.7%) and Podkarpackie (72.4%, 4.6%). The slowest increase in labor productivity was in the Śląskie (55.0%, 3.7%), Zachodniopomorskie (51.1%, 3.5%), Pomorskie (42.3%, 3.0%) and Opolskie (41.9%, 3.0%) voivodeships.
- Labor productivity in the Mazowieckie Voivodeship was much higher than the value of this macroeconomic variable in other groups of voivodeships. It grew from 96.7 thousand PLN in 2004 to 168.5 thousand PLN in 2016. In the remaining groups of voivodeships, production per employee increased from a level of 69.8 thousand PLN in 2004 to 124.8 thousand PLN in 2015, it later fell to a level of 114.0 thousand in 2016 PLN in western Poland,[6] in central Poland it grew from 65.8 thousand PLN in 2004 to 109.4 thousand PLN in 2016, and in the voivodeships of eastern Poland it increased from 49.4 thousand PLN up to 85.7 thousand PLN.
- It is also worth noting that the level of labor productivity in the voivodeships of eastern Poland in 2017 was significantly lower than the value of this variable in the Mazowieckie Voivodeship in 2004 and was comparable with the production per employee in western or central Poland from 2009 to 2010.
- In 2004, labor productivity in the voivodeships of western Poland accounted for 72.2% of the value of this variable in the Mazowieckie Voivodeship, while in 2016 it was only 67%. Similar indicators for the remaining groups of voivodeships are as follows: in central Poland, 68.1%

and 64.9%, while in eastern Poland, 51.1% and 50.9%. This means that in terms of labor productivity (similar to the GDP per capita analyzed in Chapter 3), the gap between the Mazowieckie Voivodeship and the rest of the country is widening.

- In contrast to GDP or to per capita GDP, which are variables both in the Polish economy as a whole and in groups of voivodeships, the workforce productivity increased the fastest before the global financial crisis, while the slowest growth performance during the crisis itself (of work forced productivity) was in the Mazowieckie Voivodeship and the voivodeships of eastern Poland. It grew the fastest during the global financial crisis (at an annual average rate of 6.6% in the Mazowieckie Voivodeship and 6.1% in eastern Poland, respectively), and growth was slower before and after the financial crisis. What's more, also in the voivodeships of central and western Poland, production growth rates for those employed after 2013 dropped (from 4.1 to 3.5% in central Poland and from 5.3 to −0.5% in western Poland, respectively). This can be explained by the hypothesis of unemployed economic growth (cf. e.g. Kwiatkowski et al. 2004 or Kotlorz, Sojka 2017). During the global financial crisis, the Polish economy experienced a significant slowdown in economic growth – the GDP growth rate fell below the rate of labor productivity growth resulting from capital accumulation and technological progress. This resulted in a decrease in labor demand, a decrease in employment and an increase in unemployment. This effect was an increase (with positive GDP growth rates) in labor productivity. However, after 2013, the demand for labor in Poland began to increase, which led to a decrease in the rate of labor productivity growth.

Map 7.2 presents the average levels of wages in voivodeships in the years 2004–2017, Figure 7.6 – the trajectories of this variable in groups of voivodeships. The following conclusions can be drawn from Map 7.2 and Figure 7.6 (see also Tokarski 2005b, 2012; Roszkowska, Rogut 2007; Adamczyk et al. 2009; Misiak, Tokarski 2012 or Adamczyk 2015):

- As in the case of GDP per capita or labor productivity, the highest wages were also recorded in the Mazowieckie Voivodeship (on average in 2004–2017 PLN 4,654.48). In the Śląskie (3,813.20 zlotys), Dolnośląskie (3,725.98 zlotys) and Pomorskie (3,707.35 zlotys) voivodeships, wages were higher than 3,500 PLN. The lowest level of wages (below PLN 3,200) was recorded in the Podkarpackie (PLN 3,125.46), Warmińsko-Mazurskie (PLN 3,126.35) as well as Lubuskie (3,181.68 PLN) and Kujawsko-Pomorskie (PLN 3,181.91) voivodeships.
- Comparing the spatial diversity of wages with the diversity of labor productivity (Map 7.1) and unemployment rates (Map 7.3), it turns out that in voivodeships with a higher level of labor productivity and lower unemployment, wages were higher The correlation coefficient between

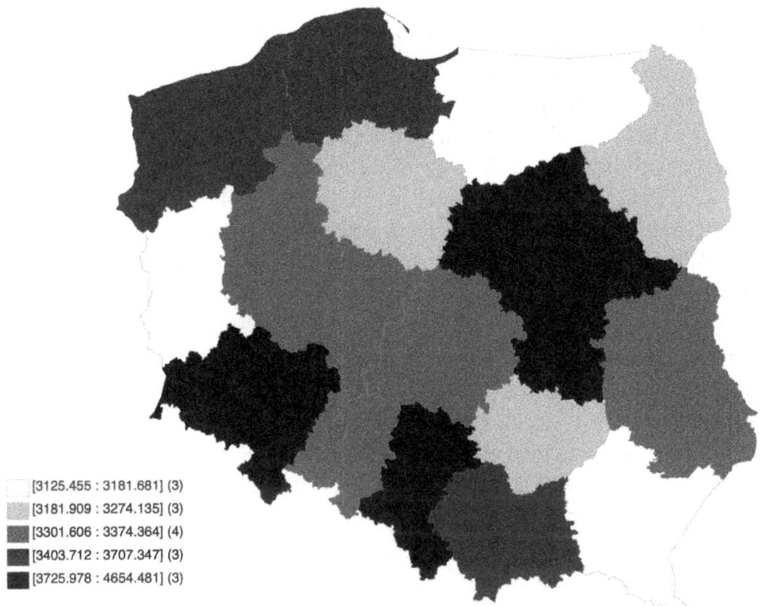

Map 7.2 Wages in Polish voivodeships in 2004–2017 (PLN, according to 2015 prices).
Source: Our own estimates based on: https://bdl.stat.gov.pl/BDL/start (access: 2019-12-30).

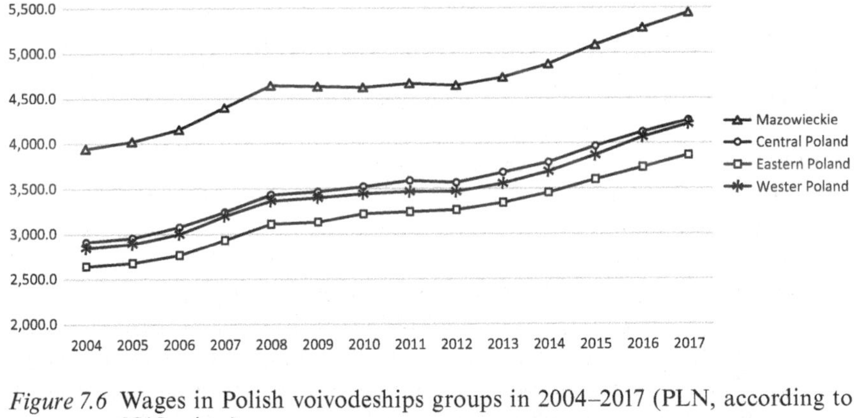

Figure 7.6 Wages in Polish voivodeships groups in 2004–2017 (PLN, according to 2015 prices).
Source: Our own estimates based on: https://bdl.stat.gov.pl/BDL/start (access: 2019-12-30).

voivodeship wages and labor productivity (in 2004–2016) was 0.886, and between wages and unemployment rates, 0.716.

- In 2004–2017, overall wages in all Polish voivodeships were characterized by an upward trend. The highest (exceeding 50%) wage increases were recorded in the Dolnośląskie (53.1%), Małopolskie (52.1%) and Łódzkie (51.2%) voivodeships, whereas the lowest growth rate of this macroeconomic variable was recorded in the Świętokrzyskie (43.2%), Śląskie (29.6%) and Mazowieckie (38.3%) voivodeships.
- Comparing wages in the Mazowieckie Voivodeship with the value of this feature in the other groups of voivodeships, it turns out that the wages in this voivodeship in 2004 (amounting to PLN 3,939.26) were slightly lower than the wages in the central (PLN 4,252.79) and western (PLN 4,205.69) voivodeships and higher than wages in eastern Poland (PLN 3,862.94) in 2017.[7]
- Before the global financial crisis (2004–2009) wages in the voivodeships of central and western Poland grew at an average annual rate of 3.6%, in eastern Poland, 3.5% and in the Mazowieckie Voivodeship, 3.3%. An increase in unemployment during this crisis reduced the wage dynamics in Poland. The average annual growth rate of wages in 2010–2013 fell to 1.6% in eastern Poland, 1.5% in central Poland, 1.3% in western Poland and only 0.5% in the Mazowieckie Voivodeship. The economic recovery after 2013 combined with falling unemployment translated into a significant acceleration of the growth rate of the macroeconomic variable analyzed here in Poland. Wages in western Poland increased in 2014–2017 at a rate of 4.3%, in central and eastern Poland at a rate of 3.7% and in the Mazowieckie Voivodeship at a rate of 3.6%.

The spatial differentiation of unemployment rates in Poland in 2004–2017 is shown on Map 7.3. In contrast, Figure 7.7 shows the trajectories of this macroeconomic variable in groups of voivodeships. The following conclusions can be drawn from Map 7.3 and Figure 7.7 (see also Tokarski 2005a, b, Kwiatkowski, Tokarski 2007, Tokarski 2008, Misiak, Tokarski 2012, Dykas et al. 2013, Majchrowska et al. 2013, Trojak, Tokarski 2013, Trojak 2015, Gomółka et al. 2017 or Pastuszka, Tokarski 2017):

- The highest unemployment rates in the research period were in the Warmińsko-Mazurskie (20.0%), Zachodniopomorskie (17.2%) and Kujawsko-Pomorskie (16.5%) voivodeships. The first two of these voivodeships and partly also the Kujawsko-Pomorskie Voivodeship are voivodeships which formerly possessed many (communist) state-owned collective farms. Thus, the liquidation of these state-owned farms (Państwowe Gospodarstwo Rolne, PGR) at the beginning of the transformation of the economic system led to high structural unemployment (see: Rogut, Tokarski 2001, 2002), which to a large extent still persists.[8]

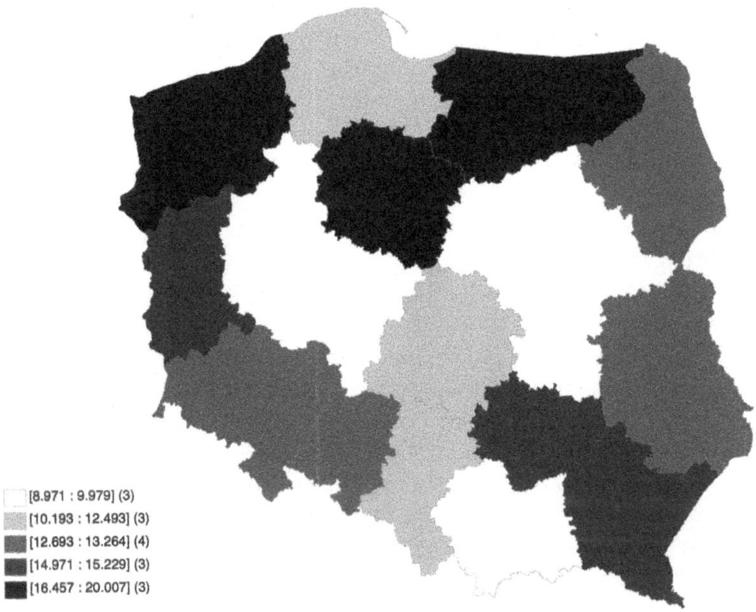

Map 7.3 The unemployment rates in voivodeships in 2004–2017 (in %).

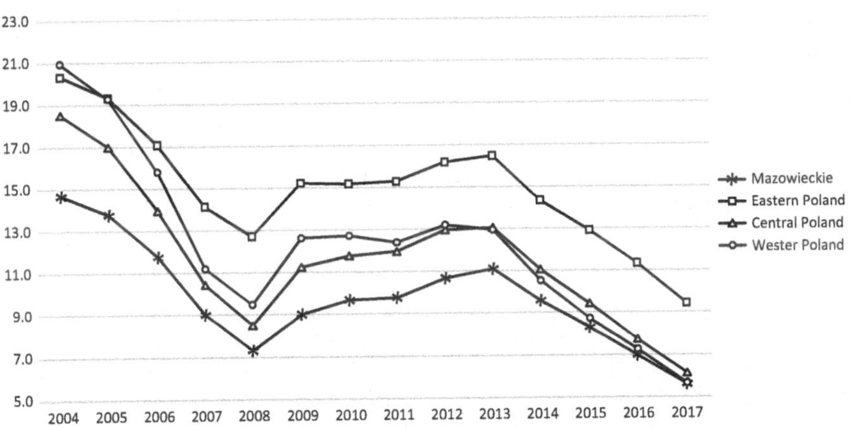

Figure 7.7 The unemployment rates in groups of voivodeships in 2004–2017 (in %).
Source: Our own estimates based on: https://bdl.stat.gov.pl/BDL/start (access: 2019-12-30).

- The lowest unemployment rates were recorded in the following voivodeships: Wielkopolskie (9.0%), Mazowieckie (9.8%), Małopolskie (10.0%) and Śląskie (10.2%).
- In all voivodeships, the unemployment rates in 2017 were significantly lower than at the beginning of the research period. These rates fell most in those regions which liquidated state-run collective farms such as in the[9] Lubelskie (from 25.6 to 5.6%), Zachodniopomorskie (from 27.5 to 8.5%) and Warmińsko-Mazurskie (from 29.2 to 11.7%) voivodeships, and the least in three voivodeships of eastern Poland (Podlaskie from 16.1 to 8.5%, Lubelskie from 17.8 to 8.8% and Podkarpackie from 19.1 to 9.6%) as well as in the Mazowieckie (from 14.7 to 5.6%) and Małopolskie (from 15.0 to 5.3%) voivodeships.
- In 2004–2008, that is, immediately after Poland's accession to the European Union, the good situation of the economic cycle led to an increase in labor demand, an increase in employment and a decrease in unemployment. At that time, the unemployment rate in eastern Poland fell from 20.3 to 12.8%, in western Poland from 21.0 to 9.5%, in central Poland from 18.5 to 8.5% and in the Mazowieckie Voivodeship from 14.7 to 7.3%.
- The global financial crisis has led to a significant slowdown in economic growth in Poland. This, in turn, translated into a decrease in demand for work and an increase in unemployment. The unemployment rate in eastern Poland increased until 2013, reaching 16.2%, in western Poland it increased to 13.2%, in central Poland it increased to 13.0%, and in the Mazowieckie Voivodeship it rose to 10.7%.
- The good economic cycle in 2014–2017 increased the demand for work, leading to an increase in employment and a decrease in unemployment. Unemployment rates in 2017 were at a level of 5.6% in the Mazowieckie Voivodeship and in western Poland, 6.1% in central Poland and 9.5% in eastern Poland.

Figure 7.8 presents the coefficient of the variation of labor productivity, wages and unemployment rates in Poland in the research period (defined as the relationship of standard deviations to the unweighted arithmetic mean of the analyzed variables). From this figure, the following conclusions can be drawn: First, the spatial diversity of wages was much smaller than the differences in labor productivity or unemployment rates. This resulted from the fact that wages in the public sector are loosely related to both the level of labor productivity and unemployment in a given voivodeship. Second, the spatial diversity of wages in 2004–2017 was characterized by a certain convergence tendency (the coefficient of variation of this variable fell from 0.117 to 0.102). Third, the spatial diversity of unemployment rates in Poland in times of prosperity grows, while in weak economic conditions it decreases. Fourth, the spatial diversity of labor productivity is relatively stable.

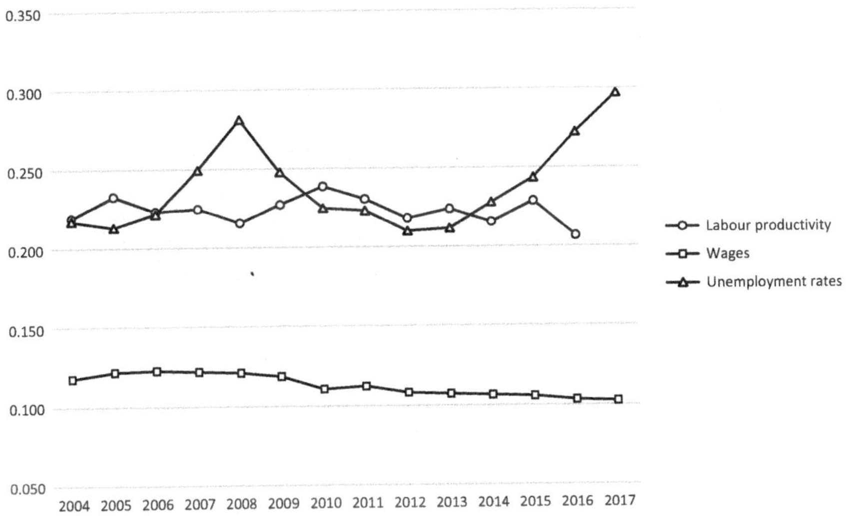

Figure 7.8 Coefficients of the variability of labor productivity, wages and unemployment rates in Poland in 2004–2017.

Source: Our own estimates based on: https://bdl.stat.gov.pl/BDL/start (access: 2019-12-30).

7.3.2 Differentiation in labor productivity, wages and unemployment rates in Ukraine

Map 7.4 presents the spatial differentiation of labor productivity in the oblasts of Ukraine in 2004–2017.[10] Trajectories of this variable in oblast groups are illustrated in Figure 7.5. Map 7.4 and Figure 7.9 show the following (see also Pustovoit 2016, Chugaievska et al. 2017, Chugaievska, Tokarski 2018 or Tokarski et al. 2019):

- As in the case of GDP per employee, the highest level of labor productivity was also recorded in Kyiv (364.4 thousand UAH). A high value of this trait, in Ukraine, was also characteristic of the Dnipropetrovsk (172.1 thousand UAH) and Poltava oblasts (164.9 thousand UAH) in central Ukraine, Donetsk (157.6 thousand UAH) in eastern Ukraine and Kyiv (147.0 thousand UAH) in the north of Ukraine.

In the case of the Autonomous Republic of Crimea and Sevastopol in 2004–2013.

- The lowest (less than 80 thousand UAH) labor productivity was recorded in the Kherson Oblast (77.7 thousand UAH) in the south of Ukraine and in the Ternopil (74.7 thousand UAH), Zakarpattia (69.2 thousand UAH) and Chernivtsi (62.9 thousand UAH) oblasts in western Ukraine.

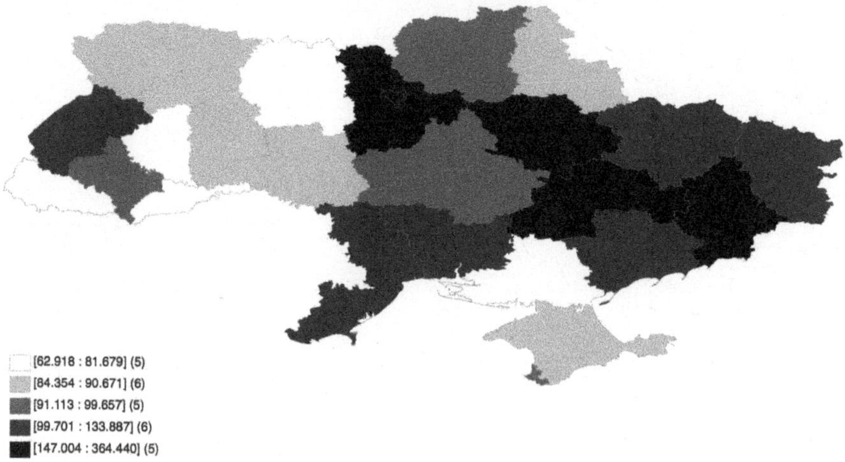

Map 7.4 Labor productivity in the oblasts in the years 2004–2017 (1,000 UAH, prices 2016).

Source: Our own estimates based on: http://www.ukrstat.gov.ua/ (access: 2019-12-30).

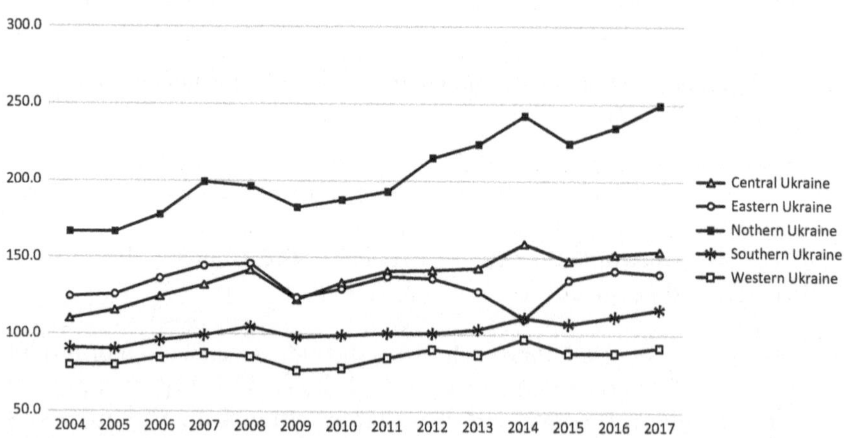

Figure 7.9 Labor productivity in oblast groups in 2004–2017 (1,000 UAH, according to 2016 prices).

In the case of the Autonomous Republic of Crimea and Sevastopol in2004–2013.

Source: Our own estimates based on: http://www.ukrstat.gov.ua/ (access: 2019-12-30).

- This is because Left-bank Ukraine and the Odesa and Mykolayiv oblasts are characterized by a higher capital-labor ratio of labor and (often) stronger gravitational effects than Right-bank Ukraine (Chugaievska et al. 2017), so the level of labor productivity in these areas was generally higher than in the west of Ukraine.

- In 21 out of 25 Ukrainian oblasts (excluding the Autonomous Republic of Crimea and Sevastopol) labor productivity in 2017 was higher than in 2004 (although in the Ivano-Frankivsk Oblast production per employee increased only by 1.7%, i.e., 0.1% annual average).
- The highest (exceeding 30%) increases in this macroeconomic variable were recorded in the Kyiv Oblast (73.9%, 4.3% on average per year) and Kyiv City (44.1%, 2.8%) in the north of Ukraine and in the Vinnytsya (37.3%, 3.4%) and Cherkasy (40.9%, 2.7%) oblasts in the center of the country. The highest increases in labor productivity were recorded in the Kyiv Oblast (73.9%, 4.3% on average per year) and the City of Kyiv (44.1%, 2.8%) in northern Ukraine and the Vinnytsya (54.4%, 3.4%) and Cherkasy (40.9%, 2.7%) oblasts in central Ukraine. Labor productivity in the Autonomous Republic of Crimea increased in 2004–2013 by 24.4% (2.5% on average per year), while in Sevastopol by 32.9% (3.2%).
- Similar trends in labor productivity can be seen in all the oblast groups (except in eastern Ukraine). In the years 2004–2008 the value of this variable increased, and in 2009 it decreased significantly. This decrease was the result of both the global financial crisis and the gas conflict with Russia. In 2010–2014 (and thus until the Euro-Maidan) the GDP per working person began to grow again. In 2015, the level of this variable decreased. The increase in labor productivity in 2016–2017 was due to the fact that the Ukrainian economy recorded the first symptoms of economic recovery after the crisis caused by the political perturbations after the Euro-Maidan (in 2016 the Ukrainian GDP increased by 2.4%, and in 2017 by 2.5%).
- By far the highest level of GDP per working person was recorded in the regions of northern Ukraine, where the value of this variable increased from 166.6 thousand UAH in 2004 to 249.2 thousand UAH in 2017. In eastern Ukraine, labor productivity increased from 124.4 thousand UAH to 139.7 thousand UAH, in central Ukraine from 110.0 thousand UAH to 154.4 thousand UAH, in the south from 91.3 thousand UAH to 116.6 thousand UAH, and in the west from 80.0 thousand UAH to 91.5 thousand UAH. Thus, the value of this variable grew the fastest in the best-developed northern Ukraine (3.1% on average per year), and the slowest in the industrial and mining oblasts of eastern Ukraine (0.9%).

Map 7.5 presents the spatial diversity of wages in Ukraine, while Figure 7.10 shows the trajectories of this variable in oblast groups in 2004–2015. The following conclusions can be drawn from the map and graph (see also, for example, Chugaievska et al. 2017, Bolińska, Gomółka 2017 or Tokarski et al. 2019):

- As in the case of labor productivity, the highest wages were recorded in the capital of Kyiv (on average in 2004–2017 8386.05 UAH). The Donetsk (5,990.33 UAH), Dnipropetrovsk (5,481.32 UAH), Kyiv (5,330.82 UAH) and Zaporizhzhya (5,239.78 UAH) oblasts also had a high value of the macroeconomic variable analyzed here.

- The lowest wages occurred in the Chernivtsi (4,012.08 UAH), Volyn (4,005.88 UAH) Ternopil (3,763.51 UAH) and Kherson (4,009.66 UAH) oblasts in the west of Ukraine and in the Chernihiv (4,000.78) UAH) Oblast in the north of the country.

Map 7.5 Wages in Ukrainian oblasts in 2004–2017 (UAH, according to 2016 prices).
Source: Our own estimates based on: http://www.ukrstat.gov.ua/ (access: 2019-12-30).

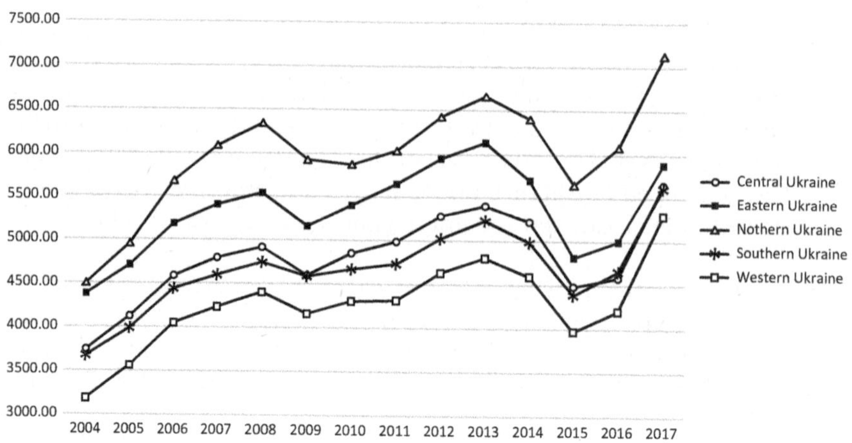

Figure 7.10 Wages in groups of oblasts in 2004–2017 (UAH, according to 2016 prices).
Source: Our own estimates based on: http://www.ukrstat.gov.ua/ (access: 2019-12-30).

- In all oblasts, wages in 2017 were higher than at the beginning of the research period. The fastest value of this variable grew in the Ternopil (by 85.2%, 4.9% on average per year), Volyn (83.7%, 4.8%, respectively) and Khmelnytskiy (83.4%, 4.8%) oblasts in western Ukraine and in the Vinnytsya (82.1%, 4.7%) Oblast in central Ukraine. The lowest wage increases were recorded in the Dnipropetrovsk (34.6%, 2.3%) Oblast in central Ukraine and the Zaporizhzhya (32.4%, 2.2%) and Luhansk (27.3%, 1.9%) oblasts in the eastern Ukraine. In the Autonomous Republic of Crimea, wages in 2004–2013 increased by 41.1% (3.9% on average per year), while in Sevastopol by 41.0% (3.9%).

In the case of the Autonomous Republic of Crimea and Sevastopol in 2004–2013.

- The spatial diversity of wages in Ukraine largely coincided with the diversity of labor productivity. The correlation coefficient between these variables was 0.946. On the other hand, the correlation coefficient between wages and unemployment rates considered below is 0.586.
- Wage trajectories in oblast groups were similar in shape to both the trajectory of GDP and labor productivity. This is due to the fact that labor productivity has largely affected the level of wages in Ukraine.
- In Ukraine northern, wages increased from 4,499.27 UAH in 2004 to 7,130.00 UAH in 2017, in the east from 4,373.79 UAH to 5,881.58 UAH, in central Ukraine from 3,741.65 UAH to 5,654.84 UAH, in the south from 3,669.01 UAH to 5,614.69 UAH, while in the poorest region, that is western Ukraine, from 3,176.35 UAH to 5,291.34 UAH. Thus, the highest average annual wage dynamics were observed in the group of western Ukraine oblasts (4.0%), while the lowest in eastern Ukraine (2.3%).

Map 7.6 illustrates the spatial differentiation of unemployment rates in Ukrainian oblasts (on average in 2004–2017), while Figure 7.11 shows trajectories of this macroeconomic variable in groups of oblasts. The following conclusions can be drawn from the aforementioned map and figure (see also, e.g., Lysiuk, Kaflevska 2012, Paniuk 2013, Homiak 2015, Yarova 2015, Chugaievska et al. 2017, Chugaievska, Tokarski 2018 or Tokarski et al. 2019):

- The lowest average unemployment rates in the period under consideration were recorded in the two cities with a special status (Sevastopol 5.0% and Kyiv 5.3%) and the Autonomous Republic of Crimea (5.7%) and in the Odesa Oblast (5.9%) in southern Ukraine. The highest level of this variable was recorded in the Zhytomyr Oblast (10.1%) in the north of Ukraine, as well as in the Ternopil (10.3%) and Rivne (10.4%) oblasts in western Ukraine. High unemployment rates also occurred in the Chernihiv Oblast (9.8%) in the north and the Kirovohrad Oblast (9.7%) in central Ukraine.

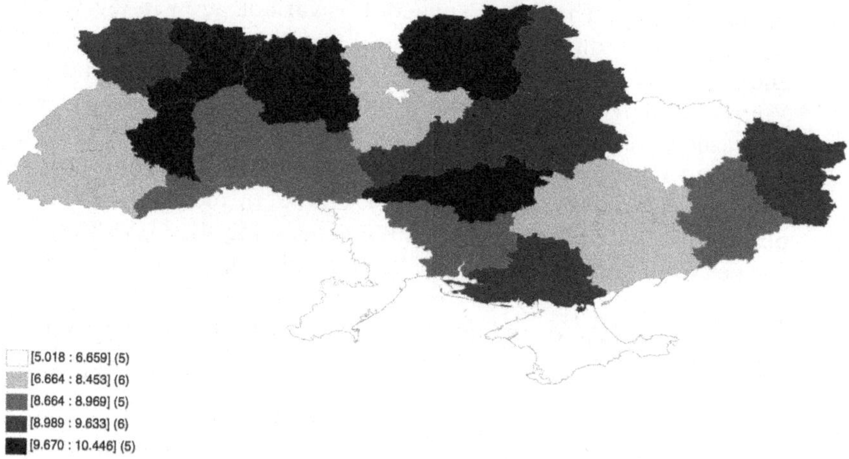

Map 7.6 The unemployment rates in oblasts in 2004–2017 (in %).
Source: Our own estimates based on: http://www.ukrstat.gov.ua/ (access: 2019-12-30).

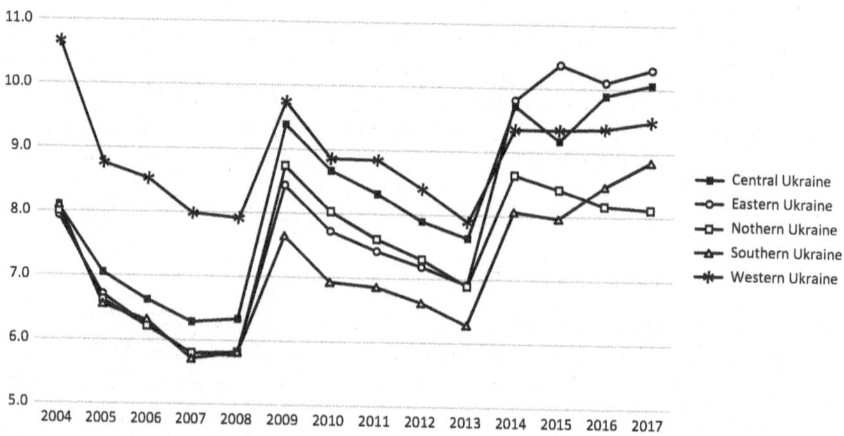

Figure 7.11 The unemployment rates in group of oblasts in 2004–2017 (%).
Source: Our own estimates based on: http://www.ukrstat.gov.ua/ (access: 2019-12-30).

In the case of the Autonomous Republic of Crimea and Sevastopol in 2004–2013.

- The spatial differentiation of unemployment rates in Ukraine partially coincided with the spatial differentiation of labor productivity and wages in the sense that the higher the labor productivity or wages, the lower the unemployment rates were. The correlation coefficient between these rates and labor productivity was −0.499, and between unemployment rates and wages −0.586.

- In 12 Ukrainian oblasts, unemployment rates in 2017 were lower than in 2004, while in the remaining 13 they were higher. The group of oblasts in which unemployment rates fell included the following regions: Chernivtsi, Khmelnytskiy, Ivano-Frankivsk, Lviv, Rivne and Ternopil in western Ukraine; Kyiv, Sumy and Zhytomyr in the north of Ukraine; Kharkiv in the east of Ukraine; Mykolayiv in the south; and the Cherkasy Oblast in central Ukraine. The largest decreases in unemployment rates were recorded in the following regions: Chernivtsi by 3.8% points (from 12.2% in 2004 to 8.4% in 2017), Lviv by 2.5% points (from 10.0 to 7.5%) and Khmelnytskiy by 2.4% points (from 11.1 to 8.7%), while the highest increases were in the Poltava by 4.5% points (from 7.4 to 11.9%), Donetsk by 7.1% points (from 7.4 to 14.5%) and Luhansk oblasts by 7.4% points (from 9.2 to 16.5%). In the Autonomous Republic of Crimea, the unemployment rate fell from 6.9 to 5.9% in 2004–2013, while in Sevastopol it increased from 5.3 to 5.7%.
- A period of relative prosperity in the Ukrainian economy (2004–2008), when the GDP grew quickly, translated into an increase in employment combined with a decrease in unemployment in all groups of oblasts. Unemployment rates fell the fastest in western Ukraine (by 2.7% points), in northern and southern Ukraine (2.3% points) and in eastern Ukraine (2.1% points), and the slowest in central Ukraine (1.7% points). As a result, the difference between the group of oblasts with the highest value of this variable (western Ukraine) and the group with its lowest value (eastern Ukraine) fell from 2.7% points in 2004 to 2.1% points in 2008.
- The global financial crisis, combined with the Russian-Ukrainian gas conflict, translated into a one-year recession, which also resulted in a significant increase in unemployment rates in all oblast groups. At the time, these rates rose the fastest in the oblasts of central Ukraine (by 3.1% points), then in the northern (3.0% points) and eastern (2.6% points) oblasts. The slowest increase was in the south and west of Ukraine (by 1.8% points).
- Economic growth in Ukraine in the years 2010–2013 again led to a decrease in the variable analyzed here, in all oblast groups. The highest decreases in unemployment rates were then recorded in western Ukraine (1.9% points), while the lowest in southern Ukraine (1.4% points).
- The economic, political and military crisis after the Euro-Maidan caused a surge in unemployment rates in all groups of Ukrainian oblasts. These rates increased from 7.9% in 2013 to 9.4% in 2014 in western Ukraine, from 7.6 to 9.7% in central Ukraine, from 6.9 to 9.8% in eastern Ukraine, from 6.9 to 8.6% in the north and from 6.3 to 8.6% in southern Ukraine.
- In 2015–2017, the unemployment rates in all groups of Ukrainian oblasts stabilized, except for the oblasts of northern and southern Ukraine. In the north they began to rise slightly, while in the south they fell insignificantly.

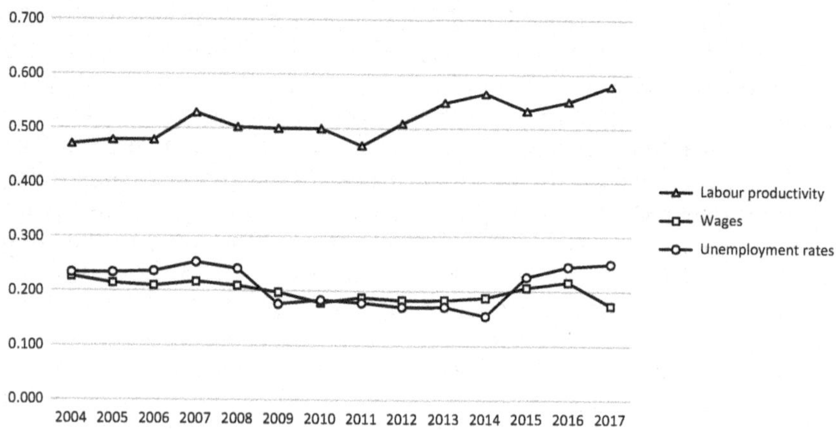

Figure 7.12 Coefficients of variability of labor productivity, wages and unemployment rates in Ukraine in 2004–2017.

Source: Our own estimates based on: http://www.ukrstat.gov.ua/ (access: 2019-12-30).

Figure 7.12 presents the coefficients of variation of the analyzed macroeconomic variables in Ukrainian oblasts in 2004–2017. The following conclusions can be drawn from this figure: First of all, labor productivity was much more spatially diverse than wages and unemployment rates. Second, the diversity of labor productivity in Ukraine was greater than the diversity of this macroeconomic variable in Poland. Third, the spatial diversification of labor productivity in Ukraine (as a trend) increased. Fourth, the differences in wages and unemployment rates were similar and quite stable.

7.4 Determinants of the increase in unemployment rates and gross real wages – a theoretical approach and empirical verification

In order to determine the main determinants of the increase in unemployment rates, one can rely on the definition of the unemployment rate of the equation $u_{it} = \frac{U_{it}}{U_{it} + L_{it}}$ (where U_{it} and L_{it} means the number of unemployed and working persons in the *i*-this voivodeship or oblast respectively in a given year *t*). Differentiating this equation (after time t) and making simple transformations, we conclude that:

$$u'_{it} = (1 - u_{it}) \cdot \left[\frac{N'_{it}}{N_{it}} - \frac{L'_{it}}{L_{it}} \right]. \tag{7.1}$$

Equation (7.1) shows that the increase in the unemployment rate u'_{it} depends on its u_{it} level and the difference between the labor supply growth rate N'_{it}/N_{it} and the employment growth rate L'_{it}/L_{it}.

Assuming that the employment growth rate L'_{it}/L_{it} is higher, the higher the product growth rate g and by using the relationship (7.1), we arrive at an equation for the growth of the unemployment rate of the form of (see also Dykas et al. 2013):

$$u'_{it} = (1 - u_{it}) \cdot \left[\frac{N'_{it}}{N_{it}} - f(g) \right], \tag{7.2}$$

where $\frac{L'}{L} = f(g)$ and $f'(g) > 0$. This equation (7.2) shows the following conclusions: First, an increase in the unemployment rate is a decreasing function of the product growth rate g and second if the labor supply rate is higher (lower) from the employment growth rate, the increase in the unemployment rate is a decreasing (increasing) function of the unemployment rate.

While analyzing the factors determining wages, the following reasoning can be used, resulting from the Solow 1979 efficiency wage model and the neoclassical Solow 1956 economic growth model and its generalizations (Tokarski 2005a, b or Dykas, Misiak 2014). This model shows that the higher the regional level of wages is, the higher the regional labor productivity is, and the lower the regional unemployment rate is as well. So we have the following equation:

$$w_{it} = \alpha_0 - \alpha_1 \cdot u_{it} + \alpha_2 \cdot y_{it}, \tag{7.3}$$

where w_{it} means wages in the region i and in a year t, y_{it} is labor productivity, and u_{it} is the unemployment rate.

Statistical analyzes of the impact of the real GDP growth rate (labor productivity) on the unemployment rate (gross real wages) in 2004–2017 were conducted based on panel data for Poland and Ukraine:

- Poland – 16 voivodeships, corresponding to the NUTS2 classification
- Ukraine – 27 oblasts, while for the Autonomous Republic of Crimea and Sevastopol, data refer to the period of 2004–2013.

The simple theoretical models presented in point 7.3 show that the impact of the GDP growth rate on the increase in unemployment rates as well as the impact of the unemployment rate and the level of labor productivity on the level of gross real wages can be established using the following equations:

$$\Delta u_{it} = \beta_0 - \beta_1 u_{it-1} + \beta_2 d_{\Delta u} u_{it-1} + \beta_3 \Delta \ln Y_{it}, \tag{7.4}$$

and:

$$\ln w_{it} = \alpha_0 - \alpha_1 u_{it} + \alpha_2 \ln y_{it}, \tag{7.5}$$

where u_{it} is the unemployment rate in the voivodeship (oblast) and in a given year t, Δu_{it} is the increase in the unemployment rate, and $d_{\Delta u}$ is the dummy variable taking the value 1 when the unemployment rate in the voivodeship (oblast) i and in a year t increased, zero in other cases; $\Delta \ln Y_{it}$ is the real GDP growth rate in the voivodeship (oblast) i in a year t; w_{it} is the average gross real wage in a voivodeship (oblast) and i in a year t; y_{it} is the level of labor productivity in the voivodeship (oblast) i in a year t; β_0 is a constant that has no direct economic interpretation; $\beta_1 > 0$ measures the strength of the impact of the unemployment rate on the increase in the unemployment rate when the rate is not rising; $\beta_2 > 0$ measures the impact of the unemployment rate on the increase of this rate when the unemployment rate increases; β_3 describes the impact of the real GDP growth rate on the increase in the unemployment rate; α_0 is constant without direct economic interpretation; α_1 is a relative decrease in wages in the voivodeship (oblast) i and in a year t resulting from an increase in the unemployment rate by 1% point; α_2 is wage flexibility in terms of labor productivity.

The above equations were estimated in two variants:

i In Variant I, Eqs. (7.4) and (7.5) were estimated using a two-step estimator based on the First Differences Generalized Method of Moments (FDGMM) by Arellano and Bond 1991.
ii Eqs. (7.4) and (7.5) were estimated in variant II using the System Generalized Method of Moments Estimator (SGMM) (Blundell and Bond 1998).

The results of this estimation of the parameters of these Eqs. (7.4) and (7.5) for variants I and II are summarized in Tables 7.1 and7.2.

From the estimation results summarized in Table 7.1 the following conclusions can be drawn:

- The estimated parameters of the equation for the increase in unemployment rates using both FDGMM and SGMM, when statistically significant, are also consistent with theoretical postulates as to the direction of the impact of explanatory variables on the increase in unemployment rates for both Poland and Ukraine.
- However, the values of estimated parameters for Poland and Ukraine differ significantly. Analyzing the results of estimation using FDGMM estimators, one can notice a large asymmetry of the impact of unemployment rates from the previous period, on the increase in unemployment rates depending on whether the previous unemployment rates increased or decreased. They had a more significant impact from the previous period, when they had a downward trend rather than an upward trend. This observation applies to both estimated parameters for Poland and Ukraine, with the difference that for Ukraine, the estimated parameter of the impact of the unemployment rate from the previous year, when the unemployment rate was falling, was not statistically significant.

Table 7.1 Estimate of the parameters of the equation for increasing unemployment rates for Poland and Ukraine

Explanatory variables	*Poland*				*Ukraine*			
	FDGMM		*SGMM*		*FDGMM*		*SGMM*	
	Coef.	*t-stat*	*Coef.*	*t-stat*	*Coef.*	*t-stat*	*Coef.*	*t-stat*
Δu_{it-1}	0.2139	5.46	0.0778	2.5	−0.6030	−2.64	0.01979	0.39
		(0.0000)		(0.024)		(0.014)		(0.702)
constant	0.0639	10.60	0.02412	5.67	−0.0037	−0.38	0.02047	5.89
		(0.0000)		(0.0000)		(0.710)		(0.0000)
u_{it-1}	−0.5230	−16.28	−0.2431	−6.41	0.02332	0.19	−0.31315	−7.37
		(0.0000)		(0.0000)		(0.852)		(0.0000)
$d_{\Delta u} u_{it-1}$	0.1155	8.13	0.15270	11.60	0.1486	8.70	0.24950	14.86
		(0.0000)		(0.0000)		(0.0000)		(0.0000)
$\Delta \ln Y_{it}$	−0.11617	−2.30	−0.1808	−3.40	−0.0770	−6.51	−0.0341	−3.92
		(0.0036)		(0.004)		(0.0000)		(0.001)
Test AR(1)	−3.21		−3.11		−3.92.		−3.96	
	(0.001)		(0.002)		(0.000)		(0.0000)	
Test AR(2)	0.35		0.31		−1.44.		0.35	
	(0.724)		(0.753)		(0.149)		(0.726)	
Hansen test	0.04		15.01		0.32.		24.15	
	(0.836)		(0.182)		(0.571)		(0.190)	
Test F	676.85		104.02		380.52.		149.94	
	(0.000)		(0.000)		(0.000)		(0.0000)	
Number of observations	176		176		316		316	
Number of instruments	6		16		6		24	

Source: Our own calculations based on data from the websites of the Statistical Offices of Poland and Ukraine.
The levels of significance of *t*-Student statistics are given in brackets.

Table 7.2 Estimate of the parameters of the gross real wage equation for Poland and Ukraine

Explanatory variables	*Poland*				*Ukraine*			
	FDGMM		*SGMM*		*FDGMM*		*SGMM*	
	Coef.	*t-stat*	*Coef.*	*t-stat*	*Coef.*	*t-stat*	*Coef.*	*t-stat*
$\ln(w_{it-1})$	0.79099	28.43 (0.0000)	0.75017	25.65. (0.0000)	0.6940	27.31 (0.0000)	0.6279	37.36 (0.001)
constant	1.4899	14.72 (0.0000)	1.7524	12.11. (0.0000)	1.9113	9.12 (0.000)	2.5636	14.15 (0.0000)
$\ln(y_{it})$	0.0783	1.94 (0.072)	0.0894	2.35. (0.0000)	0.1659	3.86 (0.001)	0.1408	3.87 (0.001)
u_{it}	−0.7083	−15.68 (0.0000)	−0.76229	−13.82. (0.0000)	−0.8605	−3.01 (0.006)	−0.6182	−2.98 (0.006)
Test AR(1)	−2.17 (0.030)		−2.09 (0.037)		1.10 (0.271)		1.19 (0.233)	
Test AR(2)	0.85 (0.394)		0.81 (0.416)		−4.73 (0.000)		−4.81 (0.000)	
Hansen test	0.7 (0.952)		14.74 (0.195)		25.99 (0.002)		26.59 (0.097)	
Test F	3699.56 (0.0000)		862.5 (0.0000)		458.06 (0.0000)		675.37 (0.0000)	
Number of observations	192		192		343		343	
Number of instruments	8		15		13		22	

Source: Our own calculations based on data from the websites of the Statistical Offices of Poland and Ukraine.
The levels of significance of statistics are given in brackets.

- Under decreasing unemployment rates, each subsequent percentage point of decrease in the unemployment rates in the previous year (ceteris paribus) reduced the increase in the unemployment rates in Poland by 0.243% points in an estimations using the SGMM and by 0.523 in estimates using the FDGMM, and in Ukraine by 0.313% points correspondingly, and in the estimations using the FDGMM this parameter was not statistically significant. However, in conditions of rising unemployment, each subsequent percentage point of increase in the unemployment rate in the previous year increased the growth of this variable in Poland by 0.153 (0.116) of a percentage point in an estimation using the SGMM estimator (FDGMM), and in the Ukrainian economy respectively by 0.25 (0.15) of a percentage point.
- An increase in the real GDP growth rate of 1% point resulted in a decrease in the unemployment rates of 0.181 of a percentage point in Poland and by 0.034 of a percentage point in Ukraine in estimations using the SGMM estimator and by 0.12 of a percentage point in Poland and by 0.08 of a percentage point in Ukraine in estimates from using the FDGMM estimator.
- Valuations employing the SGMM estimator several times (about 5.3 times) were more significantly influenced by an increase in the unemployment rate in Poland than in Ukraine.
- Analyzing the estimated parameters using the SGMM estimator, one can observe a smaller asymmetry of the impact of delayed unemployment rates, both in Poland and Ukraine. The difference in estimated parameters of the impact of economic growth rates was also smaller. For Poland, this parameter was about 56% higher, and in Ukraine about 56% lower compared to the parameters estimated using the FDGMM.
- The instruments in both estimation variants were properly selected, as indicated by the Hansen test values. The obtained Hansen test statistics, as well as the significance levels obtained in variants I and II for both Poland and Ukraine, do not provide grounds for rejecting the zero hypothesis that all instruments in the model are exogenous.
- Satisfactory Arellano-Bond test values for AR (1) and AR (2) were also obtained, which indicate that a negative, statistically significant first order autocorrelation and a statistically insignificant second order autocorrelation were obtained in all estimation variants for both Poland and Ukraine. This demonstrates the compliance and effectiveness of the estimators used.
- Analyzing the results of the estimation of gross real wage equations using both FDGMM and SGMM estimators for Poland and Ukraine (summarized in Table 7.2), the following conclusions can be drawn:
- The estimated values of the parameters of the real wage equation using the FDGMM estimator for Poland and Ukraine were significantly different. The estimated values of the labor productivity impact parameter for Ukraine were almost two times higher than for Poland, suggesting

that the increase in labor productivity in Ukraine determined the increase in wages more significantly than in Poland. This parameter in assessments using the SGMM estimator for the Ukrainian economy was about 58% higher than for Poland.

- Estimates using the SGMM estimator show that when labor productivity increased by 1%, real wages increased by 0.09% in Poland and by 0.14% in Ukraine.
- The estimated parameters of the impact of the unemployment rate on gross real wages, using the SGMM estimator, indicate that the unemployment rate in Poland exerted a more robust impact by approximately 23% on wages than in the Ukrainian economy.
- The parameters obtained using the SGMM for Poland and Ukraine are consistent with the theoretical assumptions made.
- According to an analysis of the Arellano-Bond test values for AR (1) and AR (2) for Poland, a statistically significant first-order autocorrelation and a statistically insignificant second-order autocorrelation were observed. The Hansen test values confirm that the instruments were correctly selected.
- In the estimation of the equation parameters of gross real wages for Ukraine, it can be stated that based on the Arellano-Bond tests for AR (1) and AR (2) a negative statistically significant second-order autocorrelation was observed. These Arellano-Bond test values for AR (2) significantly undermine the received estimates of the parameters of the gross real wage equation in Ukraine, and indicate that the obtained values could be significantly influenced by autocorrelation.

7.5 Summary

The considerations in this chapter can be summarized as follows:

i Among the voivodeships, the highest levels of labor productivity were recorded in (the Mazowieckie, Dolnośląskie and Wielkopolskie voivodeships. The smallest value of the discussed variable was recorded in three voivodeships of eastern Poland: Podlaskie, Świętokrzyskie and Podkarpackie).

ii In the Ukrainian economy, the highest level of labor productivity was recorded in (the capital of the country – Kyiv. The Dnipropetrovsk, Poltava and Donetsk oblasts also belonged to a group of high labor productivity oblasts. The lowest value of GDP per working person was in the Kherson, Ternopil and Zakarpattia oblasts).

iii The highest wages, in 2004–2017, occurred in the following voivodeships: (Mazowieckie, Śląskie and Dolnośląskie. On the other hand, the lowest wages in the Polish economy were recorded in the Podkarpackie, Warmińsko-Mazurskie and Lubuskie voivodeships).

iv In oblasts as a group, the highest wages occurred in the (capital City of Kyiv and in the oblast surrounding it – the Kyiv Oblast. High wages also occurred in the Dnipropetrovsk Oblast, whose capital, Dnipro, is the center of financial services in Ukraine. On the other hand, the lowest wages in the Ukrainian economy occurred in western Ukraine: in the Chernivtsi, Volyn and Ternopil oblasts).

v In the Polish economy, in the years 2004–2017, the highest unemployment rates were recorded in the following voivodeships: Warmińsko-Mazurskie, Zachodniopomorskie and Kujawsko-Pomorskie. The Wielkopolskie, Mazowieckie and Małopolskie voivodeships were characterized by the lowest unemployment rates in the research period.

vi The lowest average annual unemployment rates were recorded in those cities with a special status (Sevastopol and Kyiv) and in the Autonomous Republic of Crimea. The highest values of this variable, in 2004–2017, occurred in the Zhytomyr, Ternopil and Rivne oblasts.

vii In the conditions of decreasing unemployment rates, each subsequent percentage point of a decrease in unemployment from the previous year translated into a decrease of this variable in the current period, for the Polish economy, depending on the estimation method, by approx. 0.24–0.52 of a percentage point, and for the Ukrainian economy by approx. 0.31 of a percentage point (for the SGMM estimates). However, in conditions of rising unemployment, each subsequent percentage point of increase in the unemployment rate from the previous year translated into an increase of approx. 0.15–0.12 of a percentage point (in the case of Poland) and by approx. 0.15–0.25 of a percentage point (in Ukraine) of the current unemployment rate.

viii An increase in the real GDP growth rate by 1% point, using the SGMM estimator, translated in the case of the Polish economy to a decrease in the unemployment rate by approx. 0.181, and in the Ukrainian economy by approx. 0.034 of a percentage point. However, when using the FDGMM estimator, these decreases were as follows: 0.12 of a percentage point for Poland and 0.08 of a percentage point for Ukraine.

ix Labor productivity statistically and significantly determined the level of wages in both the Polish and Ukrainian economy. Assessments using the SGMM estimator show that wage flexibility in relation to labor productivity was about 0.09 for Poland and by about 0.14 for Ukraine.

Notes

1 United Nations Economic Commission for Europe, data base: *Labour Force & Wages* (https://w3.unece.org/PXWeb2015/pxweb/en/STAT/STAT__20-ME__3-MELF/, access: 2019-12-30).

2 Source: Macrotrends (2019), https://www.macrotrends.net/countries/POL/poland/gdp-growth-rate, and The World Bank Group, Indicators, (2019).

3 https://bank.gov.ua/markets.

4 The quarrel began in March 2005. The situation returned to normal in January 2006. The next conflict began in October 2007 and lasted until 2009.

5 In 2013, the population of the Crimean Peninsula numbered about 2.4 million people (5.2% of the population of Ukraine), and about 1.1 million people were employed there (5.3% of Ukraine's workforce). Similar indicators for the Donbas

are 6.6 million inhabitants (14.5% of the population of Ukraine) and 3.0 million employed (14.6% of those employed in Ukraine).

6 The decline in labor productivity in the voivodeships of western Poland in 2016 was mainly due to the fact that the number of employed there grew faster than the GDP. In 2016, the GDP in this group of voivodeships increased by 3.2%, while the number of those employed by as much as 12.9%. A similar process took place in the Mazowieckie voivodeship in 2014, when the GDP increased by 4.2% and the number of employed by 8.8%.

7 In 2015, wages in the voivodeships of central Poland amounted to PLN 3 960.16 and western Poland to PLN 3 869.11, and were therefore lower than the wages in the Mazowieckie voivodeship in 2004.

8 Areas with high structural unemployment are also significant parts of the Dolnośląskie and Lubuskie voivodeships and the areas of the former Słupsk voivodeship in the western part of the Pomorskie voivodeship (for more on this topic, see: Misiak, Tokarski 2012 or Majchrowska et al. 2013

9 Government Agriculture Farm.

10 Data on the Autonomous Republic of Crimea and Sevastopol illustrated on Maps 5.4–5.6 (due to Russia's annexation of the Crimean Peninsula in 2014) are average values of the analyzed variables from 2004 to 2013.

8 Simulations of voivodeship and oblast development trajectories. An analysis based on the gravity growth model

Svitlana Chugaievska, Katarzyna Filipowicz, Tomasz Tokarski and Rafał Wisła

8.1 Introduction

This analysis of the most important determinants of the spatial diversity of labor productivity in Poland and Ukraine was carried out on the basis of the gravitational model of economic growth proposed in the work by Mroczek et al. 2014 (cf. also Filipowicz 2019) and is a compilation of the gravitational trade models of Linnemann 1963, Poyhonen 1963 and Pulliainen 1963 with the neoclassical model of economic growth of Solow 1956.

The model under consideration is assumed to be, amongst others, an assumption that labor productivity depends both on the capital-labor ratio (as is the case in the neoclassical Solow growth model) and on the gravity effects affecting a given region. These (as in Newton's law of universal gravitation) are directly proportional to the economic potential of a given region (voivodeships or oblasts) and the economic potential of other regions, and is inversely proportional to the square of the geometric mean [geomean] of the distance between the capital of a given region and the capitals of other regions.

The gravitational growth model was used, inter alias, for analyzing the spatial diversity of the economic development of Polish voivodeships (Mroczek et al. 2014; Filipowicz 2019), Ukrainian oblasts (Chugaievska et al. 2017), the Balkan countries (Mroczek et al. 2015) and the EU countries (Wisła et al. 2018).

8.2 Gravitational growth model

In the gravitational model of economic growth, the following submissions are made regarding the long-term functioning of the economy (after Mroczek et al. 2014, see also Filipowicz 2019):

1 Labor productivity function (resulting from the Cobb-Douglas production function) is given by the formula:[1]

$$\forall i \quad y_i(t) = a\left(g_i(t)\right)^{\beta}\left(k_i(t)\right)^{\alpha}, \tag{8.1}$$

where $y_i(t)$ means labor productivity in the region i (i.e., in the Polish voivodeship or Ukrainian oblast) at the moment t, $a>0$ is a certain constant that has no direct economic interpretation, $g_i(t)$ are aggregate gravity effects, $k_i(t)$ is capital-labor ratio, and $\alpha \in (0,1)$ and $\beta \in (0,1)$ are elasticities of labor productivity in relation to capital-labor ratio and total gravitational effects. We also assume that $\beta < \frac{1-\alpha}{2}$, which means that the nontrivial steady state point of the system of differential equations (8.6) is (by the Grobman–Hartman theorem) asymptotically stable.

2 Total aggregate gravity effects affecting the region i are the geometric mean of individual gravity effects connecting this region with the other regions, therefore:

$$\forall i \quad g_i(t) = \sqrt[N-1]{\prod_{j \neq 1} g_{ij}(t)}, \tag{8.2}$$

where $g_{ij}(t)$ means individual gravity effects connecting the region i with the region j.

3 The individual gravitational effects connecting the region i with the region j are directly proportional to the ratio of the economic potential of these regions (measured by their capital-labor ratio) and inversely proportional to the square of the distance between them (and exactly between their capitals). It follows that individual gravitational effects can be written as follows:

$$\forall i, \quad j \wedge i \neq j \quad g_{ij}(t) = \frac{k_i(t)k_j(t)}{d_{ij}^2}, \tag{8.3}$$

where d_{ij} is the distance between the capital of the region i and region j (this distance was calculated from the Pythagorean theorem in a straight line connecting the capitals of voivodeships or oblasts).

4 The increase in capital-labor ratio k_i is described by the Solow equation:

$$\forall i \quad k_i(t) = s_i y_i(t) - \mu_i k_i(t), \tag{8.4}$$

Where $s_i \in (0,1)$ is the investment rate in the region i, and $\mu_i > 0$ is the decrease rate of the capital-labor ratio (which is the sum of the depreciation rate of capital and the growth rate of employment).

From Eqs. (8.1) to (8.3) we obtain the function of labor productivity:

$$\forall i \quad y_i(t) = a \frac{(k_i(t))^{\alpha+\beta} \prod_{j \neq 1} (k_j(t))^{\beta/(N-1)}}{\bar{d}_i^{2\beta}}, \tag{8.5}$$

where $\bar{d}_i$ is the geometric mean distance from the capital of the region i and from the capitals of the other regions. By inserting Eq. (8.5) into the equations for the increase of capital-labor ratio (8.4), we arrive at the following system of differential equations:

$$\forall i \quad \dot{k}_i(t) = s_i a \frac{\left(k_i(t)\right)^{\alpha+\beta} \prod_{j \neq 1} \left(k_j(t)\right)^{\beta/(N-1)}}{\bar{d}_i^{2\beta}} - \mu_i k_i(t). \tag{8.6}$$

The system of differential equations (8.6) has two steady state points: trivial at the beginning of the N-dimensional coordinate system and non-trivial in which dependencies are met (after Mroczek et al. 2014).

$$\forall i \quad \ln k_i^* = \frac{\frac{\beta}{(N-1)(1-\alpha-2\beta)} \sum_j \ln \frac{a s_j}{\mu_j \bar{d}_j^{2\beta}} + \ln \frac{a s_i}{\mu_i \bar{d}_i^{2\beta}}}{1-\alpha-\frac{N-2}{N-1}\beta}. \tag{8.7}$$

As already mentioned, using the Grobman–Hartman theorem (Grobman 1999: 219–221) it can be shown that the non-trivial stationary point determined by Eq. (8.7) is characterized by an asymptotic stability (Mroczek et al. 2014). So, this point sets the long-run equilibrium of the gravitational model of economic growth.

The following conclusions can be drawn from Eq. (8.7). The level of capital-labor ratio in the i-region k_i^* is higher when the investment rate in this region s_i is higher, of the decrease rate of investment in other regions s_j and the lower the capital decrease rate in i-the region μ_i and the decrease rate in other regions μ_j. The size of the long-term capital-labor ratio in each region is also affected by its geographical location, which follows from the fact that the more centrally located region (i.e., the lower the average geometric distance $\bar{d}_i$), the higher is the long-term capital-labor ratio.

8.3 The diversity of the capital-labor ratio, gravitational effects and investment rates

Since the key variables in the gravitational model of economic growth are capital-labor ratio and gravitational effects, before simulating the trajectory of labor productivity in voivodeships and oblasts, a brief description of the spatial diversity of these macroeconomic variables in Poland and Ukraine seems appropriate. These analyses (due to the availability of relevant statistical data on the websites of the Polish and Ukrainian Statistical Offices) concern the years 2004–2015 (in the case of Poland) and 2004–2017 (in the case of Ukraine).

8.3.1 Poland

In the years 2004–2016 there were significant disproportions between voivodeships due to the level of capital-labor ratio. This variable (on average over the whole period of time studied) ranged from 129,800 PLN in the

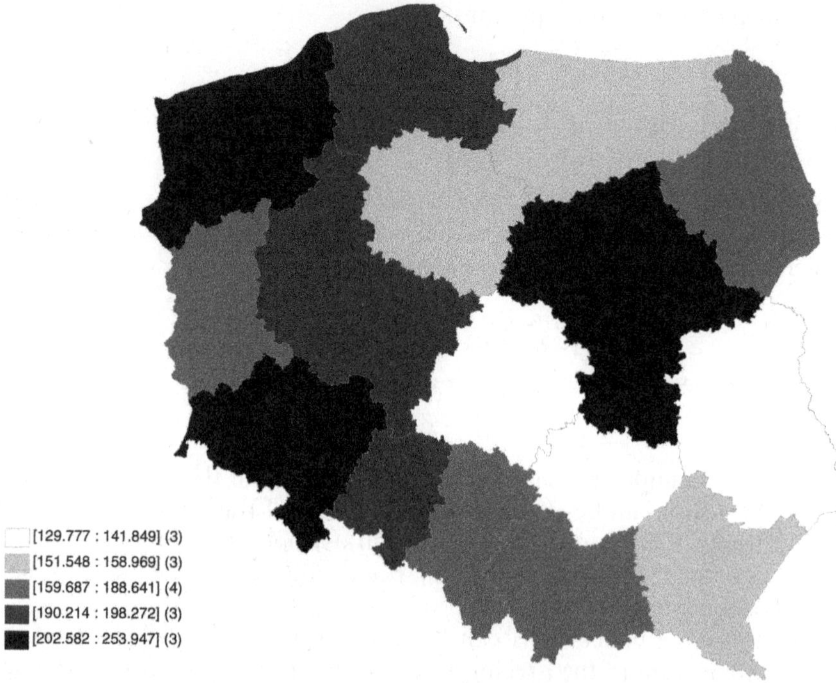

Map 8.1 Diversification of capital-labor ratio in voivodeships in 2004–2016 (thousand PLN, according to 2014 prices).

Source: Our own estimates based on: https://bdl.stat.gov.pl/BDL/start (access: 2019-12-30).

Lubelskie Voivodeship up to 253,900 PLN in the Mazowieckie Voivodeship. In addition to the capital of the Mazowieckie Voivodeship, the capital-labor ratio exceeded a level of 200,000 PLN in the Zachodniopomorskie (213,000 PLN) and Dolnośląskie (202,600 PLN) voivodeships. The following voivodeships all exceeded a level of 190,000 PLN, that is, the Opolskie (198,300 PLN), Pomorskie (190,400 PLN) and Wielkopolskie (190,200 PLN) voivodeships. The lowest levels of this variable, however, were in the Łódzkie (141,800 PLN) and Świętokrzyskie (133,900 PLN) voivodeships. The capital-labor ratio did not exceed a level of 160,000 PLN in the following voivodeships: Małopolskie (159,700 PLN), Warmińsko-Mazurskie (159,900 PLN), Kujawsko-Pomorskie (157,700 PLN) and Podkarpackie (151,500 PLN, see Map 8.1).

Hence, we may come to a more general conclusion that (except for the Łódzkie and Świętokrzyskie voivodeships) the voivodeships west of the Vistula (Wisła) river were characterized by a higher level of capital-labor ratio.

The spatial diversity of gravitational effects is the result of two factors. These factors are the economic potential of a given region (measured by its capital-labor ratio) and its geographic location.

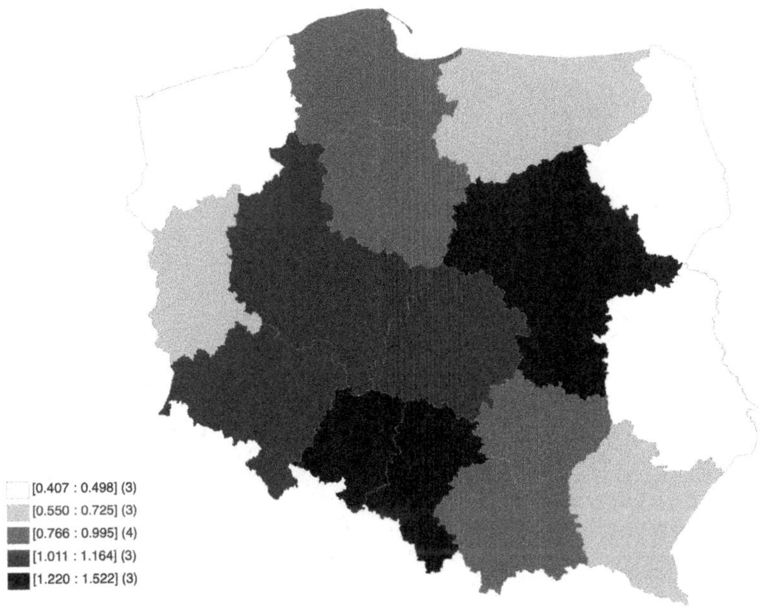

Map 8.2 Differentiation of gravitational effects in voivodeships in 2004–2016 (million PLN^2/mingeo^2 according to 2014 prices).

Source: Our own estimates based on: https://bdl.stat.gov.pl/BDL/start (access: 2019-12-30).

The highest levels of gravitational effects in Poland were found in the following voivodeships:[2] Mazowieckie (1.522 million PLN^2/mingeo^2), Śląskie (1.243 million PLN^2/mingeo^2) and Opolskie (1.220 million PLN^2/mingeo^2). The high level of the feature in question was also characteristic of the Łódzkie (1.164 million PLN^2/mingeo^2), Dolnośląskie (1.075 million PLN^2/mingeo^2) and Wielkopolskie (1.011 million PLN^2/mingeo^2) voivodeships. Low and very low levels of gravitational effects were found in peripheral regions, both in the east and in the west of Poland. These were the following voivodeships: Warmińsko-Mazurskie (0.725 million PLN^2/mingeo^2), Podkarpackie (0.573 million PLN^2/mingeo^2), Lubuskie (0.550 million PLN^2/mingeo^2), Lubelskie (0.498 million PLN^2/mingeo^2), Zachodniopomorskie (0.424 million PLN^2/mingeo^2) and Podlaskie (0.407 million PLN^2/mingeo^2, see Map 8.2).

In the following numerical simulations of labor productivity, in addition to internal gravitational effects, external gravitational effects were also included, connecting voivodeships with Poland's largest economic partner, that is, Germany.[3] These effects are also included in the estimation of production function parameters and used to determine the development trajectories of voivodeships under various scenarios regarding the economic growth in Germany.

External gravitational effects indicate which voivodeships are potentially most affected by the German economy. By far the highest external

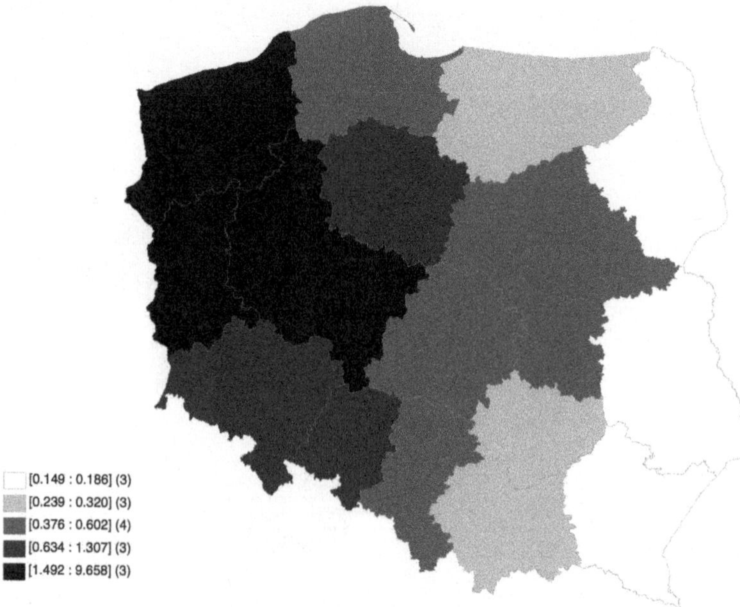

Map 8.3 External gravitational effects in voivodeships in 2004–2016 (million PLN^2/ $mingeo^2$ according to 2014 prices).
Source: Our own estimates based on: https://bdl.stat.gov.pl/BDL/start (access: 2019-12-30).

gravitational effects were characteristic of the border voivodeships in the west of Poland: the Zachodniopomorskie (9.658 million PLN^2/$mingeo^2$) and Lubuskie (4.435 million PLN^2/$mingeo^2$) voivodeships. The Wielkopolskie (1.492 million PLN^2/$mingeo^2$) and Dolnośląskie (1.307 million PLN^2/$mingeo^2$) voivodeships also achieved a high level of this feature. Low external gravitational effects were observed in the following voivodeships: Małopolskie (0.320 million PLN^2/$mingeo^2$), Warmińsko-Mazurskie (0.302 million PLN^2/$mingeo^2$) and Świętokrzyskie (0.239 million PLN^2/$mingeo^2$). The weakest benefits from the impact of the German economy were recorded in the peripheral voivodeships in eastern Poland, that is, in the Podkarpackie (0.186 million PLN^2/$mingeo^2$), Podlaskie (0.166 million PLN^2/$mingeo^2$) and Lubelskie (0.149 million PLN^2/$mingeo^2$, see Map 8.3) voivodeships.

Because, according to Solow's Neoclassical Growth Model (1956) (but also in accordance with Mankiw et al. growth models (1992), and Nonneman's, Vanhoudt's (1996), or the gravitational model of economic growth used here), the investment rate is a key variable that determines the rate of capital accumulation and the rate of economic growth, one should also look at the spatial diversity of this variable in Polish voivodeships and Ukrainian oblasts.

In the years 2004–2015, the range between the highest and lowest investment rate (calculated as the share of investment in GDP) in voivodeships

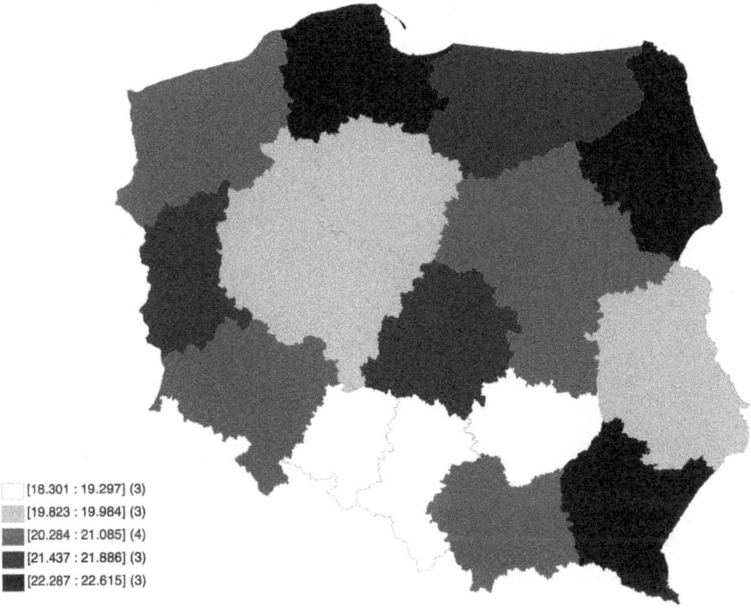

Map 8.4 Investment rates in voivodeships in 2004–2015 (%).
Source: Our own estimates based on: https://bdl.stat.gov.pl/BDL/start (access: 2019-12-30).

was 4.3 percentage points, as these rates ranged from 18.3% (Śląskie Voivodeship) to 22.6% (Podlaskie Voivodeship). In as many as 11 voivodeships, investment rates exceeded 20%. These were the following voivodeships: Podlaskie (22.6%), Podkarpackie (22.4%), Pomorskie (22.3%), Warmińsko-Mazurskie (21.9%), Lubuskie (21.6%), Łódzkie (21.4%), Zachodniopomorskie (21.1%), Dolnośląskie (20.4%), Małopolskie (20.3%), Mazowieckie (20.3%) and Kujawsko-Pomorskie (20.0%). The lowest investment rate was recorded in the Śląskie Voivodeship (18.3%, see Map 8.4).

8.3.2 Ukraine

Map 8.5 illustrates the spatial differentiation of capital-labor ratio in Ukraine. We can reach the following conclusions from this map: By far the highest level of capital-labor ratio was in the City of Kyiv (670,600 UAH). The group of oblasts with a high value of this feature also included the Kyiv Oblast (256,300 UAH) in northern Ukraine, and the Donetsk (243,500 UAH) in the east of Ukraine, and Dnipropetrovsk (227,100 UAH) and Poltava (191,000 UAH) oblasts in central Ukraine. A high (for Ukrainian conditions) value of this feature was recorded in the Zaporizhzhya (190,400 UAH), Luhansk (181,300 UAH) and Kharkiv (169,700 UAH) oblasts in

Map 8.5 Diversification of capital-labor ratio in oblasts in 2004–2017 (thousand UAH, according to 2016 prices).

In the case of the ARC and Sevastopol in 2004–2013.

Source: Our own estimates based on: http://www.ukrstat.gov.ua/ (access: 2019-12-30).

eastern Ukraine and the city of Sevastopol (184,300 UAH), Odesa Oblast (179,900 UAH) and the Autonomous Republic of Crimea (169,700 UAH) in the south. Thus, all oblasts with the highest or high value of capital per employee were located in Left-bank Ukraine or on the Black Sea.

The group of oblasts with the lowest level of capital-labor ratio was composed of the following oblasts: Zakarpattia (102,900 UAH) and Ternopil (104,100 UAH) in western Ukraine, Kherson (104,300 UAH) in the south and Zhytomyr (104,500 UAH) and Sumy (108, 600 UAH) in the north of Ukraine. A low level of capital-labor ratio also characterized the Vinnytsya (109,700 UAH) and Cherkasy (117,300 UAH) oblasts in central Ukraine, the Volyn (117,300 UAH), Chernivtsi (121,500 UAH) and Khmelnytskiy (130,100 UAH) oblasts in the west of the country, and the Chernihiv (119,300 UAH) Oblast in the north of Ukraine. Thus, oblasts with a low or very low level of capital-labor ratio were located mainly on the Right-bank of Ukraine.

Map 8.6 illustrates the spatial differentiation of national gravitational effects in Ukraine. This map shows that the highest national gravitational effects were observed in the oblasts located in the Dnieper valley (Kyiv 1.628 million $UAH^2/mingeo^2$ and Kyiv Oblast[4] 0.698 million $UAH^2/mingeo^2$, Dnipropetrovsk 0.452 million $UAH^2/mingeo^2$, Poltava 0.388 million $UAH^2/mingeo^2$ and Kirovohrad 0.380 million $UAH^2/mingeo^2$). This resulted both from their central geographical location and from the very high economic potential (in particular) of Kyiv and the Kyiv and Dnipropetrovsk oblasts (see also Chugaievska et al. 2017).

Map 8.6 Differentiation of national gravitational effects in the oblasts in 2004–2017 (million UAH^2/mingeo^2, according to 2016 prices).

In the case of the ARC and Sevastopol in 2004–2013.

Source: Our own estimates based on: http://www.ukrstat.gov.ua/ (access: 2019-12-30).

In contrast, the group of oblasts with the lowest national gravitational effects was composed of the following oblasts: Zakarpattia (0.074 million UAH^2/mingeo^2), Volyn (0.188 million UAH^2/mingeo^2) and Lviv (0.189 million UAH^2/mingeo^2) in the west of Ukraine; Luhansk (0.114 million UAH^2/mingeo^2) in the east; and Sumy (0.173 million UAH^2/mingeo^2) in the north of the country.

When analyzing the impact of external gravitational effects on Ukrainian oblasts, two of Ukraine's most important economic partners, that is, Russia and Poland, were taken into account.[5]

The external gravitational effects flowing from Russia are illustrated in Map 8.7. The following conclusions can be drawn from this map: First of all, Kyiv had by far the highest level of these effects (1.437 million UAH^2/mingeo^2). Second, a very high level of these effects was recorded in the Kharkiv (0.781 million UAH^2/mingeo^2), Donetsk (0.685 million UAH^2/mingeo^2), Poltava (0.661 million UAH^2/mingeo^2) and Dnipropetrovsk (0.625 million UAH^2/mingeo^2) oblasts, located in eastern and central Ukraine. Third, the lowest value of this feature was observed in the oblasts located in the west of Ukraine, in particular in the Zakarpattia (0.059 million UAH^2/mingeo^2), Ternopil (0.093 million UAH^2/mingeo^2), Chernivtsi (0.104 million UAH^2/mingeo^2), Ivano-Frankivsk (0.105 million UAH^2/mingeo^2) and Volyn (0.109 million UAH^2/mingeo^2) oblasts. Fourth, the external gravitational effects flowing from Russia had a much stronger impact on the Left-bank Ukraine and the Odesa and Mykolayiv coastal regions than on the rest of the country. This was due to historical (stronger economic links of the Left-bank of Ukraine with the rest of the Romanov Empire before World War I

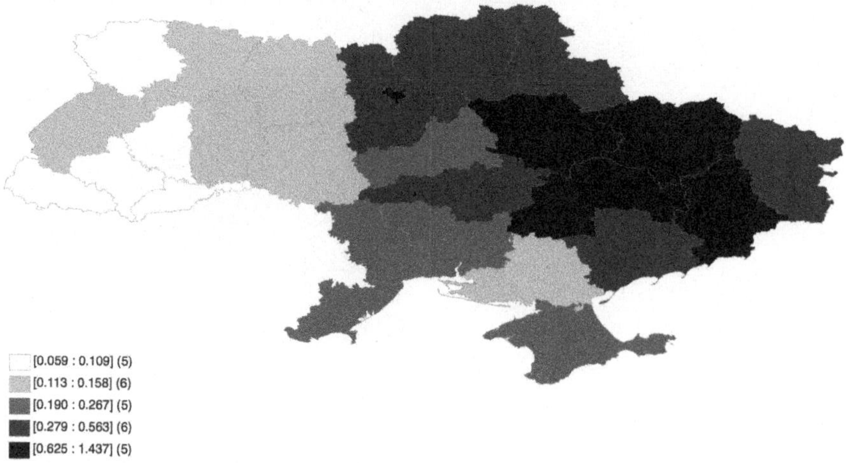

Map 8.7 External gravitational effects from Russia in oblasts in the years 2004–2017 (million UAH^2/mingeo^2, according to 2016 prices).
In the case of the ARC and Sevastopol in 2004–2013
Source: Our own estimates based on: http://www.ukrstat.gov.ua/ (access: 2019-12-30).

and with the other Soviet republics after the October Revolution in Russia), geographical (these oblasts are closer to Russia) and economic connections (they are usually characterized by a higher level of economic development than from the Right-bank of Ukraine).

Considering the external gravitational effects flowing from Poland (Map 8.8), the following conclusions can be drawn: These effects had the strongest impact on the Lviv (1.584 million UAH^2/mingeo^2), Zakarpattia (1.073 million UAH^2/mingeo^2), Volyn (0.884 million UAH^2/mingeo^2) and Ivano-Frankivsk (0.866 million UAH^2/mingeo^2) oblasts in western Ukraine and on the City of Kyiv (1,166 million UAH^2/mingeo^2). The impact of these effects on the Lviv, Volyn and Ivano-Frankivsk oblasts (but also on the Rivne 0.688 million UAH^2/mingeo^2 and Ternopil 0.574 million UAH^2/mingeo^2) resulted both from historical reasons (these regions belonged to Poland in the interwar period) and geographical causes (their close proximity to the Polish border). The substantial impact of gravitational effects in the Zakarpattia Oblast was due to a geographical factor (although it seems that this oblast, for historical reasons, is more strongly influenced by Hungary, Slovakia or Czechia than Poland), and in Kyiv due to its economic potential. The weakest external gravitational effects flowing from Poland affected the eastern oblasts of Luhansk (0.086 million UAH^2/mingeo^2) and Kharkiv (0.109 million UAH^2/mingeo^2) in the east of Ukraine, in the south the Kherson Oblast (0.098 million UAH^2/mingeo^2) and the Autonomous Republic of Crimea 0.099 million UAH^2/mingeo^2) and the Sumy Oblast located in northern Ukraine (0.087 million UAH^2/mingeo^2). Thus,

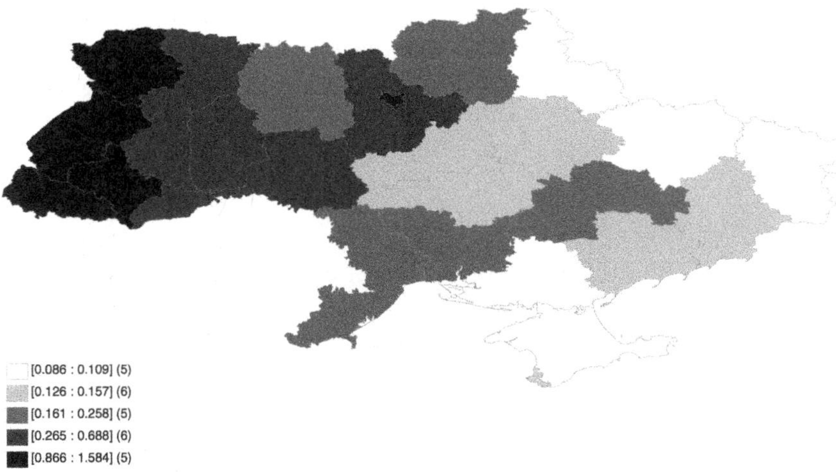

Map 8.8 External gravitational effects from Poland in oblasts in the years 2004–2017 (million UAH^2/mingeo^2, according to 2016 prices).
In the case of the ARC and Sevastopol in 2004–2013.
Source: Our own estimates based on: http://www.ukrstat.gov.ua/ (access: 2019-12-30).

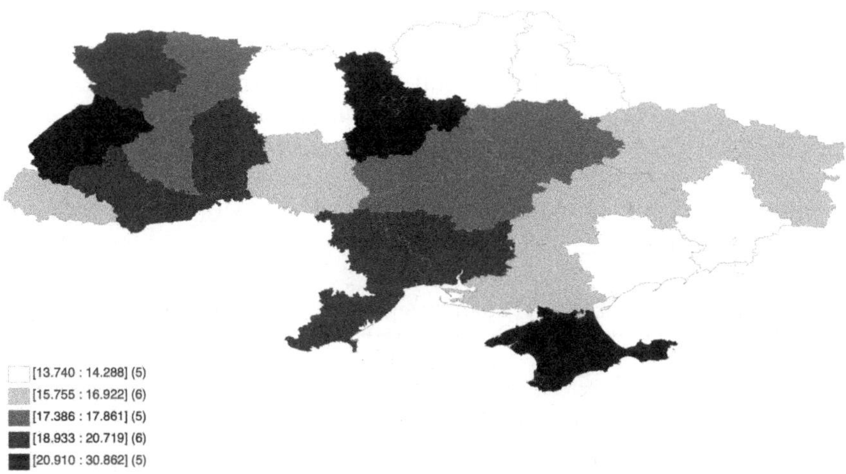

Map 8.9 The investment rates in Ukrainian oblasts in 2004–2017 (%).
In the case of the ARC and Sevastopol in 2004–2013.
Source: Our own estimates based on: http://www.ukrstat.gov.ua/ (access: 2019-12-30).

due to both geographical and historical factors, the external gravitational effects flowing from Poland had a significantly greater impact on western Ukraine than on other oblasts.

The average investment rates in the oblasts in 2004–2017 are illustrated on Map 8.9. This map shows that the Autonomous Republic of Crimea (30.9%) and Sevastopol (20.9%) had the highest level of this value in the south of

Ukraine, while the Kyiv Oblast (30.5%) and the City of Kyiv (23.8%) had the highest value of this feature in northern, and the Lviv Oblast (21.3%) in western Ukraine. The lowest shares of investment in GDP were recorded in the Sumy (13.7%), Chernihiv (14.0%) and Zhytomyr (14.2%) oblasts in northern Ukraine as well as the Zaporizhzhya (14.2%) and Donetsk (14.3%) oblasts in the east of Ukraine.

8.4 Calibration of model parameters

The parameters of the gravitational model of economic growth were calibrated based on historical data for voivodeships from 2004 to 2015 or oblasts from 2004 to 2017. The labor productivity function includes both domestic gravitational effects and foreign gravitational effects related to the impact of the German or Russian or Polish economy. In the case of Poland, this function is described by the following equation:

$$y_{it} = a(k_{it})^{\alpha}(g_{it})^{\beta}(g_{it}^{N})^{\gamma}$$

or after log in:

$$\ln y_{it} = \ln a + \alpha \ln k_{it} + \beta \ln g_{it} + \gamma \ln g_{it}^{N}, \tag{8.8}$$

where: $a > 0$ means total factor productivity, k_{it} is capital-labor ratio in the i-this region in year t, g_{it} is the total national gravitational effects in the i-this region in year t, g_{it}^{N} is the foreign gravitational effects from Germany in the i-this region in the year t. The parameters of this Eq. (8.8) were estimated by two methods – the ordinary least squares (OLS) method and the generalized method of moments (GMM). The results of the estimates are presented in Table 8.1.

Table 8.1 Estimates of the parameters of Eq. (8.1) for Poland

Explanatory variables	*OLS*	*GMM*
$\ln a$	0.532^{**} (2.325)	0.437^{*} (1.759)
$\ln k_{it}$	0.783^{***} (17.963)	0.802^{***} (16.957)
$\ln g_{it}$	0.115^{***} (6.594)	0.113^{***} (6.132)
$\ln g_{it}^{N}$	0.0206^{***} (2.877)	0.0187^{**} (2.433)
adjusted R^2	0.852	0.847

Source: Our own calculations based on https://bdl.stat.gov.pl/
Student's t-statistics are given in brackets under the estimates. *** statistically significant variables were determined at a 1% level of significance, ** at a 5% level, * at a 10% level. In the estimates of the generalized method of moments, instrumental variables are dependent and independent variables delayed by a year.

All estimated parameters of Eq. (8.8) were statistically noteworthy at least at a significance level of 10%. In the numerical simulations the labor productivity function was adopted; the parameters of which were obtained by averaging the values of the parameters obtained OLS and GMM. This function has the following form:

$$y_{it} = 1{,}623 k_{it}^{0{,}793} g_{it}^{0{,}114} \left(g_{it}^{N}\right)^{0{,}0197}. \tag{8.9}$$

Function parameters (8.9) can be given the following economic interpretation: Capital-labor ratio (i.e., the internal potential of that province) had the strongest impact on labor productivity in a given voivodeship, the national gravitational effects were much weaker, and the external gravitational effects exerted the least influence. The impact of national effects was more than five times stronger than external effects related to the German economy.

Similar estimates of equation parameters (8.8) for Ukrainian regions are given in Table 8.2.

The estimates of equation parameters (8.8) presented in Table 8.2 for Ukraine show that all independent variables in this equation had a statistically substantial effect on the dependent variable at least at a 5% significance level.

After averaging the parameter estimates, we get the equation:

$$y_{it} = 32{,}346 k_{it}^{0{,}341} g_{it}^{0{,}0649} \left(g_{it}^{R}\right)^{0{,}239} \left(g_{it}^{P}\right)^{0{,}0663}. \tag{8.10}$$

The calibrated parameters of the Eq. (8.10) for Ukraine show that the level of labor productivity in the Ukrainian oblasts was most strongly affected

Table 8.2 Estimates of the parameters of Eq. (8.1) for Ukraine

Explanatory variables	*OLS*	*GMM*
$\ln a$	3.190***	3.763***
	(11.089)	(12.518)
$\ln k_{it}$	0.380***	0.302***
	(8.030)	(6.154)
$\ln g_{it}$	0.0505**	0.0794***
	(2.060)	(3.153)
$\ln g_{it}^{P}$	0.0464***	0.0862***
	(3.236)	(5.607)
$\ln g_{it}^{R}$	0.211***	0.268***
	(9.078)	(10.832)
Adjusted R^2	0.773	0.786

Source: Our own calculations based on www.ukrstat.gov.ua
Student's *t*-statistics are given in brackets under the estimates. *** Statistically significant variables were determined at a 1% level of significance, ** at a 5% level, * at a 10% level. In the estimates of the generalized method of moments, instrumental variables are dependent and independent variables delayed by a year. g^P, g^R means external gravitational effects flowing (respectively) from Poland and Russia.

by peripheral capital-labor ratio, followed by gravitational effects flowing from Russia, next from Poland, and finally, by the national gravitational effects. It can be assumed that this is due to the fact that what is happening in eastern Ukraine is more strongly influenced by the economic situation of Russia, and in the west by Poland.

Comparing the calibrated parameters of the labor productivity function (8.8) for Poland (8.9) and Ukraine (8.10), it turns out that in Poland, labor productivity was much more strongly influenced by the amount of capital per employee and national gravitational effects than in Ukraine.

When simulating the trajectory of labor productivity, a system of difference equations was used, analogous to the systems of Eq. (8.6). It looks like this:

$$\forall i \;\; \Delta k_i = s_i a \frac{k_{it}^{\alpha+\beta} \prod_{j \neq 1} k_{jt}^{\beta/(N-1)}}{\bar{d}_i^{2\beta}} \left(g_{it}^F\right)^{\gamma} - \mu_i k_{it-1} \qquad (8.11)$$

where the subscript t refer to subsequent years, g_{it}^F means foreign gravitational effects, while the other designations as in the case of a system of Eq. (8.6) parameters α, β, γ were calibrated as in Eqs. (8.9) and (8.10). Using the system of Eq. (8.11), capital-labor ratio was calculated in subsequent regions in subsequent years, which allowed for the calculation of total gravitational effects and levels of labor productivity in regions and years.

8.5 Simulation of labor productivity trajectories

8.5.1 Poland

It seems that before presenting the results of simulations of labor productivity until 2050, it is necessary, at least briefly, to describe the diversity of labor productivity in the last year in which regional statistical data on this macroeconomic variable are available. Spatial diversity of labor productivity in Poland in 2015 is shown on Map 8.10.

In 2015, the Mazowieckie (145,900 PLN), Wielkopolskie (135,300 PLN) and Dolnośląskie (134,000 PLN) voivodeships were characterized by the highest labor productivity. Labor productivity over 120,000 PLN was also found in the Śląskie (126,500 PLN) and Zachodniopomorskie (122,200 PLN) voivodeships. The lowest levels of labor productivity were found in the Świętokrzyskie (72,500 PLN) and Lubelskie (67,000 PLN) voivodships. Labor productivity below 90 thousand was also found in the following voivodeships, that is, the Podkarpackie (88,600 PLN), Łódzkie (88,300 PLN), Warmińsko-Mazurskie (86,100 PLN) and Podlaskie (82,200 PLN) voivodeships.

Using the gravitational model of economic growth, labor productivity simulations up to 2050 were carried out in eight alternative development scenarios. The scenarios differed in assumptions regarding investment rates, rate of capital depreciation per employee in voivodeships and German GDP growth rates.

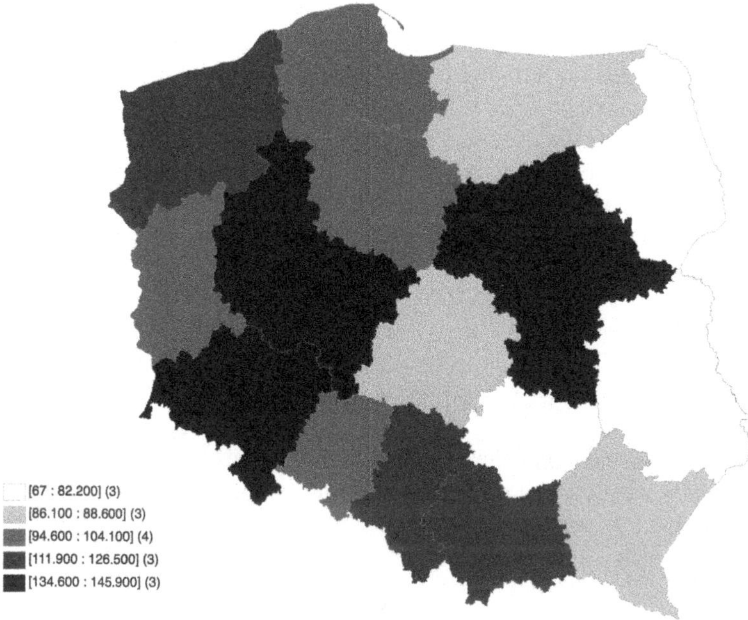

Map 8.10 Diversification of labor productivity in voivodeships in 2015 (thousand PLN, according to 2014 prices).

Source: Our own estimates based on: https://bdl.stat.gov.pl/BDL/start (access: 2019-12-30).

The considered scenarios are as follows (see also Filipowicz 2019):

I In the following years, the investment rate in all voivodeships will be at a level of 20.3% (equal to the average investment rate in Poland in 2004–2015), and the rate of decrement of capital-labor ratio will be equal to 7%. In addition, Germany's GDP will change at a pace equal to the average dynamics of this variable in 2004–2015.

II In scenario II, the assumption that the same rate of decrement of capital per employee was the same in all voivodeships was rescinded. This variable was dependent on the growth rates of people of working age forecast by the Central Statistical Office (GUS) (i.e., it was assumed that the growth rate of the number of employed will coincide with the growth rate of the number of people of working age forecast by the GUS).

III Scenario III assumes that voivodeships are characterized by constant, over a given timeframe, investment rates as well as capital decrement rates per employee. In addition, it is assumed that the German economy will develop at the same pace as in the years 2009–2015. This scenario differs from scenario I, only under the assumption regarding the GDP growth rate of the German economy.

IV In the next scenario, it is assumed that investment rates are the same in all voivodeships, the German economy's GDP growth rates are equal to the average for 2009–2015, and the rate of decrement of capital-labor ratio is based on data on the projections of the number of people of working age. Scenario IV differs from scenario II only by an assumption regarding the pace of GDP changes in the German economy.

V Investment rates in voivodeships will be at a level equal to the average for individual voivodeships from 2004 to 2015. In this scenario (as in scenario I) it is assumed that the capital decrement rates per employee are the same for all voivodeships and that the German economy is growing at an average pace of that of 2004–2015.

VI In the next scenario, it is assumed that not only investment rates are different in individual voivodeships, but also capital decrement rates per employee are different (based on projected GUS data on the number of people of working age). In addition, the scenario under consideration assumes that the German economy will develop economically at a rate equal to the average from 2004 to 2015.

VII Scenario VII adopts the same assumptions as in scenario V with one exception; in other words, it is assumed that the German economy will develop at a slightly faster pace, that is, at a level of the average from 2009 to 2015.

VIII In this scenario, it is assumed that the spatial structure of investment rates is shaped as it was in 2004–2015; in addition, the rate of capital loss per employee (based on forecasts regarding the number of people of working age) also varies and the average GDP growth rate of the German economy is at the average level of 2009–2015.

Table 8.3 presents data on the level of labor productivity in 2015 both in individual voivodeships and groups of voivodeships, as well as the results of numerical simulations of this macroeconomic variable in 2050 in subsequent, previously characterized scenarios. Table 8.3, however, presents the average levels of average annual growth rates of labor productivity in various simulations.[6]

Tables 8.3 and 8.4 draw the following conclusions:

- In scenario I, with the same investment rates and rate of decrement of capital-labor ratio in all voivodeships, the highest (exceeding 650,000 PLN) level of labor productivity in 2050 should be characterized by the Wielkopolskie, Dolnośląskie and Opolskie voivodeships located in the west of Poland, and the Mazowieckie Voivodeship and the Śląskie Voivodeship in central Poland. The group of voivodeships with the lowest level of labor productivity will be composed of the Pomorskie Voivodeship and four out of the five voivodeships of eastern Poland, that is, the Warmińsko-Mazurskie, Podkarpackie, Lubelskie and Podlaskie (see: Map 8.12 in the annex) voivodeships. The fact that the Pomorskie

Table 8.3 Labor productivity in 2015 and simulations of labor productivity in 2050

Voivodeship	*Labor productivity in 2015 (in thousand PLN, according to 2014 prices)*	*Labor productivity in 2050 in the script (in thousand PLN, according to 2014 prices)*							
		I	*II*	*III*	*IV*	*V*	*VI*	*VII*	*VIII*
Dolnośląskie	134.6	681.3	663.4	684.6	666.6	710.0	691.4	713.5	694.8
Kujawsko-Pomorskie	94.6	589.5	570.1	592.4	573.0	574.1	555.4	577.0	558.1
Lubelskie	67.0	361.8	369.3	363.5	371.1	346.8	354.1	348.5	355.8
Lubuskie	95.4	578.0	562.4	580.8	565.1	711.9	692.5	715.4	695.9
Łódzkie	88.3	617.1	627.9	620.2	631.0	748.8	761.4	752.6	765.2
Małopolskie	111.9	589.2	511.9	592.1	514.4	603.2	524.2	606.2	526.7
Mazowieckie	145.9	686.1	585.4	689.4	588.2	698.9	596.4	702.3	599.3
Opolskie	96.6	652.8	716.6	656.0	720.1	573.4	630.2	576.2	633.2
Podkarpackie	88.6	433.1	411.8	435.2	413.8	595.2	566.2	598.2	569.0
Podlaskie	82.2	357.6	360.8	359.3	362.5	498.9	502.8	501.4	505.3
Pomorskie	104.1	497.0	430.2	499.4	432.2	673.2	583.8	676.6	586.8
Śląskie	126.5	681.1	701.8	684.4	705.2	514.4	530.9	516.9	533.4
Świętokrzyskie	72.5	502.8	528.3	505.3	530.9	439.3	462.0	441.4	464.2
Warmińsko-Mazurskie	86.1	478.3	477.9	480.6	480.2	613.1	612.3	616.2	615.3
Wielkopolskie	135.3	693.3	619.7	696.7	622.8	659.7	589.6	662.9	592.5
Zachodniopomorskie	122.2	550.3	544.6	552.9	547.2	626.2	619.6	629.3	622.6
Coefficient of variation	0.229	0.200	0.204	0.200	0.204	0.180	0.167	0.180	0.167
Group of voivodeships	Labor productivity in 2015 (in thousand PLN, according to 2014 prices)	Labor productivity in 2050 (in thousand PLN, according to 2014 prices)							
Central Poland	78.1	641.6	615.6	644.9	618.8	646.7	622.7	650.0	625.9
Western Poland	138.8	684.9	661.1	688.4	664.4	701.0	676.4	704.6	679.9
Eastern Poland	94.7	441.5	447.9	443.7	450.1	510.0	518.5	512.7	521.2

Source: Our own estimates.

Table 8.4 Average annual growth rates of labor productivity in 2016–2050 in subsequent scenarios (%)

Voivodeship	*Scenario*							
	I	*II*	*III*	*IV*	*V*	*VI*	*VII*	*VIII*
Dolnośląskie	4.8	4.7	4.8	4.7	4.9	4.8	4.9	4.8
Kujawsko-Pomorskie	5.4	5.3	5.4	5.3	5.3	5.2	5.3	5.2
Lubelskie	4.9	5.0	5.0	5.0	4.8	4.9	4.8	4.9
Lubuskie	5.3	5.2	5.3	5.2	5.9	5.8	5.9	5.8
Łódzkie	5.7	5.8	5.7	5.8	6.3	6.3	6.3	6.4
Małopolskie	4.9	4.4	4.9	4.5	4.9	4.5	4.9	4.5
Mazowieckie	4.5	4.0	4.5	4.1	4.6	4.1	4.6	4.1
Opolskie	5.6	5.9	5.6	5.9	5.2	5.5	5.2	5.5
Podkarpackie	4.6	4.5	4.7	4.5	5.6	5.4	5.6	5.5
Podlaskie	4.3	4.3	4.3	4.3	5.3	5.3	5.3	5.3
Pomorskie	4.6	4.1	4.6	4.2	5.5	5.0	5.5	5.1
Śląskie	4.9	5.0	4.9	5.0	4.1	4.2	4.1	4.2
Świętokrzyskie	5.7	5.8	5.7	5.9	5.3	5.4	5.3	5.4
Warmińsko-Mazurskie	5.0	5.0	5.0	5.0	5.8	5.8	5.8	5.8
Wielkopolskie	4.8	4.4	4.8	4.5	4.6	4.3	4.6	4.3
Zachodniopomorskie	4.4	4.4	4.4	4.4	4.8	4.7	4.8	4.8
Group of voivodeships								
Central Poland	5.2	5.1	5.2	5.1	5.3	5.1	5.3	5.2
Western Poland	5.0	4.9	5.0	4.9	5.1	4.9	5.1	5.0
Eastern Poland	5.1	5.1	5.1	5.1	5.5	5.6	5.5	5.6

Source: Our own estimates.

Voivodeship (with the very robust Tri-City agglomeration of Gdańsk, Gdynia and Sopot) will be found in this group of voivodeships results from the fact that in this scenario, investment rates in all voivodeships will be at 20.3%, that is, 2 percentage points lower than the investment rate that was recorded in the Pomorskie Voivodeship in 2004–2015.

- In this scenario, those voivodeships located quite close to Warsaw should develop the fastest in 2016–2050, that is, the Łódzkie (5.7% average annual average), Świętokrzyskie (5.7%), Kujawsko-Pomorskie (5.4%) and Opolskie (5.6%) voivodeships. The lowest average annual growth rates of labor productivity should be found in the Mazowieckie (4.5%), Zachodniopomorskie (4.4%) and Podlaskie (4.3%) voivodeships.
- This scenario should also lead to a convergence of labor productivity, as the coefficient of the variability of labor productivity should decrease from 0.229 in 2015 to 0.200 in 2050.
- In Scenario I, labor productivity in the central Poland Voivodeship group should increase from 73.8% of labor productivity in the Mazowieckie Voivodeship in 2015 to 93.5% in 2050, in the voivodeships of western Poland from 85.5% to 99.8%, and in eastern Poland from 53.5% to 64.3%.

- In scenario II (the same investment rates, different rate of decrement of capital-labor ratio), the quartile group with the highest labor productivity in 2050 should be composed of the following voivodeships: the Opolskie and Dolnośląskie in western Poland as well as the Łódzkie and Śląskie in central Poland. In contrast, the quartile group with the lowest labor productivity in 2050 coincides with the one obtained in scenario I (Map 8.13 in the annex).
- In the scenario considered here, the highest growth rate of labor productivity should be recorded in the Łódzkie (5.9%), Opolskie (5.9%) and Świętokrzyskie (5.8%) voivodeships, and the lowest in the Podlaskie (4.3%), Pomorskie (4.1%) and Mazowieckie (4.0%) voivodeships.
- This scenario will also lead to a convergence of labor productivity, as the coefficient of variation of this variable should fall to 0.204.
- In 2050, the level of labor productivity in the group of voivodeships from western Poland should be 12.9% higher than in the Mazowieckie Voivodeship, and 5.2% higher in central Poland, and 13.5% lower in eastern Poland than in the Mazowieckie Voivodeship. In this scenario, in the group of western Poland voivodeships, the level of labor productivity should be higher than in the Mazowieckie Voivodeship from around 2025, while in central Poland from approximately 2045 (see Figure 8.2 in the Annex).
- In scenario III, which differs from scenario I only by the assumption concerning the growth rate of the German economy (in scenario I a 1.5% yearly average, in scenario III 1.7%), the spatial diversity of labor productivity in 2050 should be very similar to that which was obtained in scenario I (see Map 8.14 in the annex). Labor productivity in voivodeships of central Poland should increase to 93.5% of the value of this variable in the Mazowieckie Voivodeship, in western Poland to 99.9% and in eastern Poland to 64.4%. The coefficients of variation of this variable, similar to variant I, should drop to 0.200.
- In scenario IV, which differs from scenario II only by assuming the growth rate of the German economy, performance simulations were obtained that were very similar to those obtained in scenario II (Map 8.15 in the annex).
- In scenario V, in which it is assumed that the investment rates will be different between voivodeships, the rates of capital deprecation – the same in all voivodeships – and the German economy will develop as on average in 2004–2015; these simulations indicate that the highest level labor productivity in Poland in 2050 should be recorded in the following voivodeships: Łódzkie (almost 750,000 PLN), Lubuskie and Dolnośląskie (about 710,000 PLN) and Mazowieckie (almost 700,000 PLN). At the same time, the lowest level of this macroeconomic variable should be characterized by three voivodeships of eastern Poland: the Podlaskie (approx. 500,000 PLN), Świętokrzyskie (approx. 440,000 PLN) and Lubelskie (just below 350,000 PLN, see Map 8.16 in the annex).

- In this variant the Łódzkie Voivodeship should develop the fastest (the average annual labor productivity growth rate should be 6.3%), followed by the Lubuskie (5.9%) and Warmińsko-Mazurskie (5.8%) voivodeships. The lowest rates of growth in labor productivity should be recorded in the Wielkopolskie (4.6%), Mazowieckie (4.6%) and Śląskie (4.1%) voivodeships.
- Labor productivity in the voivodeships of central Poland should increase to 92.5% of the value of this variable in the Mazowieckie Voivodeship, in western Poland to 100.3% and in eastern Poland to 73.0%. In this scenario, there would also be a stronger convergence than in scenarios I–IV, as the coefficient of this variation would drop to 0.180.
- In scenario VI (varied investment rates and the varied rate of decrement of capital-labor ratio), as in scenario V, the highest value of labor productivity in 2050 should be in the Łódzkie Voivodeship (about 760,000 PLN) and three voivodeships in western Poland: Lubuskie (around 690,000 PLN), Dolnośląskie (690,000 PLN) and Opolskie (around 630,000 PLN). At the same time, the lowest level of this macroeconomic variable should be characterized by three voivodeships of eastern Poland: the Podlaskie (approx. 500,000 PLN), Świętokrzyskie (approx. 460,000 PLN) and Lubelskie (just below 350,000 PLN see Map 8.17 in the annex).
- Under these conditions, the highest rates of growth in labor productivity, as in scenario V, should be found in the following voivodeships: Łódzkie (6.3%), Lubuskie (5.8%) and Warmińsko-Mazurskie (5.8%). At the same time, the lowest growth rates of this macroeconomic variable should occur in the following voivodeships: the Mazowieckie (4.1%), Śląskie (4.2%) and Wielkopolskie (4.3%).
- In the VI scenario, the GDP for people working in the group of western Polish voivodeships should be higher than in the Mazowieckie Voivodeship starting from around 2025, while in central Poland from 2045. In 2050, the labor productivity in western Poland should be higher than the value of this variable in the Mazowieckie Voivodeship by 13.4%, in central Poland by 4.4%, while in eastern Poland by 13.1%.
- In this scenario, a more rapid convergence should occur than in scenario V (the coefficient of the variation in labor productivity should fall to 0.167).
- Scenarios VII and VIII differ from (respectively) scenarios V and VI only by their assumption about the growth rate of the German economy. Therefore, these scenarios lead to simulations of the spatial differentiation of production per employee analogous to that which occurs in scenarios V and VI.

8.5.2 Ukraine

Map 8.11 presents the spatial differentiation of labor productivity in the oblasts of Ukraine in 2017.

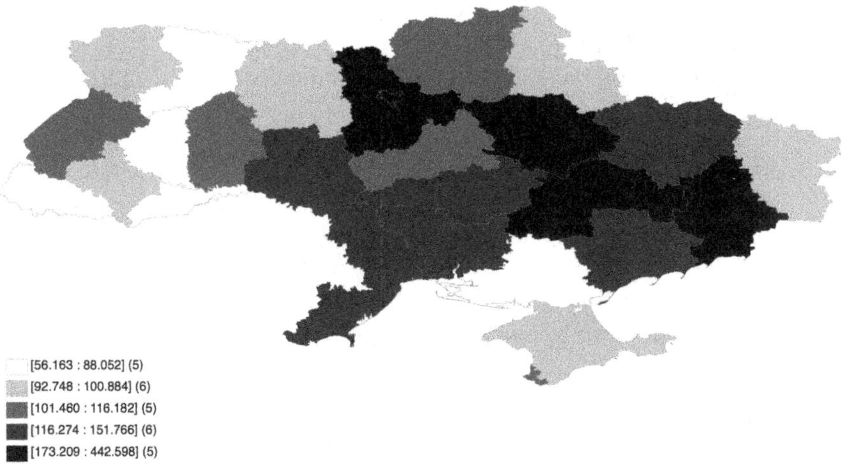

Map 8.11 Diversification of labor productivity in oblasts in 2017 (thousand UAH, according to 2016 prices).

In the case of the ARC and Sevastopol in 2004–2013.

Source: Our own estimates based on: http://www.ukrstat.gov.ua/ (access: 2019-12-30).

We can reach the following conclusions from this map: In 2017, the highest level of labor productivity was recorded in the City of Kyiv (442,600 UAH). Next in order were the Poltava Oblast (193,700 UAH) in central Ukraine, the Kyiv Oblast (182,600 UAH) in northern Ukraine, and the Dnipropetrovsk (181,200 UAH) in central Ukraine and the Donetsk (173,200 UAH) Oblast in eastern Ukraine. The quartile group with the lowest value of this feature was composed of the Chernivtsi (56,200 UAH), Zakarpattia (64,900 UAH), Ternopil (80,700 UAH) and Rivne (86,200 UAH) oblasts in the west of Ukraine and the Kherson (88,100 UAH) Oblast in the south of the country. Thus, as in the case of many other macroeconomic variables, labor productivity in the Left-bank Ukraine and on the Black Sea, that is, the Odesa and Mykolayiv oblasts in 2017, was (generally) much higher than in the Right-bank Ukraine (including – in particular – the western Ukrainian oblasts).

Simulations of trajectories of labor productivity in the oblasts of Ukraine in 2018–2050 were carried out using the following eight scenarios:[7]

- I Investment rates in all oblasts will be equal to the average investment rate in Ukraine in the years 2004–2017 (19%), the Russian and Polish economies will develop as in the years 2004–2017 (i.e., at an annual rate of 2.4% in Russia and 3.9% in Poland), the Autonomous Republic of Crimea and Sevastopol would remain under Russian occupation.
- II Investment rates in individual oblasts are at the same level as they were in 2004–2017, other assumptions as in scenario I.

III Investment rates in all regions are 19%, the Russian and Polish economies are developing as in scenarios I–II, the Crimean Peninsula is returned to Ukraine.

IV Investment rates vary in subsequent circuits, other assumptions as in scenario III.

V The same investment rates in all regions, the Russian economy is growing at an average annual rate of 1%, Poland 3.3%, the Autonomous Republic of Crimea and Sevastopol remain under Russian occupation.

VI Different investment rates in subsequent circuits, other assumptions as in scenario V.

VII The same investment rates in all oblasts, the Russian and Polish economies are developing as in scenario VI, the Crimean Peninsula is returned to Ukraine.

VIII Different investment rates in subsequent regions, the Russian and Polish economies are developing as in the assumptions V–VII, the Autonomous Republic of Crimea and Sevastopol are returned to Ukraine.

Table 8.5 presents data on the level of labor productivity in 2017 both in individual oblasts and groups of oblasts as well as the results of numerical simulations of this macroeconomic variable in 2050 in subsequent, previously characterized scenarios. Table 8.6, however, presents the average levels of the average annual growth rates of labor productivity in various simulations in oblasts and groups of oblasts.

Tables 8.5 and 8.6 draw the following conclusions:

- In scenario I, the highest level of labor productivity in 2050 should be in the Sumy Oblast (about 400,000 UAH), Kyiv (over 370,000 UAH) and the Chernihiv Oblast (over 310,000 UAH) in the north of Ukraine, the Kharkiv Oblast (around 360,000 UAH) in the east and the Poltava Oblast (around 350,000 UAH) in central Ukraine. The lowest value of this feature should be found in the west of the country, in the Zakarpattia Oblast (about 120,000 UAH), and the Chernivtsi (almost 160,000 UAH), Ivano-Frankivsk (over 160,000 UAH) and Lviv (over 170,000 UAH) oblasts, and in the Odesa Oblast, located on the Black Sea (almost 180,000 UAH, see also Map 8.20 in the annex).
- In this scenario, the highest, exceeding 3%, average annual growth rates should be found in the Sumy Oblast (northern Ukraine, 4.3%), and the Chernihiv (northern Ukraine, 3.5%), Kharkiv (eastern Ukraine, 3.3%) and Chernivtsi (western Ukraine, 3.2%) oblasts. In Kyiv, the average annual growth rates should be negative (−0.5%), while in the Odesa (southern Ukraine), Donetsk (eastern Ukraine) and Lviv (western Ukraine) oblasts, they should not exceed 1.5%. The negative projected growth rates in Kyiv result from the fact that scenario I assumes a 19% investment rate in all oblasts, while in Kyiv in 2004–2017 this rate was 23.8%.

Table 8.5 Labor productivity in 2017 and simulations of labor productivity in 2050

Oblast	*Labor productivity in 2017 (thousand UAH according to 2016 prices)*	*Labor productivity in the year 2050 (thousand UAH, according to 2016 prices) in scenario*							
		I	*II*	*III*	*IV*	*V*	*VI*	*VI*	*VIII*
Autonomous Republic of Crimea	92.5[a]	–	–	155.4	384.9	–	–	116.3	283.9
Kharkiv Oblast	123.9	361.7	262.7	359.8	264.7	267.0	195.0	265.7	196.5
Kherson Oblast	88.1	181.4	122.9	184.3	126.4	134.5	91.8	136.7	94.3
Khmelnytskiy Oblast	103.2	197.3	193.4	192.6	191.2	146.5	143.7	143.1	142.1
Cherkasy	112.3	273.6	233.9	270.5	234.2	202.1	173.3	199.8	173.5
Chernihiv Oblast	101.5	313.0	167.9	307.5	167.1	231.1	125.3	227.1	124.7
Chernivtsi Oblast	56.2	157.1	179.3	153.7	177.6	116.6	132.9	114.1	131.7
Dnipropetrovsk Oblast	181.2	295.7	203.2	295.9	205.8	220.0	152.3	220.2	154.2
Donetsk Oblast	173.2	261.1	154.2	262,1	156.5	195.7	117.0	196.5	118.7
Ivano-Frankivsk Oblast	97.8	163.4	175.4	159,5	173.5	121.6	130.5	118.8	129.0
Kyiv Oblast	182.6	293.7	708.2	288,4	704.5	219.3	522.0	215.5	519.2
Kyiv	442.6	376.1	543.3	369,4	540.3	283.1	406.3	278.2	404.0
Kirovohrad Oblast	116.3	254.1	214.1	252,8	215.8	188.3	159.3	187.4	160.4
Lviv Oblast	110.9	172.9	206.6	168,8	204.3	128.8	153.5	125.8	151.8
Luhansk Oblast	92.7	243.5	189.1	243,9	191.7	182.2	142.3	182.5	144.2
Mykolayiv Oblast	116.4	200.8	194.4	202,3	198.3	149.3	144.7	150.4	147.6
Odesa Oblast	129.4	176.6	196.5	177,3	199.8	131.7	146.4	132.2	148.8
Poltava Oblast	193.7	350.3	288.4	348,1	290.2	259.8	214.7	258.2	216.0
Rivne Oblast	86.2	198.2	162.1	193,0	160.0	146.9	120.6	143.1	119.0
Sevastopol	112.3[a]	–	–	152,4	177.3	–	–	114.4	132.7
Sumy Oblast	99.7	402.0	204.8	398.0	205.4	295.6	152,2	292.7	152.6
Ternopil Oblast	80.7	180.1	146.8	175,3	144.9	133.6	109,4	130.1	107.9
Vinnytsya Oblast	117.5	210.9	155.6	206,6	154.4	156.4	116,0	153.2	115.1
Volyn Oblast	100.9	194.5	186.6	189,6	184.2	144.5	138,8	140.9	137.0
Zakarpattia Oblast	64.9	119.7	93.1	117,4	92.6	89.0	69.6	87.4	69.2
Zaporizhzhya Oblast	151.8	247.1	140.0	248.8	142.6	183.5	105.1	184.8	107.0
Zhytomyr Oblast	96.4	225.4	125.6	220.3	124.4	166.7	93.8	163.0	92.9
Coefficient of variation	0.568	0.311	0.606	0.324	0.586	0.310	0.601	0.323	0.581
North Ukraine	249.2	332.9	426.0	326.8	417.8	248.3	316.7	243.8	310.7
Central Ukraine	154.4	281.1	213.7	279.9	215.8	208.6	159.4	207.8	160.9
Eastern Ukraine	139.7	297.2	198.6	281.0	188.6	220.6	148.6	209.3	141.5
South Ukraine	116.6	183.9	179.2	174.9	240.4	136.9	133.5	130.4	178.3
Western Ukraine	91.5	172.3	172.6	168.6	170.7	128.0	128.3	125.3	126.9

Source: Our own estimates.
a – in the year 2013

Table 8.6 Average annual growth rates of labor productivity in 2018–2050 in subsequent scenarios (%)

Oblast	*I*	*II*	*III*	*IV*	*V*	*VI*	*VI*	*VIII*
Autonomous Republic of Crimea	–	–	1.6	4.4	–	–	0.7	3.5
Kharkiv Oblast	3.3	2.3	3.3	2.3	2.4	1.4	2.3	1.4
Kherson Oblast	2.2	1.0	2.3	1.1	1.3	0.1	1.3	0.2
Khmelnytskiy Oblast	2.0	1.9	1.9	1.9	1.1	1.0	1.0	1.0
Cherkasy	2.7	2.2	2.7	2.3	1.8	1.3	1.8	1.3
Chernihiv Oblast	3.5	1.5	3.4	1.5	2.5	0.6	2.5	0.6
Chernivtsi Oblast	3.2	3.6	3.1	3.6	2.2	2.6	2.2	2.6
Dnipropetrovsk Oblast	1.5	0.3	1.5	0.4	0.6	−0.5	0.6	−0.5
Donetsk Oblast	1.3	−0.4	1.3	−0.3	0.4	−1.2	0.4	−1.1
Ivano-Frankivsk Oblast	1.6	1.8	1.5	1.8	0.7	0.9	0.6	0.8
Kyiv Oblast	1.5	4.2	1.4	4.2	0.6	3.2	0.5	3.2
Kyiv	−0.5	0.6	−0.5	0.6	−1.3	−0.3	−1.4	−0.3
Kirovohrad Oblast	2.4	1.9	2.4	1.9	1.5	1.0	1.5	1.0
Lviv Oblast	1.4	1.9	1.3	1.9	0.5	1.0	0.4	1.0
Luhansk Oblast	3.0	2.2	3.0	2.2	2.1	1.3	2.1	1.3
Mykolayiv Oblast	1.7	1.6	1.7	1.6	0.8	0.7	0.8	0.7
Odesa Oblast	0.9	1.3	1.0	1.3	0.1	0.4	0.1	0.4
Poltava Oblast	1.8	1.2	1.8	1.2	0.9	0.3	0.9	0.3
Rivne Oblast	2.6	1.9	2.5	1.9	1.6	1.0	1.5	1.0
Sevastopol	–	–	0.9	1.4	–	–	0.1	0.5
Sumy Oblast	4.3	2.2	4.3	2.2	3.3	1.3	3.3	1.3
Ternopil Oblast	2.5	1.8	2.4	1.8	1.5	0.9	1.5	0.9
Vinnytsya Oblast	1.8	0.9	1.7	0.8	0.9	0.0	0.8	−0.1
Volyn Oblast	2.0	1.9	1.9	1.8	1.1	1.0	1.0	0.9
Zakarpattia Oblast	1.9	1.1	1.8	1.1	1.0	0.2	0.9	0.2
Zaporizhzhya Oblast	1.5	−0.2	1.5	−0.2	0.6	−1.1	0.6	−1.1
Zhytomyr Oblast	2.6	0.8	2.5	0.8	1.7	−0.1	1.6	−0.1
Group of oblasts	*I*	*II*	*III*	*IV*	*V*	*VI*	*VII*	*VIII*
North Ukraine	0.9	1.6	0.8	1.6	0.0	0.7	−0.1	0.7
Central Ukraine	1.8	1.0	1.8	1.0	0.9	0.1	0.9	0.1
Eastern Ukraine	2.3	1.1	2.1	0.9	1.4	0.2	1.2	0.0
South Ukraine	1.4	1.3	1.2	2.2	0.5	0.4	0.3	1.3
Western Ukraine	1.9	1.9	1.9	1.9	1.0	1.0	1.0	1.0

Source: Our own estimates.

- As a result of these changes, the relation of labor productivity in the oblasts of central Ukraine in comparison to northern Ukraine should increase from 62.0% to 84.4%, in eastern Ukraine from 56.1% to 89.3%, in southern Ukraine from 46.8% to 55.2% and in western Ukraine from 36.7% to 51.8%. As the coefficient of variability of labor productivity also drops from 0.568 in 2017 to 0.311 in 2050, (with the same investment rates in all regions) in Ukraine there should be a process of spatial convergence of labor productivity (see also Figure 8.9 in the Annex).
- In the second scenario (varying investment rates in the oblasts, the Crimean peninsula still under Russian occupation), the highest level of

labor productivity in 2050 should be recorded in the Kyiv Oblast (northern Ukraine, over 700,000 UAH), then in the City of Kyiv (over 540,000 UAH), in the Poltava (almost 290,000 UAH) and Cherkasy (over 230,000 UAH) oblasts in central Ukraine and the Kharkiv (around 260,000 UAH) Oblast in the east of Ukraine. The lowest value of this variable should be found in the Zakarpattia (over 90,000 UAH) and Ternopil oblasts (nearly 150,000 UAH) in the west of the country, in the Kherson (around 120,000 UAH) Oblast in the south, and the Zhytomyr (almost 130,000 UAH) Oblast in north and the Zaporizhzhya (about 140,000 UAH) Oblast in the east of Ukraine (see Map 8.21).

- In this variant, the Kyiv Oblast (4.2%) in northern Ukraine and the Chernivtsi (3.6%) Oblast in western Ukraine should definitely have the highest average annual productivity growth rates. In the Donetsk and Zaporizhzhya oblasts (in the east of Ukraine), the average annual labor productivity growth rates may be negative (−0.4% and −0.2%, respectively), while in the Dnipropetrovsk Oblast (central Ukraine), in Kyiv and in the Zhytomyr (northern Ukraine) and Vinnytsya (central Ukraine) oblasts, these growth rates will be lower than 1%.
- In this scenario, labor productivity in central Ukraine should fall to around 50% of this variable in northern Ukraine, in eastern Ukraine to 46.6%, in southern Ukraine to 42.1%, while in the west to 40.5% of the labor productivity in the northern Ukrainian oblasts. Moreover, in this scenario, the oblasts of southern Ukraine should outperform the east and the center of Ukraine in terms of labor productivity between 2030 and 2035.
- As in this scenario the coefficient of the variability of labor productivity will increase from 0.568 to 0.606, scenario II (as opposed to scenario I) will lead to a divergence of labor productivity. This divergence will most strongly affect the most industrialized oblasts of eastern Ukraine, in which investment rates (also in the highly developed heavy and mining industries) were low.
- In scenario III (in which we assume the same investment rates in all oblasts, but we also assume that the Autonomous Republic of Crimea and Sevastopol have been returned to Ukraine), the highest labor productivity in 2050 should be in the Sumy (northern Ukraine approx. 400,000 UAH), Kyiv (almost 370,000 UAH) and Kharkiv oblasts (eastern Ukraine, almost 360,000 UAH), and in the Poltava (central Ukraine, almost 350,000 UAH) and Chernihiv oblasts (northern Ukraine, almost 310,000 UAH). The lowest labor productivity should then be recorded by the Zakarpattia Oblast (less than 120,000 UAH) in the west, Sevastopol and the Autonomous Republic of Crimea in the south, as well as the Chernivtsi and Ivano-Frankivsk oblasts in the west (approx. 150–160,000 UAH, see Map 8.22 in the annex).
- In Scenario III, labor productivity should increase the fastest in the Sumy Oblast (4.3%) in northern Ukraine, then in the Chernihiv oblasts

in the north, then the Kharkiv and Luhansk oblasts in the east and in Chernivtsi Oblast in the west (an average annual increase in labor productivity of approx. 3–3.5%). In Kyiv, as in option I, the growth rate of production per employee may be, at this time, negative (around -0.5%), while in Sevastopol and the Odesa Oblast (southern Ukraine) no more than 1%.

- In scenario III, labor productivity relationships in the oblasts of central, southern, eastern and western Ukraine (compared to the value of this variable in northern Ukraine) would be at levels similar to those obtained in Option I. Also, the coefficient of the variation in labor productivity would fall to 0.324, and therefore there would be a convergence of the spatial differentiation of labor productivity in Ukraine.
- In Scenario IV, we differentiate investment rates of the oblasts, maintaining the assumption that the Crimean Peninsula has been returned to Ukraine. In this scenario, as in scenario II, the Kyiv Oblast in the north of Ukraine (about 700,000 UAH) should have the highest labor productivity in 2050. Next in line should be the City of Kyiv (about 540,000 UAH), the Autonomous Republic of Crimea (about 390,000 UAH) in the south and the Poltava region (about 290,000 UAH) in central Ukraine. The group of regions with the lowest labor productivity (below 150,000 UAH) should be composed of the following oblasts: Zakarpattia and Ternopil in the west of Ukraine, Zhytomyr in the north, Kherson in the south and Zaporizhzhya in the east (see Map 8.23 in the annex).
- In this scenario, the Autonomous Republic of Crimea (4.4%) as well as the Kyiv (northern Ukraine, 4.2%) and Chernivtsi (western Ukraine 4.6%) oblasts should enjoy the highest rates of labor productivity growth.
- As a result of these changes, labor productivity in central Ukraine in 2050 should constitute 51.7% of the value of this variable in northern Ukraine, eastern Ukraine only 45.1%, southern 57.5% and western Ukraine 40.9%. Moreover, in this scenario between 2030 and 2035, the southern oblasts of Ukraine should overtake, in terms of labor productivity, the central and eastern oblasts of this country, while the currently poorest oblasts, that is, those of western Ukraine, will have results approximating the eastern oblasts, which are presently the most developed industrially.
- In the scenario considered here, the coefficient of variation in labor productivity will increase from 0.568 to 0.586, which means that the divergence of this macroeconomic variable will slightly increase.
- Scenarios V–VIII are identical to scenarios I–IV when it comes to the differentiation or non-differentiation of investment rates and further Russian occupation or the return of Crimea to Ukraine. However, they differ in their assumptions about the growth rates of the Russian and Polish economies. We assume here that Russia's economic growth will slow down from 2.4% to 1.1%, while in Poland from 3.9% to 3.3%.

- This modification of the assumption about the slowdown in the economic growth rate of Ukraine's most important neighbors will not affect the simulations of spatial differentiation of labor productivity in this country (compared to the simulations obtained in Scenarios I–IV). However, the economic slowdown in Russia and Poland may lead to the fact that the level of labor productivity in Ukrainian oblasts will be about 25% lower than what could have been achieved, with a more rapid development of the Polish and Russian economies.
- Comparing the results of the simulation of labor productivity in Poland and Ukraine, we note that the Polish regions should develop much faster than the Ukrainian ones. This means that without deep, thorough, market-oriented reforms and further integration of Ukraine (mainly) with the EU countries, development disparities between this country and Poland and other EU countries may be constantly increasing.

8.6 Annex

Simulations of spatial differentiation of labor productivity in 2050 in voivodeships and oblasts and trajectories of simulations of labor productivity up to 2050 in voivodeship and oblast groups.

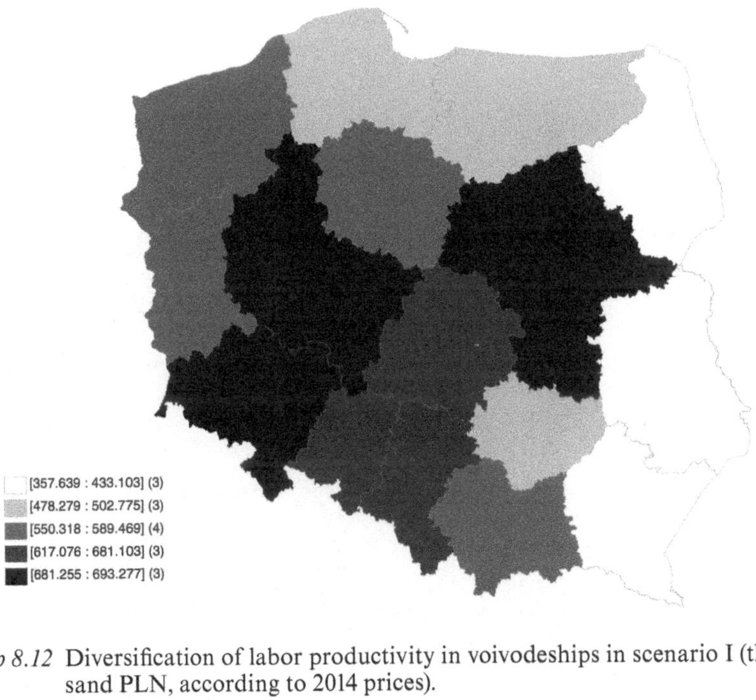

Map 8.12 Diversification of labor productivity in voivodeships in scenario I (thousand PLN, according to 2014 prices).

Source: Our own estimates.

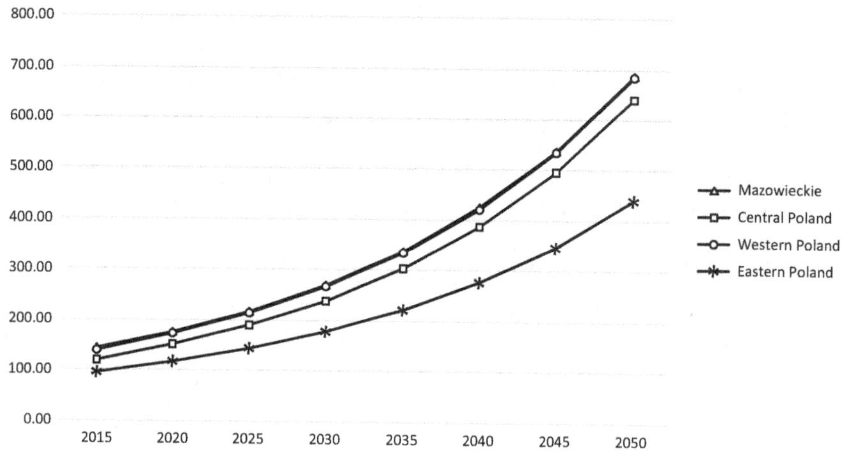

Figure 8.1 Simulation of trajectories of labor productivity in groups of voivodeships in scenario I (thousand PLN, according to 2014 prices).
Source: Our own estimates.

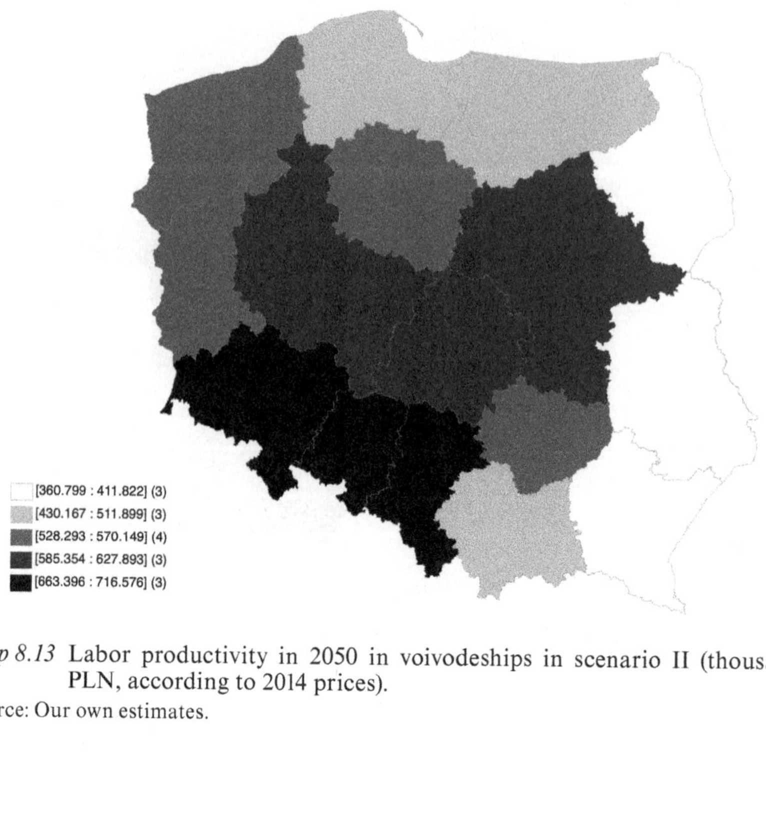

Map 8.13 Labor productivity in 2050 in voivodeships in scenario II (thousand PLN, according to 2014 prices).
Source: Our own estimates.

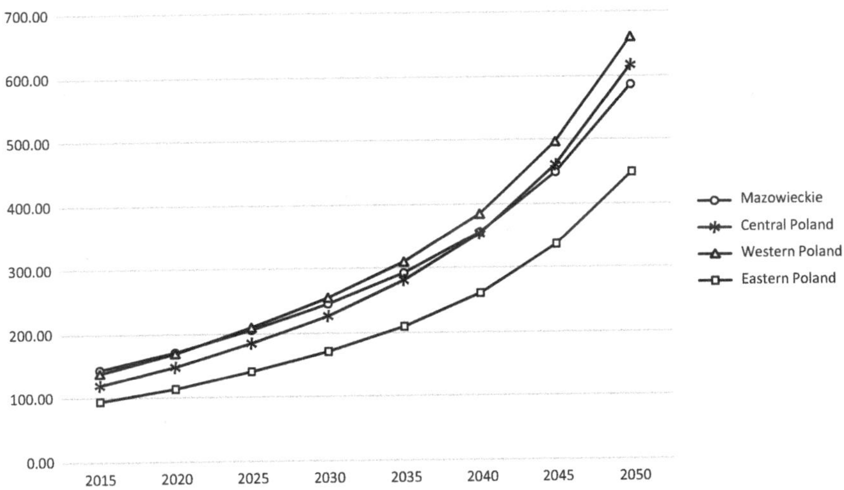

Figure 8.2 Simulation of trajectories of labor productivity in groups of voivodeships in scenario II (thousand PLN, according to 2014 prices).

Source: Our own estimates.

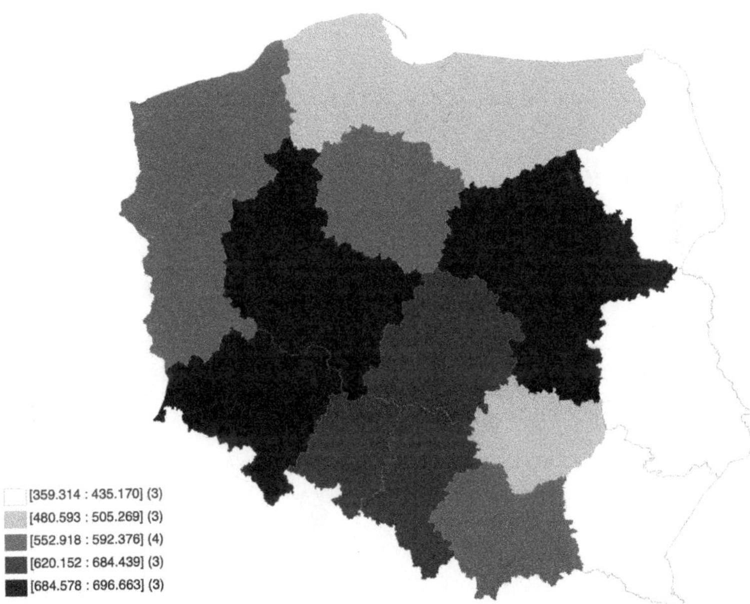

Map 8.14 Labor productivity in 2050 in voivodeships in scenario III (thousand PLN, according to 2014 prices).

Source: Our own estimates.

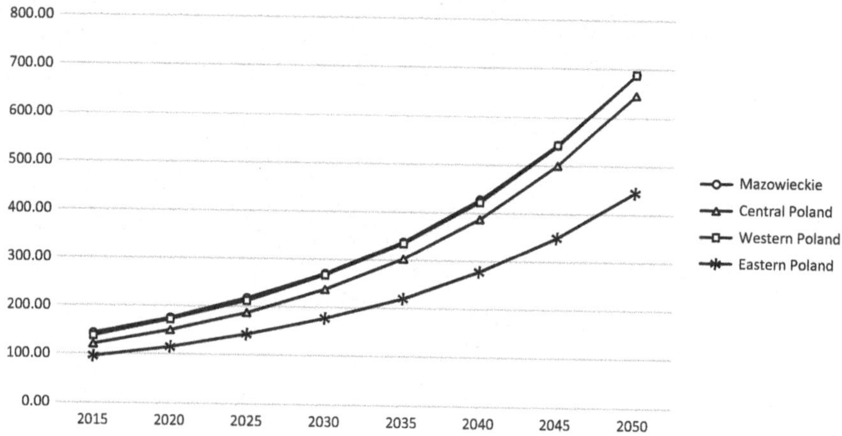

Figure 8.3 Simulation of trajectories of labor productivity in groups of voivodeships in scenario III (thousand PLN, according to 2014 prices).

Source: Our own estimates.

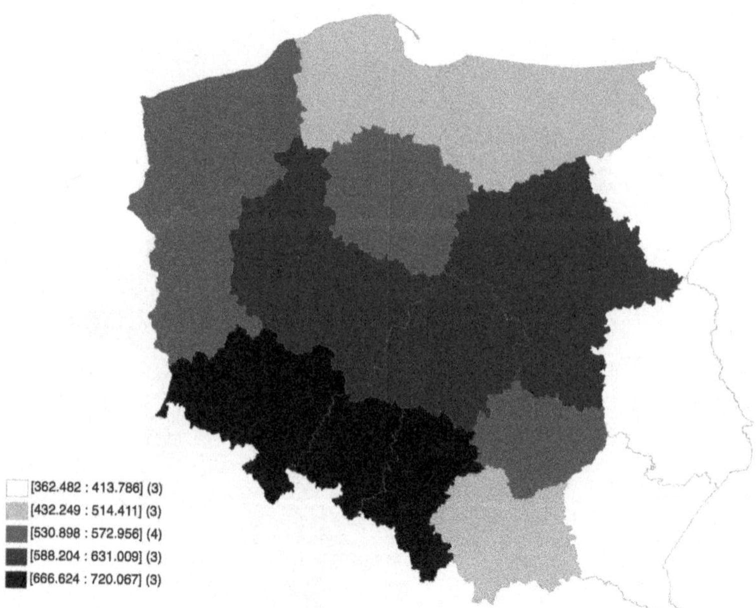

Map 8.15 Labor productivity in 2050 in voivodeships in scenario IV (thousand PLN, according to 2014 prices).

Source: Our own estimates.

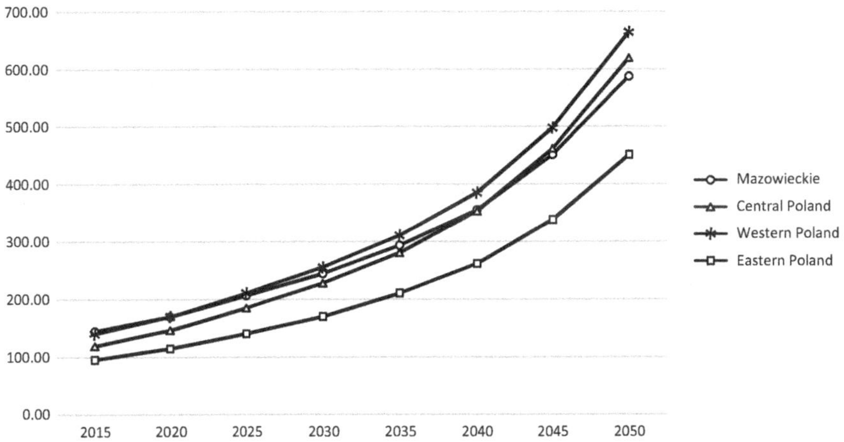

Figure 8.4 Simulation of trajectories of labor productivity in groups of voivodeships in scenario IV (thousand PLN, according to 2014 prices).

Source: Our own estimates.

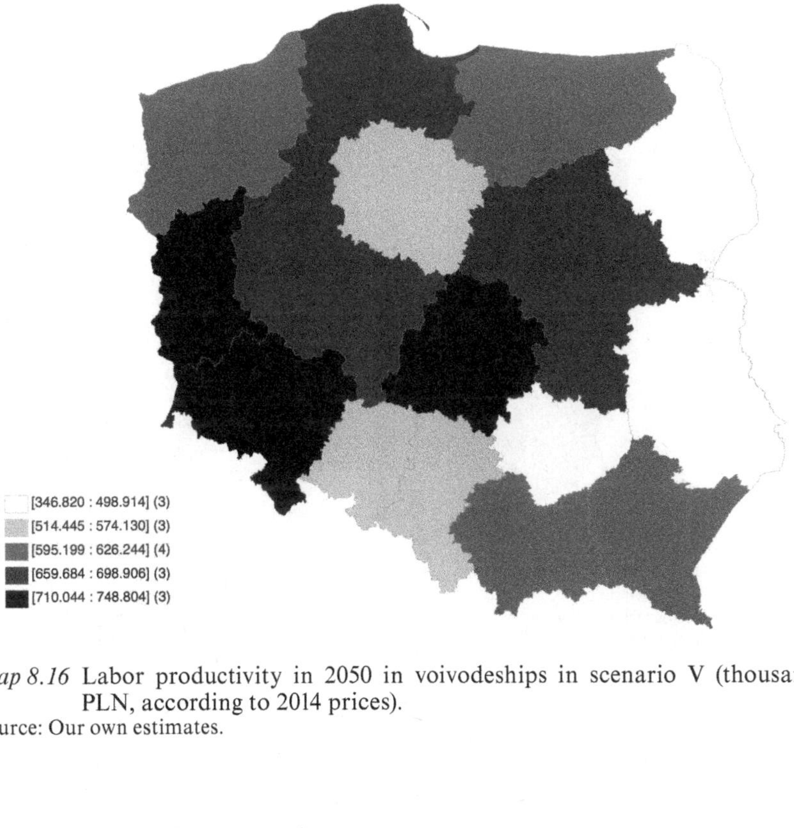

Map 8.16 Labor productivity in 2050 in voivodeships in scenario V (thousand PLN, according to 2014 prices).

Source: Our own estimates.

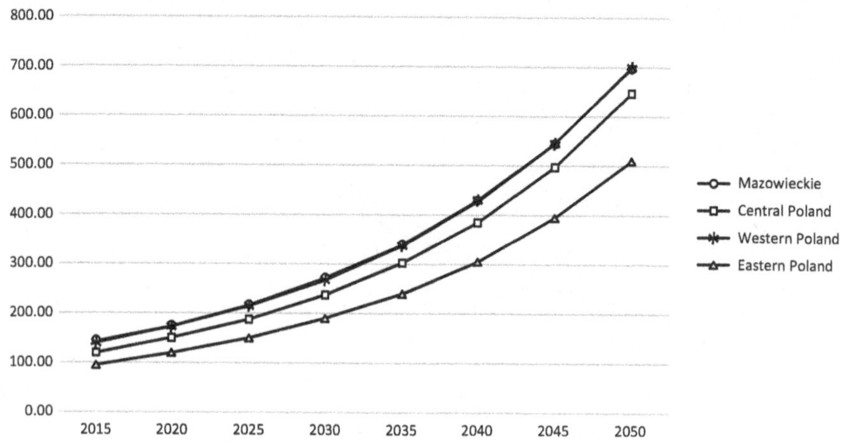

Figure 8.5 Simulation of trajectories of labor productivity in groups of voivodeships in scenario V (thousand PLN, according to 2014 prices).
Source: Our own estimates.

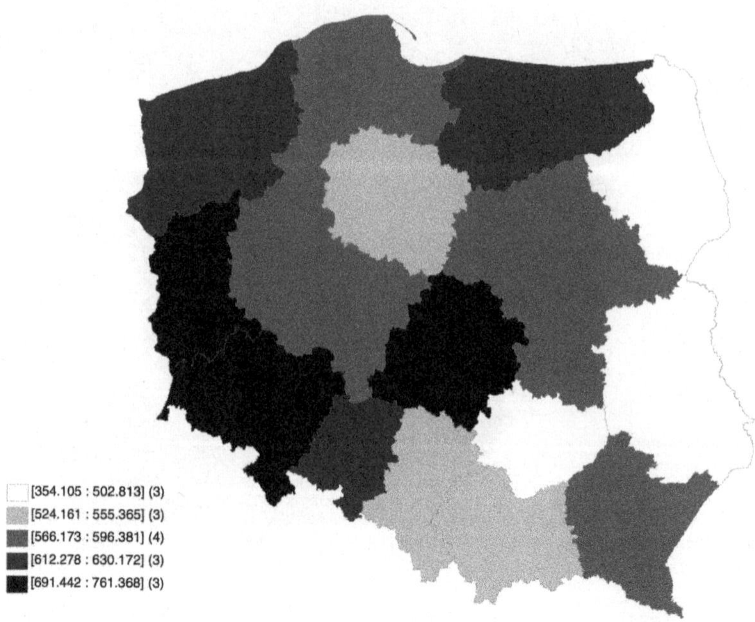

Map 8.17 Labor productivity in 2050 in voivodeships in scenario VI (thousand PLN, according to 2014 prices).
Source: Our own estimates.

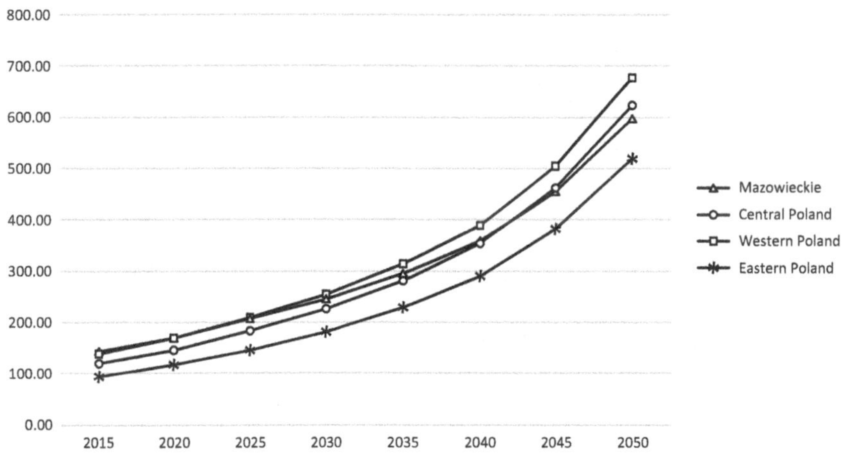

Figure 8.6 Simulation of trajectories of labor productivity in groups of voivodeships in scenario VI (thousand PLN, according to 2014 prices).

Source: Our own estimates.

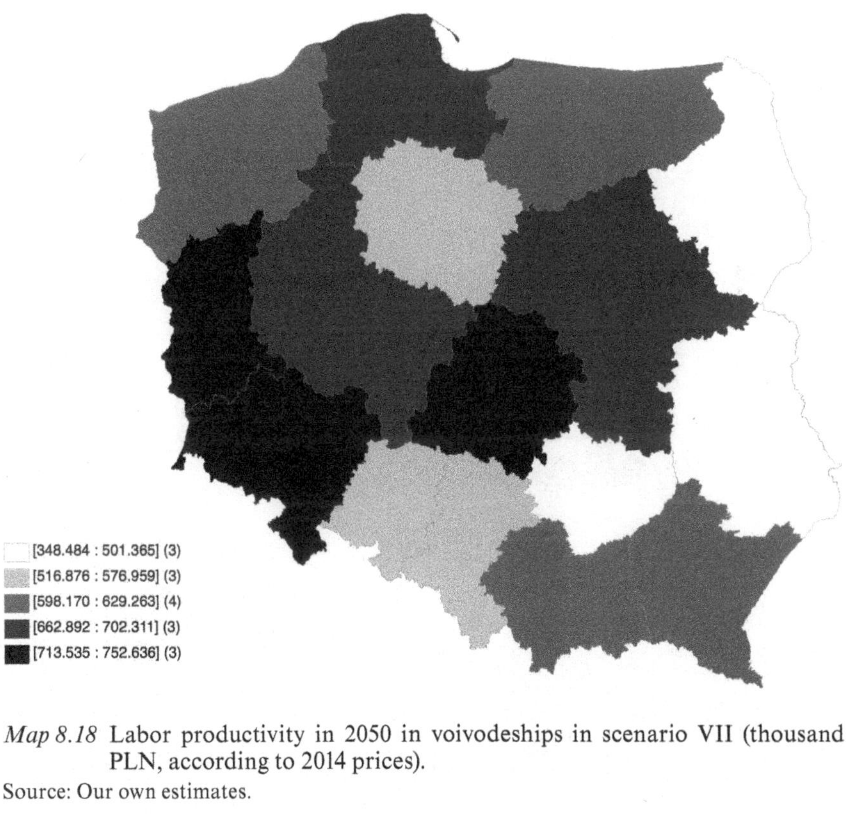

Map 8.18 Labor productivity in 2050 in voivodeships in scenario VII (thousand PLN, according to 2014 prices).

Source: Our own estimates.

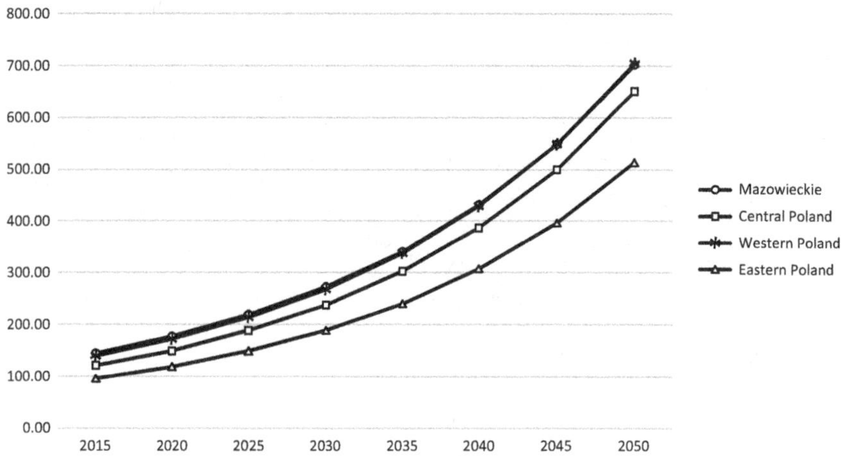

Figure 8.7 Simulation of trajectories of labor productivity in groups of voivodeships in scenario VII (thousand PLN, according to 2014 prices).

Source: Our own estimates.

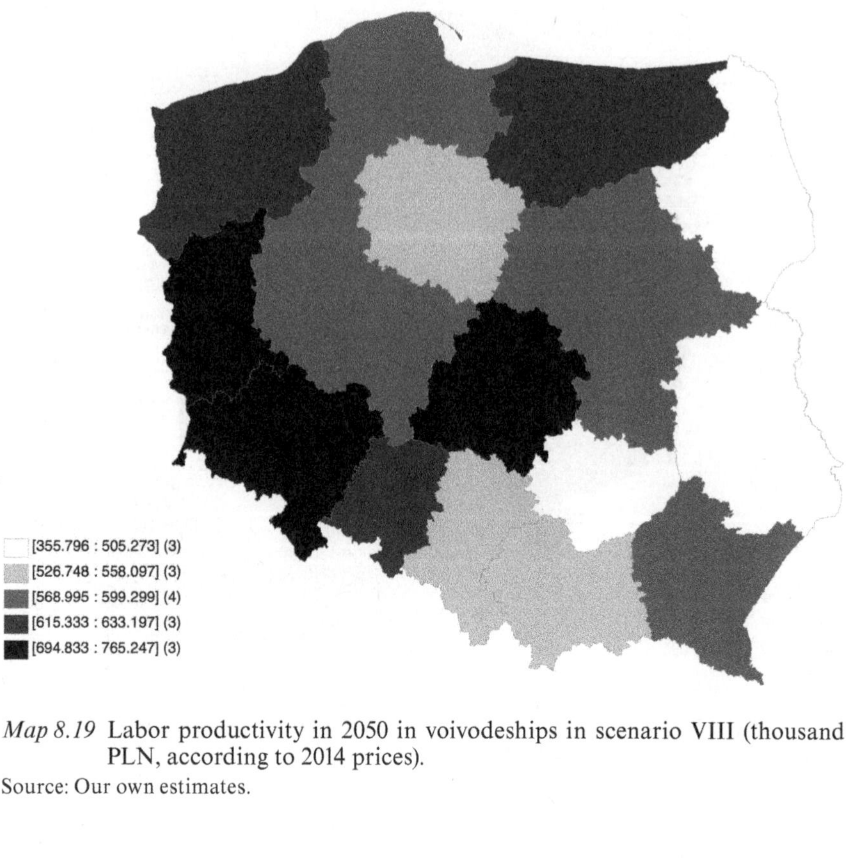

Map 8.19 Labor productivity in 2050 in voivodeships in scenario VIII (thousand PLN, according to 2014 prices).

Source: Our own estimates.

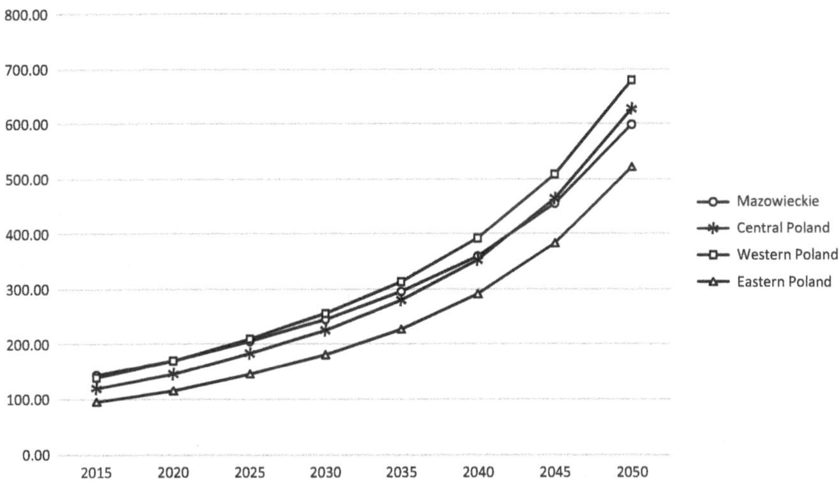

Figure 8.8 Simulation of trajectories of labor productivity in groups of voivodeships in scenario VIII (thousand PLN, according to 2014 prices).

Source: Our own estimates.

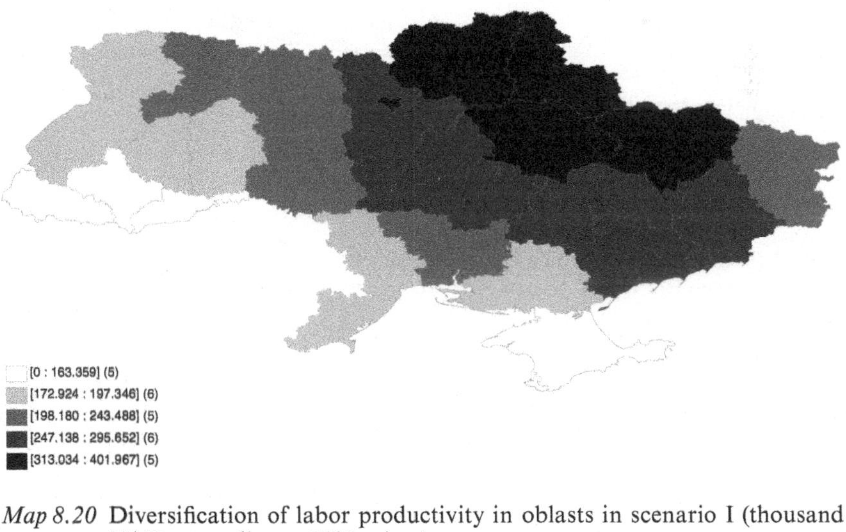

Map 8.20 Diversification of labor productivity in oblasts in scenario I (thousand UAH, according to 2016 prices).

Source: Our own estimates.

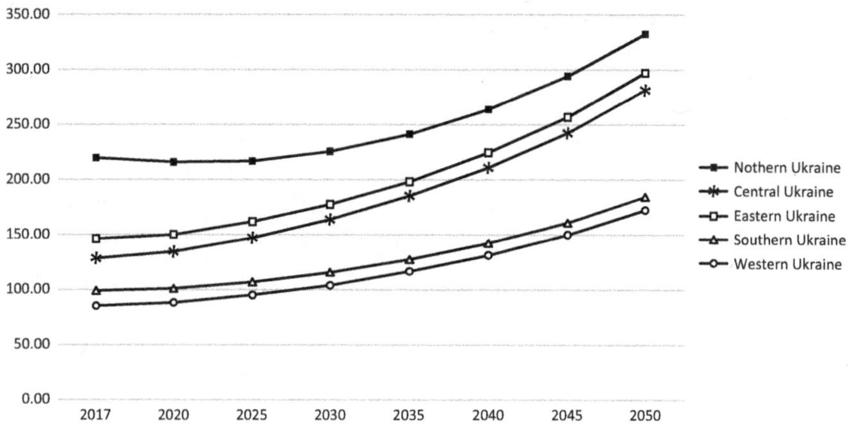

Figure 8.9 Simulation of trajectories of labor productivity in groups of oblasts in scenario I (thousand UAH, according to 2016 prices).

Source: Our own estimates.

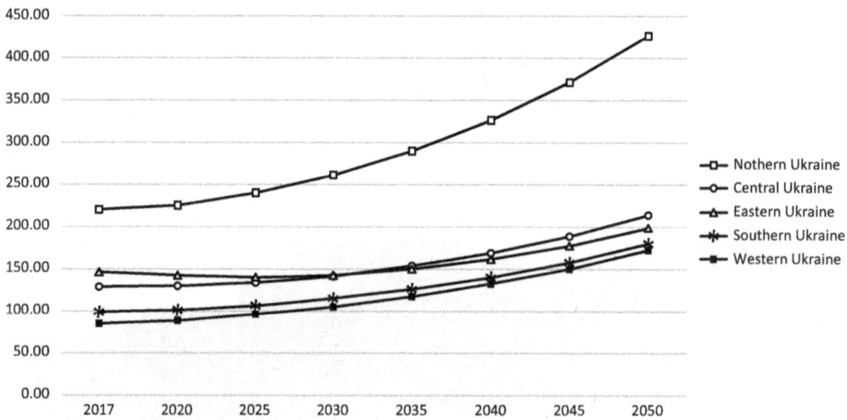

Figure 8.10 Simulation of trajectories of labor productivity in groups of oblasts in scenario II (thousand UAH, according to 2016 prices).

Source: Our own estimates.

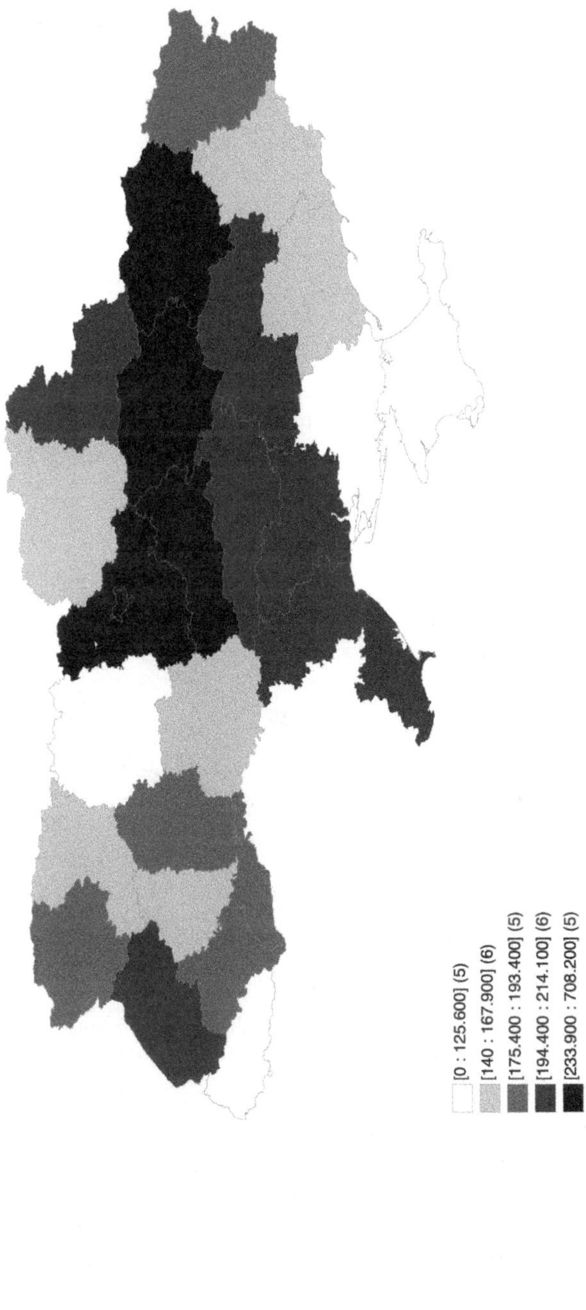

Map 8.21 Diversification of labor productivity in oblasts in scenario II (thousand UAH, according to 2016 prices).

Source: Our own estimates.

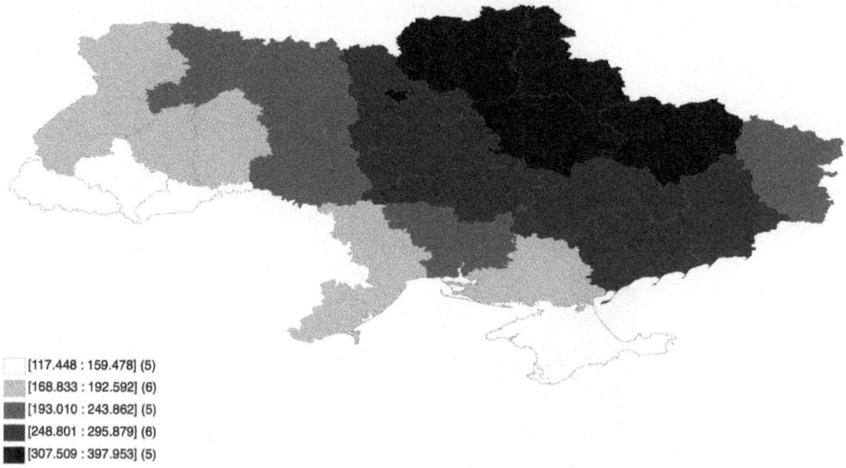

Map 8.22 Diversification of labor productivity in 2050 in oblasts in scenario III (thousand UAH, according to 2016 prices).

Source: Our own estimates.

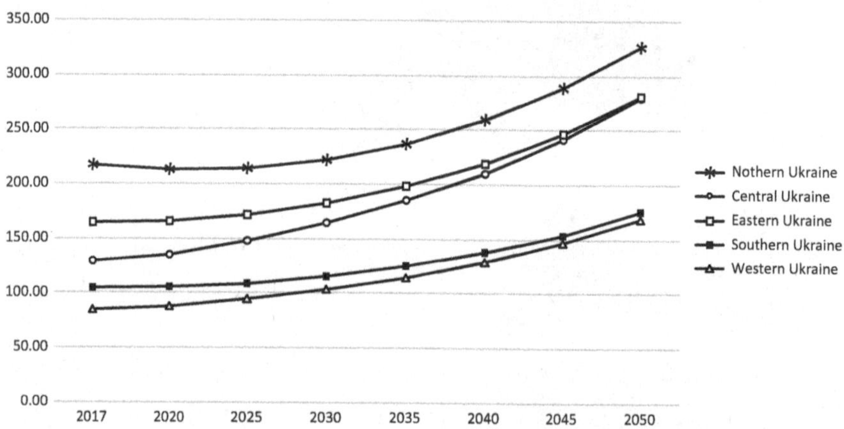

Figure 8.11 Simulation of trajectories of labor productivity in groups of oblasts in scenario III (thousand UAH, according to 2016 prices).

Source: Our own estimates.

Map 8.23 Diversification of labor productivity in 2050 in oblasts in scenario IV (thousand UAH, according to 2016 prices).

Source: Our own estimates.

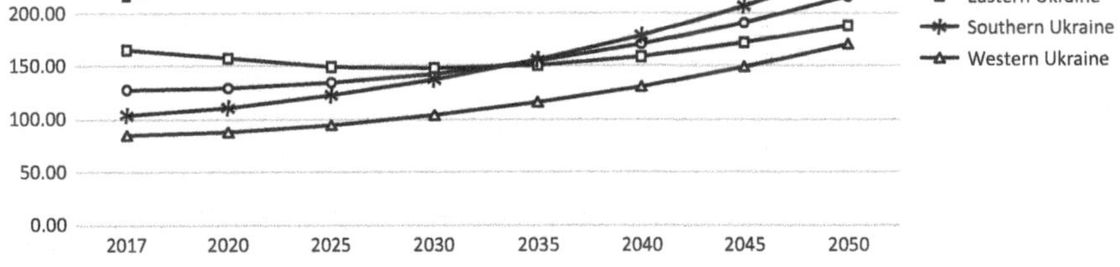

Figure 8.12 Simulation of trajectories of labor productivity in group of oblasts in scenario IV (thousand UAH, according to 2016 prices).

Source: Our own estimates.

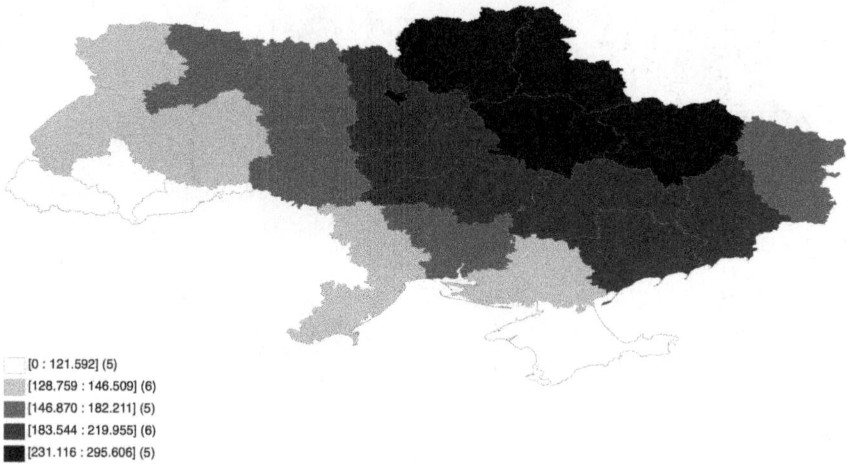

Map 8.24 Labor productivity in 2050 in voivodeships in scenario V (thousand PLN, according to 2016 prices).

Source: Our own estimates.

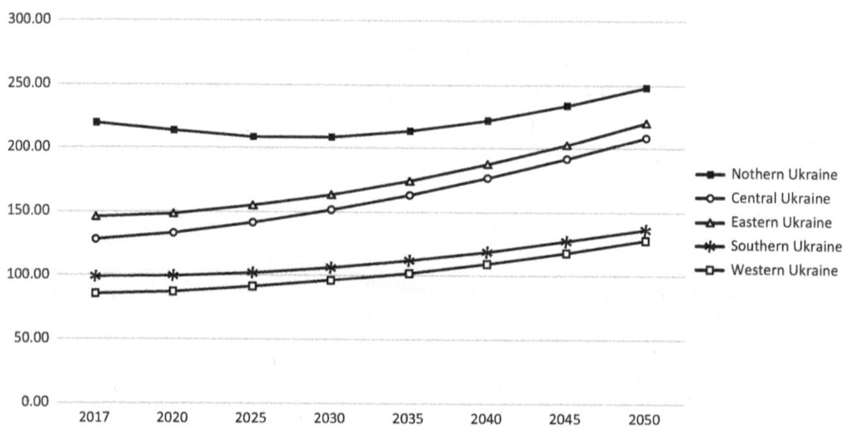

Figure 8.13 Simulation of trajectories of labor productivity in groups of oblasts in scenario V (thousand UAH, according to 2016 prices).

Source: Our own estimates.

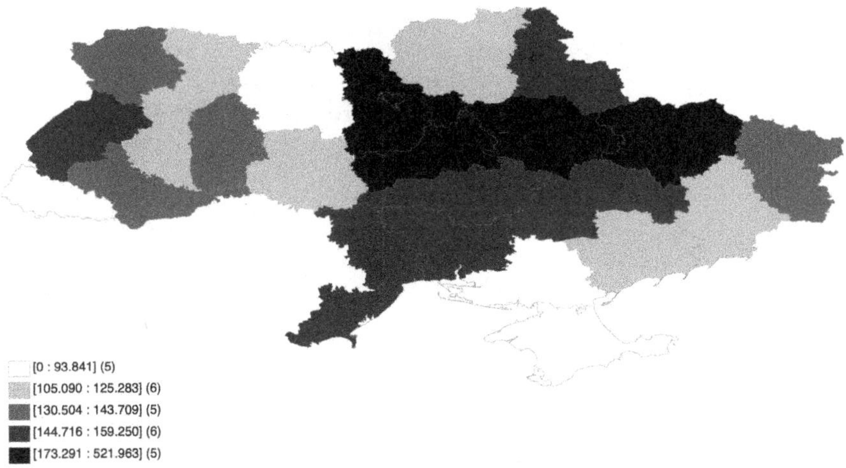

Map 8.25 Labor productivity in 2050 in oblasts in scenario VI (thousand UAH, according to 2016 prices).
Source: Our own estimates.

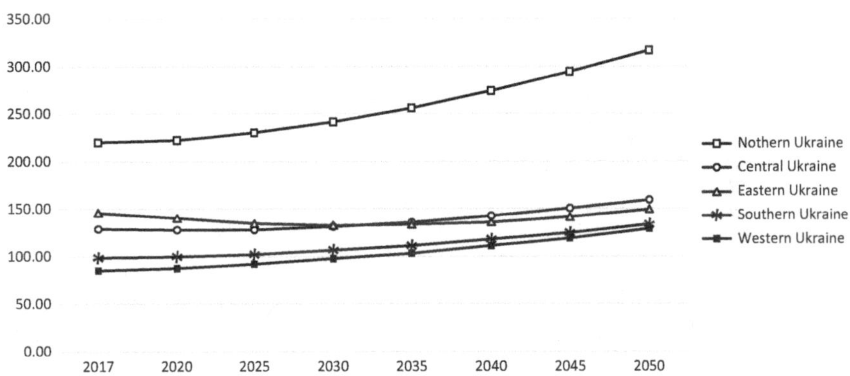

Figure 8.14 Simulation of trajectories of labor productivity in group of oblasts in scenario VI (thousand UAH, according to 2016 prices).
Source: Our own estimates.

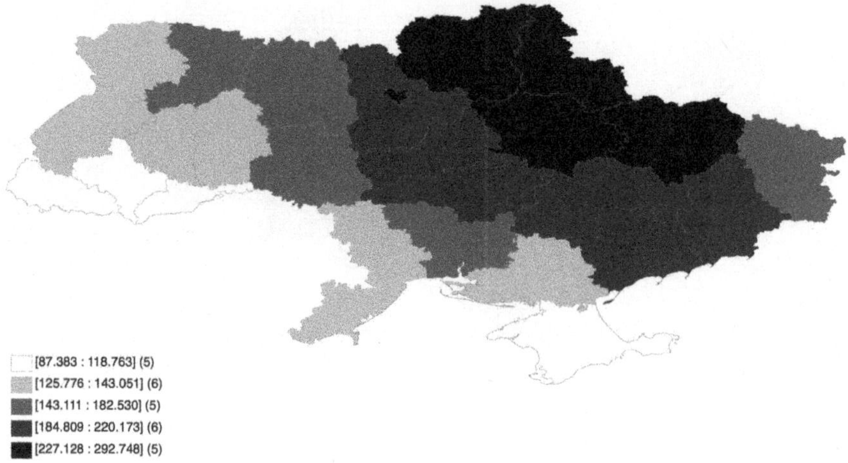

Map 8.26 Labor productivity in 2050 in oblasts in scenario VII (thousand UAH, according to 2016 prices).
Source: Our own estimates.

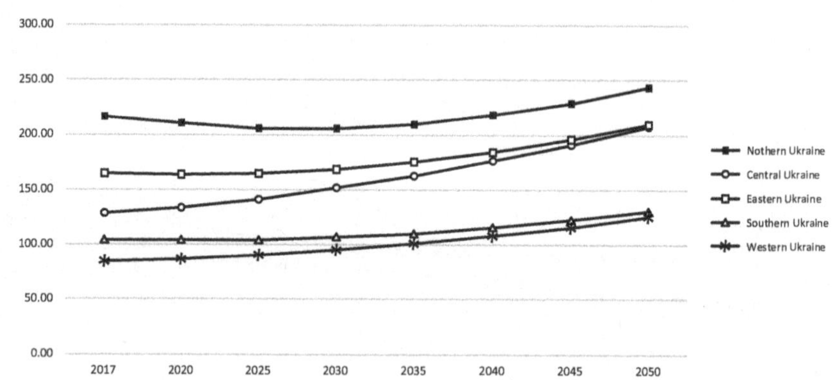

Figure 8.15 Simulation of trajectories of labor productivity in groups of oblasts in scenario VII (thousand PLN, according to 2016 prices).
Source: Our own estimates.

Map 8.27 Labor productivity in 2050 in oblasts in scenario VIII (thousand UAH, according to 2016 prices).

Source: Our own estimates.

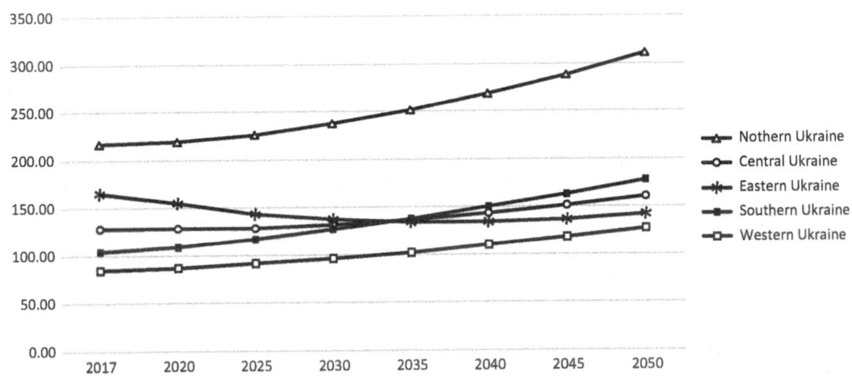

Figure 8.16 Simulation of trajectories of labor productivity in groups of oblasts in scenario VIII (thousand PLN, according to 2016 prices).

Source: Our own estimates.

Notes

1 The notation $\forall i$ will mean $\forall i = 1,2,...,N$, where $N>2$ is the number of regions analyzed. The entries will be read in the same way in $\sum_i$ and $\prod_i$. In addition, about all macroeconomic variables analyzed at this point, we assume that they are functions differentiable with respect to time t, and the record $\dot{x}(t) = dx / dt$ will mean the derivative of the variable x after time t (i.e., economically speaking, the increase in the value of the variable x at time t).

2 This is due to the fact that in the following considerations, labor productivity is expressed in thousand PLN, and the distance between provincial capitals in geographical minutes (mingeo), so the gravitational effects are expressed in million $PLN^2/mingeo^2$. The gravity effects in Ukraine are calculated similarly.

3 The external gravitational effects connecting voivodeships with other countries neighboring Poland were also counted. However, they turned out to be much weaker than those that connect these voivodeships with Germany. That is why they were omitted in the simulation analyzes.

4 When calculating the gravitational effects of the Kyiv oblast, the distance between the largest city of this oblast (Bila Tserkva) and the capitals of the other oblasts was taken into account.

5 Gravity effects from the other Ukrainian neighbors turned out to be much weaker than those from Poland or Russia. That is why they were omitted in simulation analyzes.

6 Simulations of labor productivity trajectories in groups of voivodeships or oblasts and their spatial diversity in 2050 in various scenarios are included in the annex.

7 In all scenarios, it was also assumed that the rate of depreciation of capital-labor ratio would be 14% (as it was historically).

9 The spatial differentiation of migration in Poland and Ukraine

Nataliia Chugaievska and Daniela Szczepaniak

9.1 Introduction

It is difficult to single out one reason that forces people to leave their place of residence and migrate to another country. Everything depends on the specific set of motives of a person who has the desire and right to choose an optimal place of residence and work for himself, and thus meet his material, professional and spiritual needs.

Homoncik et al. (2017) emphasize that foreign migrations are a socio-economic phenomenon that has become permanently engrained in Poland's contemporary history. The Poles' Migration for Work report (2016) indicates that 78.8% of migrants indicate higher earnings as the main reason for emigration. Other important motives are a higher standard of living (58.9%), the opportunity to travel and explore the world (44.0%), better social conditions (37.3%) and better career prospects (35.7%).

In the second decade of the 21st century, Poland became for Ukraine's citizens one of the leading labor markets among all other countries of the European Union. This is favored primarily by liberal procedures for legalizing one's stay, obtaining employment, geographical and cultural proximity, as well as the extremely attractive human potential of Ukraine (Zubik, 2014).

This chapter is part of the problem of migration research in a regional and local perspective. The analyses conducted here relate to the spatial differentiation of the rates of migration inflows and outflows as well as their determinants. Relative wages and relative unemployment rates are considered to be the main determinants of these flows.[1] The chapter estimates the impact of relative wages and relative unemployment rates on migration flows, by using regression methods.

Statistical data on the characteristics (variables) used are taken from the Local Data Bank of the Central Statistical Office and the Ukrainian Statistical Office[2] (Державна Служба Статистики України)[3] and refer to the period of 2004–2017. The choice of this time frame is determined by the availability of relevant time series at the voivodeship or peripheral level.

9.2 Spatial diversity of migration inflows and outflows rates and their determinants in Poland

9.2.1 Inflow rates

Figure 9.1 presents the evolution of annual rates of migration inflows in groups of voivodeships in the years 2004–2017. These rates are defined as the ratio of the size of migration inflows to a given group of voivodeships in relation to the population in this group of voivodeships. Figure 9.1 shows that:

- The highest migration inflow rates in the entire analyzed period were recorded in the Mazowieckie Voivodeship, and were significantly lower in western Poland than in central Poland, and the lowest rates were in eastern Poland.
- At the beginning of this research period (2004–2007), migration inflow rates were characterized by an upward trend. The highest inflow rate was recorded in the Mazowieckie Voivodeship (0.5%), followed by western Poland (0.3%), central Poland (0.25%) and eastern Poland (0.2%).
- In 2008, a sharp decline in migration inflow rates could be observed in all groups of voivodeships. In the Mazowieckie Voivodeship, the rates fell from 0.5% to below 0.4%, in western Poland from 0.32% to about 0.27%, in central Poland from 0.27% to 0.23%, while in eastern Poland from 0.24% to 0.2%. This was due to the fact that European Union countries opened their labor markets to those countries admitted in 2004. Therefore, migration trends have shifted to other countries.
- Since 2009, the rate of migration inflows to the Mazowieckie Voivodeship has oscillated around 0.4%; nevertheless, this voivodeship was characterized by the largest fluctuations of these inflows. In other regions of Poland, inflow rates remained stable.

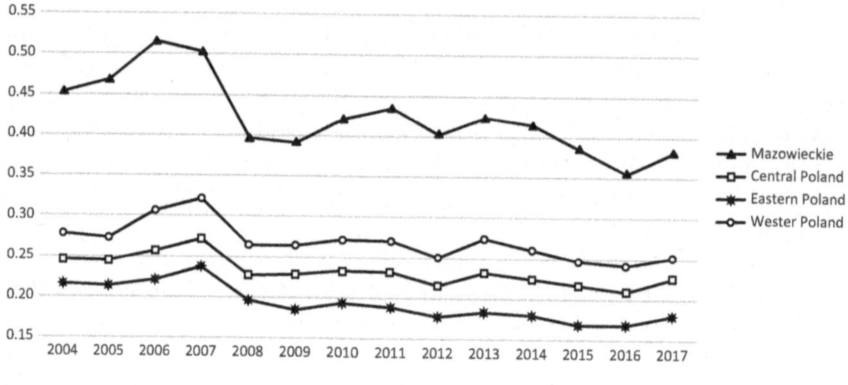

Figure 9.1 Migration inflow rates in voivodship groups in 2004–2017.
Source: Our own estimates based on: https://bdl.stat.gov.pl/BDL/start (access: 2019-12-30).

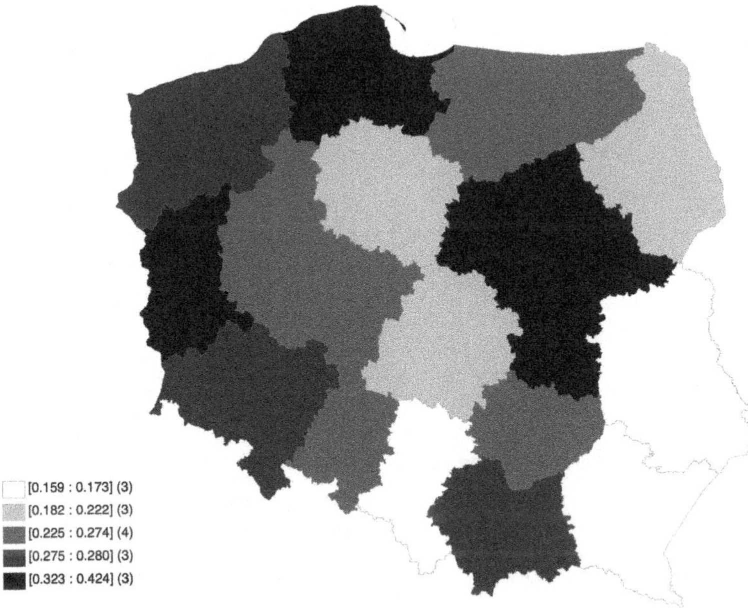

Map 9.1 Spatial differentiation of migration inflow rates in Poland in 2004–2017.
Source: Our own estimates based on: https://bdl.stat.gov.pl/BDL/start (access: 2019-12-30).

Map 9.1 presents the spatial differentiation of migration inflow rates, on average in 2004–2017. The following conclusions can be drawn from this fact:

- These inflows were characterized by the highest rates in the Mazowieckie (0.42%), Pomorskie (0.35%) and Dolnośląskie (0.28%) voivodeships.
- The lowest inflow rates, however, were found in the Lubelskie (0.16%), Podkarpackie (0.16%) and Śląskie (0.17%) voivodeships.
- It is worth noting that in the Śląskie Voivodeship, exceptionally low rates of migration inflows were observed. This phenomenon is quite surprising, as the analyzed region has relatively high relative wages and a low unemployment rate.

9.2.2 Drainage rates

Figure 9.2 presents the evolution of migration outflows in voivodeship groups (these rates are defined analogously to the inflow rates). The following conclusions can be drawn:

- In the entire analyzed period, eastern Poland was characterized by the highest outflow rates, followed by western and central Poland, and the lowest outflow rates were recorded in the Mazowieckie Voivodeship.

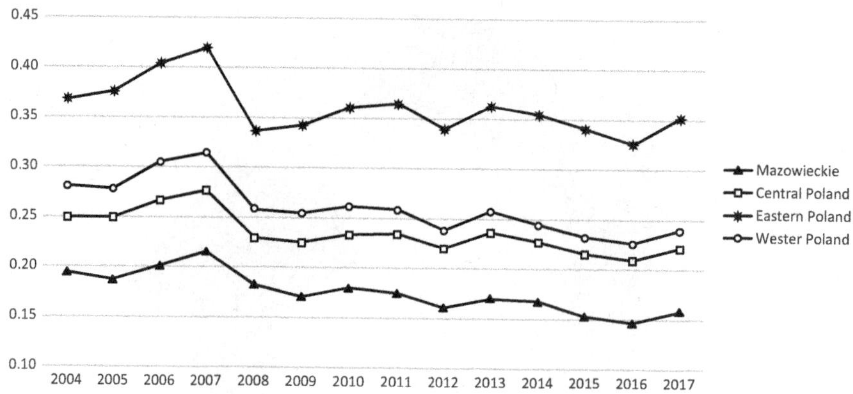

Figure 9.2 Rates of migration outflows in groups of voivodeships in 2004–2017.
Source: Our own estimates based on: https://bdl.stat.gov.pl/BDL/start (access: 2019-12-30).

- At the beginning of the period under review, that is, in the years 2004–2007, an increase in migration outflow rates can be observed in each group of voivodeships. In eastern Poland from approximately 0.37% in 2004, these outflows increased to 0.47% in 2007, in western Poland from 0.33% to 0.37%, in central Poland from 0.3% to 0.33%, while in the Mazowieckie Voivodeship from 0.29% to 0.32%.
- In 2008, a sudden drop in migration outflow rates could be observed to as high as 0.33% in eastern Poland, 0.31% in central Poland, 0.28% in western Poland and 0.28% in the Mazowieckie Voivodeship. Such large changes, as in the case of inflow rates, were influenced by the opening of the EU labor markets to the Poles.
- Fluctuations in outflow rates have not changed so radically since 2009. For each group of voivodeships, slight declines could be observed from 2013 to 2016, followed by another increase in 2017. At the end of the audited period, the outflow rates for eastern Poland were at 0.4%, western Poland 0.28%, central Poland 0.27% and the Mazowieckie Voivodeship 0.21%.

Map 9.2 presents the spatial diversity of migration outflow rates in the voivodeship. On this basis it can be concluded that:

- The Warmińsko-Mazurskie (0.46%) Voivodeship, followed by the Świętokrzyskie (0.41%) and Lubelskie (0.38%) voivodeships, had the highest rates of migration outflows.
- The lowest rates are found in the following voivodeships: Małopolskie (0.17%), Mazowieckie (0.18%) and Wielkopolskie (0.19%).

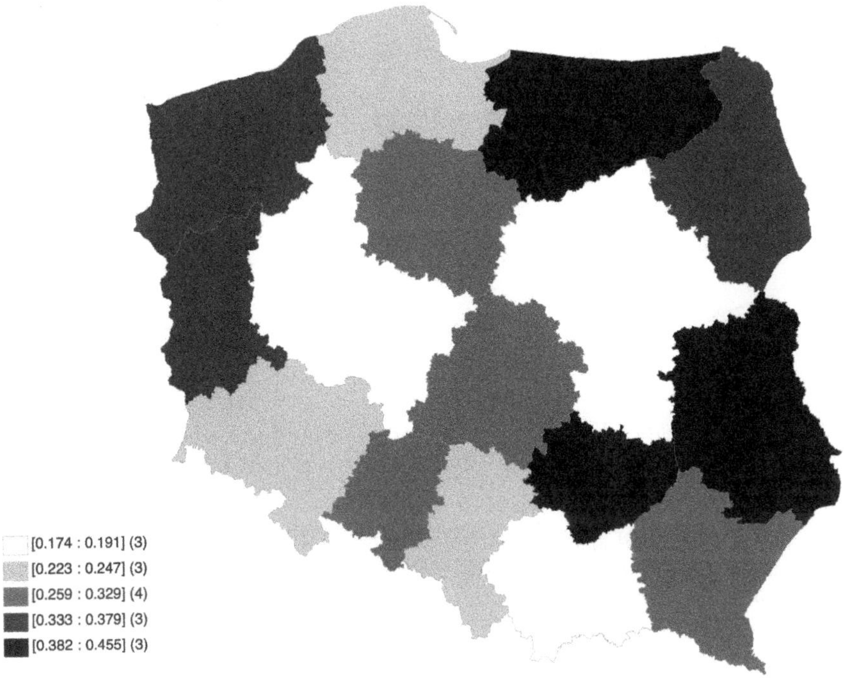

Map 9.2 Spatial differentiation of rates of migration outflows in Poland in 2004–2017.

Source: Our own estimates based on: https://bdl.stat.gov.pl/BDL/start (access: 2019-12-30).

9.2.3 Net inflow rates

Figure 9.3 shows the trajectories of net migration rates (understood as differences between inflow rates and outflow rates) in groups of voivodeships in 2004–2017. From this figure it can be concluded that:

- Over the entire period under review, the highest net migration rates were recorded in the Mazowieckie Voivodeship, while the lowest were in the voivodeships of eastern Poland. Central Poland and western Poland were characterized by similar migration balances, while in the first half of the analyzed period, that is, 2004–2010, central Poland had a higher migration balance, while from 2011 on, western Poland had higher net rates.
- The voivodeships of eastern Poland were characterized by the largest diversification of net migration inflows. In 2006, the migration balance was the lowest and amounted to about −0.9% for this part of the country. In 2008, the largest increase was observed to be around −0.7%.
- In central and western Poland, net inflow rates were not characterized by large fluctuations. Throughout the entire research period, these

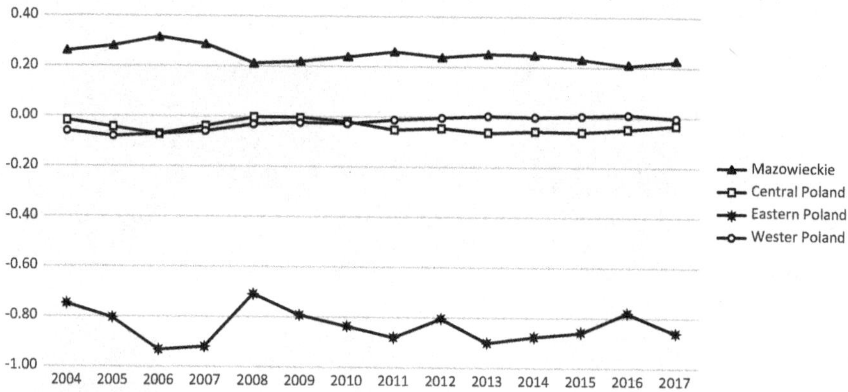

Figure 9.3 Migration balance rates in voivodeship groups in 2004–2017.
Source: Our own estimates based on: https://bdl.stat.gov.pl/BDL/start (access: 2019-12-30).

fluctuations ranged from −0.07% to 0.01%. It can be seen that since 2011, net migration rates for central Poland have stabilized at around −0.05%, and for western Poland at 0%.

- Net inflow rates in the Mazowieckie Voivodeship fluctuated around 0.25% in the whole research period with slight fluctuations. It is worth noting that at the beginning (2004–2007) net migration rates were the highest, while in 2008 there was the largest decrease, and that since then, there have been no major changes.

The spatial differentiation of migration balances was presented on Map 9.3. The following conclusions can be drawn from this map:

- The following voivodeships had the highest net migration rates: Mazowieckie (0.25%), Pomorskie (0.12%) and Małopolskie (0.10%). It is worth noting that the difference between the Mazowieckie Voivodeship and the others is substantial.
- However, the lowest levels of migration balances were found in the Lubelskie (−0.22%), followed by Świętokrzyskie (−0.19%) and Warmińsko-Mazurskie (-0.18%) voivodeships.
- Negative migration balances were also evident in the following voivodeships: Podlaskie (−0.15%), Podkarpackie (−0.10%), Śląskie (−0.07%), Kujawsko-Pomorskie (−0.07%), Łódzkie (−0.07%), Opolskie (0.07%) Lubuskie (−0.06%) and Zachodniopomorskie (−0.06%).
- Apart from the voivodeships mentioned at the beginning, only two voivodeships have positive migration balances, the Wielkopolskie (0.05%) and Dolnośląskie (0.05%), hence the conclusion that the Mazowieckie Voivodeship is dominant and absorbs the population of other voivodeships.

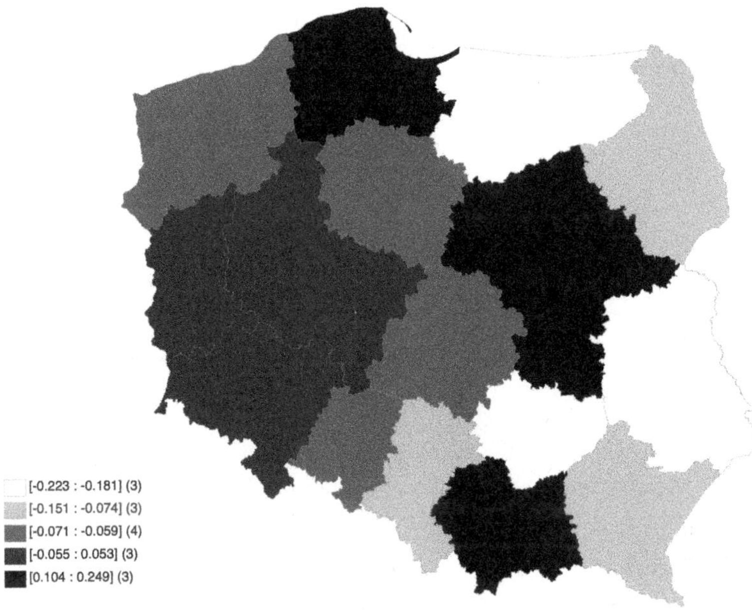

Map 9.3 Spatial diversity of migration balances in Poland.
Source: Our own estimates based on: https://bdl.stat.gov.pl/BDL/start (access: 2019-12-30).

9.2.4 Relative wages

Figure 9.4 presents the relative wages in voivodeship groups. The following conclusions can be drawn from this figure:

- The Mazowieckie Voivodeship was characterized by the highest relative wages throughout the entire research period. It is worth noting that only in this case, did we observe a downward trend in relative wages from around 1.33 in 2004 to approximately 1.25 in 2017. Nevertheless, despite the downward trend in relative wages, the gap between the Mazowieckie Voivodeship and other groups of voivodeships is quite significant.
- Central Poland came in second in terms of wages. During the whole period under review, this part of the country was characterized by a relative wage stability of around 0.98 of the national average.
- Slightly lower levels of relative wages were recorded in western Poland. In the analyzed period this variable oscillated at around 0.95 of the average value. It is worth noting that in 2017 there was a noteworthy alignment between wages in western Poland and wages in the central part of the country.
- Eastern Poland had the lowest relative wages. In this group of voivodeships, wages were around 0.88 of the national average. Similarly, to central and western Poland, this variable, except for slight fluctuations, was constant over time.

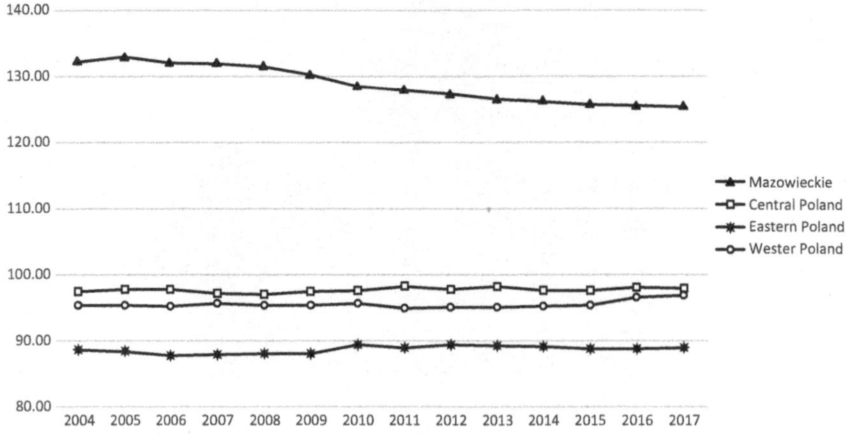

Figure 9.4 Relative wages in voivodeship groups in 2004–2017.
Source: Our own estimates based on: https://bdl.stat.gov.pl/BDL/start (access: 2019-12-30).

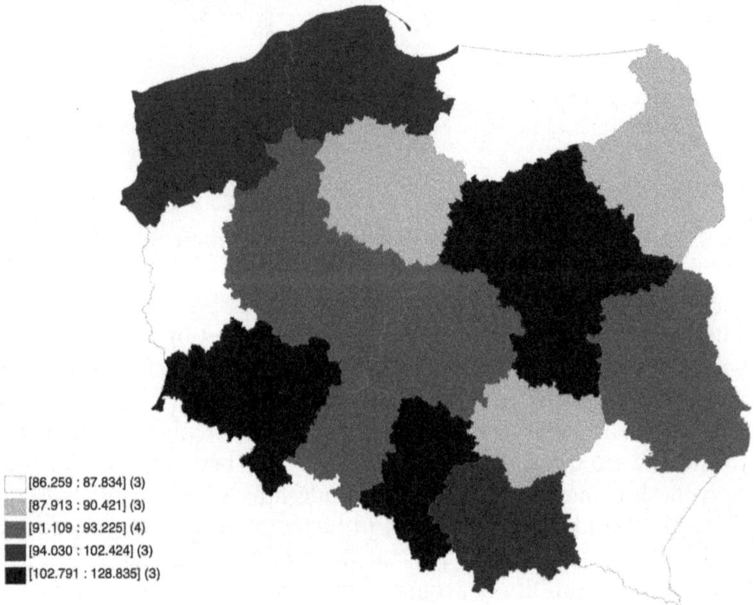

Map 9.4 The spatial differentiation of relative wages in Poland.
Source: Our own estimates based on: https://bdl.stat.gov.pl/BDL/start (access: 2019-12-30).

The spatial differentiation of relative wages is presented on Map 9.4. The following conclusions can be drawn from this map:

- The highest relative wages were recorded in the Mazowieckie (1.29), Śląskie (1.05) and Dolnośląskie (1.03) voivodeships. It is notable that there was a substantial difference – over 20% points – between the Mazowieckie Voivodeship and the remaining ones.

- The lowest wages were recorded in the Podkarpackie (0.86), then in the Warmińsko-Mazurskie (0.86) and finally in the Lubuskie (0.88) voivodeships.
- It is also important that apart from the three voivodeships with the highest relative wages, only the Pomorskie Voivodeship had wages above the national average (1.02). Therefore, it can be concluded that the Mazowieckie Voivodeship surpassed the other voivodeships in terms of wages and significantly increases the national average.

9.2.5 Relative unemployment rates

Figure 9.5 presents the relative unemployment rate in voivodeship groups. The following conclusions can be drawn:

- The relative variation in the unemployment rate was large. At the beginning of the period under review (i.e., 2004–2008), a downward trend in the relative unemployment rate can be seen for western and central Poland and the Mazowieckie Voivodeship. However, in the case of eastern Poland, a clear increase in the analyzed variable can be observed during the same period.
- Since 2009, an increase in the relative unemployment rate can be observed in the Mazowieckie Voivodeship and in central Poland. In the case of western Poland, a downward trend is still observed. In contrast, in eastern Poland there was a decrease in relative unemployment rates until 2013.
- At the end of the period under review, an increase in the relative unemployment rate in eastern Poland can again be observed. In the case of other groups of voivodeships, slight decreases of this variable can be noticed.

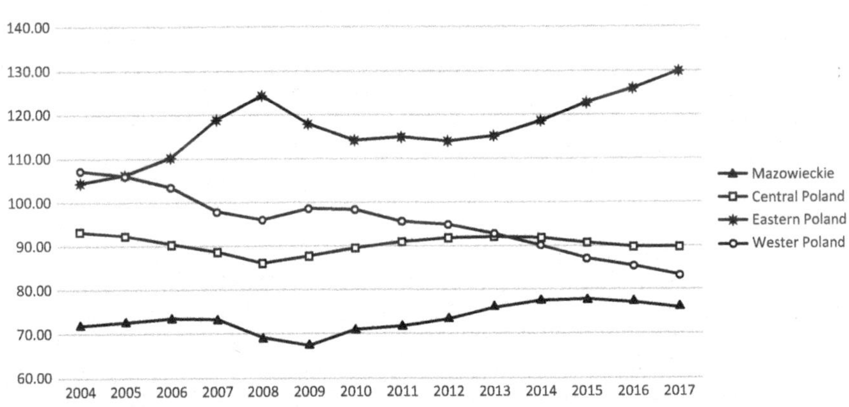

Figure 9.5 Relative unemployment rates in voivodeship groups in 2004–2017.
Source: Our own estimates based on: https://bdl.stat.gov.pl/BDL/start (access: 2019-12-30).

9.3 A spatial differentiation of migration inflow and outflow rates and their determinants in Ukraine

9.3.1 Inflow rates

Figure 9.6 illustrates the rates of inflow in groups of oblasts of Ukraine in 2004–2017. This shows that:

- Strong factors influencing internal migration include the political and social stability in a country. In particular, the observed decline in 2009 was caused by the political crisis and the global financial crisis.
- Very substantial changes in the inflow rates were recorded in 2014–2016, which resulted from the military-political conflict in southern and eastern Ukraine and the occupation of Crimea.
- The group of northern Ukraine oblasts had the highest relative rates of migration inflows, in particular a very high rate was recorded in the Kyiv Oblast (1.82%) and the City of Kyiv (1.69%).
- The substantial decline in 2016 was caused by the underdevelopment in the new law of the procedure for transferring data from the State Migration Service to the State Statistics Service of Ukraine.
- In 2014, a sharp decline in migration inflow rates in eastern Ukraine could be observed.

The reason for this was that the war began in the Luhansk and Donetsk oblasts.

Map 9.5 presents the relative inflow rates in the oblasts of Ukraine. The following conclusions can be drawn:

- The highest inflow rates were recorded in the Kyiv Oblast (1.82%), the City of Kyiv (1.69%), the Sumy Oblast (1.63%), the Poltava Oblast (1.63%) and the Kharkiv Oblast (1.61%).

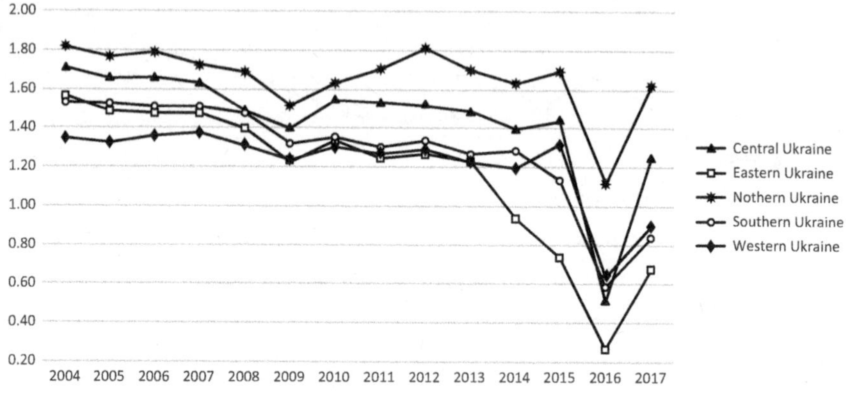

Figure 9.6 Rates of migration inflows in groups of oblasts in 2004–2017.
Source: Our own estimates based on: http://www.ukrstat.gov.ua/ (access: 2019-12-30).

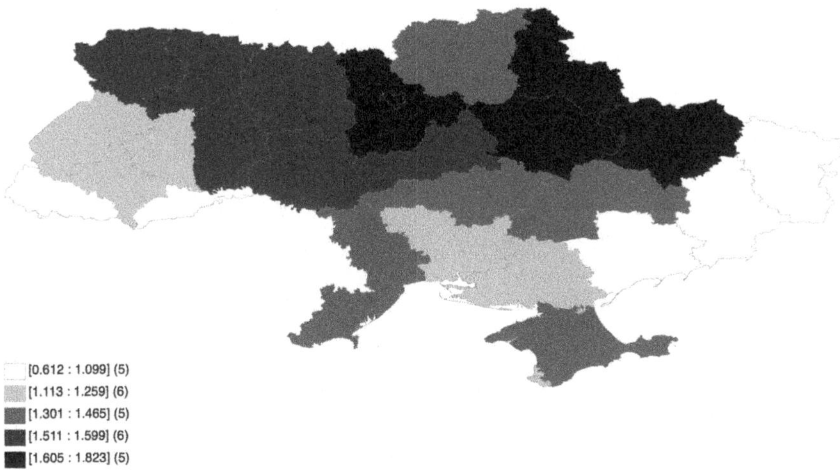

Map 9.5 Spatial differentiation of rates of migration inflows in Ukraine.
Source: Our own estimates based on: http://www.ukrstat.gov.ua/ (access: 2019-12-30).

- The lowest values of the analyzed variable were observed in the Zakarpattia (0.61%), Donetsk (0.97%), Chernivtsi (1.10%), Zaporizhzhya (1.10%) and Luhansk (1.05%) oblasts.
- In interregional migrations, the main beneficiary was the City of Kyiv and the Kyiv Oblast. In 2000, the increase in the capital's population, at the expense of other regions, reached 20,000 people for the year. During the current migration crisis, growth has decreased (from 14.4 thousand people in 2014 to about 12,000 people in 2015), but it still remains the highest in Ukraine. It is worth noting that this data applies only to officially approved migrations, and does not include temporary and forced migrations.[4]
- The observed distribution of migration inflow rates can be explained by the fact that many of the population living in small underdeveloped areas decided to move to oblasts with larger cities, where it is easier to find a job, earn a higher salary and enjoy a better lifestyle.

9.3.2 Outflow rates

The general regularity of the impact of political and social stability on migration processes of the population is reflected in the dynamics of indicators of relative outflow rates in groups of oblasts of Ukraine, which is presented in Figure 9.7.

The following conclusions can be drawn:

- The trajectories of relative rates of migration outflows in groups of oblasts of Ukraine were similar.

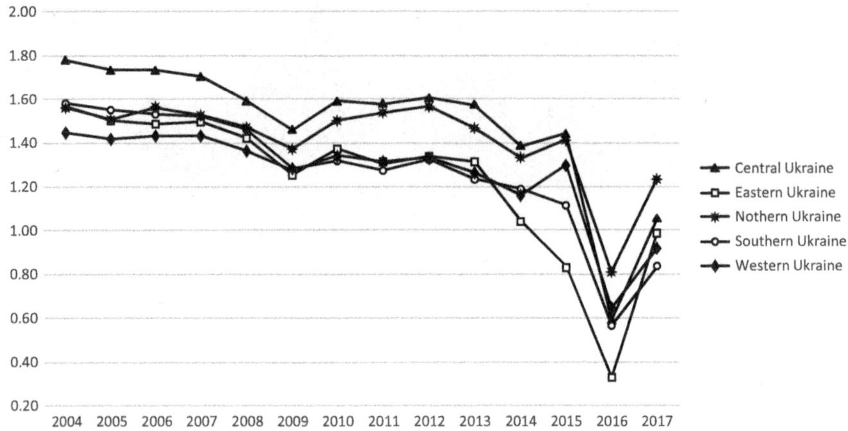

Figure 9.7 Rates of migration outflows in circuit groups in 2004–2017.
Source: Our own estimates based on: http://www.ukrstat.gov.ua/ (access: 2019-12-30).

- In 2004, central Ukraine (1.78%) had the highest relative rates of outflows, while western Ukraine (1.45%) had the lowest. At the beginning of the period under review, a slight downward trend in migration outflows can be observed in all groups of oblasts.
- After slight increases in the years 2010–2013, a significant decrease of the analyzed variable can be detected in all parts of the country, especially in western Ukraine, to a level of 0.65% in 2016. Against the background of the economic and political crisis in Ukraine, starting from 2013, the material situation of those people with medium and low incomes had deteriorated. Many people were forced to look for a job which provided a higher income. For people from western Ukraine, it was more convenient and more profitable to travel abroad (to Europe) than looking for a job in other regions of Ukraine.

The average rates of migration outflows in the oblasts of Ukraine are shown on Map 9.6. This map shows that:

- The highest relative rates of outflows were recorded in the underdeveloped oblasts of Ukraine, that is, the Poltava (1.64%), Vinnytsya (1.65%), Zhytomyr (1.69%), Rivne (1.71%), and Sumy (1.75%) oblasts.
- The lowest rates of this variable were observed in the Zakarpattia (0.69%), Sevastopol (0.83%), Chernivtsi (1.05%), and Donetsk oblasts (1.09%) and the City of Kyiv (1.10%).
- Starting from 2014, strong internal migrations in Ukraine, of a mandatory nature, were caused by the annexation of Crimea and military operations in the Donbas. According to information from the

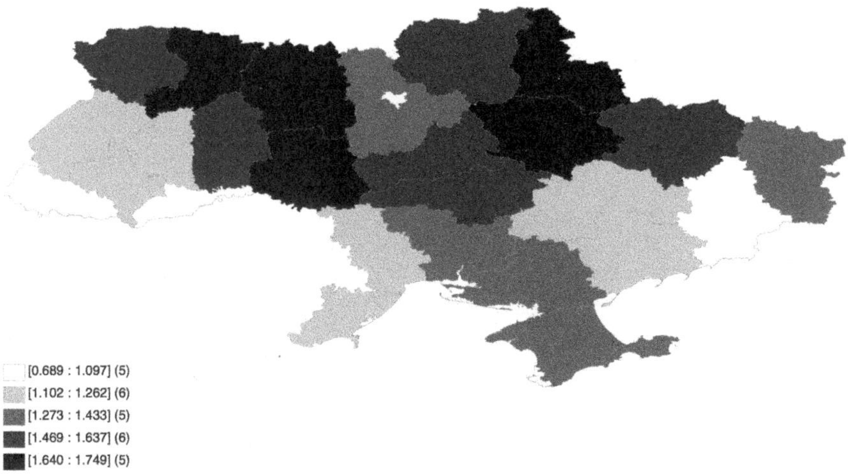

Map 9.6 Spatial differentiation of the rates of migration outflows in Ukraine.
Source: Our own estimates based on: http://www.ukrstat.gov.ua/ (access: 2019-12-30).

Inter-ministerial coordination of the staff for social security of displaced persons (HVE), as of July 20, 2016 from areas outside the Government's sphere of influence, 1,029,571 people were forced to move to other regions of Ukraine, mainly from the Donetsk and Luhansk Oblasts, who numbered 1,007,112 people; from the Autonomous Republic of Crimea and the city of Sevastopol 22,459 people. The grand total included 170,581 children and 495,093 who were either disabled or elderly.[5]

9.3.3 Net inflow rates

Net inflow rates in 2004–2017 are presented in Figure 9.8. The following conclusions can be drawn from this figure:

- Net inflow rates in 2004–2017 were very diverse.
- Northern Ukrainian oblasts have become more attractive to the migrant population. Over 14 years, this indicator for northern Ukraine increased from 0.4% in 2004 to 1.56% in 2017. This situation was affected by the war and political conflict, as many people streamed into the City of Kyiv and to the Kyiv region from eastern Ukraine.
- In northern Ukraine, in the years 2004–2013 a weak upward trend in net migration could be detected. However, since 2014 a strong decrease may be observed, which was due to the fact that the State Statistics Service of Ukraine does not provide data on the Autonomous Republic of Crimea and the city of Sevastopol, and in addition fewer, and fewer

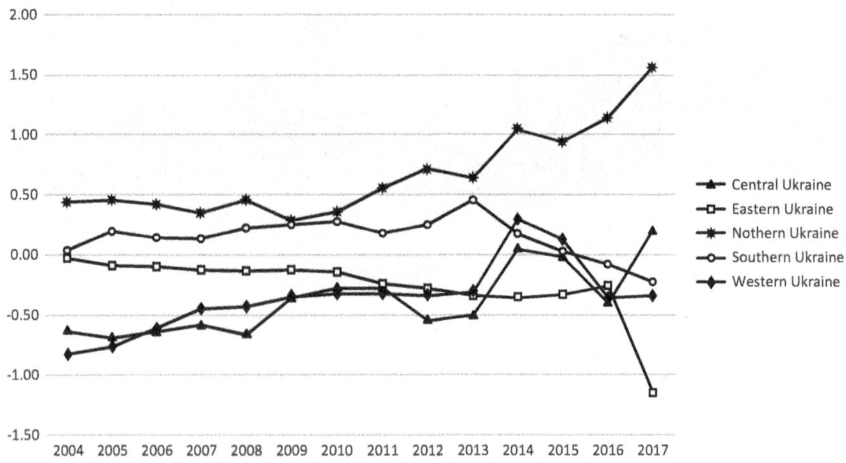

Figure 9.8 Net migration inflow rates in groups of oblasts in 2004–2017.
Source: Our own estimates based on: http://www.ukrstat.gov.ua/ (access: 2019-12-30).

people want to live close to territories where military operations are taking place.

- Net inflow rates in central and western Ukraine were at a similar level. From 2004 to 2014, these parts of the country were characterized by negative migration balances, but an upward trend can be perceived during this period. Then in 2016 it fell below zero again.

Net migration inflows in individual oblasts are presented on Map 9.7. This map shows that:

- The highest net inflow rates were recorded in the City of Kyiv (0.593%) and Sevastopol (0.431%), then in the Kyiv (0.391%), Kharkiv (0.137%) and Odesa (0.085%) oblasts.
- The lowest net inflow rates were recorded in the following oblasts: Kirovohrad (−0.248%), Luhansk (−0.220%), Kherson (−0.190%), Sumy (−0.117%) and Donetsk (−0.115%).
- In the period of 2004–2017, the directions of migration in Ukraine were caused by the hope in people that they could realize their full potential outside their then-current permanent place of residence. For most migrants, the main motive for their trip was the desire to get a (better) job, improve their employment conditions and raise their standard of living. From 2014, migrations were caused by the desire to avoid participation in military activities, which could have posed a threat to life and health, also impediments to, or a lack of, business opportunities.

Map 9.7 Spatial differentiation of the rates of net migration inflows in Ukraine.
Source: Our own estimates based on: http://www.ukrstat.gov.ua/ (access: 2019-12-30).

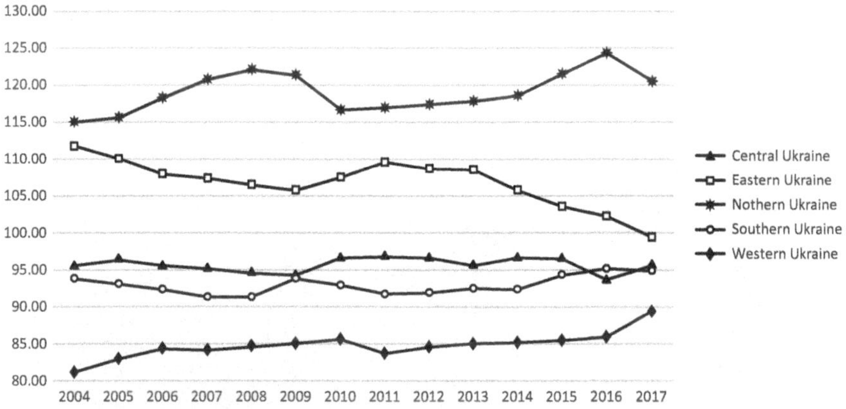

Figure 9.9 Relative wages in oblast groups in 2004–2017.
Source: Our own estimates based on: http://www.ukrstat.gov.ua/ (access: 2019-12-30).

9.3.4 Relative wages

Figure 9.9 illustrates the relative wages in groups of Ukrainian oblasts. The following conclusions can be drawn:

- The highest relative wages were recorded in northern Ukraine – in 2016 they amounted to 1.25 of the average salary in Ukraine, this was mainly due to the relatively high wages in Kyiv.

- Wages above the national average were also characteristic of eastern Ukraine, because this part of the country is largely associated with industry – there are iron and steel mills and hard (anthracite) coal mines.
- In 2004, this analyzed variable remained at a similar level in eastern and northern Ukraine, but within 14 years the disparity between the wages of these parts of the country increased to 1% in eastern Ukraine and to 1.2% in northern Ukraine in 2017.
- Relative wages below the national average were recorded in southern and western Ukraine. These are underdeveloped regions, from which many people leave in order to search for better living conditions.
- In central Ukraine, relative wages fluctuated around zero with slight changes.

Map 9.8 presents the spatial differentiation of relative wages in Ukraine. This map shows that:

- The highest relative wages were recorded in the City of Kyiv (1.67) and the Donetsk (1.19), Dnipropetrovsk (1.09), Kyiv (1.06) and Zaporizhzhya oblasts (1.05).
- The lowest indicators of this variable were recorded in the Volyn (0.79), Chernivtsi (0.80), Chernihiv (0.80), Kherson (0.80) and Ivano-Frankivsk (0.88) oblasts.

Map 9.8 Spatial differentiation of relative wages in Ukraine.
Source: Our own estimates based on: http://www.ukrstat.gov.ua/ (access: 2019-12-30).

9.3.5 Relative unemployment rates

The dynamics of the relative unemployment rate in Ukraine in 2004–2017 are presented in Figure 9.10. The following conclusions can be drawn:

- The dynamics of the relative unemployment rates in Ukraine in 2004–2017 varied widely.
- With the start of the armed conflict with Russia in 2014, in eastern Ukraine, the relative unemployment rate increased sharply to 1.19 in 2017.
- A strong downward trend in the unemployment rate can be observed in western Ukraine. However, these charts may be misleading, because people go abroad and remain registered as unemployed in Ukraine.
- Since 2011, the relative unemployment rate in northern Ukraine has been decreasing, which indicates the creation of new jobs.

At the end of 2017, 354,400 people were registered in the State Employment Service as unemployed citizens. Seven people applied for every job vacancy. However, according to national analysts, the information provided by the State Statistical Service reduces the actual level of unemployment by about five times.[6] The consequence of this is the presence of multidimensional hidden unemployment.

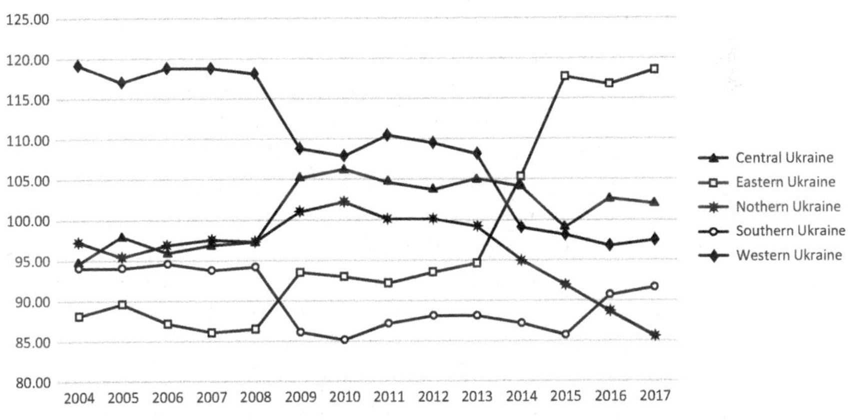

Figure 9.10 Relative unemployment rate in oblast groups in 2004–2017.
Source: Our own estimates based on: http://www.ukrstat.gov.ua/ (access: 2019-12-30).

9.4 A statistical analysis of the impact of relative wages and relative unemployment rates on migration flows

In order to examine the impact of relative wages and relative unemployment rates on migration flows, the parameters of the equations of the linear (9.1) and logistic (9.2) functions were estimated as:

$$m_{it} = \alpha + FE + \alpha_w \frac{w_{it}}{\bar{w}_t} + \alpha_U \frac{u_{it}}{\bar{u}_t}, \tag{9.1}$$

$$m_{it} = \frac{1}{1 + \exp\left(\alpha + FE + \alpha_w \frac{w_{it}}{\bar{w}_t} + \alpha_U \frac{u_{it}}{\bar{u}_t}\right)}, \tag{9.2}$$

where m_{it} is the inflow rate, outflow rate or migration balance in a voivodeship/oblast i and in year t, FE is the individual effects, w_{it} is the wages in a voivodeship/oblast i in year t, $\bar{w}_t$ is the average wage in the country in year t. u_{it} is the unemployment rate in a voivodeship/region i and in year t, and $\bar{u}_t$ is the unemployment rate in the country in the year t.

The parameters of Eqs. (9.1) and (9.2) were estimated by the following estimation methods: ordinary least squares (OLS), OLS with fixed effects in space, OLS with fixed effects in space and time, generalized method of moments (GMM), GMM with fixed effects in space, GMM with individual effects in space and time, a logistic model, a logistic model with individual effects in space, a logistic model with individual effects in space and time.

Estimates of the parameters of Eqs. (9.1) and (9.2) for Poland are presented in Table 9.1. The following conclusions can be drawn:

- In estimations in which the rate of migration inflows is the explained variable, the relative wages in most cases had a statistically significant and positive impact on these inflows. Only in the logistic model with individual effects was this interaction not significant.[7]
- The impact of the relative unemployment rate on the analyzed variable was no longer so unambiguous. In models without individual effects, this impact was positive and statistically significant. Only in the equation of the logistic function with the effects in space and time was the impact of the relative unemployment rate statistically significant and negative. Other models indicated the insignificance of this variable.
- Comparing the absolute values of Student's t statistics with the explanatory variables, it can be noticed that relative wages significantly influenced the rate of migration inflows.
- Comparing corrected coefficients of determination for models without individual effects, it can be seen that the variability of the dependent variable was best explained with the Ordinary least squares (OLS) method in approx. 39.3%, then the Generalized Method of Moments (GMM) 38.6% and the logistics model (logit model) 29.0%.

Table 9.1 Estimates of the parameters of Eqs. (9.1) and (9.2) for Poland

Independent variables	*Estimation method*								
	OLS	*OLS with fixed effects (FE) in space*	*OLS with fixed effects (FE) in space and time*	*GMM*	*GMM with fixed effects (FE) in space*	*GMM with fixed effects (FE) in space and time*	*Logistic model*	*Logistic model with fixed effects (FE) in space*	*Logistic model with fixed effects (FE) in space and time*
Dependent variable: migration inflow rate									
$w_{it}/\overline{w}_t$	0.00532	0.00355	0.00374	0.00537	0.00435	0.00476	1.798	0.43468	0.47606
	(11.816)	(2.374)	(4.498)	(11.185)	(2.233)	(4.540)	(9.480)	(0.7595)	(1.635)
$u_{it}/\overline{u}_t$	0.000886	6.17×10^{-5}	6.49×10^{-5}	0.000870	0.000175	0.000185	0.317	−0.09272	−0.09204
	(4.391)	(0.249)	(0.478)	(4.033)	(0.526)	(1.037)	(3.727)	(−0.9755)	(−1.939)
R^2	0.398	0.886	0.968	0.392	0.885	0.969	0.297	0.890	0.974
adjusted R^2	(0.393)	(0.877)	(0.963)	(0.386)	(0.875)	(0.964)	(0.290)	(0.881)	(0.970)
Number of Observations	224			208			224		
Dependent variable: migration outflow rate									
$w_{it}/\overline{w}_t$	−0.0019	0.00088	0.00104	−0.00177	0.00192	0.00185	−0.778	0.76534	0.83926
	(−4.339)	(0.574)	(1.427)	(−3.804)	(0.942)	(1.988)	(−5.214)	(1.514)	(3.897)
$u_{it}/\overline{u}_t$	0.0023	0.000412	0.000414	0.00240	0.000540	0.000528	0.784	0.18926	0.19046
	(11.679)	(1.617)	(3.494)	(11.444)	(1.557)	(3.372)	(11.73)	(2.254)	(5.425)
R^2	0.580	0.912	0.982	0.582	0.909	0.982	0.603	0.922	0.987
adjusted R^2	(0.576)	(0.904)	(0.979)	(0.578)	(0.900)	(0.979)	(0.600)	(0.915)	(0.985)
Number of Observations	224			208			224		
Dependent variable: migration balance rate									
$w_{it}/\overline{w}_t$	0.00723	0.00267	0.00270	0.00714	0.00267	0.00288	0.00729	0.00269	0.00272
	(12.108)	(2.477)	(2.442)	(11.293)	(1.952)	(2.087)	(12.09)	(2.471)	(2.436)
$u_{it}/\overline{u}_t$	−0.00141	−0.000350	−0.000349	−0.00153	−0.000338	−0.000342	−0.00142	−0.000353	−0.000352
	(−5.268)	(−1.959)	(−1.936)	(−5.401)	(−1.458)	(−1.461)	(−5.271)	(−1.958)	(−1.935)
R^2	0.616	0.979	0.979	0.621	0.980	0.981	0.615	0.979	0.979
Adjusted R^2	(0.612)	(0.977)	(0.976)	(0.617)	(0.978)	(0.978)	(0.612)	(0.977)	(0.976)
Number of observations	224			208			224		

Source: Our own estimates

- In the estimations of Eqs. (9.1) and (9.2), when the dependent variable was the rate of migration outflows, the impact of relative wages on this variable was not unequivocal. In the estimations of models without individual effects, the impact was statistically significant and negative. Only in the case of the GMM model with effects in space and time and the logistic model with effects in space and time was the impact of relative wages positive and statistically significant. Other estimation methods indicated the statistical insignificance of the variable in question.
- The impact of relative unemployment rate on migration outflows in all estimation methods turned out to be statistically positive. Only in the OLS model with effects in space and GMM with effects in space was this variable insignificant. In other cases, the relative rate had a statistically significant effect.
- Comparing the absolute values of Student's *t* statistics for independent variables, it should be stated that it was the relative unemployment rate that had a significant impact on migration outflows.
- Analyzing the corrected coefficients of determination (without individual effects), it can be seen that the variability of the dependent variable is best described by the logistics model (60.0%), then GMM (57.8%) and OLS (57.6%).
- Estimations of Eqs. (9.1) and (9.2), in which the dependent variable was the net migration rate [A2] [A2], relative wages had a positive and statistically significant effect on the net migration rate for each estimation method.
- The impact of the relative unemployment rate was negative and statistically significant in OLS estimations with and without fixed effects, the logistic model (with and without effects) and GMM without fixed effects. Only in the case of GMM models with individual effects did this variable turn out to be statistically insignificant.
- Comparing the absolute values of *t* statistics with independent variables, it should be stated that relative wages were the more significant variable.
- Analyzing the values of the adjusted coefficient of determination, it can be seen that the variability of the dependent variable was best explained by the GMM model at about 61.7%, for the OLS and the logistic model, it was 61.2%.

Estimates of the parameters of Eqs. (9.1) and (9.2) for Ukraine are presented in Table 9.2. For Ukraine, only those equations are analyzed, in which the dependent variable is the rate of migration balances, because in other cases the results were not satisfactory and their interpretation would not make sense. The following conclusions can be drawn from the estimates in Table 9.2:

Table 9.2 Estimates of the parameters of Eqs. (9.1) and (9.2) for Ukraine

Independent variables	*Estimation method*								
	OLS	*OLS with fixed effects (FE) in space*	*OLS with fixed effects (FE) in space and time*	*GMM*	*GMM with fixed effects (FE) in space*	*GMM with fixed effects (FE) in space and time*	*Logistic model*	*Logistic model with fixed effects (FE) in space*	*Logistic model with fixed effects (FE) in space and time*
Dependent variable: migration balance rate									
$w_{it}/\bar{w}_t$	0.00366	0.00504	0.00425	0.00292	0.00259	0.000217	0.00369	0.00510	0.00432
	(6.242)	(2.113)	(1.736)	(4.667)	(0.612)	(0.0497)	(6.234)	(2.130)	(1.754)
$u_{it}/\bar{u}_t$	−0.00523	−0.00358	−0.00346	−0.00593	−0.00461	−0.00470	−0.00527	−0.00361	−0.00349
	(−10.139)	(−5.633)	(−5.398)	(−10.282)	(−5.349)	(−5.409)	(−10.17)	(−5.648)	(−5.414)
R^2	0.462	0.691	0.701	0.445	0.678	0.687	0.462	0.692	0.702
adjusted R^2	(0.459)	(0.666)	(0.664)	(0.442)	(0.649)	(0.646)	(0.459)	(0.667)	(0.665)
Number of observations	370			343			370		

Source: Our own estimates.
In the case of the logistics model, the dependent variable is $1 + m_{it}$; this is because the dependent variable in the logistics function must be positive. The variable m_{it} (for any i and t) does not satisfy this condition, while the variable $1 + m_{it}$ satisfies this condition.

- Relative wages had a positive and statistically significant effect[8] on the examined dependent variable in OLS estimations (with and without effects), the logistic model (with and without effects) and GMM. In GMM estimations with individual effects, this variable turned out to be statistically insignificant.
- The impact of the relative unemployment rate was negative and statistically significant in each estimation method.
- Comparing the absolute values of Student's t statistics, it turned out that relative unemployment was a more significant variable.
- Analyzing the corrected coefficients of determination (in models without individual effects), it can be seen that the variability of the dependent variable was best explained by the OLS and logistics model in about 45.9%, while the GMM model 44.2%.

For Poland, the authors also estimated the parameters of the following equations:

$$\frac{M_{ijt}}{P_{it}} = \alpha + \mathrm{FE} + \alpha_W \frac{w_{jt}}{w_{it}} + \alpha_U \frac{u_{jt}}{u_{it}} + \alpha_D \ln\left(d_{ij}\right), \tag{9.3}$$

$$\frac{M_{ijt}}{P_{it}} = \frac{1}{1+\exp\left(\alpha + \mathrm{FE} + \alpha_W \frac{w_{jt}}{w_{it}} + \alpha_U \frac{u_{jt}}{u_{it}} + \alpha_D \ln\left(d_{ij}\right)\right)}, \tag{9.4}$$

where M_{ijt} is the number of people migrating from and to the voivodeship j in year t, P_{it} is the number of people living in the voivodeship i and in year t, w_{it}, w_{jt} is the wages in voivodeships i and j in year t, u_{it}, u_{jt} is the unemployment rate in a voivodeship i and j in year t, and d_{ij} is the distance (in a straight line) between voivodeships i and j.

The estimation of the parameters of Eqs. (9.3) and (9.4) was made using the following estimation methods: OLS, OLS with effects over time, GMM, GMM with effects over time, logistics model and logistics model with effects over time. Models with individual effects in space were not analyzed, as distances between voivodeship capitals are a linear combination of effects in space. In addition, due to a lack of data, it was impossible to create models for Ukraine.

Estimates of the parameters of Eqs. (9.3) and (9.4) are presented in Table 9.3. The following conclusions can be drawn from these estimates:

- The ratio of wages in the voivodeship j to wages in the voivodeship had a positive and statistically significant effect[9] on migration flows between these voivodeships,
- The relation of the unemployment rate in the voivodeship j to the unemployment rate in the voivodeship j had a negative and statistically significant effect on the dependent variable,
- The distance between the capitals of individual voivodeships had a negative, statistically significant impact on migration flows between those voivodeships,

Table 9.3 Estimates of the parameters of Eqs. (9.3) and (9.4)

Independent variables	*Estimation method*					
	OLS	*OLS with fixed effects (FE) in time*	*GMM*	*GMM with fixed effects (FE) in time*	*Logistic model*	*Logistic model fixed effects (FE) in time*
w_{jt}/w_{it}	0.000934	0.000935	0.000948	0.000948	0.000943	2.66991
	(29.977)	(29.992)	(26.456)	(26.458)	(29.98)	(23.53)
u_{jt}/u_{it}	-2.31×10^{-5}	-2.24×10^{-5}	-1.64×10^{-5}	-1.61×10^{-5}	-2.40×10^{-5}	−0.350844
	(−1.855)	(−1.791)	(−1.117)	(−1.094)	(−1.858)	(−7.719)
$\ln d_{ij}$	−0.000217	−0.000217	−0.000214	−0.00214	−0.000219	−1.00431
	(−28.664)	(−28.671)	(−27.019)	(−27.028)	(−28.67)	(−36.42)
R^2	0.401	0.404	0.395	0.398	0.401	0.436
Adjusted R^2	(0.401)	(0.401)	(0.394)	(0.395)	(0.401)	(0.433)
Number of observations	3,360		3,120		3,360	

Source: Our own estimates.

- When comparing the absolute values of these statistics, it should be stated that the distance between voivodeship capitals and the pay ratio were more significant variables than the unemployment rate ratio.
- Analyzing the corrected coefficient of determination (in models without individual effects) it can be seen that the variability of the dependent variable was best explained by the logistics model and OLS in about 40.1%, while GMM 39.4%.

9.5 Summary

i In Poland, the rate of migration inflows was statistically significantly positive on relative wages, while the impact of the relative unemployment rate was not so clear. Hence, one can conclude that the factor attracting migrants to a given voivodeship was the desire to find a better-paying job.

ii In the case of the migration outflow rate, the relative unemployment rate was a variable that had a positive, statistically significant effect on these outflows, while it is difficult to discern the clear impact of relative wages. This means that the factor determining migration from a given province was the inability to find a job.

iii In the net migration balance, both the relative wages and the relative unemployment rate were statistically significant. In the case of wages, the impact was positive, while unemployment was negative. It is worth noting that wages were a more important variable.

iv In the case of Ukraine, the net migration balance was negatively affected by the relative statistical rate of unemployment. The impact of relative wages was positive, but not always statistically significant, which means that the population decided to migrate because of being unable to find a job.

v The model describing inter-voivodeship migrations in Poland shows that the most important factor negatively and statistically significant for these migrations is the distance between voivodeship capitals. The ratio of wages between pairs of provinces had a slightly weaker but positive impact on migration. However, the ratio of unemployment rates had the weakest impact on the dependent variable. This means that people who decide to migrate are more likely to choose voivodeships that are closer to their current place of residence, and at the same time those where wages are higher.

Notes

1 Relative wages (the relative unemployment rate) are understood to be the quotient of wages (unemployment rates) in a given province or region and wages (unemployment rates) in the entire economy.
2 https://bdl.stat.gov.pl/BDL/start (access: 2019-12-30).
3 http://www.UKRSTAT.gov.ua/ (access: 2019-12-30).
4 International Organization for Migration, *Mihratsiia yak chynnyk rozvytku v Ukraini* (Міграція як чинник розвитку в Україні), 2016. Access: http://www.iom.org.ua/sites/default/files/mom_migraciya_yak_chynnyk_rozvytku_v_ukrayini.pdf.
5 *Mihratsiia v Ukraini: fakty i tsyfry 2016. Access:* http://iom.org.ua/sites/default/files/ff_ukr_21_10_press.pdf.
6 Sirochuk N.A. (2014), *Mizhnarodna trudova mihratsiia ukraintsiv do krain yevropeiskoho soiuzu: faktory vplyvu.* Access: http://economy.kpi.ua/files/files/12_kpi_2014.doc.
7 The variable can be considered statistically significant at a level of 5% when the absolute value of the statistics given in brackets is greater than the critical value of Student's *t*-distribution (1.65).
8 The variable should be considered statistically significant at the level of 5% when the absolute value of the statistics given in brackets is greater than 1.65.
9 The variable should be considered statistically significant at the level of 5% when the absolute value of the statistics given in brackets is greater than 1.645.

10 Spatial differentiation of the economic development of Polish voivodeships and Ukrainian oblasts

Monika Bolińska and Olesia Chornenka

10.1 Introduction

Economic growth depends on many factors. One of them is the economic development of the regions. In turn, diversification of the economic development of regions may have a direct impact on the economic development of a country (Gurgul, Lach 2011).

A statistical and taxonomic analysis of the spatial diversity of economic development of the regions of Poland and Ukraine in 2004–2016 is the main goal of this chapter. Taxonomic indicators of economic development based on five macroeconomic variables were used in the study of oblasts and voivodeships: four stimulants (GDP per capita, investment rate, wages, net migration) and one deterrent (unemployment rate).

There are many studies dealing with the spatial differentiation of development of both the Polish and Ukrainian economies, on a local as well as on a regional level. But, comparative research on these two economies is extremely rare. To a large extent they concern relations between Polish and Ukrainian regions, which are directly adjacent to each other. It is worth mentioning Kowerski's work here (2017), which uses taxonomic indicators and econometric methods to study the socio-economic development of cross-border regions. In his considerations the author dealt with the Polish-Ukrainian borderlands. The conducted research shows that both taxonomy and econometric methods are a good tool for studying the socio-economic development of these economies, and the provinces and border regions of Poland and Ukraine (except the Lviv Oblast) are not the most developed in socio-economic terms in their respective countries (Kowerski 2017).

Among the works in this area, we can see those that show a positive impact on trade and investment between border regions. One such work is a study by Mikhel (2016), which researched the impact of Poland on the development of western Ukraine. These studies show significant links between Polish and Ukrainian entrepreneurs. Mikhel (2016) also points out that the share of exports of goods from regions such as Volyn, Lviv or Ternopil to Poland is increasing every year, which fortifies the development of trade relations between the economies in question.

Based on the review of empirical research on the impact of immigrants on economic growth and development as well as the development of human capital, it may be concluded that immigrants exert a significant positive impact on these aspects in the host country. Koshulko and Koshulko (2016) were involved in research on the influence of the Ukrainian migration in Poland. In their research, they proved that most of the money earned by Ukrainians is spent mainly on living expenses in Poland, and only a small amount of the money earned in Poland is sent by wire transfer to Ukraine (Koshulko, Koshulko 2016).

The Polish and Ukrainian economies are compared not only because of their proximity to each other, nor solely due to their cultural similarity, but also because of the comparable level of GDP per capita in the 1990s. In Poland since the 1990s, an economic transformation has been taking place and since then the GDP per capita has been steadily rising, while Ukraine is still struggling with a low level of this value compared to Poland. Adarov et al. (2015) ascertain that Poland's success is not due to the change of the centrally planned economy to a free market economy that occurred in Poland at the turn of the 1980s and 1990s, but from a long-term systemic transformation process, whose echo was present until the first decade of the 20th century. In addition, the authors emphasize that the experience of the Polish economy cannot be directly implemented in the Ukrainian economy, but only part of the experience, especially that which is related to trade and openness of the economy (Adarov et al. 2015).

The chapter structure is as follows: Section 10.2 presents the methodology for constructing taxonomic indicators. Section 10.3 contains an analysis of the spatial differentiation of taxonomic indicators of the economic development of Polish voivodeships, while Section 10.4 presents the spatial differentiation of taxonomic indicators of the economic development of Ukraine's oblasts. Section 10.5 contains a comparative analysis of the spatial differentiation of the taxonomic indicators of the economic development of Polish voivodeships and Ukrainian oblasts. Chapter 10 closes with a summary and conclusions of the conducted considerations.

10.2 Taxonomic methods employed

The level of development of a voivodeship or an oblast can be characterized by many methods; one of them are taxonomic methods, which allow the classification of regions using metric measures. These measures transform the n-dimensional space of variables describing the level of development of the region into a one-dimensional real space. The need to use taxonomic measures is mainly due to the fact that there is no good order in n-dimensional spaces ($n \geq 2$), so we are not able to compare any feature vectors.

Taxonomic methods have the form of a universal algorithm and are based on the following stages (for more on the stages of building development indicators see, e.g., in Willmott and Grimshaw 1969; Wishart 1969; Grabiński et al. 1989; Zeliaś 2000):

1 the selection of diagnostic variables describing the development of a given region (diagnostic variables);
2 the determination of the nature of variables in relation to the examined properties of the structure (a division into stimulants, destimulants and nominants);
3 selection of methods for estimating values of variables and units;
4 normalization of diagnostic variables aimed at freeing them from labels, so that they are mutually comparable;
5 determination of the synthetic variable value based on the chosen method of aggregation of diagnostic variables.

The selection of diagnostic variables was based on the availability of macroeconomic variables, which were listed on the Statistics Poland (GUS)[1] and the State Statistics Service of Ukraine (ДССУ)[2] websites.

Synthetic variables (first) allow for the ordering and comparison of units (voivodeships and oblasts) and (second) these variables also allow a classification of regions into groups with a similar degree of development. In this study, the authors based their research on synthetic variables, and grouped voivodeships and oblasts into quintile groups. The next quintiles contain regions with the highest, high, medium, low and the lowest level of economic development.

At the next stage, stimulants and destimulants of economic development should be distinguished from diagnostic variables. These concepts were introduced in Hellwig's work in 1968.

A stimulant of economic development is understood as being a variable whose high values are desirable from the point of view of the characteristics of the structure under study, while low values are undesirable. A destimulants, on the other hand, is such a macroeconomic variable whose high values cause an undesirable state of the studied structure, while an increase in the value of this variable deepens this state.

Among the macroeconomic variables discussed in previous chapters, the GDP per capita, investment rates, wages and migrations were accepted as stimulants of economic development, and the destimulants were the unemployment rates.

Destimulants can become stimulants and vice versa, which allows considering a set of diagnostic variables as a stimulant or deterrent syndrome. In the subsequent analyses, this destimulants is transformed into a stimulant based on the relationship:

$$s^i_{jt} = \frac{1}{d^i_{jt}}, \tag{10.1}$$

where indexes $i = 1, 2,\ldots, 16$ (27), $j = 1, 2,\ldots, 5$) and $t = 2004, 2003,\ldots, 2016$ mean, respectively: voivodeships (oblasts), years and stimulants (s) (destimulants (d)) of economic development (see: Dykas 2009, 2017).

In the next step, the stimulants are standardized to unity, dividing the value of the j-th stimulant by its maximum value and thus excluding their labels:

$$\overline{s}_{jt}^{i} = \frac{s_{jt}^{i}}{\max\limits_{it}\left(s_{jt}^{i}\right)}, \tag{10.2}$$

where $\overline{s}_{jt}^{i}$ means a standardized stimulant. The values $\overline{s}_{jt}^{i}$ are at the same time not greater than 1 and not less than 0, which allows one to compare any standardized stimulant values.

In addition, the value of a stimulant equal to 1 is interpreted in such a way that in the i-th region in a given year t, the j-th stimulant assumed the maximum value in the group of regions studied. It also follows from this that the closer/further from 1 the value a standardized stimulant ($\overline{s}_{jt}^{i}$) attains, in a given region, the more the region was characterized by a higher/lower degree of development in terms of the variable that the stimulant represents.

The study adopts a taxonomic method based on the highest value of the sum of Pearson's linear correlation coefficients between the taxonomic indicator $\left(SK_t^i\right)$, and standardized stimulants of economic development (see: Dykas et al. 2013 or Dykas 2017).

Let's suppose it's a $D=\left[d_{ij}\right]$ matrix of variables representing stimulants, where d_{ij} is equal to the value of the j-th stimulant in region number k, where $i = k$ *(modulo)* 16 (27), therefore $i = k + p \cdot r$ ($r = 0$ for 2004, $r = 1$ for 2005,…, $r = 12$ for 2016 and $p = 16$ (27)).

Let X be a normalized matrix D, where the normalization is accomplished utilizing the following transformation[3] (see: Bolińska at al. 2018):

$$X_{\bullet,j} = \frac{D_{\bullet,j}}{\max\left(D_{\bullet,j}\right)},$$

when the j-column of the matrix D is a stimulant, and:

$$X_{\bullet,j} = 1 - \frac{D_{\bullet,j}}{\max\left(D_{\bullet,j}\right)},$$

when the j-column of the matrix D is a destimulant.

The taxonomic indicator SK_i of the development of the k-th ($i = k$ *(modulo)* 16 (27)) of the territorial unit is the following convex linear combination of normalized features:

$$SK_i = \omega_1 \cdot X_{i,1} + \omega_2 \cdot X_{i,2} + \cdots + \omega_5 \cdot X_{i,5},$$

where the value vector $\omega = (\omega_1, \omega_2,\ldots,\omega_5)$ is an argument for which the function:[4]

$$F(\omega) = \sum_{j=1}^{5} \operatorname{cor}\left(X_{\bullet,j}, X * \omega\right), \tag{10.3}$$

takes the largest value.

We interpret the indicators SK_i (for $i = 1, 2, \ldots, 16\ (27)$) in such a way that the closer (further) one they are, the better (worse) is the i-region. The value vector ω is determined based on distributed evolutionary algorithms. In addition, the individual coordinates ω_i ($i = 1,2,3,\ldots, 5$) are as follows:

- in Poland: wages – 0.260, investment rates – 0.252, GDP per capita – 0.199, unemployment rates – 0.189, migrations – 0.100,
- in Ukraine: wages – 0.244, investment rates – 0.181, GDP per capita – 0.178, unemployment rates – 0.221, migrations – 0.176,
- jointly, both in Poland and in Ukraine: wages – 0.155, investment rates – 0.240, GDP per capita – 0.168, unemployment rates – 0.230, migrations – 0.207.

10.3 Spatial differentiation of taxonomic indicators of economic development of voivodeships

Map 10.1 presents the development of the taxonomic indicator in Polish voivodeships in the years 2004–2016. We can draw the following conclusions from this map:

- The highest level of economic development in the research period was characterized by those voivodeships with a high level of GDP per capita, high wages and low unemployment rates. These were the Mazowieckie (index value of 0.722), Pomorskie (0.550) and Wielkopolskie voivodeships (0.546).
- Voivodeships with high wages and a high level of GDP were in the group of voivodeships with a high level of economic development. This group includes the following voivodeships: Dolnośląskie (0.545), Małopolskie (0.532) and Śląskie (0.518).
- The group of voivodeships with an average value of the taxonomic index included the voivodeships of Łódzkie (0.495), Opolskie (0.475), Lubuskie (0.473) and Zachodniopomorskie (0.467).
- Low values of the taxonomic indicator were recorded in voivodeships in which low wages occurred during the research period. These were the Podlaskie (0.462), Podkarpackie (0.451) and Kujawsko-Pomorskie (0.442) voivodeships.
- The group of voivodeships with the lowest value of the taxonomic index was composed of three voivodeships of eastern Poland: Świętokrzyskie (0.431), Warmińsko-Mazurskie (0.425) and Lubelskie (0.421).

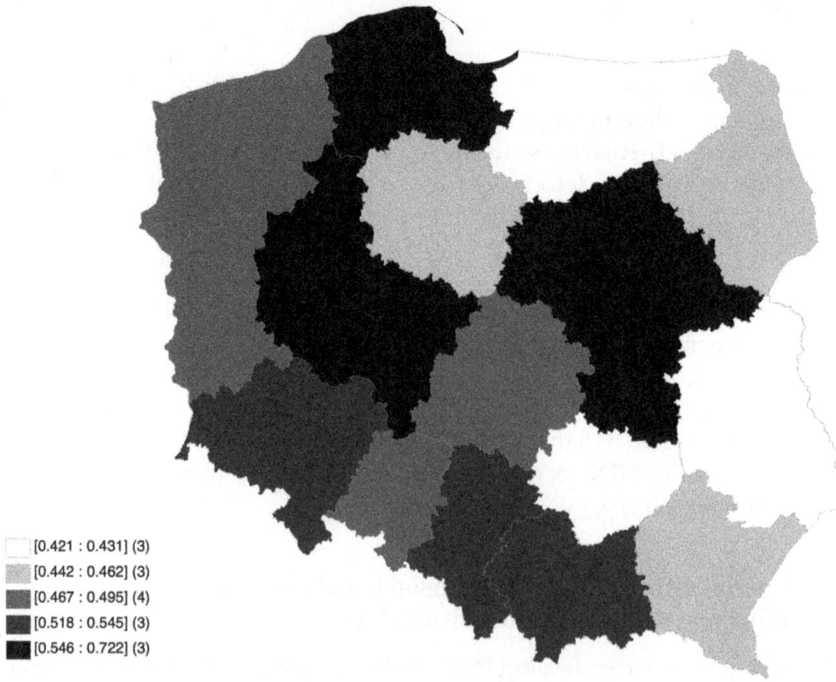

Map 10.1 Spatial differentiation of taxonomic indicators of economic development of voivodeships.

Source: Our own estimates based on: https://bdl.stat.gov.pl/BDL/start (access: 2019-12-30).

Table 10.1 summarizes the data on the development of taxonomic indicators in Polish voivodeships from specific years. This table also presents the coefficients of variation (understood as the relation of the standard deviation to the unconsidered average) of these indicators in the selected years and the correlation coefficients between the values of these indicators in subsequent years. The following conclusions can be drawn from the data contained in the table (see also Bolińska 2017):

- In all of the years singled out, the Mazowieckie Voivodeship had the highest value of the taxonomic indicator. In 2004, 2008 and 2016, the Wielkopolskie Voivodeship was in second place, while in 2013 the Dolnośląskie Voivodeship was in second place.
- The lowest value of this indicator in 2004 stood out in the Lubelskie and Warmińsko-Mazurskie voivodeships. The Warmińsko-Mazurskie Voivodeship also obtained the lowest value in 2008 and 2013. In addition, in 2013 the lowest value was also recorded in the Świętokrzyskie

Table 10.1 Taxonomic indicators of economic development in voivodeships in selected years

Voivodeship	*Years*			
	2004	*2008*	*2013*	*2016*
Dolnośląskie	0.42	0.57	0.56	0.65
Kujawsko-Pomorskie	0.35	0.48	0.43	0.47
Lubelskie	0.33	0.45	0.44	0.45
Lubuskie	0.37	0.47	0.46	0.54
Łódzkie	0.38	0.54	0.51	0.55
Małopolskie	0.43	0.57	0.52	0.61
Mazowieckie	0.61	0.77	0.71	0.81
Opolskie	0.36	0.48	0.47	0.63
Podkarpackie	0.36	0.45	0.48	0.49
Podlaskie	0.38	0.5	0.46	0.49
Pomorskie	0.42	0.61	0.54	0.64
Śląskie	0.4	0.58	0.51	0.6
Świętokrzyskie	0.35	0.46	0.42	0.46
Warmińsko-Mazurskie	0.33	0.44	0.42	0.47
Wielkopolskie	0.45	0.61	0.52	0.66
Zachodniopomorskie	0.38	0.51.	0.50	0.51
Coefficients of variation	0.170	0.163.	0.143	0.175
Correlation coefficients		Years		
		2008 and 2004	2013 and 2008	2016 and 2013
		0.960	0.942	0.906

Source: Our own estimates based on: https://bdl.stat.gov.pl/BDL/start (access: 2019-12-30).

Voivodeship. In 2016, the lowest value of this indicator was recorded in the Lubelskie Voivodeship.

- Between 2004 and 2008 (i.e., before the global financial crisis) an increase in the value of the taxonomic index was recorded in all Polish voivodeships, while the highest increase was noted in the Pomorskie, Śląskie and Łódzkie voivodeships. In these voivodeships, the increase was over 40%.
- In the period between 2008 and 2013 (i.e., the period in which the effects of the global financial crisis were most noticeable) a decrease in the taxonomic indicator was noted in 15 out of 16 voivodeships. The only voivodeship in which instead of a decrease an increase was recorded was the Podkarpackie Voivodeship. The highest decrease in the taxonomic index (by over 10%) was recorded in the following voivodeships: Pomorskie, Wielkopolskie, Śląskie and Kujawsko-Pomorskie.
- The decrease in taxonomic indicators of economic development in the aforementioned period of time resulted mainly from an increase in the unemployment rates.

- In the last analyzed period of time (i.e., in the years 2013–2016), an increase in the taxonomic index was recorded in all voivodeships, with the highest increase recorded in Opolskie (by 34.3%) and Wielkopolskie (26.7%).
- Despite a decrease in the taxonomic indicator in earlier years, in the last of the years researched, the value of the discussed indicator was higher in all voivodeships, as compared to 2004. The most rapid increases in the indicator were recorded in the Opolskie (by 72.7%) and Dolnośląskie (55.3%) voivodeships.
- The conclusion of the coefficients of variation in Table 10.1 is that in the years 2004–2013 a process of convergence of taxonomic indicators of economic development took place, and after 2013 there was a clear divergence of these indicators. On the other hand, high correlation coefficients in subsequent years suggest a significant stability of spatial diversity of those voivodeships in undergoing economic development.

Figure 10.1 presents the trajectories of changes in economic development indicators in 2004–2016 in groups of Polish voivodeships and in the Polish economy as a whole. This figure shows the following:

- Over the entire research period, the value of the taxonomic indicator followed the same trend. In 2004, the lowest values of the taxonomic indicator in groups of voivodeships were recorded in the group of voivodeships of eastern Poland and they were 1.22 times lower than the values of these indicators for the group of voivodeships of central Poland.
- In the years 2004–2008, the average annual growth rate of the taxonomic index was 7.6%. The highest average annual growth rate of the taxonomic indicator in 2004–2008 occurred in the group of voivodeships of central Poland (8.2%), and the lowest in the group of voivodeships of eastern Poland (7.0%).

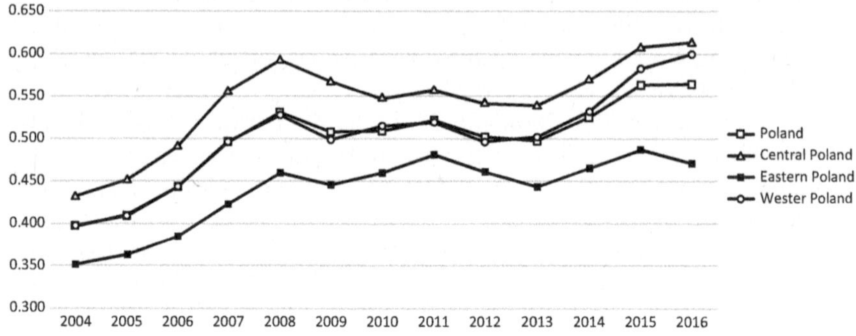

Figure 10.1 Taxonomic indicators of economic development in groups of voivodeships in 2004–2016.

Source: Our own estimates based on: https://bdl.stat.gov.pl/BDL/start (access: 2019-12-30).

- Between 2006 and 2007, the largest increase in the taxonomic index was recorded throughout the entire period considered (13%). This increase was recorded in the group of voivodeships of central Poland. The largest decrease of this indicator was recorded in the years 2008–2009 (5.5%). The voivodeships of western Poland were characterized by this decrease.
- The years 2009–2013 manifest minor changes in the taxonomic indicator in the groups of Polish voivodeships. In central Poland, this ratio fell by 5.1%, while in western Poland it increased by 0.7%.
- The value of the taxonomic indicator in the years 2014–2016 increased in all the discussed groups, with the highest (annual average) growth recorded in western Poland (6.2%), while the lowest growth rate occurred in eastern Poland (0.6%).
- The average annual growth rate of the analyzed indicators over the years 2004–2016 for the entire Polish economy was 3%, and was equal to the growth rate of this indicator in central Poland. In the same period, the growth rate in eastern Poland was 2.5%, while in western it was 3.5%. The taxonomic indicator in 2016 compared to 2004 in western Poland increased by over 50%, while the lowest increase among all respondents was in the least-developed group of voivodeships, that is, in eastern Poland (34.1%).

10.4 Spatial differentiation of taxonomic indicators of economic development of oblasts

In this part of the chapter, we will focus on the spatial differentiation of taxonomic indicators of economic development in the oblasts of Ukraine. Taxonomic indicators of economic development were based on the same macroeconomic variables as in the case of Poland.

The spatial differentiation of the values of taxonomic indicators of oblasts is shown on Map 10.2 and Table 10.2.

Map 10.2 indicates a significant spatial diversity of taxonomic indicators of economic development of the oblasts.

One may perceive a decidedly weaker economic development of western Ukraine, compared to the rest of the country. What's more, the oblasts in Left-bank Ukraine were characterized by a higher level of economic development compared to those on the right side of the Dnieper river (see also Tokarski, Chugaievska 2018 or Tokarski at al. 2019).[5]

Throughout the research period, the cities with a special status, that is, Kyiv (0.712) and Sevastopol (0.407), the Autonomous Republic of Crimea (0.397) and the oblasts of Kyiv (0.443), Odesa (0.384), Dnipropetrovsk (0.377), Kharkiv (0.359), Poltava (0.333), Donetsk (0.332) and Zaporizhzhya (0.331), were characterized by the highest taxonomic economic development rate of this indicator. In turn, the least developed in relation to this indicator were the following oblasts: Rivne (0.273), Kirovohrad (0.268), Sumy (0.267), Chernivtsi (0.256), Kherson (0.254), Zhytomyr (0.249) and Ternopil (0.247).

Table 10.2 Taxonomic indicators of economic development in oblasts in selected years

Oblast	*Years*			
	2004	*2008*	*2013*	*2016*
Autonomous Republic of Crimea	0.33	0.43	0.42	–
Kharkiv	0.36	0.41	0.35	0.32
Kherson	0.21	0.32	0.25	0.23
Khmelnytskiy	0.25	0.34	0.28	0.27
Cherkasy	0.30	0.34	0.27	0.24
Chernihiv	0.24	0.31	0.26	0.24
Chernivtsi	0.23	0.38	0.30	0.24
Dnipropetrovsk	0.37	0.42	0.37	0.32
Donetsk	0.33	0.41	0.36	0.24
Ivano-Frankivsk	0.27	0.37	0.31	0.28
Kyiv	0.34	0.50	0.50	0.47
Kirovohrad	0.24	0.29	0.28	0.25
Luhansk	0.27	0.35	0.36	0.21
Lviv	0.28	0.36	0.32	0.34
Mykolayiv	0.29	0.33	0.33	0.29
Odesa	0.36	0.45	0.39	0.34
Poltava	0.32	0.40	0.34	0.29
Rivne	0.30	0.32	0.28	0.25
Sumy	0.23	0.31	0.28	0.27
Ternopil	0.20	0.30	0.26	0.23
Vinnytsya	0.23	0.33	0.30	0.25
Volyn	0.24	0.33	0.30	0.25
Zakarpattia	0.27	0.34	0.27	0.25
Zaporizhzhya	0.32	0.38	0.33	0.28
Zhytomyr	0.20	0.30	0.26	0.24
Kyiv	0.72	0.87	0.71	0.64
Sevastopol	0.36	0.47	0.41	–
Coefficients of variation	0.334	0.291	0.280	0.314
Correlation coefficients		Years		
		2008 and 2004;	2013 and 2008;	2016 and 2013
		0.958	0.968	0.939

Source: Our own estimates based on: http://www.ukrstat.gov.ua/ (access: 2019-12-30).

Table 10.2 presents the taxonomic indicators of economic development in oblasts in selected years. The selection of those years was conditioned by the political and economic crises in Ukraine. These crises had a significant impact on the economic development of the oblasts; therefore, the following years were chosen for a detailed analysis of the taxonomic indicators of the economic development of the Ukrainian oblasts: 2004 (the Orange Revolution, November–December 2004), 2008 (the global financial crisis and gas conflict with Russia 2008–2009), 2013 (the Euro-Maidan and annexation of the Crimean peninsula and military conflict with the Russian Federation) and at the end of 2016, as a year of some stabilization of the economic

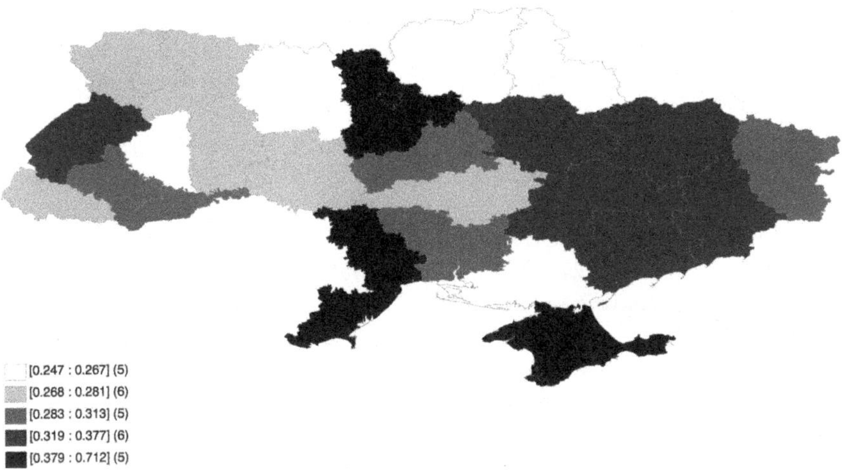

Map 10.2 Spatial differentiation of the taxonomic indicators of economic development of oblasts.

Source: Our own estimates based on: http://www.ukrstat.gov.ua/ (access: 2019-12-30).

situation in Ukraine after the economic crisis caused by the military conflict with Russia.

The year 2004 was the beginning of a period of development for the Ukrainian economy. The Orange Revolution that took place in 2004 led to a change in the political scene of Ukraine, and the election of Viktor Yushchenko as President of Ukraine (Golovko 2010). Analyzing the taxonomic indicator of the economic development of Ukrainian oblasts in 2004, we can see that by far the most developed oblasts were those of Dnipropetrovsk, Kharkiv, Odesa, the city of Sevastopol and Kyiv, all of which had the highest level of this indicator. In turn, the lowest level of the taxonomic indicator of economic development of the Ukrainian oblasts was recorded in the following regions: Zhytomyr, Ternopil, Kherson, Vinnytsya and Sumy.

The policy of President Viktor Yushchenko had a positive impact on the economy of Ukraine. Generally, in 2004–2008 (i.e., during the Yushchenko presidency) the economic growth fluctuated around 7%, measured by the taxonomic development index. The year 2008 was difficult for the economic situation in Ukraine, because in addition to the global financial crisis (which significantly affected the Ukrainian economy), there was also a political conflict with the Russian Federation related to the signing of an agreement between Ukraine and Russia, concerning the supply of Russian gas to Ukraine. The main problems that occurred at the time of the signing of this agreement were the conditions for supplying natural gas, in particular the price of the gas (Rosenberger 2012).

In 2008, the most developed with respect to the taxonomic index were the following oblasts: the City of Kyiv together with the oblast of Kyiv, Sevastopol along with the Autonomous Republic of Crimea and the Odesa Oblast. The least developed were the Kirovohrad, Zhytomyr, Ternopil, Sumy and Chernihiv oblasts.

The period 2013–2014 was the most problematic period in Ukrainian politics and the economy, after the economic crisis of the 1990s. Following the Euro-Maidan (November 2013–February 2014), Ukraine was faced with another conflict, this time of a military nature. The struggle began with the annexation of the Crimean Peninsula (March 2014), after which military operations have continued from April 2014, until the present. This time, the conflict afflicted the two most industrially developed oblasts of eastern Ukraine, namely the Donetsk and Luhansk oblasts (Klotz 2017). The Ukrainian economic situation, which was linked with politics, reacted to the above conflict with an economic crisis in the form of a decline in GDP and wages, as well as an increase in the unemployment rate. The crisis naturally contributed to a lowering of the taxonomic indicators of the economic development of the Ukrainian oblasts, in particular those directly affected by the war. The highest significance of this indicator in 2013 was recorded in the Kyiv, Odesa, and Dnipropetrovsk oblasts, the Autonomous Republic of Crimea and in the cities of Kyiv and Sevastopol. The lowest were recorded in the Zhytomyr, Ternopil, Chernihiv and Zakarpattia oblasts.

The year 2016 was distinguished by the fact that, for the first time after the economic crisis, an increase in the taxonomic indicators of economic development was recorded in most Ukrainian oblasts. During this period, the City of Kyiv and its oblast, together with the Lviv, and Kharkiv oblasts, stood out due to their significantly high taxonomic indicators. The Luhansk, Ternopil, Zhytomyr and Vinnytsya oblasts were distinguished by their low levels of taxonomic indicators.

Analyzing the coefficients of variation in Table 10.2, the following conclusions may be drawn: First, these coefficients are much higher in Ukraine than in Poland, which also means that the spatial diversity of the development of the Ukrainian economy is greater than that of Poland. Second, just like in Poland, the levels of these coefficients dropped until 2013, before rising significantly.

Considering the values of correlation coefficients between successive years, it turns out that the spatial diversity of the economic development of oblasts (like voivodeships) is stable over time.

The dynamics of taxonomic indicators of economic development in 2004–2008 once again indicate a high level of economic development over this time period. This period was characterized by an increase in taxonomic indicators in all oblasts, which proves that the economic policy at that time was rather effective. The average annual growth rate of these indicators fluctuated around 11% in the Chernivtsi, Ternopil, Kherson, Zhytomyr and

Kyiv oblasts. An approximately 8% increase was recorded in the Vinnytsya, Ivano-Frankivsk, Volyn, Khmelnytskiy and Luhansk oblasts. An increase of 3% was recorded in the following oblasts: Mykolayiv, Dnipropetrovsk, Kharkiv, Cherkasy and Rivne.

After the gas conflict and the global financial crisis, the situation in the Ukrainian economy deteriorated significantly. In the period of 2009–2014, the taxonomic decline rate of economic development fluctuated around 3.5%. It is worth noting that the decline was an element of the armed conflict with Russia. The most noticeable destabilization in the years 2009–2014 took place in the Donetsk, Chernivtsi, Luhansk, and Zakarpattia oblasts (the rate of decline in the taxonomic indicators of economic development in these oblasts fluctuated around 5%). The least noticeable decline in these indicators occurred in the following oblasts: Mykolayiv, Ivano-Frankivsk, Kirovohrad and Dnipropetrovsk (a decrease of approx. 2%).

After the most active phase of the military conflict in 2014, the economic situation in Ukraine stabilized somewhat in 2015–2016. Nevertheless, during this period, a decrease in the taxonomic index of economic development was rated at about 1.7% on a scale of the economy as a whole. It should be noted, however, that in Lviv, Donetsk, Sumy and Zhytomyr oblasts, an increase in the taxonomic indicator of economic development was perceived. At that time, the Ivano-Frankivsk, Dnipropetrovsk, Kharkiv, Zaporizhzhya and Vinnytsya oblasts still manifested an approximate 6% drop in the above indicator. Comparing, in turn, the taxonomic indicators of the Ukrainian oblasts in 2004 and 2016, we can see that their values were very similar, which proves that after the political and economic crises, the indicators of the development of the Ukrainian economy returned to their 2004 levels.

As can be seen in Figure 10.2 during a period of economic growth in the Ukrainian economy (i.e., in 2004–2008), the trajectories of the taxonomic index of economic development of oblast groups were very similar to each other. An upward trend of this indicator in the aforementioned period is also noticeable. Then in 2009 the first crisis for the Ukrainian economy, associated with the global financial crisis and the gas conflict with Russia, appeared. Another critical moment shown on the figure is at the turn of 2013–2014, and was related to the military conflict in eastern Ukraine and the annexation of the Crimean Peninsula.

In the research period, the lowest level of taxonomic indicator of economic development was recorded in the group of western Ukrainian oblasts.[6] Such a level of this indicator is conditioned by the low level of GDP per capita and wages, and the high unemployment in these regions. Generally, most of the oblasts in this group do not have a well-developed industrial and service sector. The basic types of economic activity in the western Ukrainian oblasts are agriculture, construction and tourist services. Despite the fact that this group of oblasts is the largest in terms of the number of oblasts it contains, in terms of economic development we can only distinguish the Lviv Oblast

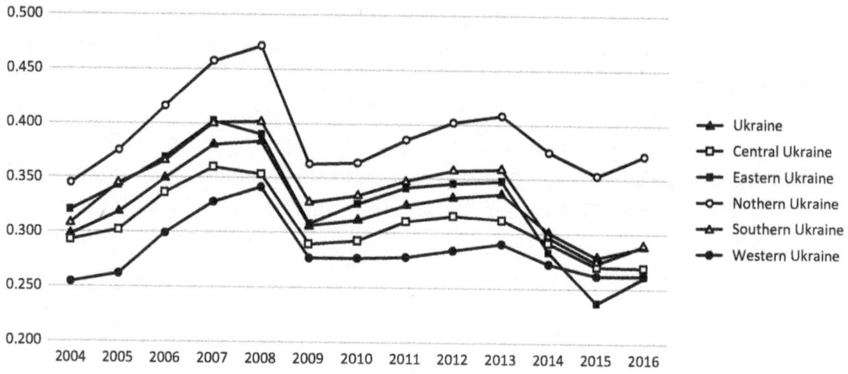

Figure 10.2 Taxonomic indicators of economic development in oblast groups in 2004–2016.

Source: Our own estimates based on: http://www.ukrstat.gov.ua/ (access: 2019-12-30).

together with the city of Lviv, which is the largest and most developed city in the western part of Ukraine, as making noteworthy economic progress.

By far the most developed oblast of central Ukraine was the Dnipropetrovsk Oblast together with the city of Dnipro, which is one of the most important financial and service centers of Ukraine. The high level of economic development of the Dnipropetrovsk Oblast has a significant impact on the level of economic development of the central Ukrainian oblast group. Among the less-developed oblasts of this group, we can distinguish Kirovohrad and Vinnytsya.

Northern Ukraine is the most developed part of the country. Despite the fact that three oblasts included in this group (Sumy, Chernihiv and Zhytomyr) in the research period were characterized by a rather low level of GDP per capita, and investment along with a rather high unemployment rate (which translated into a low level of economic development), the group had the highest level of the taxonomic indicator, mainly due to the capital City of Kyiv. Over 20% of the country's GDP is generated in Kyiv, which, combined with a highly centralized system, distinguishes this part of the country regarding economic growth; in addition, it exerts a significant impact on the spatial diversity of the economic development of the Ukrainian oblasts.

Southern Ukraine also had a fairly high level of taxonomic economic development in the period under review. This indicator was largely influenced by the very low level of unemployment in this part of the country, together with a high level of investment. Southern Ukraine having access to the Black and Azov Seas was also important in the framework of economic development, particularly with regard to the increase in tourism in this region, as well as the expansion of other commercial activities.

Eastern Ukraine is the most economically advanced part of the country. Modern heavy industry together with access to a large amount of natural resources, especially energy (gas, oil and to a great extent, coal), has caused the group of oblasts of eastern Ukraine to be one of the most developed oblasts of the country, as evidenced by the high level of the taxonomic indicator of economic development over the years 2004–2016. Precisely because of this high level of economic development, and greater integration with Russia, the oblasts of the eastern Ukrainian group were affected by the military conflict in 2014, which not only resulted in a destabilization of the region, but was the root of the economic crisis that extended throughout the country.

Analyzing the pace of economic development throughout the country, an average annual decrease of taxonomic indicators of economic development in the years 2004–2016 was noted to be approximately 0.3%. In turn, when broken down into groups of regions, we can see that the group of oblasts of western and northern Ukraine, in the analyzed period, manifested an increase in taxonomic indicators of 0.3% and 0.6%. A slowdown in economic growth in the form of declines in taxonomic indicators was recorded in the eastern, southern and central parts of the country (−1.7%, −0.6%, −0.7%, respectively).

A significant acceleration of the pace of economic development was recorded in the period of 2004–2008 in all groups of oblasts; on average in Ukraine as a whole, there was about a 7% increase in taxonomic indicators during this period. The highest increase in these indicators was noted in the western Ukrainian oblast group (7.7%), followed by the northern and southern parts of the country (7.1% and 6.7%, respectively). The weakest growth rate in the years 2004–2008 was recorded in the groups of regions of eastern (5.0%) and central (4.8%) Ukraine.

The period 2012–2015 was distinguished by a lackluster economic development rate throughout the country (approximately a 5.6% average annual decrease in taxonomic indicators). During this period, taxonomic indicators dropped in all oblast groups. A decrease of 5% was recorded in the western, northern and central Ukrainian oblast groups, while the highest decreases in these indicators were recorded in the eastern (11.8%) and southern (10.6%) parts of the country.

10.5 Spatial differentiation of taxonomic indicators of economic development of Polish voivodeships and Ukrainian oblasts

Map 10.3 presents the development of the taxonomic indicator of economic development jointly for the Polish and Ukrainian economies in 2004–2016. We can conclude from this map that (see also Bolińska, Gomółka 2018):

- Out of 43 analyzed regions, the most developed were regions in which high investments were recorded. These were the capital of Ukraine – Kyiv (0.589) and the Mazowieckie Voivodeship (0.510).

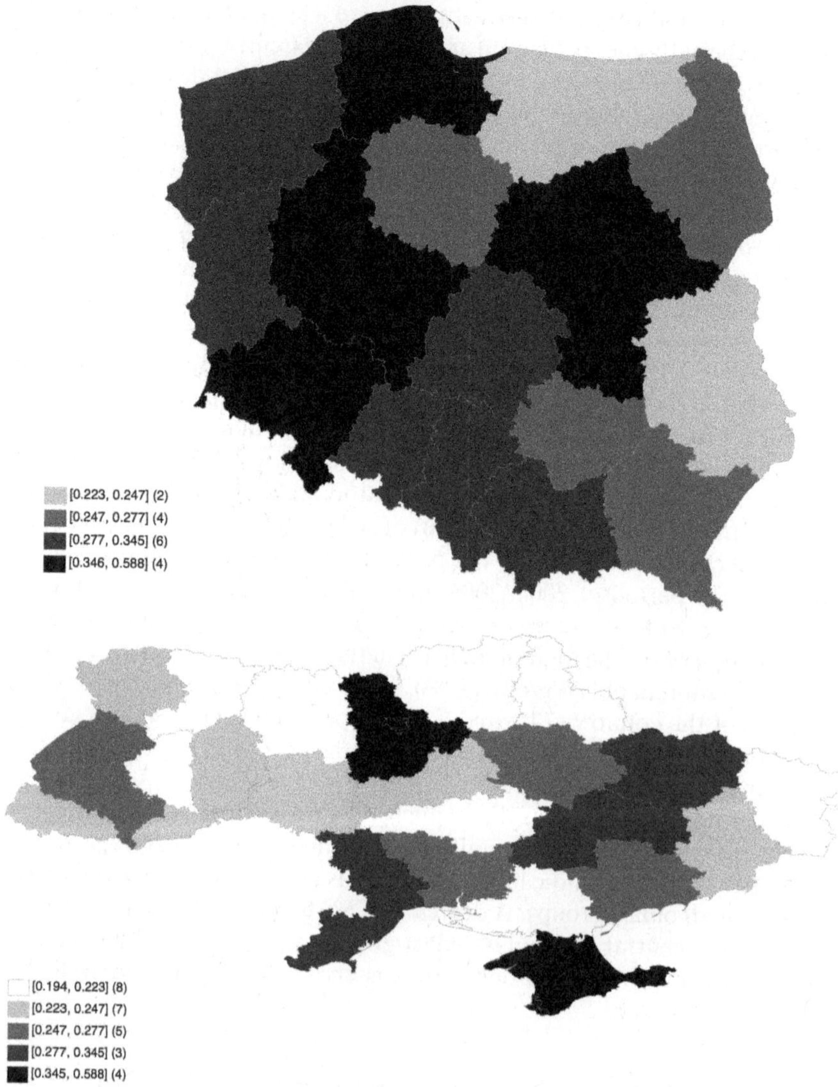

Map 10.3 Spatial differentiation of taxonomic indicators of economic development of voivodeships and oblasts.
In the case of the Autonomous Republic of Crimea and in 2004–2013.

The group of the most developed regions in the research period also included the Kyiv Oblast (0.389) as the natural economic base of the Kyiv metropolis, as well as the Wielkopolskie Voivodeship (0.357), the Autonomous Republic of Crimea (0.355), the voivodeships of Pomorskie (0.351), and Dolnośląskie (0.347) and the city with a special status, Sevastopol (0.347).

- The group of regions with a high value of this analyzed indicator was made up of three oblasts, Odesa (0.321), Kharkiv (0.296) and Dnipropetrovsk (0.292), and six voivodeships, the Małopolskie (0.346), Śląskie (0.320), Łódzkie (0.302), Opolskie (0.292), Lubuskie (0.289) and Zachodniopomorskie (0.284).
- The group of underdeveloped regions was made up of two voivodeships of eastern Poland and seven oblasts in Ukraine. This group included the Warmińsko-Mazurskie Voivodeship (0.247), Chernivtsi Oblast (0.245), Lubelskie Voivodeship (0.244) and the following oblasts: (0.237), Volyn (0.234), Cherkasy (0.229), Khmelnytskiy (0.228), Zakarpattia (0.225) and Vinnytsya (0.223).
- The group with the lowest values of the taxonomic indexes was composed of only Ukrainian oblasts. This group was made up of the following oblasts: Luhansk (0.222), Rivne (0.215), Kirovohrad (0.214), Sumy (0.206), Ternopil (0.203), Kherson (0.201), Chernivtsi (0.201) and Zhytomyr (0.194).

Table 10.3 summarizes the data on the value of the analyzed variable in all voivodeships and oblasts in the years selected as before. From the data summarized in this table, the following is evident:

- In 2004, 2008 and 2013, the highest value among all the discussed regions was in Kyiv, while in 2016 the Ukrainian capital was overtaken by the Mazowieckie Voivodeship (previously occupying second place in this ranking).
- The lowest values in all the years discussed were in the Ukrainian oblasts. In 2004, it was the Zhytomyr Oblast, in 2008 the Kirovohrad Oblast, in 2013 the Kherson Oblast, and in the last analyzed year 2016 the Luhansk Oblast.
- Between 2004 and 2008, in most of the regions analyzed (except for the Rivne and Chernivtsi oblasts in which this value remained unchanged), the level of the taxonomic index increased, while the highest increase, by 78.4%, was recorded in the Chernivtsi region. Another circuit with a high increase in this indicator was the region of Kherson (an increase of 60.2%). In Polish voivodeships, this increase was lower, with the Śląskie (13%) and Wielkopolskie (12.2%) voivodeships standing out.
- The period between 2008 and 2013 resulted in a decrease in the value of the taxonomic indicator. The effects of the global financial crisis and the gas conflict between Ukraine and Russia were most felt in the oblast, in which this indicator fell by almost 34%, that is, the Kherson Oblast, which in the previous period recorded the largest increase in the taxonomic rate of economic development between 2008 and 2013, was among those regions with the most significant decrease (32.5%). During the aforementioned period of time, in the Podkarpackie Voivodeship, a slight (4.1%) increase of the analyzed indicator was recorded, while in the Dolnośląskie Voivodeship, no change was perceived.

Table 10.3 Taxonomic indicators in Polish voivodeships and Ukrainian oblasts in selected years

Voivodeship or oblast	*Years*				*Year 2016, (year 2004 = 100)*
	2004	*2008*	*2013*	*2016*	
Dolnośląskie	0.25	0.36	0.36	0.43	171.51
Kujawsko-Pomorskie	0.21	0.29	0.26	0.3	140.49
Lubelskie	0.19	0.26	0.26	0.28	147.94
Lubuskie	0.22	0.29	0.28	0.34	153.91
Łódzkie	0.23	0.33	0.31	0.35	152.88
Małopolskie	0.28	0.37	0.34	0.41	147.82
Mazowieckie	0.43	0.53	0.51	0.57	132.85
Opolskie	0.22	0.3	0.29	0.38	170.37
Podkarpackie	0.21	0.27	0.28	0.3	140.42
Podlaskie	0.23	0.3	0.27	0.3	135.21
Pomorskie	0.27	0.38	0.35	0.43	159.9
Śląskie	0.24	0.36	0.32	0.38	159.87
Świętokrzyskie	0.21	0.28	0.25	0.29	138.00
Warmińsko-Mazurskie	0.2	0.26	0.24	0.28	145.54
Wielkopolskie	0.29	0.39	0.35	0.45	155.00
Zachodniopomorskie	0.23	0.31	0.3	0.32	142.88
Autonomous Republic of Crimea	0.3	0.39	0.37	–	122.85[a]
Vinnytsya	0.2	0.28	0.23	0.18	92.39
Volyn	0.22	0.29	0.24	0.2	93.51
Dnipropetrovsk	0.31	0.33	0.27	0.24	76.33
Donetsk	0.26	0.32	0.25	0.14	55.91
Zhytomyr	0.16	0.25	0.19	0.18	112.62
Zakarpattia	0.23	0.29	0.21	0.19	82.86
Zaporizhzhya	0.26	0.3	0.25	0.2	77.54
Ivano-Frankivsk	0.23	0.32	0.25	0.22	96.91
Kyiv	0.31	0.46	0.43	0.41	134.33
Kirovohrad	0.2	0.24	0.21	0.19	95.98
Luhansk	0.21	0.28	0.27	0.14	67.72
Lviv	0.25	0.31	0.25	0.28	113.5
Mykolayiv	0.24	0.27	0.25	0.23	92.32
Odesa	0.32	0.4	0.32	0.28	85.83
Poltava	0.27	0.33	0.26	0.22	79.16
Rivne	0.27	0.27	0.2	0.18	66.67
Sumy	0.19	0.25	0.21	0.21	113.21
Ternopil	0.17	0.26	0.21	0.18	108.37
Kharkiv	0.33	0.34	0.26	0.25	76.14
Kherson	0.17	0.28	0.18	0.18	101.4
Khmelnytskiy	0.23	0.3	0.22	0.22	93.71
Cherkasy	0.29	0.29	0.2	0.18	61.94
Chernivtsi	0.2	0.36	0.24	0.19	95.48
Chernihiv	0.2	0.26	0.19	0.18	91.68
Kyiv	0.64	0.73	0.56	0.5	78.51
Sevastopol	0.31	0.42	0.34	–	108.73[a]

Source: Our own estimates based on: http://www.ukrstat.gov.ua/ and https://bdl.stat.gov.pl/BDL/start (access: 2019-12-30).

a In 2013.

- As a result of the Euro-Maidan, there was a decrease in the value of the taxonomic indicator of economic development in 2013–2016 in most oblasts (the Khmelnytskiy region was the only one in which no change was recorded at that time). The highest decrease was recorded in the Donbas (Luhansk Oblast, a 47.2% decrease and in the Donetsk Oblast, a decrease of 42.8%).
- In 2013–2016, all voivodeships were characterized by an increase in this analyzed indicator. The highest increase of the indicator discussed here in the research period was recorded in the Opolskie (32.5%) and Wielkopolskie (29%) voivodeships.

Figure 10.3 presents the trajectories of the taxonomic indicator of economic development in groups of voivodeships, in the Polish economy as a whole, as well as in groups of oblasts and the entire Ukrainian economy in the years 2004–2016. We can draw the following conclusions from this map:

- The highest level of economic development in the first year of the analyses was recorded in the group of northern Ukrainian oblasts. The taxonomic index in the said group was 1.5 times higher than the least developed group of voivodeships in eastern Poland, at that time.
- Until 2007, all groups discussed had the same tendency to change. In 2004–2007, the highest average annual growth of the analyzed indicator was recorded in the group of oblasts of southern Ukraine, and

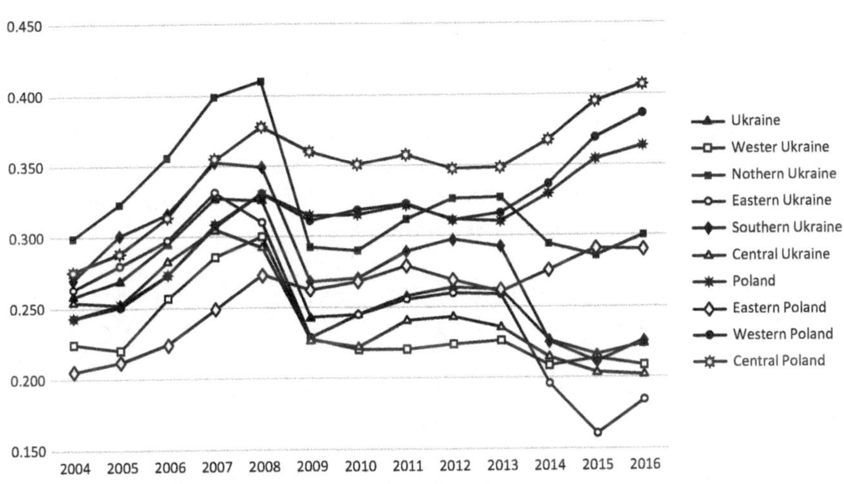

Figure 10.3 Taxonomic indicators of economic development in groups of voivodeships and groups of oblasts in 2004–2016.

Source: Our own estimates based on: http://www.ukrstat.gov.ua/ and https://bdl.stat.gov.pl/BDL/start (access: 2019-12-30).

was at a level of 9.3%. The group of oblasts of northern Ukraine (8.8%) and the group of voivodeships of central Poland (8.7%) also had a high growth rate.

- The effect of the global financial crisis and the Russian-Ukrainian gas conflict was a decrease in economic development in 2009 in all the regions discussed. In Poland, the value of the taxonomic index decreased by about 5%, while in Ukraine this decrease was already over 25%.
- The years 2009–2014 increased the rate of economic development in Poland by 1.0% and in all voivodeship groups. In the same period, Ukraine saw a decline in economic development at a rate of 1.5%. The only group of Ukrainian oblasts in which the value of the analyzed taxonomic index (equal to 1.5%) increased in the discussed period of time was the group of oblasts of northern Ukraine.
- In the entire analyzed period, the taxonomic index for the Polish economy increased by 49.3%; the largest increase among voivodeship groups was recorded in western Poland (an increase of 58.8%). On the other hand, in the Ukrainian economy in the discussed period, a decrease in the taxonomic index of 13.5% was noted, with the highest decrease recorded in the group of eastern Ukrainian oblasts (by as much as 30.2%), while the lowest decrease occurred in the northern Ukrainian oblasts (0.2%).
- The group of central Poland voivodeships had the highest value of the taxonomic index in 2016; this value was over 2.2 times higher than the value of the taxonomic index of the group of oblasts from eastern Ukraine, the country's group of oblasts with the lowest economic progress, for this year. The value of the taxonomic index in Poland in the last year subjected to our research (2016) was over 1.6 times higher than in Ukraine.

Figure 10.4 shows the trajectories of the taxonomic indicator of economic development in the Mazowieckie Voivodeship, Kyiv Oblast and the City of Kyiv, as well as in the Polish and Ukrainian economies as a whole. We can draw the following conclusions from this map:

- In the first year of our analyses, in the City of Kyiv and in the Kyiv Oblast, the taxonomic index was 1.2 times higher than in the Mazowieckie Voivodeship. In addition, this indicator in the Ukrainian economy (equal to 0.26) was higher than in the Polish economy (equal to 0.24).
- From the first year of observation to 2008, the average annual growth rate of the taxonomic index in the City of Kyiv and the Kyiv Oblast (5.5%) and the Mazowieckie Voivodeship (5.3%) was at a similar level. However, for the Polish economy as a whole, this growth was 7.9%, and in Ukraine it was slightly lower and amounted to 6%.
- During the years 2008–2009 in the City of Kyiv and the Kyiv Oblast the taxonomic index fell by almost 34%, while in the Mazowieckie Voivodeship this decrease was much smaller and amounted to less than 4%.

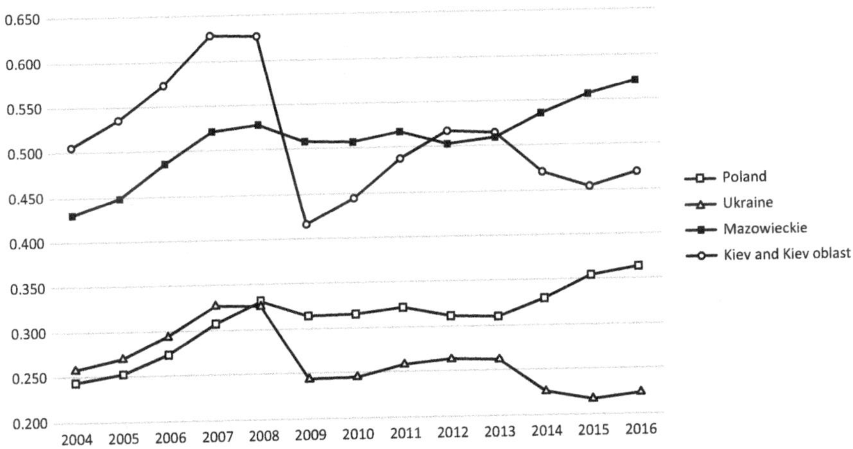

Figure 10.4 Taxonomic indicators of economic development in the Mazowieckie Voivodeship, Kyiv and the Kyiv Oblast, as well as in Poland in the years 2004–2016.

Source: Our own estimates based on: http://www.ukrstat.gov.ua/ and https://bdl.stat.gov.pl/BDL/start (access: 2019-12-30).

- In the years 2009–2013, the value of the taxonomic index increased on average by about 0.1% in the Mazowieckie Voivodeship. This increase in the City of Kyiv and the Kyiv Oblast was much higher and amounted to 5.5%. In Poland, this ratio between the discussed years did not fluctuate significantly (an average annual decrease of 0.3%), but in Ukraine the value of the discussed index increased by almost 2% on average, annually.
- The last years of observation (2014/2016) manifested a decrease in the average annual growth rate both in Ukraine (by 0.6%) as well as in Kyiv and the Kyiv Oblast (by 0.2%) and an increase of this indicator in Poland (by 5.0%) and the Mazowieckie Voivodeship (by 3.3%).
- Over the entire research period, the value of the taxonomic indicator increased in the Mazowieckie Voivodeship by almost 33%, while in the City of Kyiv together with the Kyiv Oblast, the value of this indicator decreased by 13.5%.

10.6 Summary

The considerations this chapter can be summarized as follows:

i The economic development of the Polish and Ukrainian economies is heavily dependent on socio-political stability. In the analyzed period, fluctuations in the value of the taxonomic index of the economic development of oblasts and voivodeships were associated with the global financial crisis and socio-political destabilization in Ukraine.

ii The best-developed Polish Voivodeship was the Mazowieckie Voivodeship, whereas the least-developed voivodeships were the three voivodeships of eastern Poland: the Świętokrzyskie, Warmińsko-Mazurskie and Lubelskie.

iii During the research period (i.e., in the years 2004–2016), the value of the taxonomic indicator fluctuated significantly in all Polish voivodeships, despite a decrease in the value of the taxonomic indicator after the global financial crisis (in the years 2009–2013). In the last analyzed year, an increase in economic development was recorded in all the voivodeships, with the highest increase being noted in the Opolskie and Dolnośląskie voivodeships.

iv In the discussed period, the most developed group of voivodeships was that of central Poland, whereas the lowest value of the taxonomic indicator throughout the entire research period was characteristic for eastern Poland.

v Decreases in the GDP per capita, wages and investment rates together with an increase in unemployment rates naturally contributed to the shaping of the taxonomic indicators of economic development of the oblasts. In the period under consideration, the cities of Kyiv and Sevastopol, the Autonomous Republic of Crimea and the oblasts of Kyiv, Odesa, Dnipropetrovsk, Kharkiv, Poltava, and Zaporizhzhya were characterized by a high level of taxonomic indicators. This was in contrast to the less-developed oblasts, according to the taxonomic indexes of Rivne, Kirovohrad, Chernihiv, Kherson, Zhytomyr and Ternopil.

vi This diversification of economic development is characteristic of the Ukrainian oblasts. In the years 2004–2016, significant differences were recorded in the shaping of taxonomic indicators of economic development among Ukrainian oblasts. The western part of the country is definitely the least developed, while the groups of central and eastern Ukrainian oblasts are among those with high economic growth; the northern and southern parts of the country in the research period were characterized by the highest level of taxonomic indicators of economic expansion (0.387 on average within the group during the research period). Moreover, the City of Kyiv (together with the Kyiv Oblast) attained the highest value of this indicator. To a large extent, the level of economic development of the capital (Kyiv) was affected by the highest level of GDP per capita, and wages and investment, combined with low unemployment, as well as the highly centralized system of the Ukrainian state. The regional economic policy of Ukraine, however, demands immediate change; it is necessary to emphasize a reduction of the differentiation of economic growth in the oblasts, as well as a change in the approach to state management from centralization to decentralization, which is important from the perspective of equalizing differences in economic expansion.

vii The most developed regions of all those discussed in this chapter were those of the capital of Ukraine, Kyiv, and the Mazowieckie Voivodeship. The next places were occupied by the Kyiv Oblast and the Polish voivodeship with the lowest level of unemployment – Wielkopolskie. The lowest level of economic growth among all the regions discussed was found in two oblasts of northern Ukraine, the Chernihiv and Zhytomyr oblasts.

viii Between 2004 and 2016, two voivodeships of western Poland (Dolnośląskie and Opolskie) recorded the largest increase in the taxonomic index. However, the highest decrease in economic expansion in the analyzed period was recorded in the Donetsk (eastern Ukraine) and Cherkasy (central Ukraine) oblasts.

ix Despite the fact that in the initial period of this analysis, the group of northern Ukrainian oblasts was achieving the most economic progress, in the final period, this group was overtaken by both the voivodeships of western and central Poland; only the group of voivodeships of eastern Poland (which in the first year of this analysis was the least developed) in 2016 was manifesting less growth than northern Ukraine. The remaining groups of oblasts in the last year of the analysis (2016) were making less progress than the least-developed group of Polish voivodeships.

x Comparing the best developed voivodeship of Poland and Kyiv, together with the Kyiv Oblast, we can state that in the first year of the research, the analyzed region of Ukraine, that is, Kyiv, was economically advancing at a faster rate. As a result of the Euro-Maidan and the Russian-Ukrainian gas conflict in 2016, the level of the taxonomic index of the Mazowieckie Voivodeship was 1.2 times higher than in the City of Kyiv and the Kyiv Oblast.

Notes

1 https://bdl.stat.gov.pl/BDL/start (access: 2019-12-30).
2 http://www.UKRSTAT.gov.ua/ (access: 2019-12-30).
3 For a matrix $M = \left[m_{ij}\right]$, the notation $M_{\bullet,j}$ means the j column of this matrix.
4 For $M = \left[m_{ij}\right]$ and $N = \left[n_{ij}\right]$ symbol $M * N$ signify the multiplication of the matrices.
5 Kyiv, which lies on both sides of the Dnieper, is an exception, as it attained the highest level of economic development.
6 An exception was the year of 2015, when the lowest level of this indicator was recorded in the group of oblasts of eastern.

Poland – Ukraine

Key findings

Rafał Wisła and Andrzej Nowosad

In 1990, the level of GDP per capita in Poland and Ukraine was very close to each other and (according to the World Bank) oscillated around 9.5–10.0 thousand USD (at PPP, at constant prices from 2010).

Poland was the first country in the former Soviet bloc to reject the dominance of the communist party in the partially free elections of June 4, 1989, and to transform the political, social and economic system. In the second half of December 1989, in the conditions of then-hyperinflation and economic collapse, the Polish parliament (Sejm) adopted 11 economic laws called the Leszek Balcerowicz Plan (Minister of Finance in the first post-war, non-communist government in Poland, of Prime Minister Tadeusz Mazowiecki). The plan boiled down to balancing the budget, removing most price controls, freeing most prices, introducing a rigid exchange rate of the Polish zloty against hard currencies (thanks to a stabilization fund from the IMF to the amount of approx. USD one billion) and privatizing a significant part of the economy.

The direct effects of Balcerowicz's plan seemed negative. In 1992, the GDP per capita in Poland was almost 7% lower than in 1990. Unemployment also increased, in 1993 the unemployment rate in Poland was already 14% and until 2005 it was among the highest in Europe. On the other hand, Balcerowicz's plan led to the stabilization of public finances and improved the overall macroeconomic stability of the economy, which resulted in a reduction of excessive employment (i.e., hidden unemployment) in some enterprises (mainly in the private sector) and an increase in the competitiveness of the economy. As a result of growing competitiveness and stabilization of the public finance sector, since 1993 Polish GDP and labor productivity began to grow rapidly. In 2000, GDP per capita in Poland was over 40% higher than in 1990.

Ukraine regained independence only in 1991, as a result of the collapse of the Soviet Union. A reform of the country's political, social and economic system was undertaken there as well.

However, it should be remembered that the existing Union of Soviet Socialist Republics, until 1991, was much more dependent both politically and economically on the state capital in Moscow. At that time, the Ukrainian economy was more strongly influenced by economic interconnections (including supply chains) with other former republics of the Soviet Union (including the Russian Federation) than the Polish economy.

Also, the economic reforms undertaken after Ukraine regained independence were much more conservative than in Poland. The process of ownership transformation is still far from being completed, which is widely recognized as a necessary stimulus for the development of a market-oriented political and economic system. A lack of proper control over the course of Ukrainian privatization, and corruption, caused a lot of dissatisfaction and a lack of general social consent for the continuation of this process, by the then current methods. Privatization in Ukraine is an unfinished process.

For the first two decades of the economic transformation in Ukraine, the implementation of an autonomous and transparent monetary policy in the central bank was not carried out. The central bank's independence from political pressure was illusory. Special economic zones created in Ukraine resembled tax havens, rather than solutions for managing local and regional development. The lack of transparency of state institutions and the creation of legal provisions for specific interest groups led to the emergence of a "government of the few operating mainly in their own interests" (Aristotle). The result is the "oligarchization" of the most profitable sectors of the Ukrainian economy (natural gas and the steel industry). An oligarchic group has not developed in Poland, not only because of the lack of raw materials that offer special opportunities for profit. From the early 1990s Poland has consistently pursued the goal of full EU membership. Privatization could not be inbred. It had to be open to foreign investors. The rules of privatization had to be clear. The low level of domestic savings that politicians were aware of resulted in an opening up to foreign investment capital, which the anticipated political and business stability and transparency were dependent on.

Ukrainian GDP per capita in the 1990s (as in many other post-Soviet economies) remained in a downward trend. In 1998, that is, at the beginning of the Russian financial crisis (which led, among others, to a stronger depreciation of both the Russian ruble and the Ukrainian hryvnia), Ukrainian GDP per capita was almost 60% lower than in 1990 (while the value of this macroeconomic variable in Poland increased then by almost 30%).

However, the Russian financial crisis also had a positive impact on the Ukrainian economy. Significant depreciation of the hryvnia led to an increase in the price of consumer products (but also semi-finished products and capital goods) imported from neighboring countries. Therefore, Ukrainian buyers of imported products shifted their demand from more expensive imported products to domestic products. This, in turn, as a result of the Keynesian multiplier mechanism, led to a boom in the Ukrainian economy (which was not prevented even by the Orange Revolution of 2004/2005). In the years 1998–2008, the Ukrainian GDP per capita almost doubled, while the unemployment rate dropped from over 11% to around 6.5%.

At the turn of the 20th and 21st centuries in Poland, as a result of restrictive fiscal and monetary policy and the (partly) Russian financial crisis, economic growth slowed down until 2002. Per capita GDP growth rates fell from 5–6% in the second half of the 1990s to 1–2% in 2001 and 2002. The slowdown in economic growth led to a rapid increase in unemployment. In the years 2002–2003, the unemployment rate in Poland approached 20% and was one of the highest in Europe.

Poland's accession to the European Union in 2004, the first years of full membership in the new institutional order, combined with efficient utilization of EU funds, clearly improved the economic situation in the Polish economy. GDP growth rates increased again, which translated into an increase in employment and a more than two-fold fall in unemployment rates. Another slowdown in Poland's economic development was the result of the global financial crisis of 2008. At that time, the dynamics of Polish GDP decreased, which led to an increase in unemployment (in 2012 and 2013 unemployment rates in Poland again exceeded 10%). Nevertheless, after 2013, Polish GDP growth rates increased again (to 3–5%), which resulted in a decrease in unemployment rates practically to the level of natural unemployment (4–5%). Currently, unemployment rates in Poland are among the lowest in the European Union.

In 2009, as a result of the Russian-Ukrainian gas conflict and (to a lesser extent) the global financial crisis, the Ukrainian economy was affected by another (this time one-year) recession. At that time, GDP fell by more than 10%, while the unemployment rate increased by more than 2% points. Then (similarly to the Russian financial crisis of 1998), Ukraine returned to the path of rapid economic growth, which lasted until the Euro-Maidan of 2013/2014. GDP per capita in 2013 was more than 11% higher than in 2009, while the unemployment rate fell by 1.5% points. The result of the Euro-Maidan of 2013/2014 was the Russian annexation of the Crimean Peninsula (in 2014) and the fight against the pro-Russian separatists in the Donbas. This, in turn, led to another deep recession in Ukraine. In 2015, the GDP per capita in Ukraine was over 10% lower than in 2013, while the unemployment rate increased to 9–9.5%.

***

In the 21st century (to be more precise after 2004), the best-developed Polish voivodeship (measured by the per capita GDP or the labor productivity level) was the Mazowieckie Voivodeship. This province has the cities of both Warsaw and Płock, where the largest Polish oil concern (PKN Orlen) has its headquarters. Dolnośląskie, Wielkopolskie, Śląskie and Pomorskie were also among the best developed voivodeships. These are the voivodeships in which the largest and most economically thriving urban agglomerations (Wrocław, Poznań, Śląsko-Zagłębie and the Tri-City area) are located. The lowest level of economic development was recorded in voivodeships of eastern Poland.

Moreover, with the passage of time, the development gap between the Mazowieckie Voivodeship and other groups of voivodeships, including (in particular) the group of voivodeships of eastern Poland, is increasing. For example, the GDP per capita in the group of the voivodeships of western and central Poland in 2016 was lower than in the Mazowieckie Voivodeship in 2005, while the value of this variable in the voivodeships of eastern Poland in 2016 was close to the level of this variable in western and central Polish voivodeships in 2007.

In general, the voivodeships east of the Vistula (Wisła) River (except for the right bank in Warsaw), due to the lack of larger and economically more prosperous urban centers, were characterized by a lower level of economic expansion than the voivodeships west of the river.

In Ukraine, the highest level of economic development was definitely in the capital city of Kyiv, where on average in the years 2004–2016, almost 20% of the Ukrainian GDP was generated. The Kyiv Oblast, the Dnipropetrovsk Oblast (whose capital is the center of the Dnieper financial center in Ukraine) and the oblasts of eastern Ukraine, where the heavy industry and mining of this country were concentrated, were also characterized by a high level of economic growth.

In comparison to the oblasts of Left-bank Ukraine and the coastal oblasts of Odessa and Mykolaiv, the oblasts of Right-bank Ukraine are underdeveloped, including (in particular) the oblasts of western Ukraine. This is due to the fact that in the less-developed areas of western Ukraine, there are no major cities (except Lviv) and because these areas were, until 1991, peripherally located in relation to the countries to which they belonged during the last 200 years (the Russian Empire, Austria-Hungary before World War I, the USSR, Poland and Czechoslovakia in the interwar period, and the USSR after World War II), their situation was not conducive to political-social stability nor their economic development.

Considering the dynamics of economic growth of the Ukrainian oblasts, it turns out that (mainly due to Kyiv and the Kyiv Oblast) the oblasts of northern Ukraine are developing faster than the other groups of oblasts. Moreover, since around 2011, there has been a deep recession in the most industrialized regions of eastern Ukraine, which was the result of both low investment rates (still in the first decade of the 20th century) and the armed conflict with pro-Russian separatists in the Donbas.

An equally important issue presented in this book containing our research results is labor productivity, which is one of the most important factors of long-term economic growth. An increase in labor productivity is the result of the accumulation of productive capital, human capital and process innovations used. The novelty of the approach used in this book was to take into account the fourth determinant of labor productivity – domestic and foreign gravitational effects.

The spatial differentiation of labor productivity in Poland is most strongly influenced by the spatial differentiation of capital for the working person, followed by national gravitational effects and foreign gravitational effects (flowing from Germany). The Lódzkie Voivodeship near Warsaw is the largest beneficiary of national gravitational effects, while the foreign gravitational effects are mainly of use to the voivodeships of western Poland.

In Ukraine, on the other hand, the level of product per employee (similar to Poland) is most strongly influenced by the amount of capital per employee. Then the value of this variable in Ukraine is influenced by gravitational effects flowing from Russia, national gravitational effects and (finally) gravitational effects flowing from Poland. Foreign gravitational effects from Russia mainly affect Kyiv and the regions of eastern, northern and central Ukraine, while foreign gravitational effects from Poland exert an influence on the regions of western Ukraine.

Since the voivodeships of eastern Poland and the neighboring oblasts of western Ukraine are among the poorest in these countries, further integration with the European Union (completed in the future with Ukraine's membership in the EU) should lead to an increase in Polish-Ukrainian gravitational effects, which may in turn lead to an accelerated economic development in both eastern Poland and western Ukraine.

The numerical simulations presented in Chapter 8 show that, assuming ceteris paribus, the Polish voivodeships should grow faster than the Ukrainian oblasts in the coming decades. Therefore, if the Ukrainian authorities do not undertake significant and effective structural reforms of the economy, the development distance between Poland and Ukraine may continue to increase. This, however, is not in the interest of Ukraine or Poland.

Labor productivity is an important determinant of wage levels. Hence, the spatial diversity of wages, both in Poland and in Ukraine, is largely determined by the spatial differentiation of labor productivity as well as by the spatial differentiation of unemployment rates. The higher the level of labor productivity, the higher ceteris paribus the (usually) level of wages, while the high unemployment rates of ceteris paribus are accompanied by lower wages.

In Poland, the differentiation of wages is much more strongly affected by the differentiation of unemployment rates than the differentiation in labor productivity, while in Ukraine the impact of these variables on wages is similar. This may be due to the fact that (in particular in the first decade of the 20th century) the diversity of regional unemployment rates was much larger than in Ukraine. This in turn meant that, in particular, in areas with high unemployment (including structural unemployment in some Polish voivodeships), the pressure on wage increases in the private sector (with increasing labor productivity) was much less than in well-run areas with low unemployment.

Changes in unemployment rates in the regions of the two countries studied were affected by both GDP changes and past (one year delayed) unemployment rates. GDP growth reduced unemployment rates, while in slump periods, unemployment rates rose the fastest in those regions where they were the highest (but also in those regions, unemployment rates fell the fastest in slump periods).

Migration flows were the last process analyzed. Their size in the 21st century in Poland was influenced by both relative wages (the average level of wages in a given voivodeship in relation to the average level of wages in Poland) and relative unemployment rates (defined analogously as relative wages). What's more, relative wages influenced the size of migration flows more than relative unemployment rates. In the case of migration outflows, the opposite was true. This may be due to not only the economic but also psychological conditions of the nature of these migrations. People making migration decisions move from voivodeships with high unemployment to voivodeships with low wages. It's better to have any job, than not to have one at all. Similar processes are also taking place in Ukraine.

As wages in Ukraine are among the lowest in Europe, so in the 21st century there was a rapid decline in the population of both cities and rural areas. Rural areas are being depopulated faster than cities. This means that the best-educated and most enterprising Ukrainians, not seeing any opportunities for a rapid improvement in the economic situation in their immediate surroundings or in the country as a whole, decide to make economic migrations from the countryside to the cities or to emigrate to foreign countries.

The presented results of comparative research on two neighboring countries and their economies seem to confirm the expected – on the basis of economic theory – effects of specific political and economic decisions, the adopted institutional order and geopolitical position. However, the current theoretical base of economics for creating the pillars of economic growth and development of Ukraine and Poland must take into account factors such as ecological security, digital security or structural adjustments resulting from the transformation of industry.

Bibliography

Adamczyk, A., Tokarski, T., Włodarczyk, R. W. (2009), *Przestrzenne zróżnicowanie płac w Polsce*. 'Gospodarka Narodowa', No. 9, 87–108.

Adamczyk, P. (2015), *Wewnątrzregionalne zróżnicowanie płac w Polsce*. 'Zeszyty Naukowe Szkoły Głównej Gospodarstwa Wiejskiego', No. 112, 5–14.

Adarov, A., Astrov, V., Havlik, P., Hunya, G., Landesmann, M., Podkaminer, L. (2015), *How to Stabilise the Economy of Ukraine*, (wiiw Background Study). Access: https://wiiw.ac.at/how-to-stabilise-the-economy-of-ukraine-dlp-3562.pdf.

Andriychuk, V. H. (2015), *Vyklyky ahrobiznesu: poshuk vidpovidey*. 'Ekonomika AKP', No. 5, 12–22.

Anilovska, H., Chornenka, O., Kukhar, N. (2019), *Prostorova dyversyfikatsiya VVP Ukrayiny*. 'Sotsial'no-pravovi studiyi', No. 1, 102–108.

Antoszewski, A., Kolodia, A., Kowalczyk, K. (eds.) (2010), *Transformacja w Polsce i na Ukrainie, Wybrane aspekty*. Wrocław: Uniwersytet Wrocławski, Oficyna ATUT.

Arkhireyev, S. I., (2006), *Posttransformatsiyna rynkova ekonomika: instytutsionalizatsiya fondovoho rynku*. 'Ekonomichna teoriya', No. 3, 43–54.

Arntz, M., Wilke, R. A. (2009), *Unemployment duration in Germany: Individual and regional determinants of local job finding migration and subsidized employment*. 'Regional Studies', No. 43 (1), 43–61.

Balabayeva, Z. (2015), *Grupp'i interesov v politicheskom protsesse: teoriya i praktika*. 'International Journal of New Economics and Social Sciences', No. 1 (1), 215–222.

Baltagi, B. H., Fingleton, B., Pirotte, A. (2016), *Estimating and forecasting with a dynamic spatial panel data model*. 'Oxford Bulletin of Economics and Statistics', No. 76 (1), 112–138.

Bałtowski, M. (2002), *Przekształcenia własnościowe przedsiębiorstw państwowych w Polsce*. Warszawa: PWN.

Berber, M., Özyakişar, D., Azdın, I., (eds.). (2014), *Bölgesel Kalkınma Üzerine Yazılar*, Ankara: Savaş Yayınevi.

Bessonova, O. (2006), *Razdatochnaya ekonomika Rossii*. Moskva: Rosspen.

Blien, U., Wolf, K. (2002), *Regional development of employment in eastern Germany: an analysis with an econometric analogue toshift-share technique*. 'Papers in Regional Science', No. 81 (3), 391–414.

Bolińska, M. (2017), *Przestrzenne zróżnicowanie rozwoju ekonomicznego powiatów województwa podkarpackiego*. 'Przegląd Nauk Ekonomicznych', No. 25, 49–63.

Bolińska, M., Dykas, P., Kowalczyk, A. (2018), *Przestrzenne zróżnicowanie rozwoju ekonomicznego powiatów w latach 2002–2014*. 'Studia Prawno-Ekonomiczne', No. 107, 197–219.

Bortnikow, W. (2010), *Partycypacja polityczna na Ukrainie*, in: Antoszewski, A., Kolodia A., Kowalczyk, K. (eds.), *Transformacja w Polsce i na Ukrainie, Wybrane aspekty*. Wrocław: Uniwersytet Wrocławski, Oficyna Atut, 275–286.

Bradley, S., Taylor, J. (1997), *Unemployment in Europe: A comparative analysis of regional disparities in Germany, Italy and the UK*. 'Kyklos', No. 50 (2), 221–245.

Carothers, Th. (1999), *Aiding Democracy Abroad: The Learning Curve*. Washington: Carnegie Endowment for International Peace.

Carothers, Th., Gramont, D. (de) (2013), *Development Aid Confronts Politics: The Almost Revolution*. Washington: Brookings Institution Press.

Carothers, Th., O'Donohue, A. (2019), *Democracies Divided: The Global Challenge of Political Polarization*. Washington: Brookings Institution Press.

Chenash, V. S. (2013), *Ekonomichni osnovy protsesu restrukturyzatsiyi pidpryyemstv*. 'Ekonomika: Realiyi Chasu', No. 5 (10), 55–60.

Chugaievska N., Tokarski T. (2018), *Wpływ zmian PKB na przestrzenne zróżnicowanie bezrobocia na Ukrainie*, 'Wiadomości Statystyczne', No. 3, 50–68.

Chugaievska, S., Chugaievska, N., Tokarski, T. (2017), *Analyse statistique de l'impact de l'effet gravitationnel sur la diversification du développement économique de l'Ukraine*. 'Revue Internationale Des Economistes De Langue Française', No. 2 (2), 72–95.

Coayla-Teran, E., Mohammed, S., Ruffino, P. (2007), *Hartman–Grobman theorems along hyperbolic stationary trajectories*. 'Discrete and Continuous Dynamical Systems', No. 17 (2), 281–292. doi:10.3934/dcds.2007.17.281.

Commons, J. R. (1934), *Institutional Economics*. New York: Macmillan.

Cox, K. R. (2016), *The Politics of Urban and Regional Development and the American Exception*. Syracuse: Syracuse University Press.

Dekret z dnia 20 grudnia 1946 r. o zmianie ustawy z dnia 3 stycznia 1946 r. o przejęciu na własność Państwa podstawowych gałęzi gospodarki narodowej. 'Dziennik Ustaw', No. 72, 394.

Dement'yev, V. V., Vishnevskiy, V. P. (2010), *Pochemu Ukraina ne innovatsionnaya derzhava: Institutsional'nyy analiz*. 'Zhurnal Institutsional'nykh Issledovaniy', No. 2, 81–95.

Democracy Index 2018. 'The Economist'. Access: https://www.eiu.com/topic/democracy-index.

Długosz, S. (2014), *Prywatyzacja à la Polonaise: Trzy książki o powszechnej prywatyzacji w III Rzeczypospolitej*. Warszawa: Dom Wydawniczy Elipsa.

Dolbneva, D. (2019), *Ways of transformation of the system of combating economic crimes in Ukraine with regard to the experience of the European union countries*. 'Science Rise', (2–3), 21–27.

Dolińska, A. (2019), *Socio-economic costs of systemic transformation in Ukraine in the lens of the biographical experiences of Ukrainian female migrants to Poland*. 'Qualitative Sociology Review', No. 15 (4), 140–160.

Dolzhenkov, O. (2000), *Totalitaryzm v Ukrayini: problemy formyvannya ta transformatsiyi*. Odesa: Odes'kyi instytut vnutrishikh sprav.

Dolzhenkov, O. (2002), *Ukrayins'ka nomenklatura v suspil'no - politychniy transformatsiyi*. 'Lyudyna i polityka', No. 1, 3–8.

Duma, L. V. (2017), *Imitatsiyne modelyuvannya prohnozuvannya sotsial'no-ekonomichnoho rozvytku rehioniv Ukrayiny v umovakh nestatsionarnosti.* 'Naukovyy visnyk NLTU Ukrayiny. Seriya ekonomichna', No. 2 (27), 174–177.

Duman T., Obralić M. et.al (2016), *Regional Economic Development in the Balkan Region*, Newcastle: Cambridge Scholars Publishing.

Dykas, P. (2009), *Taksonomiczne wskaźniki przestrzennego zróżnicowania rozwoju powiatów województwa podkarpackiego.* 'Studia Prawno-Ekonomiczne', No. LXXX, 200–214.

Dykas, P. (2017), *Przestrzenne zróżnicowanie lokalnych rynków pracy w województwie podkarpackim.* Kraków: Wydawnictwo Uniwersytetu Jagiellońskiego.

Dykas, P., Kościelniak, P., Tokarski, T. (2013), *Taksonomiczne wskaźniki rozwoju ekonomicznego województw i powiatów*, in: Trojak, M., Tokarski, T. (eds.), *Statystyczne analiza przestrzennego zróżnicowania rozwoju ekonomicznego i społecznego Polski*, 75–97. Kraków: Wydawnictwo Uniwersytetu Jagiellońskiego.

Dykas, P., Misiak, T. (2014), *Determinanty podstawowych zmiennych rynku pracy w polskich powiatach w latach 2002–2011.* 'Gospodarka Narodowa', No. 6, 57–80.

Dykas, P., Misiak, T., Tokarski, T. (2013), *Czynniki kształtujące regionalne zróżnicowanie stóp bezrobocia rejestrowanego w Polsce w latach 2002–2010.* 'Humanities and Social Science', No. 20 (1), 9–21.

Egger, P., Huber, P., Pfaffermayr, M. (2005), *A note on export openness and regional wage disparity in central and Eastern Europe.* 'The Annals of Regional Science', No. 39, 63–71.

Emmanuel, C., Otley, D., Merchant, K. A. (1990), *Accounting for Management Control.* London: Chapman and Hall.

Fałkowski, J., Kurek, P. (2019), *The transformation of supreme values: Evidence from Poland on salvation through civic engagement.* 'Public Choice' Access: https://doi.org/10.1007/s11127-019-00743-y 1–17.

Fedorowicz, Z. (1990), *System gospodarczy i efektywność ekonomiczna.* Warszawa: PWN.

Filipowicz, K. (2017), *Simulation des trajectoires de productive du travail dans les differentes regions de la Pologne; une analyse appuyee sur un modele de croissance gravitionnel.* 'Revue Internationale Des Economistes De Langue Française', No. 2 (2), 96–117.

Filipowicz, K. (2019), *Wpływ interakcji przestrzennych na regionalne zróżnicowanie rozwoju gospodarczego Polski (analiza oparta na grawitacyjnym modelu wzrostu).* Kraków: Wydawnictwo Uniwersytetu Jagiellońskiego.

Filipowicz, K., Tokarski, T. (2015), *Wpływ efektu grawitacyjnego na przestrzenne zróżnicowanie rozwoju ekonomicznego powiatów.* 'Wiadomości Statystyczne', No. 5, 42–61.

Finsberg, G. (1990), *Report on Poland's Application for Membership of the Council of Europe* (Rapporteur: Sir Geoffrey Finsberg, United Kingdom, Conservative), Parliamentary Assembly of the Council of Europe, Strasbourg, 19 September 1990, Doc. 6289.

Friedman, M. (1962), *Capitalism and Freedom.* [Rep. 2002] Chicago: University of Chicago Press.

Friedman, M. (1993), *Polityka i tyrania.* Łódź: Heuros.

Friedman, M. (2002), *Preface*, in: Gwartney, J., Lawson, R. (eds.) *Economic Freedom of the World: 2002 Annual Report.* Vancouver: Fraser Institute, xvii–xxi.

Gadowska, K. (2002), *Zjawisko klientelizmu polityczno-ekonomicznego, Systemowa analiza powiązań sieciowych na przykładzie sektora górniczego w Polsce*. Kraków: Wydawnictwo Uniwersytetu Jagiellońskiego.
Ganesch, F. (2018), *Regional mobility and spatial inequality: determinants of spatial labor market behavior considering firm- and region-specific factors*. 'Raumforschung und Raumordnung. Spatial Research and Planning', No. 76(6), 497–514. Access online: Springer-Verlag.
Girardin, E., Kholodilin, K. A. (2011), *How helpful are spatial effects in forecasting the growth of Chinese provinces?* 'Journal of Forecasting', No. 30 (7), 622–643.
Golovko T.V. (2010), *Ekstremizm ta radykalizm v Ukrayini: osoblyvosti formuvannya, osnovni napryamy, formy protydiyi z boku derzhavy*. 'Problemy istoriyi Ukrayiny: fakty, sudzhennya, poshuky: Mizhvidomchyy zbirnyk naukovykh prats', No. 19, 248–276.
Gomółka, A., Pastuszka, S., Tokarski, T. (2017), *Przestrzenne zróżnicowanie bezrobocia w Niemczech i w Polsce*. 'Studia i Materiały. Miscellanea Oeconomicae', No. I (3), 143–159.
Gomułka, S. (2013), *Transformacja polska, dokumenty i analizy 1991–1993*. Warszawa: Wydawnictwo Naukowe Scholar.
The Global Competitiveness Report 2015–2016. Geneva: World Economy Forum.
Gomułka, S., Kowalik, T. (eds.) (2011), *Transformacja polska, dokumenty i analizy 1990*. Warszawa: Wydawnictwo Naukowe Scholar. Access: www.weforum.org/gcr.
Goodman, D. S. G. (2016), *China's Regional Development*. Routledge.
Grabiński, T., Wydmus, S., Zeliaś, A. (1989), *Metody taksonomii numerycznej w modelowaniu zjawisk społeczno-gospodarczych*, Warszawa: Państwowe Wydawnictwo Naukowe.
Gurgul, H., Lach, Ł. (2011), *The impact of regional disparities on economic growth*. 'Operation Research and Decision', No. 2, 37–63.
Guzek, M. (1994), *Privatization in Poland*. Warsaw: Foreign Trade Research Institute.
Harriss J., Hunter J., Lewis C. (eds.), *The New Institutional Economics and Third World Development*. London: Routledge.
Harutyunyan, S. (2017), *Rynok kapitaliv v Ukrayini: problemy i perspektyvy rozvytku: Navchal'nyy posibnyk*: Odesa: Atlant.
Hayek, F. *Freedom and economic system*, [Rep. 1997] [in:] *The Collected Works of F.A. Hayek, Socialism and War: Essays, Documents, Reviews*. Caldwell, B. (ed.). 1939, Vol. 10, 189–211. Chicago: University of Chicago Press.
Hayek, F. *The Road to Serfdom*. [Rep. 1976]. Chicago: University of Chicago Press, 1944.
Hayek, F. (1960), *The Constitution of Liberty*. Chicago: University of Chicago Press.
Hellwig, Z. (1968), *Zastosowanie metody taksonomicznej do typologicznego podziału krajów ze względu na poziom ich rozwoju i strukturę wykwalifikowanych kadr*. 'Przegląd Statystyczny', No. 4, 307–326.
Holubiak, N. (2019), *External Factors of System Transformation in Poland*. 'Journal of Vasyl Stefanyk Precarpathian National University', No. 5 (3–4), 16–24.
Homiak, M. A. (2015), *Analiz suchasnoho stanu zaynyatosti ta bezrobittya v Ukrayini*. 'Aktual'ni Problemy Filosofiyi ta Sotsiolohiyi', No. 4, 141–146.
Homoncik, T., Pujer, K., Wolańska, I. (2017), *Ekonomiczno-społeczne aspekty migracji. Wybrane problemy*. Wrocław: EXANTE.

Hrycak, J. (2000), *Historia Ukrainy 1772–1999. Narodziny współczesnego narodu.* Lublin: Instytut Europy Środkowo-Wschodniej.

Hud, B. (2018), *Ukraińcy i Polacy na Naddniestrzu, Wołyniu i w Galicji Wschodniej w XIX i pierwszej połowie XX wieku.* Warszawa: Pracownia Wydawnicza.

Ichihara, M. (2017), *Japan's International Democracy Assistance as Soft Power Neo-classical Realist Analysis.* London: Routledge.

Inshakov, O, Frolov, D. (2010), *Evolyutsionnaya perspektiva ekonomicheskogo institutsionalizma.* 'Voprosy ekonomiki', No. 9, 63–77.

Jarosz, M. (2004), *Władza, Przywileje, Korupcja.* Warszawa: Wydawnictwo Naukowe PWN.

Karakılçık, Y. (2014), *Yeni Bölgeselleşme Politikaları ve Türkiye'de Bölge Yönetimi. Kuramlar, Tartışmalar ve Yeni Yaklaşımlar, Uygulama Örnekleri.* Ankara: Seçkin Yayıncılık.

Kaźmierska, K. (2019), *Thirty years after the great change. The process of social transformation in Poland.* 'Qualitative Sociology Review', No. 15 (4), 6–17.

Khoma, I. B., Kondakova, Y. V. (2013), *Restrukturyzatsiya yak element antykryzovoho upravlinnya pidpryyemstvom.* 'Naukovyy visnyk NLTU Ukrayiny', No. 23 (11), 280–286.

Klotz, M. (2017), *Russia and the Ukrainian crisis: a multiperspective analysis of russian behaviour, by taking into account NATO's and the EU's enlargement.* 'Croatian International Relation Reviev', No. XXIII (80), 259–287.

Kolodii, A. (2010), *Trajektoria demokratycznego przejścia na Ukrainie*, in: Antoszewski, A., Kolodia, A., Kowalczyk, K. (eds.), *Transformacja w Polsce i na Ukrainie, Wybrane aspekty.* Wrocław: Uniwersytet Wrocławski, Oficyna Atut, 23–38.

Kondratowicz, A. (2013), *Wolność gospodarcza, Pomiar, Percepcja, zmiany instytucjonalne.* Warszawa: Towarzystwo Ekonomistów Polskich.

Konopczyński, W. (1999), *Dzieje Polski nowożytnej.* Warszawa: Instytut Wydawniczy „Pax".

Koshulko, O., Koshulko, V. (2016), *The role of Ukrainians in the economic growth of Poland.* 'Journal World Scientific News', No. 42, 256–266.

Kotlorz, D., Sojka, E. (2017), *Wzrost gospodarczy a zatrudnienie w Polsce w latach 1995–2014.* 'Studia Prawno-Ekonomiczne', No. 105, 259–275.

Kowerski, M. (2017), *Zastosowanie metod taksonomicznych i ekonometrycznych do analizy poziomu rozwoju społeczno-gospodarczego regionów transgranicznych*, in: Miszczuk A. (ed.), *Wyzwania rozwojowe pogranicza polsko-ukraińskiego.* Lublin: Norbertinum, 11–31.

Kramorenko, M. I. (2014), *Otsenka tendentsiy ekonomicheskoy differentsiatsii regionov Severo-Zapadnogo i Tsentral'nogo federal'nykh okrugov.* 'Upravlencheskoye konsul'tirovaniye', No. 3. 89–99.

Krasnodębski, Z. (2003), *System Rywina - z Socjologii III Rzeczpospolitej.* 'Rzeczpospolita', No. 28. 2003.01.22. Access: http://niniwa22.cba.pl/krasnodebski2.htm

Krasnov, V. (2001), *Ukrayinskyy rynok kapitaliv.* 'Visnyk Natsional'noho Banku Ukrayiny', No. 2, 35–37.

Kwiatkowski, E., Roszkowska, S., Tokarski, T. (2004), *Granice wzrostu bezzatrudnieniowego w Europie i krajach WNP.* 'Ekonomista', No. 1, 39–68.

Kwiatkowski, E., Tokarski, T. (2007), *Bezrobocie regionalne w Polsce w latach 1995–2005.* 'Ekonomista', No. 4, 39–455.

Lecours, A. (2005), *New Institutionalism: Theory and Analysis.* Toronto: University of Toronto Press.

Leonov, D., Zhuk, R. (2005), *Study on Management of State-Owned Enterprises in Ukraine*. Kyiv: Ukrainian Stock Market Development Institute.

Leontev, V., Ford, D. (2012), *Mizhhaluzevyi analiz vplyvu struktury ekonomiky na navkolyshnie seredovyshche*. 'Ekonomika i Matematychni Metody', No. 8 (3), 370–400.

Liebscher, K., Christl, J., Mooslechner, P., Ritzberger-Grunwald, D., (eds.) (2005), *The Economic Potential of a Larger Europe*. Cheltenham Glos, Northampton: Edward Elgar Publishing.

Lin, J. Y. (2012), *New Structural Economics: A Framework for Rethinking Development and Policy*. World Bank Publications. Access: http://siteresources.worldbank.org/DEC/Resources/84797-1104785060319/598886-1104951889260/NSE-Book.pdf.

Lipov, V. V. (2012), *Institutsional'naya komplementarnost' kak faktor formirovaniya sotsial'no- ekonomicheskikh system*. 'Zhurnal Institutsional'nykh Issledovaniy', No. 1, 25–43.

Lisnichuk, O. V. (2002), *Hrupy interesiv u bahatoskladovomu suspil'stvi. Politolohichnyy analiz: avtoreferat dysertatsii*: *Politolohichnyy analiz*: *avtoreferat dysertatsii*. Kyiv: NANU Instytut politychnykh i etnonatsional'nykh doslidzhen'.

Longhi, S., Nijkamp, P. (2007), *Forecasting regional labor market developments under spatial autocorrelation*. 'International Regional Science Review', No. 30 (2), 100–119.

Lowndes, V., Roberts, M. (2013), *Why Institutions Matter: The New Institutionalism in Political Science* (*Political Analysis*). London: Red Globe Press.

Lysiuk, O. S., Kaflevska, S. G. (2012), *Bezrobittya yak sotsial'no-ekonomichna problema naselennya Ukrayini*. 'Ekonomichni nauky', No. 4 (70), 48–53.

Madej, Z. (1998), *Polski rynek kapitałowy*. Warszawa: Wydaw. Prywatnej Wyższej Szkoły Businessu i Administracji.

Majchrowska, A., Mroczek, K., Tokarski, T. (2013), *Zróżnicowanie stóp bezrobocia rejestrowanego w układzie powiatowym w latach 2002–2011*. 'Gospodarka Narodowa', No. 9, 69–90.

Maksimets, N. V., Bukatina, Ye. G. (2016), *Dinamika pokazateley ekonomicheskogo rosta regionov Privolzhskogo federal'nogo okruga*. 'Vestnik Povolzhskogo Gosudarstvennogo Tekhnologicheskogo Universiteta'. No. 1, 75–86.

Mankiw, N. G., Romer, D., Weil, D. N. (1992), *A contribution to the empirics of economic growth*. 'Quarterly Journal of Economics', No. 107 (2), 407–437.

Marelli, E., Patuelli, R., Signorelli, M. (2012), *Regional unemployment in the EU before and after the global crisis*. 'Post-Communist Economies', No. 24 (2), 155–175.

McMillan, M., Rodrik, D., Sepúlveda, C. (2016), *Structural Change, Fundamentals, and Growth. A Framework and Case Studies*. Washington: International Food Policy Research Institute.

Mikhel, R. (2016), *Poland's impact on the development of Ukraine's western region under the Ukraine-EU Association agreement*. 'Handel Wewnętrzny', No. 363 (4), 162–174.

Misiak, T., Tokarski, T. (2012), *Wewnątrzregionalne zróżnicowanie rynku pracy w Polsce*. 'Wiadomości Statystyczne', No. 12, 68–89.

Miszewski, M. (2001), *Transformacja gospodarcza Polski*. Bytom: Wyższa Szkoła Ekonomii i Administracji w Bytomiu.

Mroczek, K., Nowosad, A., Tokarski, T. (2015), *Oddziaływanie efektu grawitacyjnego na zróżnicowanie wydajności pracy w krajach bałkańskich.* 'Gospodarka Narodowa', No. 2, 15–53.

Mroczek, K., Tokarski, T. (2013), *Przestrzenne zróżnicowanie technicznego uzbrojenia pracy, wydajności pracy i łącznej produkcyjności czynników produkcji w Polsce w latach 1995–2009.* 'Studia Prawno-Ekonomiczne', No. 88, 333–357.

Mroczek, K., Tokarski, T., Trojak, M. (2014), *Grawitacyjny model zróżnicowania rozwoju ekonomicznego województw.* 'Gospodarka Narodowa', No. 3, 5–34.

Natsional'na komisiya z tsinnykh paperiv ta fondovoho rynku. Access: http://www.ssmsc.gov.ua/.

Nikulin, V. (2012), *Oleksandr Rakhmanov. Vlasnyky velykoho kapitalu yak sub'yekt sotsial'no-ekonomichnykh peretvoren' v Ukrayini.* Kyiv: Instytut sotsiolohiyi NAN Ukrayiny.

Nonneman, W., Vanhoudt, P. (1996), *A further augmentation of the solow model and the empirics of economic growth.* 'Quarterly Journal of Economics', No. 111 (3), 943–953.

North, D. C. (1990), *A transaction cost theory of politics.* 'Journal of Theoretical Politics', No. 2, 355–367.

North, D. C. (1992), *Institutions, Ideology, and Economic Performance.* 'Cato Journal', No. 11 (3), 477–496.

North, D. C. (1993), *Institutional change: A framework for analysis*, in: Sjostrand, S.-E. (ed.). *Institutional Change: Theory and Empirical Findings.* New York: M.E. Sharpe. Armonk, 35–46.

North, D. C. (1995), *The new institutional economics and third world development*, in: J. Harriss, J. Hunter, C. Lewis (eds.), *The New Institutional Economics and Third World Development.* London: Routledge.

Nosova, O. V. (2012), *Problemy privlecheniya inostrannogo kapitala v Ukraine.* 'Zhurnal Institutsional'nykh Issledovaniy', No. 3 (2), 14–22.

Nowosad, A. (2016), *Wolność polityczna w Europie*, in: Nowosad A., Wisła, R. (eds.), *Zróżnicowanie rozwoju współczesnej Europy.* Kraków: Wydawnictwo Uniwersytetu Jagiellońskiego, 155–182.

Ofitsiyne tlumachennya chastyny pershoyi statti 133 dyv. v Rishenni Konstytutsiynoho Sudu No. 11-rp/2001 vid 13.07.2001.

O nezavisimosti Kryma: Postanovleniye ot 17 marta 2014 goda. No. 1745–6/14: Verkhovnaya Rada Avtonomnoy Respubliki Krym. Access: https://www.rada.crimea.ua/act/11748.

Osmańczyk, E. J. (1982), *Encyklopedia ONZ i stosunków międzynarodowych.* Warszawa: Wiedza Powszechna.

Paniuk, T. (2013), *Vykorystannya svitovoho dosvidu dlya vyrishennya problem rynku pratsi v Ukrayini.* 'Ekonomika ta Menedzhment', No. 10, 178–187.

Paskhaver, O. Y., Verkhovodova, L. T., Aheieva, K. M. (2008), *Ukrayins'ka pryvatyzatsiya: hrupy interesiv, prychyny kryzy, shlyakhy yiyi podolannya.* Kyiv: Tsentr ekonomichnoho rozvytku.

Pastuszka, S. (2016), *Polityka rozwoju wschodnich Niemiec – cele, narzędzia, efekty.* 'Optimum. Studia Ekonomiczne', No. 6 (84), 56–74.

Pastuszka, S. (2017), *Długookresowe przemiany w rozwoju społeczno-gospodarczym wschodnich Niemiec.* 'Samorząd Terytorialny', No. 3, 60–79.

Pastuszka, S., Tokarski, T. (2017), *Przestrzenne zróżnicowanie PKB i bezrobocia w Polsce i we Włoszech.* 'Wiadomości Statystyczne', No. 3 (670), 49–70.

Pejovich, S. (1995), *Economic Analysis of Institutions and Systems.* Dordrecht: Kluwer A. P.

Pustovoit, O. W. (2016), *Ukrayins'ka ekonomika: khaotychni ta tsyklichni kolyvannya navkolo dovhostrokovoho trendu zrostannya.* 'Ekonomika i Prohnozuvannya', No. 2, 86–109.

Richter, R., (2005), *The new institutional economics: its start, its meaning, its prospects.* 'European Business Organization Law Review', No. 6 (2), 161–200.

Rogut, A., Tokarski, T. (2001), *Regional diversity of wages in Poland in the 90's.* 'International Review of Economics and Business', No. 68 (4), 556–582.

Rogut, A., Tokarski, T. (2002), *Regional diversity of employment structure and outflows from unemployment to employment in Poland.* 'International Journal of Manpower', No. 23 (1), 62–76.

Rosenberger, C. (2012), *Die Energiepolitik der Ukraine.* 'KAS Policy Paper', No. 18. Access: https://www.kas.de/c/document_library/get_file?uuid=24279150-b32d-0726-bdfd-7a9b20fa1ea5&groupId=252038.

Roszkowska, S., Rogut, A. (2007), *Rozkład płac i kapitału ludzkiego w Polsce.* 'Gospodarka Narodowa', No. 11–12, 55–84.

Serczyk, W. A. (2001), *Historia Ukrainy.* Wrocław, Warszawa, Kraków: Zakład Narodowy im. Ossolińskich.

Smalej, O. (2016), *Poland, after 25 Years of Transformation, Compared to Other Countries. Analysis of Selected Indicators, Managing Innovation and Diversity in Knowledge Society Through Turbulent Time.* Proceedings of the MakeLearn and TIIM Joint International Conference 2016, 197, ToKnowPress.

Sobkowiak, L. (1998), *Legitymizacja polityczna,* in: Jabłoński, A. W., Sobkowiak, L. (eds.) *Studia z teorii polityki.* Wrocław: Wydawnictwo Uniwersytetu Wrocławskiego, Vol. II.

Solow, R. M. (1956), *A contribution to the theory of economic growth.* 'Quarterly Journal of Economics', No. 70 (10), 65–94.

SPFZ – State Property Fund of Ukraine Rapport, http://www.spfu.gov.ua/

Staniek, Z. (2017), *Ekonomia instytucjonalna, dlaczego instytucje są ważne.* Warszawa: Difin.

Staniszkis, J. (2001), *Postkomunizm. Próba opisu.* Gdańsk: Wydawnictwo 'Słowo, Obraz terytoria'.

Stępniak-Kucharska, A. (2015), *Przekształcenia własnościowe polskiej gospodarki w latach 1990–2012,* 'Nierówności Społeczne a Wzrost Gospodarczy', No. 41, 136–147.

Szczepaniak, D., Tokarski, T. (2018), *Ekonomiczne determinanty migracji międzywojewódzkich.* 'Wiadomości Statystyczne', No. 2 (681), 44–59.

Teleshun, S. O., Reyterovych, I. V. (2008), *Vplyv finansovo-politychnykh hrup na prynyattya stratehichnykh rishen' u sferi polityky ta ekonomiky: ukrayins'ki realiyi.* Kyiv: Kherson.

Tokarski, T. (2005a), *Regionalne zróżnicowanie rynku pracy.* 'Wiadomości Statystyczne', No. 11, 67–88.

Tokarski, T. (2005b), *Statystyczna analiza regionalnego zróżnicowania wydajności pracy, zatrudnienia i bezrobocia w Polsce.* Warszawa: Wydawnictwo Polskiego Towarzystwa Ekonomicznego.

Tokarski, T. (2008), *Przestrzenne zróżnicowanie bezrobocia rejestrowanego w Polsce w latach 1999–2006.* 'Gospodarka Narodowa', No. 7–8, 25–42.

Tokarski, T. (2009), *Matematyczne modele wzrostu gospodarczego (ujęcie neoklasyczne),* Kraków: Wydawnictwo Uniwersytetu Jagiellońskiego.

Tokarski, T. (2012), *Przestrzenne zróżnicowanie płac w polskich powiatach*. 'Studia Prawno-Ekonomiczne', No. 85, 287–308.

Tokarski, T., Chugaievska, S., Chugaievska, N. (2019), *Determinanty przestrzennego zróżnicowania płac na Ukrainie*. 'Wiadomości Statystyczne', No. 64 (5), 17–33.

Trojak, M. (ed.) (2015), *Regionalne zróżnicowanie rozwoju ekonomicznego Polski*. Kraków: Wydawnictwo Uniwersytetu Jagiellońskiego.

Trojak, M., Tokarski, T. (eds.) (2013), *Statystyczna analiza przestrzennego zróżnicowania rozwoju ekonomicznego i społecznego Polski*. Kraków: Wydawnictwo Uniwersytetu Jagiellońskiego.

Ustawa z dnia 3 stycznia 1946 r. o przejęciu na własność Państwa podstawowych gałęzi gospodarki narodowej (1946), 'Dziennik Ustaw', No. 3, 17.

Veblen, T. (1899), *The Theory of the Leisure Class: An Economic Study of Institutions*. New York: The Macmillan Company.

Vyshnevskyi, V., Dementiev, V. (2010), *Innovatsii, instytuty ta evoliutsiia*. 'Pytannia ekonomiky', No. 9, 41–62.

Webster, A., Dunning, J. H. (eds.) (2013), *Structural Change in the World Economy*. London: Routledge.

WEF (2015), *The Global Competitiveness Report 2015–2016*. Geneva: World Economic Forum. Access: http://www3.weforum.org/docs/gcr/2015–2016/Global_Competitiveness_Report_2015–2016.pdf.

Williamson, O. E. (1985), *The Economic Institutions of Capitalism*. New York and London: The Free Press and Collier Macmillan Publishers.

Williamson, O. E. (2000), *The new institutional economics: taking stock, looking ahead*. 'Journal of Economic Literature', No. 38 (3), 595–613.

Willmott, A. J., Grimshaw, P. N. (1969), *Cluster Analysis in Social Geography*, in: Cole, A. (ed.), *Numerical Taxonomy*. New York: Academic Press, 272–281.

Wishart, D. (1969), *A Generalization of Nearest Neightbour which Reduce a Chaining Effect*, in: *Numerical Taxonomy*. New York: Academic Press, 282–311.

Wisła, R., Filipowicz, K., Tokarski, T. (2018), *Zróżnicowanie rozwoju ekonomicznego krajów UE na podstawie grawitacyjnego modelu wzrostu*, in: Cole, A. (ed.),. 'Wiadomości Statystyczne', No. 7 (686), 37–55.

Wisła, R., Tokarski, T. (2016), *Przestrzenne zróżnicowanie rozwoju ekonomicznego powiatów województwa śląskiego*. 'Wiadomości Statystyczne', No. 8 (663), 45–63.

Wiszka, E. (2007), *Systemy Polityczne Ukrainy*. Toruń: Wydawnictwo Naukowe Uniwersytetu Mikołaja Kopernika.

The World Bank Open Data (2019), data.worldbank.org

Wu, Y. (2016), *Regional Development and Economic Growth in China* (Series on Economic Development and Growth Book 7). eBook Collection (EBSCOhost).

Wyszczelski, L. (2015), *Konflikty narodowe i wewnętrzne II Rzeczpospolitej. Konflikt z sąsiadami, opór mniejszości narodowych, strajki chłopskie i robotnicze. Mroczne obszary dziejów II RP*. Warszawa: Bellona.

Yarova, L. G. (2015), *Analiz rivnya bezrobittya v Ukrayini ta napryamky yoho podolannya*. 'Hlobal'ni ta Natsional'ni Problemy Ekonomiky', No. 4, 752–755.

Zakaradze, E. (2019), *Regional and international development policy of Georgia International Formats of the Black Sea and Georgia*. 'Ovidius University Annals: Series Economic Sciences', No. 19 (2), 75–78.

Zakon Ukrayiny Pro pryvatyzatsiyu derzhavnoho mayna, Vidomosti Verkhovnoyi Rady Ukrayiny (1992), No. 24.

Zalewa, P. (2008), *Transformacja ustrojowa a kształt polskiego systemu ekonomicznego*. Lublin: Wydawnictwo Uniwersytetu Marii Curie-Skłodowskiej.
Zeliaś, A. (2000), *Metody statystyczne*. Warszawa: Polskie Wydawnictwo Ekonomiczne.
Zubik, A. (2014), *Suchasna trudova mihratsiia ukrainskoho naselennia v Polshchu*. 'Naukovi zapysky', No. 1, 107–113.
Zvit pro robotu Fondu derzhavnoho mayna Ukrayiny ta khid pryvatyzatsiyi derzhavnoho mayna u 2017 rotsi (2017). Access. http://www.spfu.gov.ua/userfiles/pdf/zvit-2017-final_12577.pdf.

Index

Note: **Bold** page numbers refer to tables; *Italic* page numbers refer to figures and page numbers followed by "n" denote endnotes.